I0362660

Integrating Archaeology and Ethnohistory: The Development of Exchange between Yap and Ulithi, Western Caroline Islands

Christophe Descantes

BAR International Series 1344
2005

Published in 2016 by
BAR Publishing, Oxford

BAR International Series 1344

Integrating Archaeology and Ethnohistory: The Development of Exchange between Yap and Ulithi, Western Caroline Islands

ISBN 9781841716909 paperback
ISBN 9781407327730 e-format
DOI https://doi.org/10.30861/9781841716909
A catalogue record for this book is available from the British Library

BAR Publishing is the trading name of British Archaeological Reports (Oxford) Ltd. British Archaeological Reports was first incorporated in 1974 to publish the BAR Series, International and British. In 1992 Hadrian Books Ltd became part of the BAR group. This volume was originally published by Archaeopress in conjunction with British Archaeological Reports (Oxford) Ltd / Hadrian Books Ltd, the Series principal publisher, in 2005. This present volume is published by BAR Publishing, 2016.

BAR
PUBLISHING

BAR titles are available from:

BAR Publishing
122 Banbury Rd, Oxford, OX2 7BP, UK
EMAIL info@barpublishing.com
PHONE +44 (0)1865 310431
FAX +44 (0)1865 316916
www.barpublishing.com

Abstract

This book presents a model of the exchange history between Yap and Ulithi Atoll of the Western Caroline Islands. This study also integrates archaeological and ethnohistoric data from these islands, which historically had important roles in what was the most extensive exchange system (*sawei*) in Micronesia. This integration contributes to the resolution of epistemological issues about the use of archaeological and ethnohistoric data for interpreting past exchange behaviors in the Pacific Islands. Organizing both data sources enriches our understanding of the developing island interaction, including later European impacts. Ethnohistoric records supply complementary context and interaction events for insights into the strong role of exchange in the dynamic social, political, and ideological domains of these island societies. Archaeological data provide diachronic evidence pertaining to the long-term practices of Yapese exchange on Mogmog. Ubiquitous Yapese earthenware potsherds from radiocarbon dated contexts are used to track the interaction between Gachpar Village, Yap and Mogmog, Ulithi Atoll. Significant ceramic attributes of the potsherds include assemblage densities, mineralogy, and chemical characterization obtained through instrumental neutron activation analysis (INAA).

The history of interaction between Yap and Mogmog was dynamic. Evidence as early as the seventh century A.D. from Mogmog implies simple trading, but beginning in the fifteenth century, before European entanglements, the interaction intensified. I propose that population pressures on Yap, which are corroborated by archaeological and ethnohistoric records, led to the intensification of taro cultivation, the extension of coastal Yapese land, internecine warfare, and an increase in social complexity. In turn, the intensification of taro cultivation resulted in ceramic technological changes, specifically the emergence of Laminated ware. Yapese ideology and the intensification of exchange between Yap and Mogmog for prestige-goods – which materialized in the form of shell valuables, raised stone platforms, and stone money imported from Palau – became increasingly important in the sociopolitical economies of both islands. Following increased European presence, formalized exchange relations persisted between the two islands despite the catastrophic depopulation in Yap and Mogmog, until the final *dénouement* of the "traditional" *sawei* exchange system at the beginning of the twentieth century.

Acknowledgements

I wish to thank everyone who has helped me through the different stages of this research. First, I would like to express my gratitude to my dissertation committee for their guidance: Professors Aletta Biersack, Gordon G. Goles, Steadman Upham, and especially my advisor, Professor William S. Ayres. Drs. Hector Neff (now at the California State University at Long Beach) and Michael D. Glascock, Senior Research Scientists at the Missouri University Research Reactor Facility (MURR), facilitated the archaeometric studies. I received important assistance from William R. Dickinson, Professor Emeritus at the University of Arizona, who conducted petrographic analyses on the Micronesian clays and pottery sherds reported in this dissertation. A special debt of gratitude is extended to Professor Michiko Intoh of the National Museum of Ethnology in Japan for allowing me to analyze her Yapese clay samples. Pacific archaeologists J. Stephen Athens, William S. Ayres, Michiko Intoh, Richard Olmo, and Richard Shutler Jr. are also thanked for allowing me to analyze Micronesian ceramics in their collections.

I wish to acknowledge those who permitted and facilitated the fieldwork stage of this research in the Federated States of Micronesia. They include the Council of Pilung, the Council of Tamol, Chief Debay, Chief Hapathey, the late Yap Historic Preservation Officers Andrew Kugfas and John Tharngan, Dr. Rufino Mauricio, Anthony Tareg, and William Yad. I am especially grateful to the people of Gachpar and Mogmog for their hospitality and assistance, in particular the families of Hosey Sugroy, Paul Beengin, Robert Beengin, and William Yad. While in the field, I received crucial assistance from Fran Defngin, Marjorie Falanruw, George Falutache, Andrew Figirmaad, Augustine Fithingamow, Suzann Gamnang, Augustine Gilbeengin, Jessie Gilchalmed, Moses Hatol, Finian Ifang, the late Anthony Marliol, Bernadette Mityay, Michael Ruetaman, Jim and Debbie Stevenson, Hosey Sugroy, William Yad, and Augustine Yanruw. In the different laboratories: Elizabeth Bigler, Robin Campbell, James Cogswell, Shannon Dion, Bruce Floyd, Sergio Herrera, Jim Meacham, Greg Nelson, Molly Ringle, Michael Shaffer, Lori Suskin, and Maria Thomas are thanked for their assistance.

Professor Richard J. Pearson from the University of British Columbia and Dr. Carla Sinopoli from the University of Michigan Museum of Anthropology assisted in the identification of historic Asian ceramics. I also would like to thank Rodrigue Lévesque for his correspondence about Micronesian history and Father Francis Hezel for sending me Father Juan Antonio Cantova's invaluable letters.

This research would not have been possible were it not for the generous financial assistance from the National Science Foundation (SBR-9412851, SBR-9503035), Sigma Xi, The Scientific Research Society, the U.S. Department of Energy (DE-FG02-95NE38135), and the Center for Asian and Pacific Studies and the Graduate School, both of the University of Oregon. Analytical cost reductions from the NSF Arizona AMS Facility and MURR are also greatly appreciated.

My special thanks to my mother, Isolde Hager, for her support and care packages while I was in the field and Greta Wichman for her love, support, and editing.

Hosa chig chig - Thank you

Kum magaragath - Thank you all

Preface

This book was previously prepared as a partial fulfillment of the requirements for the degree of Doctor of Philosophy at the University of Oregon in 1998. Since its original publication by University Microfilms Inc., it has undergone revisions, editing, and updating for publication as a British Archaeological Report. New data, for example, exist on archaeological and paleoenvironmental studies in the Western Pacific. The revisions of the dissertation were made while a postdoctoral fellow at the Archaeological Research Facility at the University of California, Berkeley and an adjunct assistant professor in the Department of Anthropology at San Francisco State University. Publications resulting from this dissertation research have been included (see Descantes 2002; Descantes et al. 2001, 2002, 2004); more are in progress. As in the original dissertation, radiocarbon dates have been calibrated with the OxCal v2.18 software program using the Gröningen (van der Plicht 1993) 1986 calibration curve.

April 8, 2003

Table of Contents

List of Figures

List of Tables

Chapter I

Introduction

Permeating all aspects of island life, exchange is integral to human island adaptations. The primary research goal of this book is to construct a diachronic model of exchange between the residents of Gachpar Village (Yap) and Mogmog Island (Ulithi Atoll) through the integration of archaeological and ethnohistoric data. Both island societies were involved historically in an extensive exchange system called *sawei*. This model contributes to our understanding of past Pacific Island inter-societal networks and their role in the development in two culturally distinct island societies.

I use the term "exchange" instead of "trade" to refer to past island interactions because it is a more inclusive term. According to the *Dictionary of Anthropology*, exchange:

> ... refers to the establishment and maintenance of relationships between persons. In order for social relationships to exist we must exchange something – whether it is the communicative exchange of language, the economic and/or ceremonial exchange of goods or the exchange of spouses [Seymour-Smith 1986:106-107].

Trade, on the other hand, is the transfer of commodities where the economic aspect of the transaction is paramount (Seymour-Smith 1986:279). I use the term "history" in two ways. The first use of the term refers to recorded events while the other more general use of "history" refers to all events of the past.

Internal and external exchange influence societies in many ways. People can acquire ideas, diseases, genes, language, materials, people, and services through exchange. Exchange also "underwrites or initiates social relations" whether they be symmetrical or asymmetrical (Sahlins 1972:186). Interaction and exchange result in more than just the transfer of tangible and intangible products or the formation of relations; they also embed transformative principles in the participating societies (e.g., Fajans 1993; Munn 1986; Narotzky 1997; Renfrew and Cherry 1986; Small 1995). Through exchange practice, society reproduces itself and through those reproductions is transformed. At the nexus of culture change, interaction between peoples serves as a mechanism to explain the reproduction and transformation of societies through time.

The study of exchange is central in archaeology because it is an important factor in explaining culture change. Certain exchange products survive the depredations of time and through characterization studies can be shown to have originated from particular areas enabling archaeologists to demonstrate human interaction. This is particularly significant in the absence of other information, e.g., ethnohistoric records. Exchange is also linked to other cultural domains, such as craft production and political organization. An understanding of exchange can also lead to an appreciation of other cultural realms, all important for explaining how people lived in the past.

Pacific Islands have long served as fertile ground for generating new anthropological method and theories (e.g., Alkire 1989; Hage and Harary 1991; Malinowski 1922; Weiner 1988). As relatively small bounded land masses, islands provide laboratory-like qualities that facilitate the study of inter-island exchange practices and their concomitant effects on the societies involved.

Engaged in uncovering past lifeways and culture change, Oceanic archaeologists face the major task of constructing exchange network models from archaeological data (Kirch and Green 1987:442; Terrell et al. 1997:175). The antiquity of external inter-island exchange extends well before the end of the Pleistocene in the Bismarck Archipelago of Melanesia (Kirch 1991:142). Not surprisingly, exchange systems in this part of the world have changed through time. Archaeological research into present Pacific Island exchange systems has shown major discontinuities between their present and prehistoric manifestations (e.g., Ambrose 1978; Egloff 1978; Irwin 1985; Kirch 1986). Exchange systems, indeed societies, have undergone major transformations before and after European entry into the Pacific.

Micronesia, a myriad of islands in the northwest tropical Pacific, first inhabited approximately 3500 years ago, has for the most part been a neglected geographical area in archaeological studies of exchange (but see Ayres et al. 1997; Fujimura and Alkire 1984; Graves et al. 1990; Intoh 1996). Melanesia and Polynesia have received considerably more research and dominate the archaeological literature (see Green and Kirch 1997; Kirch 1991). The research presented here contributes to the archaeological exchange literature between two islands in the Western Caroline Islands, part of a historically well known exchange system called *sawei*.

Sawei

Yap and Ulithi belonged to the most extensive exchange system in Micronesia called *sawei*. *Sawei* is the popular term for the formal bicultural exchange system that existed between the resource-rich high island of Yap and its neighboring low coral islands. The historic *sawei* exchange between Gachpar Village, Ulithi Atoll, and the coral Outer Islands of present-day Yap State is well documented (Alkire

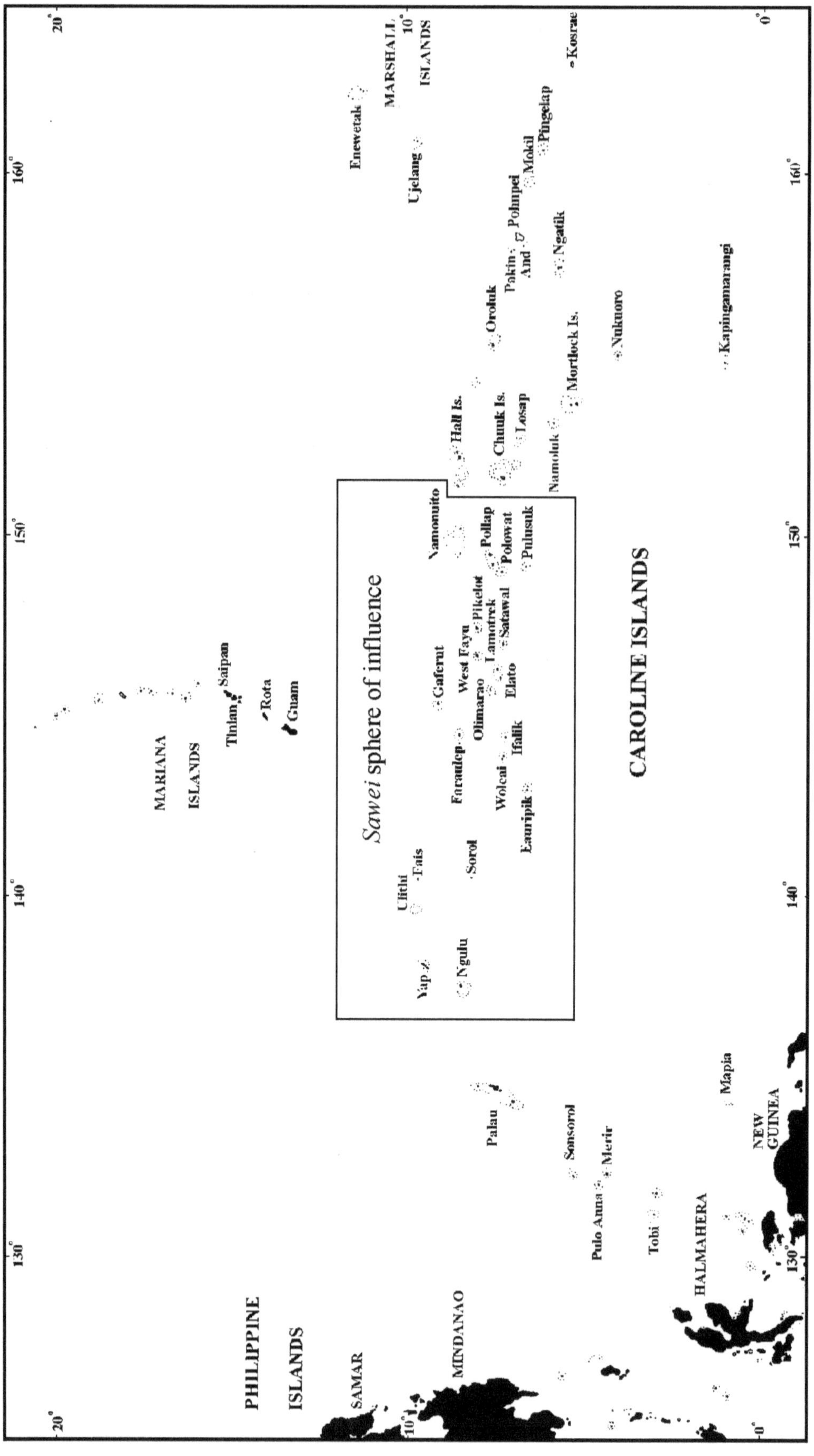

FIGURE 1. Caroline Islands and the *sawei* sphere of influence.

1978:122-124; Lessa 1950c; Lingenfelter 1975:147-155; Ushijima 1987b:55-79). Ushijima (1987b:77) claims that in prosperous years, Outer Islanders visited Yap during February and March (*Julijul* and *Mal*) after the *liefan* (latter half of the year) period when the eastern winds started blowing.

At the height of the system, 15 coral island communities extending over approximately 1,300 km belonged to what has been called the "Yapese Empire" (Figure 1). Coral islands in the Yapese sphere of exchange and influence included Ngulu, Ulithi, Fais, Woleai, Eauripik, Sorol, Ifalik, Faraulep, Lamotrek, Elato, Satawal, Polowat, Pollap, Pulusuk, and Namonuito. Ngulu is often not reported in the list of islands practicing *sawei* with Gachpar because it had *sawei* ties with Guror Village in the Gilman District of southern Yap. I include Ngulu because it practiced *sawei* with Gachpar before a chief's daughter and *sawei* privileges were given to Guror (see Lingenfelter 1975:147).

I use the term "*sawei*" generically to refer to the formalized gift exchange between the Outer Islanders and the Yapese. The system was a large socioeconomic system made up of smaller units (Ushijima 1987b:55). To be precise, "*sawei*" referred to a single gift component of the three-part exchange system. Literally, "*sawei*" in Ulithian refers to the baskets that were used to transport gifts (Lessa 1950c:32). The other two components of the almost annual visits to Yap included political (*pitigil tamol*) and religious (*mepel*) tribute (Lessa 1950c:31).

Yap was superordinate to the coral islands and at the head of what Lessa (1986) has called the "Yap Empire". There was, however, no monarch or political head with absolute control over the Outer Islands as is implied by the word "empire." A more accurate term may be the "Yapese Alliance System" (see Hunter-Anderson and Zan 1996). Gachpar Village headed the system with Ulithi as its intermediary to the other coral island communities. Coral island peoples made tributary visits to Gachpar and received many essential materials during their stay every two or three years (Lessa 1986:36). Both sides exchanged numerous items, some tangible, others not. Most of the material items were perishables and not preserved in the archaeological record. Pottery is an exception. I use earthenware pot sherds found on the coral island of Mogmog in Ulithi Atoll to indicate interactions between Yap and Ulithi. Manufactured by low caste Yapese women, earthenware pots were included as *sawei* gifts (de Beauclair 1974, Müller 1917). Women were involved in all but the preparation of a few gifts, e.g., canoe building and coconut-husk rope making.

Sawei was gift exchange and reciprocal hospitality between the people of Gagil Municipality and the Outer Islanders based on owner-tenant and caste relationships (Lessa 1950c:23). Ushijima (1982:71-72) refers to *sawei* as land tribute, but Lessa (1950c:32) states that *sawei* was neither tribute nor rent because Outer Islanders received more from the exchanges than did the Yapese. Lingenfelter (1975:147) notes the *sawei* relationship is,

TABLE 1. Goods Exchanged Between Yap and Ulithi (Outer Islands)

Yap to Ulithi (Outer Islands)	Ulithi (Outer Islands) to Yap
Bamboo	Banana fiber mats
Bananas	Bird feathers
Breadfruit	Breadfruit resin for caulking
Canoes	Canoes
Ceramic pots (from Gitam Village)	Cloth (*lavalava*)
Cloth (nylon/cotton)	Coconut candy
Coconut shell graters	Coconut-husk rope
Coconut string pouches	Coconut oil
Combs	Coconut shell jewelry
Flint stones for starting fires	Coconut syrup
Grass baskets	*Conus* shells
Iron pots	Decorative ornaments
Mahogany wood for canoes	Fais tobacco
Mirrors	Fermented Breadfruit
Ochre	Fish
Polynesian chestnuts	Iron
Squash	Leg ornaments
Steel for starting fires	*Machi* loincloths
Steel knives	Mother-of-pearl shells
Sweet potatoes	Pandanus loin mats
Taro and yams	Pandanus sails
Tridacna shells	Shell belts
Turmeric powder bundles	Sleeping mats
Weapons	*Spondylus* shells
Whet stones	Tortoise shell bands and rings

Sources: Alkire 1980; de Beauclair 1967; Damm 1938; von Kotzebue 1821; Kubary 1895; Lessa 1950c; Lingenfelter 1975; Müller 1917; Ushijima 1982, 1987b.

> ... best expressed by the giving of food and shelter while the outer islanders reside on Yap and supplying lumber and other of Yap's resources not available on the atolls. Whenever these people come to Yap they are cared for by particular clan estates as if they were children of that patriclan.

While on Yap, Outer Islanders or *pilmathou* (my spelling; the people of the sea) as they were called by the Yapese were considered *milingay ni arow*, of low social position, but not the lowest (Ushijima 1987b:63). These Outer Island "children" had a number of prohibitions while on Yap, such as chewing betel nut, eating certain foods, speaking Yapese, marrying Yapese women, and wearing combs, ornaments, red loin cloths, and turmeric powder (Lessa 1950c:44; Ushijima 1987b:63).

Archaeological research is dependent upon the recovery of materials for interpreting the past, so information about the material characteristics of the historic exchange practice is essential. Gifts between Yap and the Outer Islands included services (navigation, tattooing) and material and non-material items. Non-material gifts could include Ulithian labor, songs, and navigational knowledge or Yapese magic aid and prayers. Most exchange items were perishables. Table 1 lists gifts exchanged between the people of Gachpar and the Outer Islands.

Provenance

As physical manifestations of exchange, archaeological potsherds offer a longitudinal perspective into earlier interactions in the Western Caroline Islands. As noted earlier, I rely predominantly on ceramic potsherds as material evidence of inter-island exchange. Organic materials associated with the potsherds are dated for vital chronological information. The use of ceramics as a proxy for the entirety of interaction is problematic (cf. Blinman and Wilson 1992:67), however, the ubiquity, preservation, and ability to apply provenance studies on ceramics make it the most valuable artifact type with which to address questions of exchange behavior in the Western Carolines.

The provenance of earthenware from dated archaeological contexts plays a large role in my construction of a diachronic model of exchange between the Yapese and the Ulithians. Instrumental neutron activation analysis (INAA) on potsherds recovered in Gachpar and Mogmog is used as the analytical technique to characterize and find the provenance of the ceramics. Dickinson's petrographic mineralogical work on the ceramics in this study serves as a complementary analytical technique for addressing provenance issues.

Diachronic Perspective

Ethnohistoric records of *sawei* exchange are all recollections of people from specific spatio-temporal contexts and explain the dynamics of exchange and its political significance following European contact. Several researchers have sought to understand the extensive *sawei* exchange system (e.g., Alkire 1989; Berg 1992; Hunter-Anderson and Zan 1996; Lessa 1950c; Lingenfelter 1975). Most of the works, however, lack archaeological information and rely upon ethnographic and ethnohistoric data when modeling past *sawei* exchange. To avoid what Thomas (1996:9) calls the "misrecognition of consequences of colonial penetration," I have synthesized ethnohistoric and archaeological evidence to focus on the interaction between Yap and Ulithi after European entry into the Pacific (see also Carucci 1988). This endeavor is part of a trend to historicize anthropological inquiry (see Biersack 1991; Kirch 1992; Sahlins 1992; Thomas 1996).

Chronological control is imperative when discussing culture change. Words such as "traditional" or "original" for describing different manifestations of Western Carolinian exchange practices are confusing and imply that exchange practices are detached from time or that these societies were for the most part unchanging until contacted by Europeans (cf. Thomas 1996). I rely only on archaeological data to build a model of Yap-Ulithi exchange before European contact. Archaeological and ethnohistoric data are integrated to explain exchange and culture change following European entry into the Pacific.

Given the centrality of exchange in Pacific Island societies, a longitudinal understanding of inter-island, indeed inter-cultural exchange, leads to insights about the role of exchange in the reproduction and transformation of the respective societies. A long-term perspective offered by archaeological investigations with an integration of ethnohistoric data divides the temporal scale of resolution into smaller units. Archaeological explanations stand to benefit from the addition of cultural processes or events that operate at shorter time scales, which may not be visible in the archaeological record. Social anthropologists, on the other hand, stand to gain from the long time scale archaeology provides by gaining an appreciation of the changes societies have undergone.

Much has been written about how the formalized *sawei* exchange system of the past operated, but little is known about the development of the interactive behaviors between the island societies. Most of what we do know about past exchange practices has been extrapolated from ethnographic and ethnohistoric data. These interpretations are representative of points in time when they were collected, but are unlikely to be indicative of earlier exchange practices. Even though all the evidence of the past exists in the present, archaeological data from earlier contexts are necessary for an appreciation of earlier exchange behavior and an understanding of culture change.

Field Studies

I chose to investigate Gagil and Ulithi for a number of reasons: (1) Ulithi is the closest atoll to Yap; (2) Yap and Ulithi held the two highest positions in the *sawei* exchange system; (3) the assumption that their exchange relationship had the greatest antiquity; (4) extensive ethnographic work about *sawei* had been conducted on Yap (Lingenfelter 1975) and Ulithi (Lessa 1950c; Ushijima 1987a); and (5) the ability to correlate properties on both islands on which past living groups practiced exchange. Given Craib's (1980) previous archaeological investigations on Ulithi and Intoh's (1996) excavations on Fais, a coral island just 70 km east of Ulithi, ceramic-bearing archaeological deposits were expected.

I lived for a total of seven months in Yap and five months in Ulithi, where with the help of the local people I conducted my research. While in Yap I lived in Gachpar Village and while in Ulithi Atoll I lived on Mogmog; both villages claim important roles and rights in the past *sawei* system. Before my doctoral fieldwork, I had been in Yap for three months and visited Ulithi for a day in 1993.

Canoe fleets of Outer Islanders no longer visit Yap for *sawei* exchanges. Nonetheless, the *sawei* practice of the past has left an indelible mark on Yap-Outer Island relations, still manifested today, which previous social anthropologists have ably demonstrated (e.g., Alkire 1981, 1989). Most, if not all, of the contemporary interactions between Yap and Outer Islanders on Yap and Mogmog that I witnessed or heard about between 1993 and 1995 involved people from Gagil still exercising some level of influence over Outer Island peoples, predicated on the Yap-Outer Island relations of the past. Unlike in the past, there is now a permanent and growing Outer Island population on Yap in Daboch, Maadrich and Ruu‘.

People from both islands believe that the rank, power, and prerogatives of groups of people, such as *sawei* privileges, are invested in stone house platforms (*dayif*) and not in particular individuals. Land is regarded as permanent, while people are considered the temporary voices for the land (Lingenfelter 1975). Earlier publications about Gachpar and Mogmog have presented in one form or another the names of platforms and properties with accompanying maps (Cordy 1986; Damm 1938; Price 1975; Ushijima 1982, 1987b); in one case the platform owners' names are given (Lessa 1950c). My village maps represent only part of the complex history of land ownership and rights. I present only the names of the *dayif* properties from maps which have been approved by John Tharngan, the late Yap Historic Preservation Officer, in consultation with chiefs from both villages. Previous ethnographic works on Yap that omitted particular *sawei* relations have angered those affected.

I recognize the ideological importance of mytho-histories in past island interactions. Mytho-historical information includes mythical and legendary indigenous histories recorded by outsiders and local people. Indigenous mytho-historical data have been collected by me and others, but my study does not rely heavily on these data. Information of this sort is not less important, just less familiar to the author.

In one instance, I investigate the mytho-historical contention that Ruu‘ Village once headed the *sawei* exchange system. However, when I use mytho-history in a model about the past I am really only using my interpretation of the myth and not necessarily the variant implied meanings of the text. Metaphors from earlier time periods need careful deconstruction and interpretation in order for their meanings to be understood. If the meanings I attribute to the mytho-historical text are unknown, then I am only testing my misinterpretation of the data and not the oral histories. My work, then, is not a test of the validity of Yapese or Ulithian mytho-history. I plan to incorporate more of these important data in future work.

Book Structure

The book is organized in the following manner. First, the theoretical and methodological approaches for past and present Pacific Island exchange are reviewed in Chapter II; this focuses on what has been written about inter-island exchange in the Western Carolines. From the review, I outline the appropriate theoretical and methodological approaches I use to address my research concerns. The environmental setting and conditions people lived in on both islands are presented in Chapter III. A historical ethnography of past Carolinian interactions based on documentary evidence is constructed to understand the historical development of Yap-Ulithi interactions following European contact in Chapter IV. Chapter V is a review of archaeological evidence for the Western Carolinian Islands, with particular emphasis on Yap and Ulithi. Archaeological remains of island interaction between Yap and Ulithi are investigated in Chapter VI. Archaeological and ethnohistoric data are finally integrated in Chapter VII to model the interaction history between Yap and Ulithi. In addition, my integration method of the archaeological and ethnohistoric data and the pertinence of my work to exchange theory are discussed. Finally, my conclusions are reviewed in Chapter VIII.

Conventions

There are many Ulithian and Yapese words in this book. Many identical words are spelled differently by different researchers. A dictionary and approved orthography does not exist for the Ulithian language. A Yapese dictionary and reference grammar exist, but the presence of two spelling systems, one familiar to the older people, and the other to the younger people, is confusing. Where possible, this book relies upon Lessa's spelling for Ulithian words and Jensen's (1977) spelling for Yapese words. Quotations from the German Südsee-Expedition publications of Damm (1938), Hambruch (1912), and Müller (1917, 1918) are exact except for my omission of diacritics. Cited page numbers from all the non-English texts refer to the original page numbers, as in the case of the German texts, which despite being translated into English are unpublished by the Human Relations Area Files (HRAF).

Summary

This book attempts to explain the development of exchange relations between the two culturally distinct societies of Yap and Ulithi, Western Caroline Islands. Much has been written about past interactions between Yap and Ulithi, both members of a larger exchange system known as "*sawei.*" This study contributes to the long-term effort of research on interactions between Yap and the coral atolls of the Western Caroline Islands by adding ceramic analyses from archaeological contexts and diachronic explication of the ethnohistoric data pertaining to exchange. Continuing from Intoh's (1988, 1990) extensive Yapese ceramic analyses, I add chemical characterization data from Yapese and Ulithian contexts to address questions about ceramic exchange and culture change. Before integrating the fragmentary archaeological and ethnohistoric records of exchange, ethnohistoric records are independently analyzed and structured into a diachronic paradigm. Archaeological and ethnohistorical records are integrated to construct a model of past Yap-Ulithi exchange. This model encompasses the time period between the earliest archaeological evidence of interaction on Mogmog (cal A.D. 620, AA-21212) to the end of the nineteenth century, when inter-island voyages were forbidden by the German and later the Japanese colonial governments. Finally, the distinct epistemologies of archaeological and ethnohistoric records of exchange are examined to understand the possible integration of these vital data.

(Schneider 1957:13).

Ethnographers find exchange integral in Pacific Island societies. In Palauan society, DeVerne Smith (1983:135) notes that exchange forms and affirms relationships:

> Exchange, then, is the process and medium through which the principles of social structure – descent, matrilineal consanguinity, and patrilineal concepts of "blood"; cross-siblingship as the units of exchange and matrilineal definition; exchange as a principle of kin definition; and alliance – function, intersect, and ultimately are shaped through action at different points in the diachronic process of exchange that friends are made into cross-siblings, affines become "blood," affines become tied through mutually shared lands, and affines are defined as a source for future alliances.

An absence of exchange leads to a breakdown of relationships and invariably a loss of property, rights, and reputation. Similarly, in Gawa, *kula* transactions also begin with relatives in other island communities and keep inter-island relations peaceful. Greediness leads to visits by cannibalistic witches who inflict heavy illness on the culprits (Munn 1986).

A necessary distinction is needed between the valuables and utilitarian materials of gift-exchanges because they can have different social roles in the interacting societies. Anthropologists recognize the importance of the ceremonial exchange of valuables or prestige-goods in living cultures (e.g., Dalton 1977; Malinowski 1922; Strathern 1971) that are usually a prerogative of higher ranking people. Before outside incursions, Dalton (1977:204-205) decides ceremonial exchanges of "primitive valuables" in non-state societies to be of two basic sorts: (1) exchanges intimately connected with alliance formation and maintenance and (2) competitive exchanges "to settle rivalries for leadership positions or settle animosities" in a non-lethal fashion.

The exchange and display of items in Oceania also serve to differentiate between peoples in terms of rank and prestige. The *moka* institution of the New Guinea Highlands, for example, involves competitive gift giving in the circulation of goods between regular male partners. *Moka* exchange is seen as a channel for peaceful relations between affines in hostile communities. Participants in the exchange can maintain their egalitarian relations or choose to "rubbish" their counterparts by giving more esteemed return gifts to claim social superiority.

Exchange relations between Pacific Island peoples play a large role in political economical interpretations. Jonathan Friedman (1981, 1982) stresses the central role of exchange systems, particularly prestige-good exchange in the transformation of Oceanic societies. Friedman (1981:184) proposes that "a general model of prestige-good systems can render the historical distribution of Melanesian social types comprehensible within a larger model for the transformation of Oceanic social systems"; in other words, the manifestation of Pacific social forms belong to a single continuum of structural transformations. Essentially, he argues that, based on linguistic and archaeological evidence, the Austronesian ancestors of present-day Pacific island societies had prestige-good economies. Through time the trade density in Melanesia increased, leading to fragmented short-distance exchange and a breakdown of prestige-good monopolies and political hierarchy leading to Big-Man systems (Thomas 1996:91). Eastern Polynesia underwent a sort of "devolution" where prestige-good exchange was halted because of the increased water distances between the islands. Political dominance shifted trajectory in Eastern Polynesia with new mechanisms for distinguishing political hierarchy, such as food feasting (agricultural intensification), warfare, rank exogamy, and sacred chiefs leading to "theocratic feudalism" (Freidman 1982:192).

Thomas (1996) questions Friedman's Oceanic social evolution model on several points. Based on archaeological evidence, he argues that early Western Polynesian societies were integrated prestige-good systems only quite recently (Thomas 1996:92). Second, Thomas (1996:93) counters, that while the distances between island groups in Eastern Polynesia are magnitudes higher than those in western Oceania, Friedman ignores the exchange between islands in Polynesian archipelagoes, such as in the Hawaiian, Marquesas, Society, and Tuamotu Islands.

Structure and Practice of Exchange

Pacific ethnologists recognize the reproductive and transformational qualities of exchange systems (e.g., Fajans 1993; Munn 1986; Petersen 1982). Exchange events are viewed as dialectic interactions between structure and practice. According to Giddens's (1979) theory of structuration, practice is situated in time and space, and is a product of the dialectic between the structure and the practice, where the duality of the structure is simultaneously the medium and the outcome of practice. As such, structures of exchange and other cultural domains develop through human actions (Bourdieu 1977; Giddens 1979). Through time then, structure and practice mutually transform and reproduce themselves, and manifest themselves as changing cultural behavior. Applying this model to Pacific cultures, social anthropologists have insights into the reproduction and transformations of island societies. Munn (1986), for example, applied a synthetic symbolic analysis to inter-island *kula* exchange in the Massim of Papua New Guinea to identify the reproduction and transformation of social values through exchange practice. Petersen (1982) in his study of Pohnpeian society also interprets the production and exchange of goods as continually reproducing the island polity.

Time is an important dimension in the dialectic of structure and practice. Biersack (1991:13) notes that exchange is inextricable from practice; as a cultural scheme, it "works itself out only in and through time" (Bourdieu 1977:6). At a much longer time scale, Malinowski (1922:327) finds that the behavior of past generations, particularly from the mythical past (what the Annalistes might call the *mentalité*), guides the Trobrianders in their exchange behavior. In more recent ethnographic work, Weiner (1988:156) states that a Trobriand "villager transcends the history of his or her own ancestral lineage and becomes part of *kula* history". In other words, not only can the dialectic between structure and practice form new structures and practice, but different structures and practices can also co-exist. Similarly, Strathern (1991) writes that *moka* exchanges in the New Guinea Highlands are an expression and redirection of history.

When unprecedented inter-cultural encounters take place, such as European contact, the "structures of the conjonctures" of the interacting societies and the dialectic between structure and practice become more conspicuous (Sahlins 1981, 1985). Sahlins's analysis of post-contact Hawaiian society demonstrates the dynamic between structure and practice at these historic junctures. During these novel interactions, individuals relied on their pre-existing local structures to understand the practices of the "other". In time, the interchange between the practice and the structure, transforms the structure and the practice, resulting in a history of structured events.

Ethnographic work has shown that exchange is embedded in societies and can be explained in relation to a number of different factors, all important in contributing to a holistic understanding of exchange. The challenge of studying past exchange systems lies in constructing models of behavior with the residue of past interactions. The following section details what we know about past *sawei* practice.

Archaeological Approaches to Exchange

Archaeologists face difficult challenges in interpreting past exchange behavior. Preserved material remains are the most permanent evidence remaining of interactions in the past. Some archaeologists today favor contextual analyses to consider "the broader economic, social, political, and ideological forms in which the exchange is embedded" (Earle 1982:7-8). In addition, regional perspectives are employed to better appreciate the complexity of interactions and full spatial extent of interactions and their effects.

A contextual approach requires using archaeological data and other ancillary data, such as documentary evidence. Foreign artifacts in archaeological contexts represent more than just exchange activities. Torrence (1986:6) notes that exchange practice may not have material correlates, but that related practices, notably production and consumption of exchange goods, do leave material remains. Investigations into the production and consumption of materials and the sub-systems of exchange provide additional information on the organization of exchange and its relevance to the societies. Production studies into the amount of standardization of exchange items, for example, can give clues about the relations of production. Artifacts in association with archaeological features and other artifacts also imply their use in societies, that is whether for ritual, utilitarian activities, or both.

Trade and exchange have played different roles in archaeological explanations. Like their social anthropological counterparts, archaeologists have explained exchange systems as buffering mechanisms against seasonal and geographic fluctuations (Baugh and Ericson 1992:7). Buffering explanations, however, can have low explanatory power because they are implicit functions of many types of interaction systems (Blinman and Wilson 1992:71). Buffering-type explanations then need to be made explicit so cultural-ecological relationships can be investigated.

Earle (1982:3-4) identifies three broad tasks for archaeologists interested in describing past exchange systems: (1) source, that is determine the provenance of exchange objects; (2) describe the distribution of the exchange goods; and (3) reconstruct the organization of the ancient exchange system. The following sections briefly discuss these three tasks. Identifying evidence of exchange is the first step in an archaeological study. To establish the presence of exchange, archaeologists can quantify the chemical, mineralogical, and stylistic attributes of artifacts and compare them to the probable source. Identifying external, as opposed to internal exchange, is ideally more straight forward if the exchange goods are made of exotic materials. Provenance analysis is the study determining the origin of an artifact. Physicochemical properties of archaeological remains in provenance analysis make inferences about the origin and exchange of artifacts (Neff 1992). Provenance work is based on the following postulate "that there exist differences in chemical composition between different natural sources that exceed, in some recognizable way, the differences observed within a given source" (Weigand et al. 1977:24). After compositional data are collected, statistical algorithms are used to define physicochemical groups and determine the probability that certain artifacts come from known sources.

Before attempting to reconstruct the organization of an exchange system, the spatial and chronological extents of the materials are necessary. Spatial patterning of exchanged artifacts allows one to examine relationships of distance, centrality, and intensity of interaction. There are a number of approaches for achieving this such as regional point scatters, regression analysis, and trend-surface analysis (Earle 1982:5). Any description of the spatial patterning of exchange materials is dependent upon the archaeological spatial representation.

Reconstructing how exchange systems operated through time and affected the societies involved is the biggest challenge facing exchange studies. Renfrew (1975) proposes mathematical models for quantitative patterning of trade goods, such as direct access, down-the-line, central place distribution, and emissary trading. However, archaeological patterns can imply more than one model.

Using a contextual analysis, archaeologists rely on varied data to suggest organizational models for a practice that influenced and was affected by other cultural domains such as subsistence, craft specialization, worldview, and social and political organization. Model building requires interpreting the spatial patterning of the exchange goods. Documentary evidence can contribute to the mechanisms and exchange behavior of a certain area at a particular point in time. Clearly, exchange models that depend on numerous approaches contribute context and interpretations for the archaeological material record.

Plog's Exchange Model-Building Method

Plog (1977) offers an explicit methodology suitable for developing a wide range of exchange models, which has been applied to prehistoric Oceanic exchange systems e.g., Green and Kirch (1997) and Weisler (1997). Plog (1977:129) identifies nine critical structural variables to model exchange networks: (1) content; (2) magnitude; (3) diversity; (4) size; (5) temporal duration; (6) directionality of the exchange goods; (7) symmetry of the exchange; (8) centralization; (9) complexity.

The first content variable refers to the actual materials transferred. As mentioned earlier, this is reliant upon preservation conditions. Magnitude is a measure of the volume or quantity of goods exchanged. Diversity, the third variable, relates to the different kinds of items exchanged. Size of the exchange network describes the actual area of the network. Chronological control is necessary to determine the temporal duration of the exchange system under study. Directionality, the sixth variable, pertains to whether the flow was one or two ways. The seventh variable, symmetry refers to the balance of the exchange, and can be a measure of the goods that flowed in one direction as opposed to another. Centralization designates certain loci that have greater quantities of the resources. Complexity, the last variable, "refers to variation in symmetry, directionality, centralization, and diversity over the territory covered by the network" (Plog 1977:129).

Plog's variables are a good beginning point for describing exchange systems, but like all categorical variables, they are mechanistic. It is important to accommodate more continuous approaches in explaining exchange systems' changes by including variables that focus on historical contingencies and causation (Upham 1990).

Culture Change

Archaeologists are interested in the transformative power of interaction and exchange on societies. Since early on, archaeologists have applied cultural diffusionist models to explain certain parallels in different societies. Diffusion models usually rely upon a dominant society to influence inferior people, who then adopt traits from the more dominant culture (e.g., Childe 1934). These models can be problematic in that their generality suits many archaeological circumstances. Therefore, unless the social conditions and the process of diffusion are explicitly explained, traditional diffusion type explanations demonstrate very little.

Processualist or new archaeology paradigms tend to minimize the role of interaction and exchange in culture change and instead explain the adaptation of cultural systems by focusing on the economy, demography, and energy. More recent post-processualists, on the other hand, have re-introduced socio-cultural variables (some at the expense of more materialist perspectives), and include interaction and exchange as major components of culture change (Baugh and Ericson 1992:9). New models are formulated focusing on unequal exchange relations. The prestige-goods type model relies upon unequal access to prestige valuables to explain the emergence and maintenance of social hierarchies. Frankenstein and Rowlands (1978) for example, use the control of prestige-goods from the Mediterranean world to explain the development of paramount German chiefdoms.

Exchange mechanisms in archaeology have also been couched in world-systems models (Wallerstein 1974). This macroregional perspective focuses on dominant core and dependant periphery interactions for explaining economic alignments and culture change. The long distance movement of valuables is suggested as playing a significant role in the development of interdependent alliances in the Southwest and a rationale for political expansion in Mesoamerica (Upham et al. 1992:446). A high degree of centralization is necessary for the core to systematically exploit the periphery. I do not think this ever existed in Yap. World-systems theory, however, may be more appropriate to examine the colonial history in the Western Carolines.

Peer polity interaction (PPI), on the other hand, is an explanatory model that relies on the interaction of more or less equal polities to account for change, notably increased political complexity. Competition, competitive emulation, warfare, transmission of innovation, symbolic entrainment, ceremonial exchange of valuables, flow of commodities, and language and ethnicity are possible forms of PPI that can be used to explain the development of complex societies. Exchange in PPI models ensures that lines of obligation between polities are reaffirmed and do not disintegrate. Indeed, Renfrew and Cherry (1986:8) use an increase in exchange goods as indicative of interaction between peer polities. Certainly, an increase of exchange goods can be indicative of a number of things. Despite the fact that the PPI model is mostly applied to explain the emergence of state level societies, it has also been applied successfully to less complex societies, notably the Eastern Caroline Islands (Bryson 1989).

Pacific Archaeological Exchange Systems

Inter-island exchange is a major interest of Oceanic archaeologists. Irwin's (1992) model of exploration and colonization of the Pacific demonstrates the feasibility of maintaining relations through ocean-voyaging. Inter-island exchange has been viewed as an indispensable practice between islands not only to acquire essential raw goods, but also integral to evolutionary trajectories of island societies (e.g., Kirch and Green 1987; Terrell et al. 1997). The section briefly covers theoretical frameworks used in past exchange studies in the Pacific.

Neither the archaeological nor the rich ethnographic records contain all of the possible exchange practices of the past. The increasing archaeological work on past Oceanic exchange systems demonstrates that interaction and exchange patterns of the past differ from those of the ethnographic and ethnohistoric records in Melanesia and Polynesia (e.g., Ambrose 1978; Egloff 1978; Kirch 1986; Lilley 1988). Ethnographic manifestations of exchange then should be viewed as synchronic endpoints rather than as indicative of much earlier exchange practices.

Pacific archaeologists rely heavily on the material record for interpretations about exchange, even when there are few preserved artifacts that represent past exchange practices. Some preserved exchange artifacts include chert flakes, fine-grained basalt artifacts, obsidian, pottery, shell valuables, vesicular basalt oven stones, and volcanic glass. While archaeometric methods in the Pacific are widely used and spatial patterns of exchange goods understood, explanatory models of the past are perhaps the least developed (Earle 1982; Hunt and Graves 1990). Most of the difficulty lies in the fact that a number of different hypothetical exchange behaviors can be related to a particular manifestation in the archaeological record.

Recent Lapita studies employing Plog's (1977) exchange modeling variables have shown exchange distinctions in different Oceanic areas (e.g., Green 1996; Green and Kirch 1997; Kirch 1991; Torrence and Summerhayes 1997). No single exchange network ever joined all of the Lapita communities (Green and Kirch 1997:19). Instead, the area has been depicted in terms of four Lapita provinces: Far Western, Western, Southern, and Eastern, each with their own chronological array of defining features. Green and Kirch (1997) use historical antecedents, economic and adaptive advantages, social factors, and ideological considerations fostering identity to explain change in Plog-derived exchange variables. Kirch (1988:114) argues that long-distance exchange was an essential component of the Lapita dispersal and colonization strategy, where a formal exchange system was based on the acquisition of prestige goods such as shell valuables, obsidian, and adzes. Kirch (1987) in the Mussau Islands, Egloff (1978) in the Trobriands, and Irwin (1978, 1985) in the Massim, have shown that through time there was a tendency for exchange networks to reduce in size and become more localized. Future exchange work in Oceania will undoubtedly involve detailing past Oceanic exchange systems to explain how people with one constellation of exchange variables changed into another.

Network analysis of archaeological data and island location has proven a useful heuristic approach in the Pacific Islands. Investigating exchange, Irwin (1978, 1985), for example, investigates the development of the Mailu area of the southeast coastal Papua New Guinea interaction system. He uses connectivity analysis to quantify the relative centrality of sites to propose that Mailu emerged as a central location that coincided with its economic specialization in potting and trading.

Hunt and Graves (1990:110) propose an evolutionary paradigm, as applied to biology, to interpret exchange because "appealing to sociocultural anthropology has yielded few theoretical insights for prehistorians." An evolutionary interpretive framework of exchange allows possible explanations for the following: (1) explaining the rapid colonization of remote Oceania in offering selective advantages for colonizing new environments; (2) explicating the persistence of ancestral traits and the slow rate of cultural divergence; and (3) providing a mechanism involved in the emergence of sociopolitical hierarchy (Hunt and Graves 1990:111). They find access to resources the most significant characteristic in interpreting exchange relations. Not denying the importance of resources, we must be cautious of simplistic ecological adaptationist explanations (Allen 1985; Irwin 1985; Kirch 1991). A society's past is equally important in determining the strategy a community chooses to adopt.

Limitations of Ethnographic Analogies in Models about the Past

Limitations in using ethnographic analogies from ethnoarchaeological, ethnographic, or ethnohistoric studies for archaeological interpretations have been discussed by many (e.g., Upham 1987; Wylie 1985). Similar to other cultures, Pacific Island societies underwent major transformations induced by contact before documentation. Uncritical use of ethnographic analogies can erroneously lead to assumptions of cultural continuity (e.g., in demography, economy, and politics) between the ethnographic present and the past (Upham 1982) and identical rates of change in different cultural spheres. For example, Ambrose (1978) criticizes the appropriateness of ethnographically-derived models for explaining prehistoric Lapita exchange behavior by comparing recent Admiralty Islands exchange and the distribution of obsidian from recent and prehistoric times. Similarly, Egloff (1978:433) reporting from archaeological work in the prehistoric Collingwood Bay settlements of Papua New Guinea ascertains that the influence of historic foreign contacts must be assessed before prehistoric exchange models can be effectively described or analyzed.

Carolinian ethnohistoric data have limitations similar to those of ethnographic data. Collected after European contact, the ethnohistoric records represent island societies following major socio-political and demographic transformations. Indigenous narratives and European reports have the added complication of having been produced by people with unidentified biases and agendas. In the historical ethnography chapter of this book, I describe and evaluate the contexts of production of the ethnographic and ethnohistoric records before integrating them in the exchange history model presented in the discussion chapter.

Despite the above noted limitations, ethnohistoric data are essential in my research by providing a beginning point for model building. Ethnohistoric records offer synchronic information about prehistoric exchange behaviors and emic understandings about exchange between Yap and Ulithi at particular points in the past. If nothing else, a testable model generated from ethnohistoric data tests the archaeologist's interpretation (or misinterpretation) of the evidence. For that reason, it may be better to distinguish between tests of ethnohistoric data and tests of the archaeologist's interpretation of the ethnohistoric data.

Integrating Archaeological and Ethnohistoric Records

It is not new for archaeological studies to incorporate non-material, e.g., documentary and ethnographic records, to interpretations of the past. Recently, however, there has been a renewed interest in combining different records to historicize anthropology (e.g., Bintliff 1991; Feinman 1997; Knapp 1992a; Wilson 1993). I borrow concepts from an integrative inter-disciplinary Annales approach to integrate archaeology and ethnohistory in my research. An Annales-based approach is a French intellectual movement founded by Marc Bloch and Lucien Febvre in 1929 that attempted to combine historical and social science approaches to the past. According to Knapp, the goal of the Annales school "is to generate an interdisciplinary, multivariate, human science that incorporates a broad spectrum of material, documentary, and behavioral variables" (Knapp 1992a:xv-xvi).

Fernand Braudel, one of the contributors to the Annales School, introduced a hierarchical temporal rhythm perspective that has been adopted by some archaeologists. Braudel believes that history is the interplay between at least three groups of processes that operate contemporaneously at different time scales: the history of individual events (*événements*), the structural history of medium term (*conjonctures*), and long term (longue durée) processes (Bintliff 1991:6). He attributes the smallest time scale to microprocesses or events, such as exchange interactions and sociopolitical events, and calls them *l'histoire événementielle*. Medium-term structures are for longer processes (macroprocesses) such as demographic and socioeconomic cycles. The third time scale, perhaps the most popular amongst archaeologists, is the long-term, which typifies for Braudel geographic and environmental structures, but also includes stable technologies, the history of civilizations, and worldviews (Bintliff 1991:6). The sorting of processes into the three different time duration scales is somewhat arbitrary and can fluctuate.

Braudel's (1972) temporal perspective has been adopted and altered by archaeologists, historians, and social theorists. The environmental determinism of the *longue durée* has been called the weakest link in Braudel's trinitarian chain (Knapp 1992b:6). In addition, the static determinism of the structures has been transposed with a dialectic between structure and agency (Bourdieu 1977; Giddens 1979; Le Roy Ladurie 1979; Moreland 1992) as a way in which to integrate the "mixed epistemologies" and overcome the "explanatory dilemma" (terms used by Wilson [1993] and Leonard [1993] respectively). Knapp (1992c) in his study of the factors affecting independent and imperial polities in the Bronze Age Levant used an Annales-based framework "to consider individually and reciprocally short-term events (typically documentary) and longer-term processes (typically archaeological)" (Knapp 1992c:85). This removes the determinism and functionalism of the structure, usually of the *longue durée*, and injects the contingency of historical events, such as the European "discovery" of the Pacific.

Inter-cultural contacts provide unique opportunities for witnessing the conspicuous and dynamic transformation of culture through the dialectic of cultural structure and events. At these junctures, societies interpret new events into their pre-existing structure. In turn, the event transforms the structure. Invariably, trade at these historic encounters is identified as a central element structuring the encounter process (Wilson 1993). Examining the dialectic of structure and practice during European contact with the ancient Hawaiians, Sahlins (1981) recognizes the "structure of the conjuncture" and identifies disparate European and Hawaiian concepts of exchange. British exchange was sexual and economic while Hawaiian exchange was ritualistic and political.

***Sawei* Exchange Models**

Much has been written about the past *sawei* exchange system (e.g., Hunter-Anderson and Zan 1996; Lessa 1950c), all of it important to understand the complex post-contact expression of exchange relations between Yap and its neighboring coral islands. Even though *sawei* voyaging fleets stopped visiting Yap in the beginning of the twentieth century, informants recollected much about their past exchange relationships to anthropologists. It is important to know what form the data are in and when they are collected in order to avoid projecting historical exchange practices too far into the past. Despite the data limitations, researchers hypothesize about the past based on the present. Explanations that project the recollected past on earlier times suppose these complex systems were in only two states: the defunct state of the "ethnographic present" and the state represented in the memory culture. In so doing, the exchange system, indeed the society, is denied any dynamism. Below are explanations of inter-island exchange in the Carolines, particularly, between Yap and the Outer Islands.

The ecological contrasts and resource disparities between Yap, a high island, and its neighboring coral island communities have always been highlighted as important reasons for the existence of the formal *sawei* exchange system (Alkire 1978; Hage and Harary 1991; Lessa 1950c; Mason 1968). Some of the items exchanged by the island communities originate from their specific environmental habitats. In addition, low coral islands are likely to suffer more devastation and recuperate less quickly than high islands after unpredictable natural disasters, such as a typhoon (Schneider 1957:10). Alkire (1980) elaborates on this explanation to include political and economical motivation for the Yapese participation in an uneven *sawei* exchange system.

Hage and Harary (1991:18, 1996:1) claim to reconstruct the *sawei* network and explain the formation of island networks by viewing island societies as "elements of communication systems" relying upon the 1908-1910 Hamburg Südsee-Expedition reports and graph theoretic models of centrality, betweenness, and the neighborhood of a point. They believe ethnohistoric records "afford glimpses of the system in its *original* state" (Hage and Harary 1991:73, emphasis added). I would argue that their connectivity analysis of issues of centrality and access in relation to the German ethnohistoric material is only indicative of the exchange practices extending at best into the nineteenth century, that is the period which the ethnohistoric data represent. As explained in fuller detail in Chapter IV, the Südsee-Expedition began collecting ethnohistoric data about *sawei* exchange after *sawei* practice had already ended.

The inter-cultural exchange system between the Yapese and Outer Islanders was couched in fictive and biological kinship terms. A similar relationship existed on Yap between the high caste (*piiluung*) and low caste villagers (*pimilngaey*), where the *piiluung* provided food and land to their lower caste "children" (Labby 1976:85). The extension of the parent-child metaphor to the Outer Islanders is particularly interesting because the peoples were culturally and linguistically distinct. As explained in the introduction, high caste Yapese were considered the "parents" of their Outer Island "children." For Lessa, *sawei* is "best understood in terms of gift-exchange and reciprocal hospitality between groups maintaining the attitude that they are 'parent' and 'child' " (Lessa 1950c:23). Whenever a Ulithian found himself or herself on Yap, he or she showed filial respect (Lessa 1950c:37, 43). Along with the child status were associated a number of proscriptive behaviors. At the same time, Gagil parents treated their Outer Island children as if they were their first-born. In fact, Gachpar informants told me that on occasion Yapese hid essential items (e.g., baby food) from visiting Outer Islanders so that they would not feel compelled to give essential items away.

In the absence of archaeological evidence, Friedman (1981) suggests a long-distance prestige-good trade system for the Yapese Empire similar to that of Western Polynesia between Fiji, Samoa, and Tonga. Focusing on the characteristics of social reproduction, Friedman (1981:287) claims Western Polynesia resembles Western Micronesia "from large scale regional exchange systems ... to asymmetrical dualism in both kinship and politics". Similarly, Small (1995) uses the *sawei* system to examine the role of past external economies in the process of social evolution. According to Small (1995:76), the *sawei* system, an ethnographic example unlike its *kula* counterpart, provided the "hierarchical armature for the development of fixed ranked relations between communities within the larger political entity of Yapese control". The peripheral location of an island and the small choice of possible exchange partners in a exchange network induced trade scarcity and the imposition of a political economic monopoly.

Numerous researchers use *sawei* exchange as a prestige-goods system to explain Gagil district's rise to political supremacy on Yap (Alkire 1980; Berg 1992; Hage and Harary 1991; Lingenfelter 1975). Lingenfelter contributes political economic considerations to rationalize the formalized exchange system from a Gagil (Wanyan) perspective. Wanyan, a neighboring village of Gachpar in Gagil, had numerous *sawei* ties. Lingenfelter proposes that Outer Island tribute was a primary source of political capital, where the distribution of prestige-goods, such as *lavalavas* (woven loincloths), were used as a trading mechanism to "shift goods from areas of plenty to areas of scarcity" (Lingenfelter 1975:153). The Yapese acquired political capital while Outer Islanders benefited in economic ways.

Alkire (1980) also later added a Yapese component to his earlier work that emphasized the economic gains Outer Islands received from the *sawei* exchange system. He argues that protected Outer Island navigational knowledge was a commodity sought by the Gagil Yapese. Outer Island navigational knowledge was vital for sailing to acquire stone money from Palau, which played an important role in the political dynamics of Yap. In return, Outer Islanders received pottery, wood, food, and relief supplies for typhoon survivors. Ultimately, Alkire (1980) believes the control of information and material economic goods played a role in the development of the centralized "Yapese Empire." For Lessa (1950c:43) the primary impetus behind Outer Islanders voyaging to Yap in the past was also economic.

Berg (1992) proposes a history of the *sawei* network based on elements of legendary and genealogical evidence from Puluwat and Satawal collected by the Hamburg Südsee-Expedition. Similar to Lingenfelter's political economical focus on Yap, Berg (1992:160) describes *sawei* exchange as simple trading between Yap and the Outer Islands in the twelfth and thirteenth centuries; tribute voyaging in the fourteenth and fifteenth centuries; intensive tribute associated with the Yangolab cult to offset *fei* (Yapese stone money from Palau); and increased fighting in Yap in the sixteenth to eighteenth centuries. The introduction of stone money by Rull and Tamil, offset the prevalence of the Yapese shell valuable called *gau* (*Spondylus*) obtained from the Outer Islands, notably, Eauripik (Berg 1992:155). Today, Yapese shell valuables are kept by their owners as well as displayed in meeting houses and sacred locations. Broken fragments of shell are also sometimes found near *dayif* features.

Hunter-Anderson and Zan (1996) have recently challenged a number of proposed hypotheses about the traditional *sawei* exchange system. Like in earlier hypotheses, "traditional" refers to the time period of informant recollections and European ethnohistoric accounts. Unlike Hage and Harary (1991, 1996), Lingenfelter (1975), and Small (1995), they suggest that the island participants in the "Yapese Empire" were more heterarchical than hierarchical. Hunter-Anderson and Zan recognize the island communities were ranked, but argue that the "Yapese Empire" was neither centralized, nor stratified, and consisted of many autonomous islands. The overlapping layers of kin groups, political alliances, communication networks, eating ranks, and villages surely made the political organization complex, to say the least. In addition, they argue that Outer Island navigation expertise (Alkire 1980) and valuables (Lingenfelter 1975) could not have been transformed into political or economic power on Yap. Instead, *sawei* obligations and valuables communicated "alliance worthiness" to other competing alliances and bodies in the complex political organization of Yap (Hunter-Anderson and Zan 1996:38).

Hunter-Anderson and Zan (1996:28-33) offer a compelling scenario to explain the formation of the *sawei* exchange system based primarily on ethnographic evidence and cost/benefit type arguments. Using demographic and environmental factors, they believe the extension of Yap's alliance system into the coral island communities to the east was an adaptive response to acute population density in the resource-limited environment of Yap. Increases in population density were met with agricultural intensification. Intense competition eventually led to internecine warfare and the formation of complex ceremonial and alliance system between flexible socio-territorial (village) groups, from which a three-centered geo-political alliance system containing Gagil, Rull, and Tamil developed. While Hunter-Anderson and Zan (1996) propose that it is Gagil's assumption of *sawei* obligations to its Outer Island alliance partners that led to its rise in the Yapese geo-political system, I think valuables such as shell valuables and stone money, particularly in the post-contact period, were important in displaying rank distinctions and Gagil's extensive alliance system.

Religious ideology legitimized *sawei* exchange relations between the Yapese and the Outer Islanders. Ethnohistoric records recount the powerful religious ideology that validated Yap-Outer Island relations. Yap was the sacred center for the Caroline Islands to the east. Numerous origin myths link the creation of Ulithi with Gachpar and the *sawei* exchange practice. Yap also had powerful magicians. If the magic was white, it could "produce an abundance of food and fish, make women fertile and ward off calamity"; if the magic was black, it could "bring on typhoons, epidemics and plagues of ants" (Ushijima 1982:67). Lessa (1956:70-71) believes sorcery and economics were more important than the myths for what he calls "blackmailing" the Outer Islanders into their tributary position.

Research Questions

Much has been recorded about the ethnohistory of the *sawei* exchange system and even more has been hypothesized about how the system functioned in the past. This study proposes to contribute longitudinal exchange information from an understudied area in the Pacific, Micronesia. Previous archaeological explorations into Pacific exchange systems have shown the limitations of using the ethnographic or ethnohistoric records to represent the deep history of these island societies. Cultures are dynamic, not static. The exploration of theoretical and methodological approaches into past and present Pacific exchange systems has demonstrated the centrality of exchange and how it is integral in the reproduction and transformation of societies.

Cultural-ecological models based on ethnographic evidence help explain the benefits of exchange, but without diachronic data cannot address concerns about the origins of inter-island exchange or account for the factors involved in transforming the exchange. There is no question that the limited and unpredictable natural environments on coral islands encouraged inter-island ties (Alkire 1989:12; Hage and Harary 1991; Lessa 1956). In fact, I know of no model that does not include as one component or another the disparity of coral island resources for explaining socioeconomic relations between a high island and neighboring coral islands. Cultural-ecological explanations for the past are useful in identifying the needs people must have met in order to live, but they are also reductionist in omitting other less obvious factors such as history, which also served in forming and perpetuating an exchange system. From what we know about the historical manifestations of exchange systems in the Pacific, they were imbued with complex social, political, and ideological behaviors.

This book attempts to understand the history or transformations of exchange between Yap and Ulithi. A diachronic history of exchange practice is necessary not only for an understanding of the development of exchange between these two societies, but also to comprehend how other cultural domains affected and were influenced by exchange practices. Specifically, this research examines the evidence for exchange interactions between Yap and Ulithi to explain when and how interisland interactions began and intensified. Numerous hypotheses are formulated and tested to understand the details about past interaction between Yap and Ulithi. Part of the exchange history between these two islands includes the entanglement of European goods and presence. Therefore, outsider-generated ethnohistoric documents are integrated with archaeological evidence to understand the most recent 400 years of exchange.

Theoretical and Methodological Perspectives

The theories and methods I use to address the aforementioned research questions are eclectic because of the variety in data records. Some of the overarching theory and general methods are covered in this section; the rest are mentioned in the chapters in which the theory and methods are actually applied.

The theoretical design I use to examine culture history derives from the Annales historical movement. However, I do not use an Annaliste approach because a single Annales approach does not exist (see Moreland 1992:126). I view peoples' past as exhibiting the dialectic process of structure and events of different time duration. First, there are short-term events; second, processes of medium duration; and third, process of long duration. An event can be an exchange interaction between two persons of different cultures, while a process of medium duration can be the worldview of an individual or society.

The overall paradigm I use to explain past cultural transformations is the dynamic dialectic process of structure and agency (Bourdieu 1977; Giddens 1979). I believe that culture change comes about from the interplay between cultural structures and practice. As mentioned earlier, this removes any determinism from the explanations of culture change and accounts for the individual, social mediation, and historical contingency. The movement between the structure and practice in societies needs not necessarily lead to transformations, much less ones visible in the archaeological record. However, for there to be even a relative cultural stasis, a continual dialectic between the structure and practice is still necessary. The primary archaeological and ethnohistoric data represent both structure and practice, but I do not differentiate between structure and practice because of their duality (Giddens 1979); that is at once being structure and practice. Therefore, I take the archaeological record and ethnohistoric events as being both a representation of structure and practice, the difference being that the resolution of the ethnohistoric events are microscopic while "moments" in the archaeological record are macroscopic.

In the protohistory of past exchange between Yap and Ulithi, that is in the early contact period, I exploit the overlap between history and archaeology or what Sahlins (1992:1) calls a "privileged intellectual space." Ethnohistory, an ethnological study based on historical documents and indigenous histories, lends non-material contextual information about island interactions of a short time span while archaeological evidence, on the other hand, provides a representation of exchange practices in much longer time duration or what the Annaliste historians call the medium term and long term duration processes (Bintliff 1991:6; Braudel 1980:27).

Before integrating any records of past exchange behaviors, I appreciate the many transformations the data can undergo. The sedimentation of exchange practices in both islands and the ethnohistoric data relating to inter-island exchange, all exist in the present and have undergone various transformations before being recorded or collected. These transformations must be identified and teased out of the data to construct as accurate a model as possible.

Similar to other types of evidence, archaeological data undergo alterations and transformations beginning with the production of the artifacts to later post-depositional alterations. Geochemical properties of potsherds, for example, can be influenced by their clay source, ceramic recipe, use, and finally by their depositional context. The contexts of production for the historical records must also be examined before incorporating their information into historical models to understand their bias and limit misinterpretation.

My interpretations of past pre-contact exchange behaviors rely on archaeological evidence alone. I take material culture to be the product of human agency "both the medium and outcome of social practice", that is "socially determined individual production (Marx 1973:84)" (Moreland 1992:116). In other words, the material records are representations of human actions and are "points of articulation with social, politico-economic, or ideational structures" (Knapp 1992b:10). Analyses of exchange have shown the centrality of exchange in cultural processes. For this reason, ancillary archaeological materials with information on agricultural intensification, population pressures, and the materialization of worldview are included in the longitudinal model of exchange.

Archaeological data are fragmentary records of structure and practice and indicate the transformative nature of interaction and exchange between the people of Gachpar and Mogmog. In the absence of other evidence, Yap-Ulithi interactions are most visible in the Ulithian archaeological record because exotic artifacts are conspicuous in the coral atoll.

Ethnographic and ethnohistoric data can contribute to interpretations of the remote past. Studies discussed in the beginning of this chapter demonstrate the centrality of exchange in present and past societies and show the linkages of exchange with other cultural domains.

Interpretations of the past that depend only on the archaeological record must be mindful of the possible complex linkages of exchange with other cultural domains, such as the worldview and the social and political systems.

Summary

Exchange is central and vital in the lifeways of island peoples. Archaeological, ethnohistoric, and ethnographic records of exchange offer much to an understanding of present and past exchange practices. I examine the archaeological manifestations of exchange where there is an overlap of ethnographic and ethnohistoric records back in time to a point where only the archaeological record exists. Archaeological data give a crucial material and diachronic dimension to the exchange model.

Ethnohistoric data exist on the inter-island relations between Yap and Ulithi for its most recent history. Those records are integrated into the discussions of exchange behavior to understand the development of exchange in the last 400 years. Previous works on the exchange behaviors between Yap and its Outer Islands have relied more on synchronic ethnographic data than diachronic archaeological data. A potential outcome of considering archaeological data is the identification of exchange patterns not found in the ethnographic or ethnohistoric accounts.

Chapter III

Environmental Setting of Yap and Ulithi

This chapter reviews geological, biotic, and climatic characteristics of the natural environments of Mogmog, Ulithi and Gachpar, Yap. The environmental descriptions identify conditions to which the island inhabitants adapted and environmental conditions affecting the archaeological deposits. Ocean current and wind data describe the conditions for sailing between Yap and Ulithi. Finally, the periodicity and damage wrought by tropical storms are outlined.

Western Caroline Islands

Micronesia comprises approximately 3,000 islands with a total land area of 2,700 km^2 in an area of 7.4 million km2 of Pacific Ocean (Craib 1983:922). The Caroline Island archipelago of Micronesia spans approximately 3,200 km from Palau (Belau) to Kosrae in the northwest region of the Pacific Ocean. It is made up of 960 islands and atolls spread between 1° and 10° north latitude and between 164° and 131° east longitude (see Figure 1). High islands in the Western Carolines include Palau and Yap. The rest of the islands are either high coral islands or low coral atolls. Today these islands make up the states of Yap and part of Chuuk in the modern island nation of the Federated States of Micronesia.

Physiographic Island Types

Alkire (1989:12) notes three physiographically distinct island types within the Western Carolines: (1) volcanic-continental; (2) raised coral; and (3) coral atoll. All of the volcanic-continental high islands in the Western Carolines lie on the western edge of Micronesia and are part of the Asian continental plate. The continental nature of volcanic-continental islands makes them compositionally diverse and geologically complex. Raised coral islands, the second type, lack a lagoon, and are uplifted coral atolls. In the Western Carolines, Yap and Palau are volcanic-continental islands; Fais and Satawal are raised coral islands. All of the other islands, including Ulithi, are coral atolls – the most abundant landforms in Micronesia.

Wiens (1962:8) defines coral atolls, Alkire's (1989) second physiographic type, as:

> ... a more or less continuous emerged or slightly submerged calcareous reef surrounding a distinctly deeper lagoon or several such lagoons without emerged volcanic islands, which stand apart from other islands, and whose upper seaward slopes rise steeper than the repose angle of loose sediments from a generally volcanic foundation too deep for the growth of reef corals.

Alkire's (1989:14) description of a low coral atoll island fits Mogmog well:

> Proceeding from the lagoon side to the ocean side of an atoll island one will usually see a low sandy beach facing on the lagoon which rises to an elevation of approximately six or eight feet [1.8 - 2.4 m]. Moving inland, the beach levels off into a plain which either continues beyond the midpoint of the island or decreases in elevation, thus forming a swampy area one or two feet [0.3 or 0.6 m] above sea level. Beyond the swamp the land usually rises again at a more rapid rate, reaching its greatest elevation in the vicinity of the ocean beach. The lagoon beach is sandy, the interior swamp chiefly humus, and the ocean side composed primarily of coral cobbles, beach rock, and boulders.

Sea-Level Fluctuations

Local rising and falling land and sea data are vital for understanding the changing Pacific island landscapes pertinent to human adaptation and the preservation conditions of archaeological resources. Sea-level fluctuations, variable in both space and time (Pirazzoli 1991:6), are the result of eustatic, hydro-isostatic, and tectonic forces in the western Pacific (Dickinson 2001). Other than Johnson et al.'s (1960:82) comment that there is no evidence of sea-level change on Yap, no past sea-level data are available for the Yap and Ulithi region so I present only general comments about the history of Carolinian sea-levels.

Dickinson (1999, 2001) has recently published work on the relative Holocene sea levels on Pacific Islands. Yap and Ulithi have not received direct field measurements; however, theoretical suggestions can be made. Depending on the paleoshoreline record (paleo-low-tide, paleo-high-tide) of nearby islands, Dickinson (2001) argues a mid-Holocene (4000 B.P.) high-stand of 1.0 to 1.4 m above present MSL in the area, after which human colonization would have started. For Yap in particular, Dickinson (2001:222) suggests that despite the mid-Holocene hydro-isostatic highstand, the Yap arc likely subsided during the Holocene. In respect to Ulithi, Dickinson finds that Ulithi Atoll was mostly likely awash during the highstand and that the monotonic and linear sea level decline, absent tectonic effects, began no earlier than about 3500 BP, as it did in the Marianas (personal communication, 2002). Earlier studies interpreted exposed coral reef platforms as lithified storm deposits and not as evidence for emergence. More recent studies in Chuuk, Kosrae, the southern Marianas, and Pohnpei rely on the exposed platforms to argue that the sea level has risen at least one meter in the late Holocene

(Pirazzoli 1991:143). Therefore, Yap and Ulithi do appear to have had higher sea-levels than those found today.

Yap

Yap consists of a tight cluster of four resource-rich high islands, Yap, Gagil-Tomil, Map, and Rumung, situated at 9° 25' to 9° 46' north latitude and 138° 3' to 138° 14' east longitude (Intoh 1990:36). The Yap Islands will be referred to simply as the island of Yap. The western shores of Yap are fronted by the Philippine Sea; the eastern shores are fronted by the Pacific Ocean (Figure 3). Yap's four islands are separated by narrow water passages and form one land mass 31 km long and 12 km wide with a combined area of 7925 ha (Hunter-Anderson 1983:3). A broad fringing reef surrounds Yap. "Reef corals are colonial animals and their reef-building derives from their ability to precipitate calcium carbonate (lime) and to grow upon the skeletons of their predecessors" (Wiens 1962:90). Reef-building organisms need warm, relatively shallow, clear, saline water to grow (Wiens 1962:10).

Geological Traits of Yap

The four islands of Yap are part of a series of intra-oceanic arc-trench systems, which extend from Palau to the Mariana Islands and separate the Philippine plate from the Pacific plate (Rytuba and Miller 1990:413). Yap is at the southern end of the West Caroline Geanticline submarine ridge (Hess 1948). Unlike the islands to the east, Yap has a more complex geological history and lies west of the Andesite Line.

The Andesite Line distinguishes the geological composition of the landmasses on either side. To the left (or west) of the line lie arcs of andesitic volcanic island chains that comprise mixed submerged continental rocks displaying much folding and faulting, also containing "metamorphic rocks as slate, gneiss, and schist; such sediments as coal and clay; and such intrusive and volcanic rocks as andesite, high in silica and alumina" (Thomas 1967:4). The volcanic islands to the east of the Andesite Line, which lie in the deep Pacific Basin are characterized by "submerged volcanic mountains, and

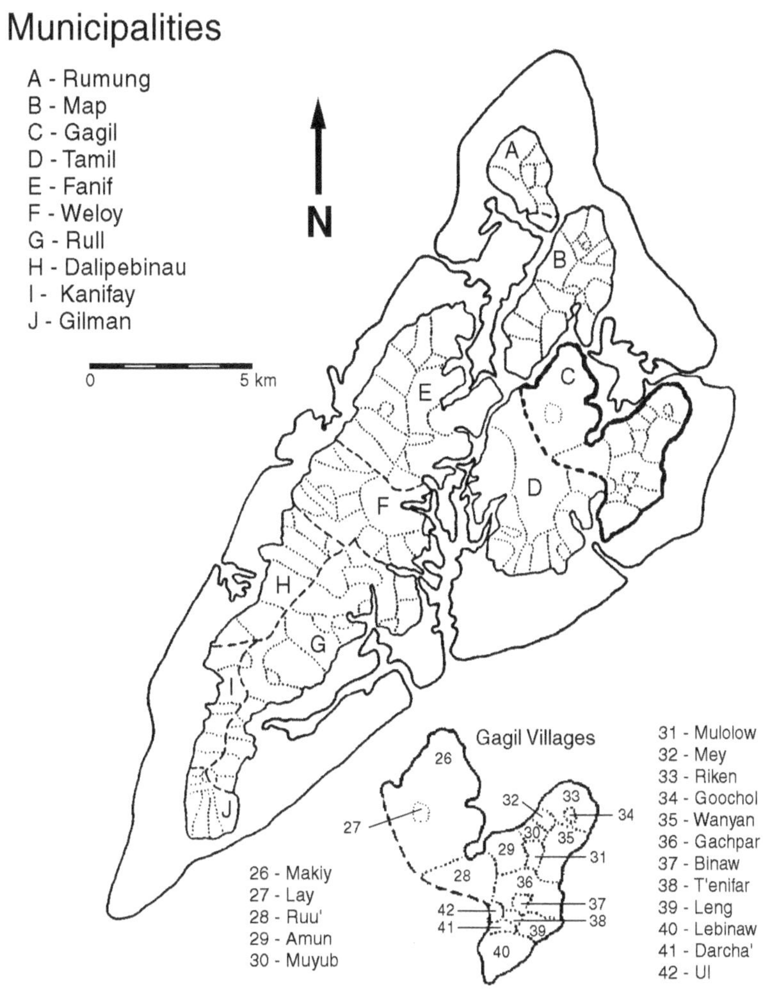

FIGURE 3. Yap (adapted from Intoh and Leach 1985:3).

oceanic volcanic islands predominantly composed of heavy dark basalt, which also comprise the platforms capped by reef corals and atolls" (Thomas 1967:3-4). The Andesite Line

> ... follows southward the arcs of the Aleutian, Kurile, Bonin, Mariana, and Palau Islands, all volcanic chains, and then turns sharply southeastward to the Fiji Islands where it makes another sharp bend southwestward to include New Zealand within the andesitic realm [Wiens 1962:13].

Yap has three main geological formations (Figure 4): (1) the Yap Formation; (2) the Map Formation; and the (3) Tomil Volcanics (Johnson et al. 1960). Yap has exposures of a pre-Tertiary metamorphic basement called the Yap Formation, dominated by greenschists and amphibolites with intrusive ultramafic rocks (Johnson et al. 1960:61). The rocks of this formation weather to clays, some of which include "ironstone concretions from fine sand to gravel in size" (Johnson et al. 1960:64). Overlying the basement rocks in the northeastern part of the islands is a mass of breccia, partly tectonic and partly sedimentary of Tertiary age called the Map Formation. Intoh (1988:66) states the Map Formation includes "angular fragments of actinolite schist, hornblende, diorite, hornblendic feldspathic gabbro, pyroxenite, serpentinite, and diopsidic marble" (Johnson et al. 1960; Hawkins and Batiza 1977:221). The Tomil "Volcanics" geological unit, probably Miocene in age, comprises "andesitic and basaltic volcanic breccias, conglomerates, lava flows, and tuffs", most of which deeply weather to a kaolinitic clay (Johnson et al. 1960:75).

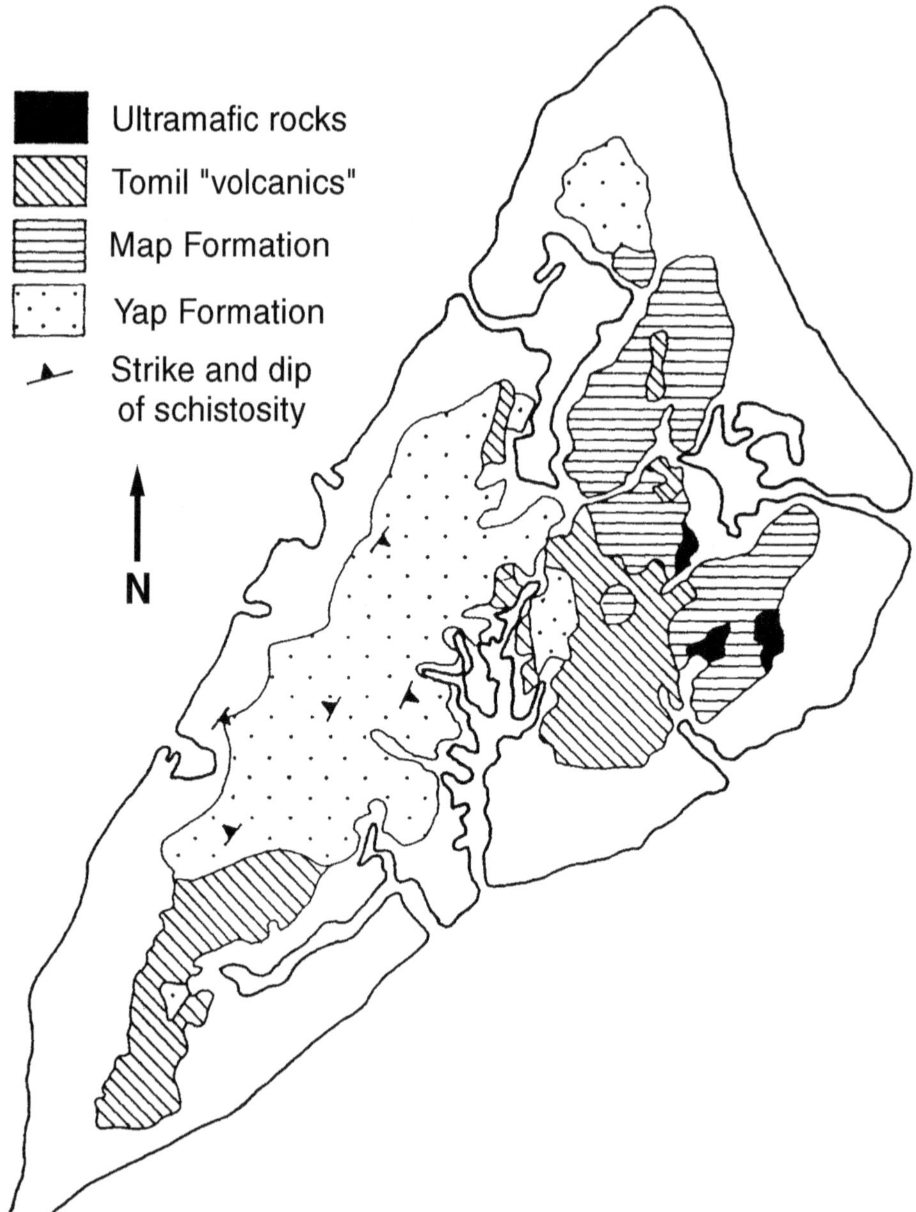

FIGURE 4. Geological formations in Yap (Hawkins and Batiza 1977; Intoh 1988:65).

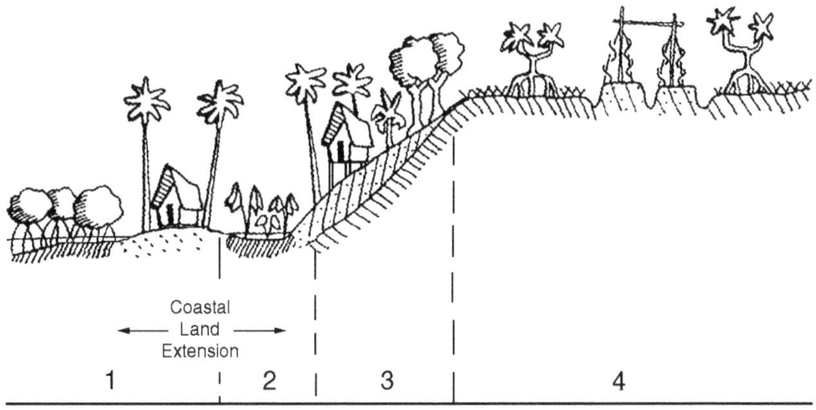

FIGURE 5. Yap environmental zones: (1) mangrove and coconut palms in the Sandy Shore zone; (2) mangrove and aroids in the Taro and Mangrove Swamps zone; (3) coconut palms, Inocarpus, and bananas in the Tree-Covered Gradual Slopes zone, and; (4) Pandanus and yam gardens in the Grassy Savanna zone (adapted from Barrau 1961:28; Craib and Price 1978:6). I have added a habitation to the third zone (see also Cordy 1986:11) and identified the coastal land extension area.

Gachpar Village Environmental Zones

Gagil is one of ten municipalities in Yap and includes the coastal village of Gachpar and sixteen other villages. Cordy's (1986:62) categorization of the Gachpar Village environmental zones is presented in Figure 5, which is similar to that of Barrau (1961:28), Craib and Price (1978), and Müller (1917:8). According to Cordy (1986:62), Gachpar exhibits four environmental zones. Beginning from the water's edge to the center of the island, the zones include (1) Sandy Shore; (2) Taro and Mangrove Swamps; (3) Tree-Covered Gradual Slopes; and (4) Grassy Savanna. The environmental zones are differentiated by elevation, vegetation (Barrau 1961), soils (see C. Smith 1983), and human settlement patterns (Cordy 1986; Craib and Price 1978).

The sandy shore or coastal flats zone make up the first zone and can be as much as 100 m wide (Cordy 1986:62). It is occupied by coconut groves and mangrove. Johnson et al. (1960) call the beach deposits alluvial mats composed of wet silty sands, mud, and calcareous sand from coral reefs, subject to flooding during storms because of their low-lying nature. The diversity of plant species on the shore is much less than that inland because of poor soil and salt spray exposure (Mason 1968:301).

A complex interplay of natural and cultural forces is responsible for the reclamation of lagoonal land. Mangrove upper intertidal tropical ecosystems, which colonize saline lagoonal land at alluvial rich estuaries, contribute to the shoreline progradation (Bloom 1970; Edwards 1995:220). Anthropologists and others have recognized yet another force behind the progradation of the coast (Cordy 1986:79; Falanruw 1990:233; Intoh 1988:40; Labby 1976:12; Müller 1917) where besides alluvial deposits and mangrove ecosystems accreting the coastal fringes, people (anthropogenic agents) have extended the coast into the lagoon flats. In Gachpar, as in other coastal-fronting villages of Yap, people in the past extended the coast by erecting stonewalls and infilling the lagoon flats and mangrove swamps with coral heads, debris, and sand.

Behind the Sandy Shore zone is the Taro and Mangrove Swamps zone where the present main staple giant swamp taro (*Cyrtosperma chamissonis*) is grown. Mangrove swamps can either be at the edge of the shore or further back in the second zone with the aroid cultigens. Mangroves are halophytic communities found in estuarine swamps and along coasts where alluvium has been deposited by streams and where fringing reefs protect coastlines from erosional wave action. Cordy (1986:62) estimates the Taro and Mangrove Swamps zone to be approximately 50 m wide. Alluvium within this zone includes muck, sand, silt, and clay rich in organic content (Johnson et al. 1960).

Higher ground behind the taro swamps, in the Tree-Covered Gradual Slopes zone, contains valleys and hillsides planted with coconut groves and forested with trees, such as breadfruit, banyan, mango, Tahitian chestnut, custard nut, pandanus, areca palms, citrus, and grasses. The fourth Grassy Savanna ecological zone is less fertile and includes high exposed areas where pandanus, grasses, and ferns grow. For more information on the vegetation of Yap, see Falanruw et al. (1987, 1990).

Soils

According to Johnson et al. (1960:96), Yap's geological soil composition of old volcanic lava and metamorphic rocks has the following generalized soils: (1) latosols; (2) planosols; (3) lithosols; and (4) alluvial soils (Figure 6):

Latosols: reddish, granular, well drained acid clays, with gravelly, limonitic surfaces locally; underlain by very deep weathered, clay-textured volcanic rocks.

Planosols: Brownish or olive, impermeable, very plastic, imperfectly drained clays, with gravelly limonitic surfaces locally; moderately shallow to schist or breccia bedrock; includes dispersed areas of lithosols.

Lithosols: Dark-brown silty clay loam, stony in places; thin olive-brown silty clay subsoils locally; shallow to schist or breccia bedrock.

Alluvial soils of coastal flats, valley bottoms and inland depressions: Deep, well to imperfectly drained calcareous sands on coastal flats; mixed with clay or silt in places, surfaces high in organic content. Deep, very poorly drained, grayish, mottled clays in valley bottoms. Reddish, granular, imperfectly drained clays and deep deposits of dark-brown limonitic gravel in lowlands with depressions. Coastal swamps and tidal flats [Johnson et al. 1960:100].

Gachpar Soils

Gagil soils are underlain by schist and conglomerate in the north and east; the soils in the south are on a highly dissected bench and are underlain by very soft volcanic breccia (C. Smith 1983:1). Christopher Smith describes Gagil soils as rich in aluminum (1983:26), clayey (1983:75), gravelly loam (1983:83), and having severe seepage (1983:81). Additionally, Gachpar has large lateritic nickeliferous iron ore deposits derived from nickel-bearing serpentine which were mined by the Japanese South Seas Development Company (commonly known as NANTAK; Johnson et al. 1960:66, 87-88).

Smith's Gachpar soil classification loosely fits the environmental zone boundaries of Gachpar (Table 2). Smith (1983) identifies the soils in the Sandy Shore zone as Dublon loamy fine sand (No. 501). This sand is of moderate slope, very deep, somewhat poorly drained, and has poor soil fertility with a high water table at a depth of 38-90 cm year-round. Beach deposits have medium to coarse-grained calcareous sand drained from coral reefs. The beach area is well drained and generally poor in organic content except in marshy mangrove areas.

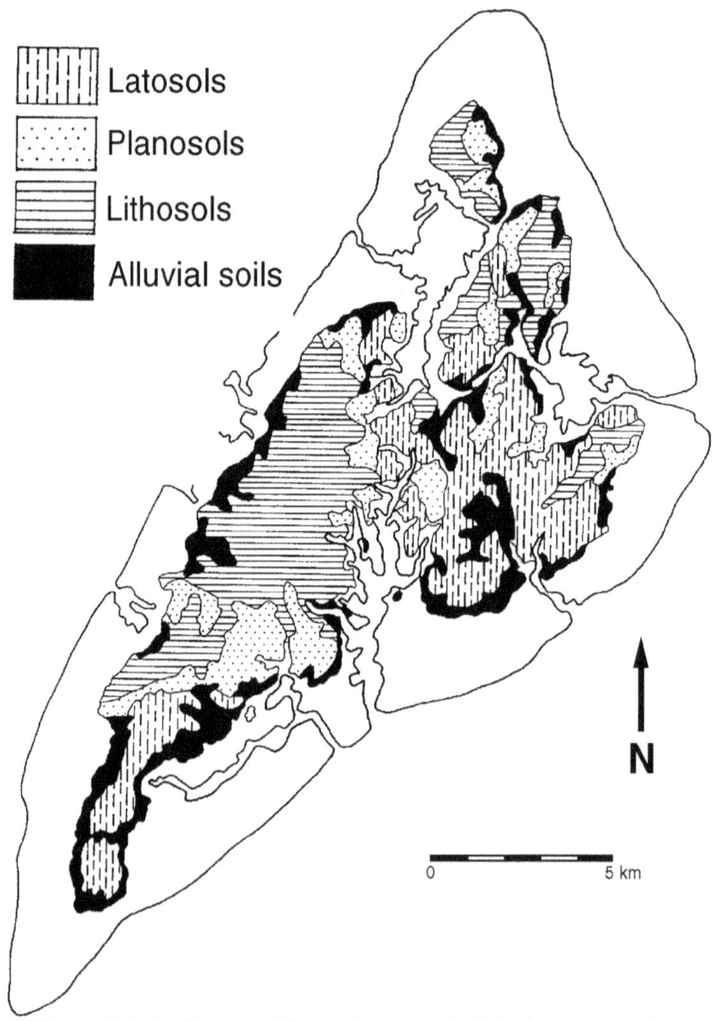

FIGURE 6. Soil distribution of Yap (Johnson et al. 1960:100; Intoh 1988:67).

TABLE 2. Characteristics of Gachpar Environmental Zones (Source: C. Smith 1983)

Environmental Zones	Gachpar Soil Type	Salinity (Mmhos/cm)	Permeability (cm/hr)	Enriched elements	Soil pH
Coastal Sandy Shore	Dublon Ngedebus Variant	< 2	15 - 50		7.4 – 8.4
Taro and Mangrove Swamp	Dublon Variant	< 2	0.5 - 5		6.6 – 7.8
Tree-Covered Gradual Slopes	Dechel	< 2	0.5 - 15	Ni, Fe	5.1 – 7.3
Grassy Savanna	Yap	< 2	5 - 15		5.1 – 6.5

The second environmental zone, Taro and Mangrove Swamps, located on the coastal flats, is between the uplands and the coast. Smith (1983:10) classifies the soil in this zone as Dublon Variant sandy clay loam (No. 502). This deep sandy clay loam soil is somewhat poorly drained and has moderate permeability. Smith (1983:10) states "[i]t formed in alluvium derived dominantly from wave-deposited coral sand, volcanic rock, and schist."

Dechel mucky silt loam (No. 500) is found behind the Taro and Mangrove Swamp zone in the Tree-Covered Gradual Slopes environmental zone (see C. Smith 1983:9-10). This deep soil is poorly drained and has moderately slow permeability. "The soil formed in alluvium underlain by volcanic material and schist" (C. Smith 1983:9). The remainder of the third environmental zone, i.e., the remainder of Gachpar and the Grassy Savanna zone has Yap silty clay loam soils (Nos. 527 and 528). These soils are very deep, well drained on low-lying broad ridges, with low fertility, and formed in "residuum derived dominantly from volcanic breccia and tuff" (C. Smith 1983:23).

Yapese Clays

Earthenware pots are complex mixtures of water, clay, non-plastic natural inclusions, and non-plastic temper. "Temper" refers to non-plastic inclusions added by potters. This section focuses on the Yapese distribution of these essential ingredients.

Clays are sedimentary deposits from the products of weathering and disintegration of older parental rocks (Rice 1987:36). Clays are mostly fine particles of hydrous aluminum silicates and irons, alkalies, and alkaline earths. There are two types of clays: primary and secondary (Rice 1987:37). Primary or residual clays are defined as those remaining more or less where they formed while secondary, transported or sedimentary clays, are those found some distance from the parental rocks. Agents involved in the transportation of clays can include erosion, streams, tides, waves, and wind (Rice 1987:37).

Intoh (1990:40) notes that the distribution of clays on Yap is somewhat restricted and that planosols are most likely to contain clays necessary for pottery manufacture. Derived mostly from Yap Formation schists, and to a lesser degree from breccias of the Map Formation, planosols are characterized as the least extensive of the major soil groups, "moderately deep, comparatively shallow to bedrock, imperfectly drained soils with brown, mottled, very plastic tight, very slowly permeable clay subsoils" (Johnson et al. 1960:97).

Intoh's raw clay source examination classifies two Yapese clay groups: montmorillonite-rich clay and kaolinite-rich clay deposits, both of which are found in Yapese ceramics. Montmorillonite-rich clay minerals belong to the smectite group and have a three-layer structure comprising an alumina layer sandwiched between silica layers (Rice 1987:482). Montmorillonite-rich clays have a small particle size, great plasticity, large drying shrinkage, and large dry strength (Intoh 1988:73). Intoh (1990:40) notes that montmorillonite-rich clays derive from both the metamorphic Map and the Yap Formations (Kawachi 1985:199-200).

In contrast, kaolinite clay minerals have two-layer structures of silica and alumina (Rice 1987:477). Unlike the montmorillonite clays, kaolinite clays have larger particle sizes, small drying shrinkage, small plasticity, small dry strength, and require higher firing temperatures for complete dehydration of the clay (Intoh 1988:73). Intoh (1990:40) notes that kaolinite-rich clays derive from the Tomil Volcanics Formation and sedimentary rocks, such as those in the southern plateau of Yap (Kawachi 1985:199-200). Clay samples from the southern plateau of the Yap Formation have greater quartz contents than do clays collected from other areas (Intoh 1988:70).

Yap has distinctive geological characteristics relevant for clays and ceramics. Dickinson and Shutler (1979:1670-1671, 1684-1685) include Yap in their Tectonic Highland Temper group, which is important for sourcing ceramics with inclusions or temper. Geological materials are characteristically metamorphosed by tectonic activity on the margin of the continental and oceanic plates. "Source rocks are characteristically cherty successions and varied metasedimentary terranes, but they also include basaltic metavolcanic rocks and ophiolitic periodites or gabbros" (Dickinson and Shutler 1979:1670). Palau, on the other hand, belongs to the Andesitic Arc Temper group, and is characterized by almost exclusively rocks and minerals of volcanic origin.

Yapese Sand Deposits

Intoh (1988) examines the distribution of sand deposits because early Yapese ceramics have sand-sized inclusions. She discovered sand deposits are primarily located on the coastal beaches and riverbanks. Sand dunes do not exist on Yap and sand deposits are not extensive (Intoh 1990:42). All ten sand sediment samples from the villages of Antoh, Aringel, Bechiel, Gachpar, Gargey, Meerur, Okau, Rang, Rumu', and Yaboch presented in Intoh's (1988) work contain a combination of organic marine-derived calcareous sand and terrigenous-derived sands. Rivers are few, mostly seasonal, and flow into mangrove swamps. Very coarse alluvial sand derives mostly from the schist bedrock of the Yap Formation (Intoh 1990:42). Inorganic mineral composition varies considerably, the majority being of metamorphic origin. However, non-metamorphic quartzo-feldspathic sands, common inclusions in older ceramics, have been found in Map and the Gagil-Tomil area (Intoh 1988:78).

Ulithi

Ulithi, the largest and northernmost atoll in the Caroline Islands and Yap's closest island society, lies between the northern latitudes of 9° 46' and 10° 6' and between the eastern longitudes of 139° 34' and 139° 52'. Ulithi Atoll is

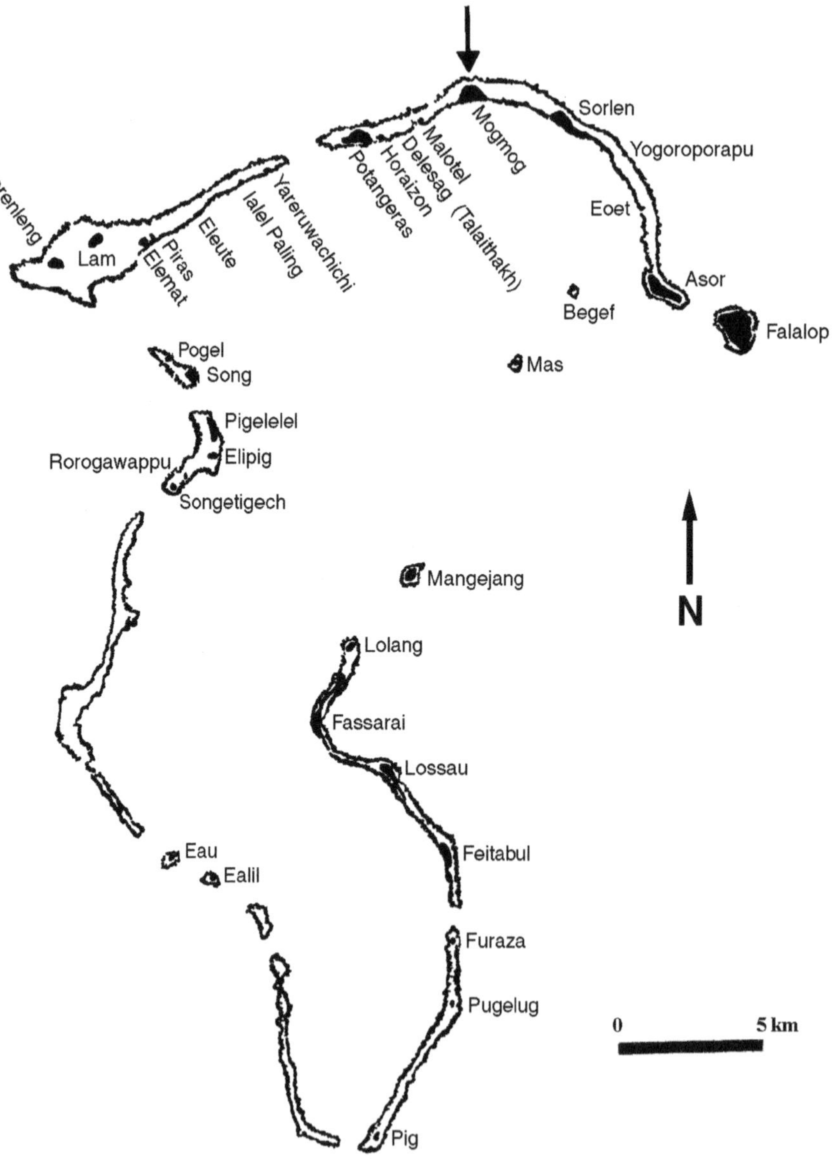

FIGURE 7. Mogmog, Ulithi Atoll (after Lessa 1986:3).

TABLE 3. Ulithi Soil Characteristics Source (Source: C. Smith 1983)

Environmental Zones	Soil Type	Salinity (Mmhos/cm)	Permeability (cm/hr)	Elements	Soil pH
Shore soils	Ngedebus sand	< 2	15 - 50	Low Fe, Mn, an Zn High Na	7.4 – 9.0
Inland soils	Ngedebus Variant sand	< 2	15 - 50	Low Fe, Mn, an Zn High Na	6.6 – 8.4

situated 170 km northeast of Yap and 75 km west of Fais and is made up of approximately forty-one coralline islets and the largest lagoon of the Caroline Islands (Figure 7). The greatest length of the lagoon is 40 km and the greatest width about 25 km (Lessa 1986:2). Ulithi has a fringing reef and a maximum lagoon depth of 64 m (Wiens 1962:20). The lagoon is approximately 460 km^2 and the combined land area of the islets is 4.7 km^2 (Craib 1981:47). Four of the islets, Asor, Falalop, Fassarai, and Mogmog, are permanently inhabited although more islands were inhabited in the past. Mogmog is the northernmost islet of Ulithi at 10° 5' north latitude and 139° 43' east longitude with the remainder of the islets along the eastern or windward portions of the reefs as is characteristic of other atolls (Thomas 1967:26, cited in Craib 1980:7).

Ulithi Geological Traits

The most common chemical constituents of coral islet soils include calcium carbonate and magnesium carbonate (Wiens 1962:334-335, cited in Alkire 1989:13). Smith (1983) reports that the Ulithian islets of Asor and Falalop have Ngedebus (No. 513) and Ngedebus Variant (No. 514) soils, applicable to Mogmog and the other Ulithian islets (Table 3). Ngedebus soils are deep, excessively drained soils adjacent to coastal beaches and within coral island interiors; their slopes can be convex or hummocky with rapid permeability. These cobbly and sandy Ngedebus and Ngedebus Variant soils "formed in alluvium derived dominantly from wind- and water-deposited coral sand, gravel, and cobbles" (C. Smith 1983:8).

Ghyben-Herzberg Lens

Fresh water on a low island is available by the movement of rainwater through the permeable coral soils to the ground water level or Ghyben-Herzberg lens. The lens sits below the soil surface and above the salt-water surface. The size and depth of the lens is a function of the size of the coral island and the 40:41 weight differential of fresh water to salt water (Wiens 1962:44, 318).

Faunal, Floral, and Marine Resources

Terrestrial fauna on Mogmog and other coral islets in Micronesia are severely restricted. Unlike the rich marine resources associated with the biotic system of coral reefs, the only animals preceding the arrival of humans in Ulithi were fruit bats (*Megachieoptera*), oceanic birds, coconut crabs (*Birgus latro*), and insects. Pigs, dogs, cats, chickens, monitor lizards (*Veranus indicus*), and rats (*Rattus* spp.) were brought by later human colonizers.

Alkire (1978:11) notes that the range of vegetation on a coral island is related to the size, amount, and frequency of rainfall. Although floral diversity is relatively poor, vegetation density is quite rich. For Ulithi Atoll, Craib (1980:10) notes:

Density of undergrowth also varies but generally consists of tangled vines (*Cassytha filiformis*), ferns (*Asplenium nidus*, *Nephrolepis* sp.), grasses (i.e., *Chloris inflata*, *Saccharum officinarum*), and other unidentified weeds and grasses.

Some of the Ulithian islets contain *Messerschmidia* and *Scaevola* tree shrubs while forested islets contain cultivated banana, breadfruit, coconut, and pandanus (Craib 1981:49). Ushijima (1982:35) notes that the swampy taro pits near the central regions of some of the islets, such as in Mogmog, are developed out of the Ghyben-Herzberg lens.

Barrau's (1961:26) land utilization model for Tarawa islets (Figure 8) is applicable to Mogmog if one adds a large central swamp and more plants to the schematic model, including arrowroot, bananas, breadfruit, and *Alocasia* and *Colocasia* taro, to name but a few traditionally important plants. For a more complete description of the vascular plants in Ulithi atoll see Lessa (1977).

Climate of Yap and Ulithi

Yap and Ulithi of the western Pacific have similar climatic conditions. The weather patterns and their seasonality in this area are relevant in determining the environmental conditions on the islands as well as conditions affecting sailing voyages between Yap and Ulithi. The Western Pacific has a marine tropical climate with local variations in humidity, rainfall, temperature, and wind conditions (C. Smith 1983:2). Between the months of July and October, the Intertropical Convergence Zone influences the Yap and Ulithi climates (Smith 1983:2). The Intertropical Convergence Zone lies mostly in the southern hemisphere

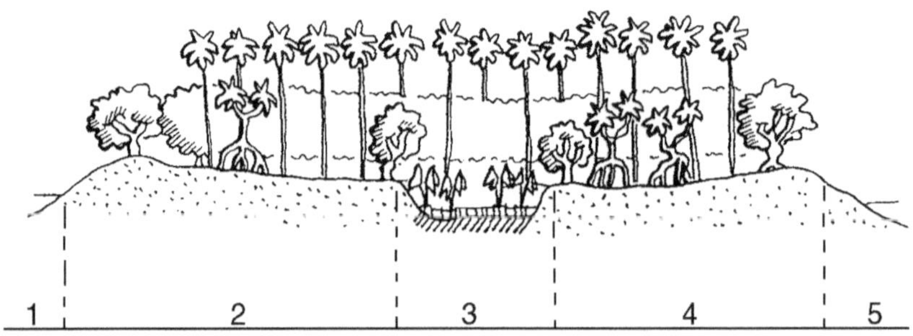

FIGURE 8. Atoll environmental zones: (1) Ocean; (2) Coral Calcimorphic Soils; (3) Cyrtosperma Central Swamp; (4) Coral Calcimorphic Soils; and (5) Lagoon (adapted from Barrau 1961:26). I have modified zone 3 to resemble Mogmog.

and is "really only in evidence during the change of the monsoons, from about mid-September to mid-November, and from about mid-April to mid-May" (Great Britain Hydrographic Department 1987:97). Smith (1983:2) notes that showers characterize this period as well as light, variable winds interspersed with heavier showers or thunderstorms with occasional strong, shifting winds. During this period, southwest and west winds predominate in the morning (0700) and afternoon (1600) on average at least 13% and at the most 27% of the time. Precipitation averages more than 360 mm of rain per month and wind speeds average to 5 knots with calm periods between 17% and 21% of the time (Great Britain Hydrographic Department 1988:38).

From November through June, the persistent and steady northeast trade winds dominate in the area. The trade winds region is typified by constant northeast prevailing winds and scattered showers mostly falling on the windward coasts of the high islands. Wind speeds average 8 knots with monthly calm periods between 1.5 to 14% of the time. From November to June, northeast and east winds predominate at least 15% and at the most 63% of the time in the morning and afternoons. Precipitation for this period averages 210 mm of rainfall (Great Britain Hydrographic Department 1988:38).

Ocean currents are always westerly between Yap and Ulithi. The rate averages between ¾ and 2 knots with always a low constancy of less than 50%. There is a slight equatorial counter current (easterly) from September to May slightly south (2°) of Yap because "[t]he zone from 10° N to the Equator is occupied by a current 'sandwich'; the E-going Equatorial Counter-current in the middle and the W-going North and South Equatorial Currents lying to the N and S of it, respectively" (Great Britain Hydrographic Department 1988:11).

Daily temperatures in Ulithi vary little and range from 80° to 85° F (27° to 29° C); humidity levels reach 84% (Craib 1980:8; Lessa 1989:2). Variation in daily temperature is 7° C while monthly variation is 2° C. Similar to Yap, there are two seasons, a dry season during the winter months lasting from December through April and a rainy season from May through November (Craib 1980:8). Craib (1980:8) reports that Ulithi receives an average of 2896 mm (114 inches) of rain per year.

Typhoons

Typhoons are unpredictable natural disasters, which can damage vegetation and property. Typhoons are important because previous researchers have used them as the reason for the existence of formalized socioeconomic exchange systems (e.g., Alkire 1989). Typhoons are powerful storms in the Pacific with torrential rains and high winds ranging from 120 to 320 km/hr. "The region to the W of 150° E probably has the highest incidence of tropical depressions in the world" (Great Britain Hydrographic Department 1988:28). Tropical storms and typhoons can occur at any time of the year, but there is a seasonal concentration between the months of June and December (C. Smith 1983:2). Typhoons are a chronic threat on Yap and Ulithi, but most pass north of the islands.

Apart from the obvious wind damage to freestanding vegetation, the most severe damage is caused by saltwater inundation of the island soils. After such an event, it can take many months before the saline concentration levels drop to a tolerable level for food production. The risk of devastation from a typhoon on a high island is minimal when compared to the wreckage a typhoon on a low atoll (Schneider 1957:10). The size of Yap allows it to recover from this natural disaster relatively quickly.

Lessa (1968) recorded the social aftermath of typhoon Ophelia that struck Ulithi 23 November 1960. Charles G. Johnson, a geologist from the U.S. Geological Survey, notes the major geomorphological effect of a typhoon is "the erosion of the lower slopes of beaches, and the deposition of much of the detritus as boulder or sand sheets onto the island slopes of the beach ridges of the islands" (Lessa 1968:339-340). The downing of all the trees and the intrusion of saltwater into the Ghyben-Herzberg lens devastatingly limits the food resources and the ability to grow food on the island.

Summary

Yap and Mogmog have similar climates and contrasting natural environments. The continental geological nature of Yap gives it a resource base and diversity advantage over raised coral islands and atolls in terms of its diverse earth materials, water supply, and biotic resources. The disparity of geological resources on both islands also allows for the identification of exotic materials of geological origin in the coral islands. Yap is the closest island to Ulithi with clay resources consisting of both montmorillonite and kaolinite-type clays for earthenware production. Ulithi's low elevation, relatively poor biodiversity, isolation, islet sizes, and location in the typhoon belt make it a less stable and less predictable environment for human adaptation.

Different depositional environments for archaeological resources exist on both islands. Yap's depositional environments, particularly inland, are deeply weathered, and corrosive to cultural remains due to their acidity. Yapese coastal soils are less acidic and better preservation environments, but cultural resources are more prone to flooding, possible typhoon destruction, and bioturbation by mangrove crabs. Given the general tectonic and sea-level activities of the late Holocene in the western Pacific, it is possible that early coastal sites on Yap are now beneath water, alluvium, and Yapese land reclamation activities. Ulithian sites, on the other hand, should not be inundated. Atoll coastal areas are more prone to storm damage and site destruction than high islands, but the uniformity of the basic (low acidity) soils makes it an excellent preservation environment for organic materials. Tree root systems can disturb archaeological sites and archaeological deposits away from human habitation areas risk bioturbation activities from land crabs (see Davidson 1967:370; 1968).

Chapter IV

Historical Ethnography of Western Carolinian Interaction

This chapter presents a historical ethnography of Western Carolinian Island interactions. It begins with the first recorded European encounters and follows through to recent ethnographic accounts. A considerable amount of the archaeological data I recovered in Mogmog and Gachpar derives from the protohistoric period (1525-1843); therefore a detailed ethnohistoric description of island interaction is given for that interval. I define "protohistory" to be the time segment between European discovery and settlement of the island societies. Ethnohistoric data on Carolinian island interactions are integral to formulating models of the exchange history between Yap and Mogmog. Ethnographic observations, by definition first-hand studies, and Carolinian informant data collected by anthropologists, colonial administrators, explorers, missionaries, and traders are included this chapter.

In this ethnographic history, I depend only on positive evidence in the ethnohistoric records. I do not introduce interpretations based on the absence of specific comments in the texts because I cannot be sure whether the lack of evidence in a report is indeed a real absence or an omission by the authors. Because the historical ethnography is dependent upon the writer's specific observations, the context in which the records were constructed is described in the following section.

Biases

Ethnographic accounts are constructions by persons from specific culture-historical contexts. Understanding the contexts of the colonial situation vis-à-vis the anthropological enterprise produces invaluable insights into the limitations of ethnographic texts (e.g., see Bashkow 1991; Clifford and Marcus 1986). Lengthy treatises could easily be written on the topic of inter-cultural encounters and the interpretation of the "Other". I give only brief descriptions of the authors' agendas and biases before addressing the specifics of the historical ethnography.

Ethnohistoric details give insight into the ideological component of past interactions that are not readily attainable from my archaeological data. I presume recorded oral histories were believed and were part of the ideology and justification for behavior at the time they were recorded. The time ethnohistorical information was collected is crucial in gathering insights about the ideology. The accounts are certainly more indicative of the time when they were collected than about any other time in question. The accuracy of the history then is not as much an issue as is an understanding of the ideologies practiced and believed at particular times in the past. Therefore, I give particular attention to when the ethnohistoric information was collected.

Sawei canoe voyages between Gachpar Village and the Outer Islands had all but ended before anthropologists began collecting reports about them. Lessa and anthropologists before him did not witness *sawei* in action because at the time of the fieldwork formal *sawei* tributary voyages and exchanges had ceased. Anthropologists recorded ethnohistory from their informants who were taught by older relatives and friends about the formalized tribute system. Therefore, the ethnographic data represent how the system was meant to operate in the nineteenth and twentieth centuries.

Historical Ethnography

The following sections explain the historical development of exchange behaviors in the Western Caroline Islands as recorded by non-Micronesians with emphasis on the relations between Yap and Ulithi. Chronological control of these primary sources provides essential glimpses of island interaction at specific points in time. Some of these fragmentary textual data are indicative of interaction at the time of their collection and need to be considered in the construction of a diachronic exchange model. Rather than use the information to accumulate an inventory of possible analogies for explaining how people interacted in the prehistoric era, I rely on these interaction events (*événements*) to illuminate how interactive behaviors that followed European contact influenced Yap-Ulithi exchange behavior.

Sixteenth Century

Early European explorers of the sixteenth and seventeenth centuries were engrossed by their investigation for wealth in the Pacific Islands. This preoccupation often distracted explorers from leaving detailed descriptions of how the indigenous peoples lived or any specifics of their encounters. European-Western Carolinian encounters in the sixteenth century were accidental, short, and usually involved trading and hostilities – typically over exchange behaviors. European crews did not tolerate islanders appropriating goods that were not given to them, but saw themselves as civilized, superior, and unlike the islanders, possessing an inherent right to take from the islands what they pleased. The political organization in the Carolines is mentioned as being feudal-like, yet the early European observers were most familiar with monarchical principles (Lessa 1962b:322).

The first written documents related to the Western Caroline Islands come from the cursory notes of European explorers. Contacts were few because "Spain established its galleon route at about the thirteenth parallel so as to purposely miss the islands to the south which were regarded at the time as little more than navigational hazards" (Hezel and Del Valle 1972:28). Early European contacts with Carolinians include Gomez de Espinosa's visit to Sonsorol in 1522, Diogo da Rocha's visit to the Islas de Sequeira (most likely Ulithi) in 1525, Ruy Lopez de Villalobos's visit to Fais in 1543, and Alonso de Arellano's visit to Ngulu in 1565. Ethnographic material from these encounters is meager, preventing any comments about Yapese hegemony or relations. Yet, wherever the location of the Islas de Sequeira, I take Barros's mention of "large *proas*" (outrigger canoes) as evidence that Western Carolinians sailed in 1525 (see Document 1525E; Lévesque 1992 I:409). Islanders told the Portuguese that the island to the west contained gold. Ulithians may well have been referring to Yapese *reang*, a yellow-orange turmeric paste that Carolinians esteemed just as highly as Europeans considered gold. Lévesque (1992 I:414) suggests the reference to gold could be yellow ocher. One hundred and seventy-one years later Father Klein witnessed castaways from Fais spreading yellow turmeric powder on their bodies before visiting a high-ranking religious official.

Despite violence and Chamorro genocide, the first inter-societal contact between Europeans and Pacific Islanders was characterized by the exchange of materials. It is obvious from early European intrusions into Micronesia that new foreign objects were sought by Micronesians, especially iron tools. "The natives hastened aboard to exchange island produce for iron, knives, and other objects" (Ibáñez 1992:25). The eagerness with which these objects were sought and their use in Micronesian island societies suggests that the introduction of these materials into existing exchange systems could have altered pre-existing exchange practices and even created new ones (e.g., Klein 1707; von Kotzebue 1821).

Seventeenth Century

The earliest European recordings of Carolinians sailing between islands came from Spanish Jesuit missionaries stationed in Island Southeast Asia. In 1669, Fr. Francisco Miedes serving on Siao, a small island off the northern end of Sulawesi (Celebes), met four Carolinians from Ifalik Atoll. Five years earlier, these four had drifted to the Moluccas while attempting to sail to Tol or Tolo (Chuuk), 700 km away, in a fleet of 30 canoes to attend a wedding. Lévesque (1995 IV:235) has recently published a copy and translation of this important document which mentions geographic locations of numerous Melanesian and Micronesian islands in the western Pacific and information on Ifalikese political organization.

Miedes's letter (Document 1664D) states,

> 8. Their sort of government is, they say, that they have a king in ***Piguilape*** (Ifalik) who rules over the surrounding islands. He is just a king in name, because he does not command other than respect as such, without anyone pressured from doing whatever he pleases [Lévesque 1995 IV:246; bold and italics in text].

Lévesque (1995 IV:15) remarks Ifalik was "apparently the center of the Carolines; the center of political power had not yet shifted to Yap." I question Lévesque's interpretation of the geographical extent of the Ifalik power base, as well as the subordinate political positions of Yap and Ulithi, approximately 750 km and 600 km away respectively. Islands subject to Ifalik may well have been the nearby islands of Eauripik, Woleai, Faraulep, Lamotrek, and Satawal, which comprise the fourth province of the Carolinian empire mentioned 57 years later by other castaways to Fr. Cantova. The four Ifalikese informants told Fr. Miedes the relative geographic positions of Ulithi (Lamolulutu) and Yap (Yape), which I take as evidence for Carolinian island interaction, but not as evidence of Yapese hegemony.

Another seventeenth century Spanish Jesuit report on the navigational feats of Carolinians comes from Fr. Paul Klein (also spelled Clain), who reported the drift voyage of 30 Carolinians from Fais. These Carolinians landed on Samar in the Philippines after attempting to return home after a visit to Lamotrek in 1696 (Klein 1707). From Klein's letter, we learn about the knowledge of 87 islands, including the location of Yap and Ulithi (Figure 9). In addition, we learn that there were 32 islands in their "nation," 29 of which were "extrémement peuplées" (extremely populated); women as well as men were passengers in ocean voyages; signs of respect and deference were shown to particular Carolinians, noting social disparities; and that Carolinians were aware of iron and valued it highly. Through the interpretation of two Carolinian women, who had voyaged to Samar sometime before, Klein understood that Lamotrek (Lamurrec) was the center of an island empire, and was where the "Roy" (king) resided (Klein 1707:125). Lessa (1962b:351) suggests that the Lamotrek political system may well have flourished inside another system because of the omission of the political position of Yap or Ulithi in Fr. Klein's letter. Indeed, Alkire (1977) describes a highly structured inter-atoll exchange system called the "hook" (*hu*) where the people of Elato and Satawal brought tribute to the paramount chief of Lamotrek. It is possible that other exchange systems of coral islands in present day Yap State co-existed with the *sawei* exchange system.

The Carolinians offered to return to their island and attract their compatriots to enter into a commerce or exchange system with the Philippines because of the abundance of exotic materials considered necessary for living (Klein 1707:134). This offer by the Carolinians is significant and suggests that there was a precedent for their interacting with other islanders to obtain exotic materials. Hezel and Del

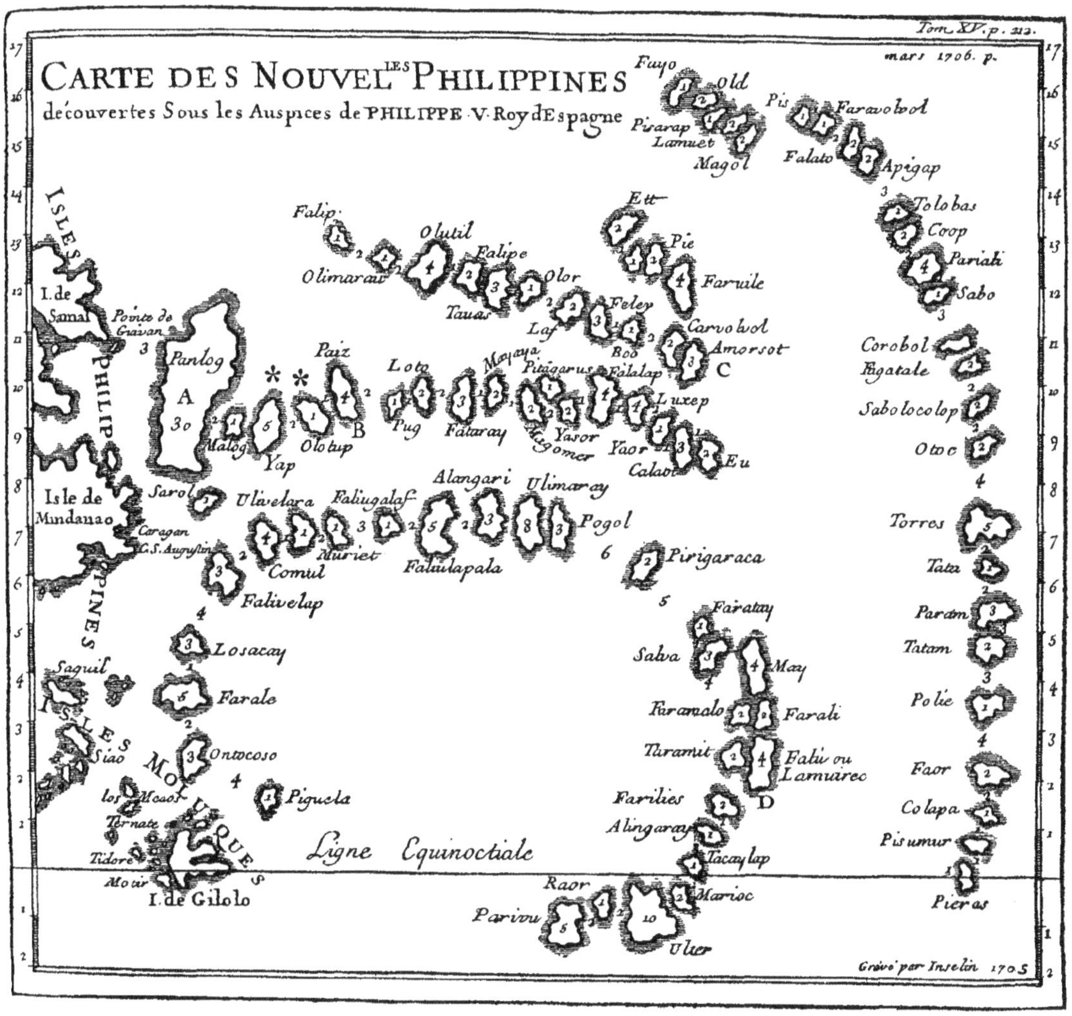

FIGURE 9. Fr. Paul Klein's map from Carolinian informants collected in 1696 (Müller 1917:3). Added asterisks indicate the locations of Yap and Ulithi.

Valle (1972:29) remark that there were "no fewer than nine different Carolinian landings in the Philippines between 1664 and 1696, and these nine must have represented merely a fraction of the actual traffic during these years." Seventeenth century ethnohistoric evidence does not establish that there was a formal exchange system in the Carolines headed by Yap; however, there is unequivocal evidence that Carolinians were voyaging extensively at this time and likely before the entry of Europeans in the Pacific Islands.

Eighteenth Century

More complete ethnographic accounts of Western Carolinian life come from European missionaries in the eighteenth century. Converting the island's inhabitants to Christianity was their primary concern – an agenda the missionaries were willing to martyr themselves for. Interest in the culture and the language of the people was essentially to destroy un-Christian-like behavior and to facilitate the conversion of the "Indians". The Italian Jesuit Father Juan Antonio Cantova (1728:221), the first to offer ethnographic details of Carolinian culture, considered the islanders possessing "almost no notion of religion," living "without culture", and therefore potential Christians. What little they did have was seen as a "ridiculous system which their fathers passed on to them by a sort of tradition" (Cantova 1728:222). Fr. Cantova's letters contain invaluable glimpses of Carolinian culture in the early eighteenth century. His negative judgement of the Carolinians may be viewed as attempts to persuade and gain permission for his Carolinian Christianization agenda from his reluctant superiors in the Philippines. His ethnographic observations and informant reports are more reliable than his impressions and conclusions. His reports are testimonies of his acute observations, right to his final note in his last letter before he was killed, where he noted reluctance on the part of the Ulithians and chose to persevere the difficult conditions in Ulithi rather than return to Guam for supplies.

The most extensive pre-nineteenth century Carolinian ethnography, what Lessa (1962b) has called an "ethnography in absentia", comes from a published letter by Cantova. An "ethnography in absentia" is a collection of ethnographic details without the author actually observing the particular society. Cantova, who lived on Guam, had

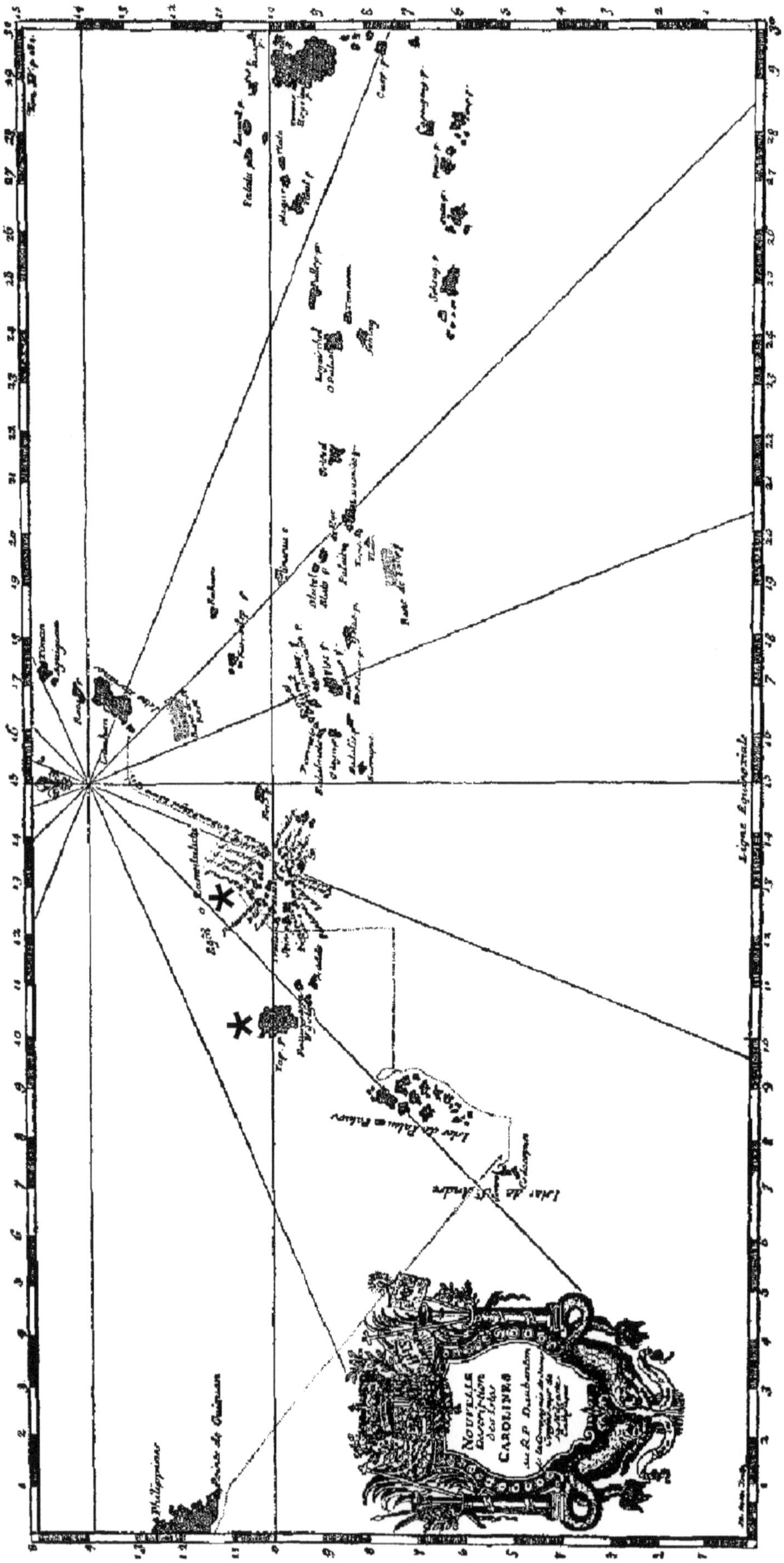

FIGURE 10. Fr. Cantova's 1722 map (taken from Müller 1917:2). Added asterisks indicate locations of Yap and Ulithi.

not visited any Carolinian societies before writing his first letter. Fr. Cantova spent eight months with thirty Carolinians from Faraulep, Lamotrek, Woleai, and Yap, who had drifted to Guam in 1721 (Hezel 1983:48-54). The information and map prepared by Cantova in 1722 once again shows the extensive knowledge these people had of their island world (Figure 10). As in earlier letters, there is evidence of chiefly authority in the Carolinian island societies, along with information about political geography, oral history, religion, division of labor, and warfare.

According to the Carolinian castaways, the political geography of the Carolines was divided into five provinces, from west to east: (1) Palau, Sonsorol, and Tobi; (2) Yap and Ngulu; (3) Ulithi, Fais, and Sorol; (4) Woleai, Lamotrek, Satawal, Ifalik, Eauripik, and Faraulep; and (5) Chuuk (Cantova 1728:210-219). Of these island societies, the high islands of Palau, Yap, and Chuuk were said to have been heavily populated.

Palau and Yap were feared at the time and were populated with peoples quite culturally distinct from Carolinian Islanders to the east. In reference to Yap, Cantova (1728:231-232) notes:

> A species of crocodile is the object of their veneration. It is under the guise of this crocodile that the Demon exercises over these people a cruel tyranny. A group of enchanters is found among them: they have contact with the evil spirit and with his help they secure sickness and even death for those whom they wish to undo.

Crocodiles are not found on Yap or known to have existed there so the informants were probably referring to large lizards (*Hydrosaurus marmoratus*) called *kaluv* (von Kotzebue 1821:189), *galuf* (Christian 1899:301; Müller 1917:8; Tetens and Kubary 1873:123), or *galuff* (Salesius 1907:21).

This venerated lizard (see Walleser 1913:615, 1053) signified many sacred characters on Yap, notably Gachpar and the Gagil's spirit called Yangolab. Half human and half spirit, Yangolab could transform himself into a man or large lizard (cf. de Beauclair 1967:23).

Evidence of possible Yapese command over other Carolinian islands is first recorded in a Cantova letter:

> It is necessary to move slowly (with lead feet), since these islands like many others of this Archipelago, are *subject to the King of Yap.* Yap is large and *very populated*, it is about 50 leagues west by southwest of these islands [Carrasco 1881:264; emphasis added].

Again, an exotic yellow dye, most likely turmeric paste, is mentioned coming from Yap (Carrasco 1881:267).

The first mention of a possible *sawei*-type voyage is made when Fr. Cantova (Carrasco 1881:265-266) tells the story of a Carolinian fleet of 35 canoes travelling from Ulithi and Woleai led by Digal. The fleet was struck by a storm in 1725 while attempting to return from Yap to Ulithi. The large fleet of Carolinian canoes sailing between Yap and Ulithi make this voyage resemble a *sawei*-type voyage.

The murder of Fr. Cantova on Mogmog, the chief island of Ulithi in 1731, may be important in illustrating the supernatural power held by the Yapese and Mogmog islanders in the Caroline Islands. Ten days after Fr. Walter, Cantova's colleague, left the Ulithian Christian mission to get more supplies from Guam, Fr. Cantova and the others in his mission, except one cabin boy, were murdered. It is not known what led to the killings, but it is possible that the teachings of the Christian mission located on Falalop threatened the superordinate position Gachpar and Mogmog islanders held over the other Carolinian islands as indicated in *sawei* ideology (cf. Tetens 1958:66). Bashkow (1991:196) has also suggested Gagil chiefs directed the murders.

Nineteenth Century

After the European imperialistic drive had claimed most of the islands, the emphasis became the collection of information. One such voyage was the Romanzov exploring expedition of 1815-1818, which was recorded by Lieutenant Otto von Kotzebue (1821), the commander of the *Rurik*, and Adelbert von Chamisso (1986), the accompanying naturalist. Both accounts of the expedition contain references about Carolinian inter-island relations from a Woleaian native named Kadu, whom the expedition had picked up in the northern Marshall Islands. Like other Woleaians more than a hundred years earlier, Kadu was familiar with the islands between Palau and Satawal and had spent a substantial amount of time on Yap (von Chamisso 1986:263, 287; von Kotzebue 1821:97-98).

In 1804, Guam Governor Don Luis de Torres visited Woleai and persuaded the Western Central Carolinians to resume annual trade visits by way of Woleai, Lamotrek, and Satawal, which Carolinians had originally requested and started in 1788. This is another example of Carolinians desiring a frequent inter-island exchange relationship with an island possessing desired goods. Carolinian boats stopped voyaging to Guam after a small fleet presumably got lost and never returned from a 1789 visit (Von Chamisso 1986:271). Carolinians stopped voyaging to Guam believing Spanish cruelty explained the disappearance of the islanders. It is possible that Carolinians interacted with Chamorros from the Mariana Islands before Spanish colonization in 1565 (Alkire 1989:135; Barratt 1988:4; Hezel and Del Valle 1972:33; Lessa 1962b:331).

After severe storms in 1810, Carolinians sailed to Guam and requested permission to live on the northern Mariana island of Saipan (Russell 1983). Earlier Spanish-Chamorro wars, European-introduced epidemics, and forced resettlement had depopulated Saipan. Spanish authorities allowed hundreds of Carolinians to settle on Saipan on the condition they embrace Christianity. This must have shaken the foundations of the ideological hegemony Yap held over coral island populations. To the people of Gachpar it may have seemed that a new island group was assuming exchange relations and providing typhoon relief once managed and provided chiefly by them. Later, in the twentieth century, the German colonial government also aided Outer Islanders by bringing storm-stricken Carolinians to Saipan.

Kadu, a Woleaian native guiding the Russian naval ships of von Kotzebue, mentioned Yapese-Outer Island interaction when he remarked that coral islanders obtained "whet-stones" from the mountains of Yap, which the Yapese use as seats of honor (von Kotzebue 1821:182). Whet-stones may refer to the tabular schist or basaltic stones the Yapese use on their platforms as backrests. Kadu described to von Chamisso (1986:285) a complex exchange system already in place in the Carolines, where the principal objects of trade were pieces of iron, boats, cloth, glass, and turmeric powder. Kadu is probably referring to the annual visits to Guam renewed by Torres:

> Those of Feis [Fais], Eap [Yap], and Mogemug [Mogmog] go to Ulea [Woleai] to purchase boats, in exchange for Curcuma [turmeric] powder. Those of the eastern islands, which have bread-fruit trees in abundance, build all their boats themselves; and those of Nugor [Lukunor] and Tuch [Chuuk] barter stuffs at Ulea [Woleai] for iron [von Kotzebue 1821:193].

Mogmog's religious and political prerogatives at this time were similar to those recorded by German anthropologists almost a century later, "[t]he boats lower their sails in sight of the island of Mogemug [Mogmog], the residence of the principal chief of the group of this name" (von Kotzebue 1821:207). The destructive magical powers mentioned almost a hundred years earlier by Cantova are reiterated by coral islanders in 1818. Yap had a reputation known for its magical arts in controlling weather; "[t]o them is ascribed the destruction of so many boats from Feis [Fais] and Mogemug [Mogmog], nay, even the gradual depopulation of these islands" (von Kotzebue 1821:205). Kadu may well be referring to the *sawei* system and its supernatural properties when he informed von Chamisso (1986:286-287) about the god or departed protective spirit (*tautup*) of Mogmog, Ngulu, Woleai, and Yap called Yangolab (Engalap). Yangolab was the spirit of *sawei*, related to the seasons of fertility, and had special temples on these islands (except for Woleai).

Von Kotzebue (1821:132-133) records from Kadu,

> [Yap] was formerly under one chief, and enjoyed peace; but now war rages between the petty chiefs of the several territories, of which Kadu named forty-six (sic); namely, Kattepar [Gachpar], Sigel, Sumop, Samuel, Sitol, Suomen, Palao, Runnu, Girrigai, Athebué, Tugor, Urang, Maloai, Rumu, Gilifith, Inif, Ugal, Umalai, Sawuith, Magetagi, Elauth, Toauwai, Ngari, Gurum, Tabonefi, Summaki, Sabogel, Samusalai, Tainefar, Thorta, Unau, Taumuti, Sul, Sütemil, Täp, Ulienger, Wutel, Laipilau, Süllang, Thelta, Urieng, Meit, Feidel, Tumunaupilau, Sop, &c.

Ruu', a village referred to in oral tradition (Müller 1917:242) said to have headed the *sawei* system before Gachpar, is not mentioned in the list. Villages beginning with the letter *"R"* in the list include: Runnu and Rumu, and probably refer to the Fanif Municipality villages of Run'uw and Rumu' respectively. Given such a detailed list, it is unlikely Kadu would not have mentioned Ruu' if Outer Islanders stayed there during their visits to Yap (although this is negative evidence). Hunter-Anderson (1983:17) notes Kattepar (Gachpar) was at the head of the 45 village list and suggests that it had already replaced Ruu' as head of the *sawei* system.

All of the information collected about Yap-Outer Island interactions, including the *sawei* system exchange practices, is of the time period when Gachpar Village regulated the exchange. Little information exists about Yap-Outer Island relations before Gachpar headed the *sawei* system except that Outer Islanders use to visit Ruu' Village when visiting Yap. Gachpar took the exchange system over after Ruu' Village was annihilated.

European traders' reports on Western Carolinian cultures preceded the European colonization of Yap and Ulithi. Impressions of the island societies at particular points in time and knowledge of European traders' actions are important for evaluating the effects of trader-islander encounters on the island societies. Driven by economic gain and adventure, early enterprising traders were forced to interact closely with natives and adapt to unfamiliar conditions. The success of the commercial missions depended upon mutual understanding and cooperation. Consequently, early trading ventures enjoyed little success. Cultural interpretations are often faulty, but their recorded observations of encounters are useful in working out characteristics of their beliefs.

Yap was virtually unknown to Europeans until the English trading captain Andrew Cheyne's two month visit to the Tomil district where he attempted to establish a bêche-de-mer (a sea slug the Chinese considered a delicacy) operation in 1843 (Hezel 1983:182). Tomil district was one of three competing geo-political areas of Yap, the other two being Rull and Gagil. As in Palau, where he was later murdered, Cheyne put himself unwittingly in the middle of island power struggles (Hezel 1983:182, 184). Cheyne notes that the Palauans and Yapese appeared to be enemies. From Cheyne's descriptions, we know the Yapese had a differentiated society with people of varying distinctions and tasks. One group of people thatched roofs, generally the low caste (*pimilngaey*) for their high caste (*piiluung*) masters (Shineberg 1971:250). Complex taboos concerning the sharing of food and fire existed (Shineberg 1971:253, 284). The conspicuous stone platforms in Yapese villages today were already in use during the 1840s when Cheyne observed raised paved areas or what he called council squares with upright backrest slabs (Shineberg 1971:264).

In 1843, Cheyne permitted one of his sick sailors to go on shore, and in effect, start an influenza epidemic, which killed fifty Tamil District inhabitants in three days (Shineberg 1971:271). This is the earliest date directly associated with Western Caroline population loss. Massive depopulation had a large impact on the Yapese social system (see Schneider 1968). The date of 1843 also indirectly implies that the high settlement densities of the reclaimed coastal extensions probably preceded the depopulation trend of the Yap Islands, which continued well into the middle of the twentieth century.

The German company of J. C. Godeffroy & Sons was the first commercial company on Yap interested in copra (dried coconut meat) and bêche de mer (Hezel 1983:267). Alfred Tetens, the company's first agent, made a number of visits to Yap and Ulithi between 1865 and 1868. Tetens was told during his first meeting in 1863 with King Karakok of Rull:

> No white man has ever been allowed to remain on Yap. It is true that foreign traders have attempted to establish themselves here, but their crews have never left the island alive [Tetens 1958:12].

Like Cheyne before him, Tetens inadvertently got entangled in the Yapese political power struggle between Gagil and Rull (cf. Berg 1992).

Tetens made many observations on the Western Carolinian societies and their inter-island relations during his visits. In his first visit of 1863, Tetens comments on exotic trade goods when he writes that the chief "seemed satisfied with the iron chisels, the only tool that the natives use and with which they accomplish everything" (Tetens 1958:14). In addition, Tetens realized that the Yapese feared Palauans (1958:10); the Yapese visited Palau to quarry stone money (1958:12, 62); graves were piled with many stones (1958:25); and men and women ate separately (1958:33). The common strife and internecine village conflicts were also mentioned often (Tetens and Kubary 1873:19; Tetens 1958:71, 97, 99).

European trader visits and new commodities unsettled the delicate power balance between the different Yapese regions (Bashkow 1991:196-197). Gagil's monopoly on Outer Island prestige goods, not to mention the new exotic goods Outer Islanders received from Europeans, gave it political power on Yap. Rull, an opposing region, welcomed foreigners, and their exotic materials in order to shift the balance of power. Gagil, on the other hand, was interested in maintaining the status quo, and did not welcome foreigners until 13 years later in 1875 (Bashkow 1991:196).

While sailing to Hong Kong, Tetens encountered most likely a Carolinian canoe on a *sawei* voyage, when he wrote, the

> event of these days was the encounter with a canoe whose occupants came from a distant island group. They were on their way to pay the tribute they owed to the Yap king. The savages had not the remotest idea where they were, did not even know in what direction Yap lay [1958:72].

Tetens (1958:63) acknowledges a tribute system resembling the formalized *sawei* exchange system recorded by later twentieth century ethnographers:

> In general the bloodthirsty Yap inhabitant is much feared by the tribes that pay him tribute, and his orders are meekly obeyed. Even the people of some distant villages on Yap itself are treated as slaves and have to do all they are ordered without pay.

Supernatural sanctions in creation myths structuring the tribute were also noted,

> the hook with which the goddess pulled the island [Fais] from the sea bottom came into the hands of the king of Yap. Therefore the island became the property of its king and was forced to pay tribute. Another saga tells of a certain goddess Isserie and of a hatchet buried on Yap, which if unearthed would cause the Ulithi Islands to be swallowed up by the sea [Tetens 1958:63].

> In consequence of this belief it is easy for the crafty Yaps to keep the group of islands constantly paying tribute. All my efforts to persuade the kings [of the Outer Islands] of the falseness of the saga were in vain; indeed they became very uncomfortable when I would not believe in the myth [Tetens 1958:66].

Irish-American trader David Dean O'Keefe, who first landed on Yap in 1871, had a large impact on Yapese society. Like Andrew Cheyne and Alfred Tetens before him, he dealt with Rull and further strengthened the district. In 1880, O'Keefe's enterprising commercialism made Yap the largest copra trading post in Micronesia. His activities provide glimpses of the Yapese late nineteenth century political and economic conditions and the importance of exotic prestige goods in the Yapese political sphere. Unlike traders before him, O'Keefe satisfied a Yapese need for Palauan stone money. He took Western Carolinians to Palau and back on his ship to quarry aragonite stone money at the cost of Yapese labor to harvest copra and bêche de mer that was later sold in Far Eastern ports (Hezel 1983:266).

Johann Stanislaus Kubary, a Polish naturalist acclaimed as the father of Micronesian anthropology (Hezel 1983:272), was the first to record detailed ethnographic observations in Micronesia (e.g., Kubary 1889; Tetens and Kubary 1873). In addition to collecting ethnographic material, Kubary speculated on the origins of Carolinian economic institutions. Here, I discuss his observations pertaining to

Western Carolinian island interaction and Yapese hegemony.

In 1882, Kubary witnessed four hundred Yapese quarrying aragonite to shape into stone money near Koror (Berg 1992:150) and noted "all the important settlements on Yap would be provided with stone money, which they used to keep other settlements dependent upon them" (Berg 1992:150, cited in Kubary 1889:3-5). Kubary (1889:2) mentions that an exchange system between Yap and its eastern coral island neighbors was well established. Yapese turmeric powder bundles were exchanged for woven hip belts, thread, sails, and jewelry made out of coconut shells. Kubary (1889:3) remarks that the reddish *gau* (*Spondylus*) shells, which were exotic to Yap and predated the popularity of Palauan stone money, were the oldest and highest valued exchange goods. *Gau* is thought to have been exclusively from the Western Carolinian island of Eauripik.

Symbols of rank and prestige, Yapese stone money was valued according to its material, size, shape, history, tools used to mine and shape the stone, and mode of transportation (de Beauclair 1963:153). Yapese stone money was important in ceremonial exchanges and belonged to villages, municipalities, and chiefs. Before Europeans frequented Yap, it was labor intensive to mine and shape aragonite rocks with shell tools and perilous to raft over 400 km of open ocean. The Yapese in Palau performed *corvée* labor and were treated in a subservient fashion for the right to quarry the stone from the chiefs of Koror (Müller 1917:27). "The quarrying of stones on a large scale comes to an end with the outbreak of World War I" (de Beauclair 1963:156).

Twentieth Century

I rely heavily on ethnographic data collected by anthropologists subsidized by different governments with colonial agendas. Many ethnographic texts are the results of recent acquisitions by colonial governments unfamiliar with the local cultures (e.g., Damm 1938; Lessa 1950a; Müller 1917; Peabody Museum 1949; Yanaihara 1934). To administer the islands more effectively, research agendas were broad in order to gain a general understanding of the island societies.

Though they entered the area much earlier, the Spanish colonial period in the Western Carolines officially started in 1885. The Spanish had a passive colonial agenda for Yap and Ulithi, unlike that for New Spain (Mexico) and the Philippines. With no political or commercial goals, the Spanish brought no imperial development to the Carolines, beyond its Catholic faith (Christmann et al. 1991:175).

The German colonizing effort and resulting effects on the island societies was greater than that of their Spanish predecessors. Unlike the Spanish, the German administration had economic interests in the Carolines. The German administration established ten geopolitical districts (or municipalities) and forbade the common inter-village wars on Yap (Müller 1917:10; Salesius 1907:83), ending one of the modes for improving a village's rank. In an attempt to better govern Yap and improve its commercial viability, the new German colonists built roads and constructed the Tageren canal across the island to join the Pacific Ocean to the Philippine Sea.

The German colonial government also made significant changes in Ulithi. They forcibly moved island populations from eight islets to four in order to facilitate colonial control (Ushijima 1982:35). In 1906, the German government moved several hundred natives from the over-populated islands of Bur, Merir, Sonsorol and Mogmog to Palau and Saipan (Damm 1938:295). Once a prerogative of Gachpar Village, the Germans provided relief for a 1907 typhoon by again moving populations from Mogmog and other devastated islands (Damm 1938:295). The German administration forbade the ocean voyage from Mogmog to Yap and other island voyages because many canoes were being lost at sea and the male population and potential labor force was decreasing rapidly (Damm 1938:324-325); in addition, the cost of repatriating castaways was expensive (Müller 1917:10). Some defied the injunction despite the German regulations.

The German Südsee-Expedition of 1908-1910 was the most extensive Pacific anthropological project of its time and followed the purchase of the Carolines in 1899. At the time, German anthropologists believed less culturally evolved peoples were destined for extinction. Indeed, the Yapese population was decreasing at an alarming rate. The German Südsee-Expedition practiced salvage ethnography "to observe and record the final phases of an old, indigenous culture as long as it still had vitality and retained any remnants of old times that were little changed" (Thilenius 1927:12, cited in Berg 1988:95). In the large Südsee-Expedition multi-volume set, expedition members often lamented at the loss of traditional culture.

Paul Hambruch, an ethnologist with the Südsee-Expedition, gave the first modern detailed ethnographic description of Mogmog. In a short stay of only 15 days in 1910, Hambruch collected much information. Unfortunately a map of Mogmog village was lost when a boat capsized during a storm while returning from Mogmog to the mother ship *Peiho* anchored in the lagoon. After Hambruch's death in 1933, Damm (1938) edited and published Hambruch's report.

Apart from the ethnohistoric data and legendary history from Ulithian informants, Hambruch offers considerable detail about the tribute voyages from the Outer Islands to Yap (Damm 1938:323-324; 330). Hambruch did not call this exchange *sawei*, but the exchange practice is the same as that described by Lessa (1950c), who first used the term, "*sawei*." Preparations for the exchange involved magic spells and invocations to the spirit Faluth (Damm 1938:330). Upon arrival in Yap, a quarantine of four days and more magic cleansing spells ensued before the Outer Islanders visited their respective *sawei* "parents" in Yap for the exchange of gifts (Damm 1938:324).

Wilhelm Müller (1917, 1918), another German ethnologist of the Südsee-Expedition, stayed ten months on Yap between June 1909 and April 1910. One of his chief informants was Ruepon, a high priest from Gachpar who resided at the Numurui estate (C36-16), the *taliw* (taboo) abode for the spirit Yangolab. Müller's choice of Ruepon as his main informant is fortuitous because of Ruepon's knowledge and association with the prevalent Yangolab cult. According to legend Yangolab founded the *sawei* exchange system. As a major figure in the *sawei* tribute system, Ruepon "claimed half of Ifaluk [Ifalik], half of Sorol and the entire atolls of Lamotrek, Elato, Olimarao, Pulap [Pollap], Satawal and Puluwat [Polowat]" (Berg 1992:157). Ruepon described much about the supernatural *raison d'être* or ideology behind the formal exchange practices between Gachpar and the Outer Islanders (Müller 1917, 1918).

The Mogmog ethnography contains much mytho-history concerning the creation of Ulithi Atoll and the origins of Yapese-Ulithian social and economic relations (Damm 1938). Hambruch did not provide the identity of his informants, but did say that information was filtered through a Yapese male interpreter. Unsurprisingly, Gachpar Village plays a central role in the oral histories collected. Hambruch notes that the Mogmog inhabitants did not speak freely and often heard from Mogmog informants, "[w]e have too much in our heads, and we get confused; the Yap Islanders know everything" (Damm 1938:300). Frustrated at collecting religious information, Hambruch comments, "[a]fter a three hour conversation I have learned that the inhabitants do not know anything" (Damm 1938:349). Clearly, his informants were not willing to part with what they knew and this shows Gachpar's influence at this time. It is not until Lessa's (1950c) ethnographic fieldwork 38 years later that a more Ulithian version is represented.

Unlike Hambruch who had difficulties collecting certain information on Mogmog (Damm 1938), Lessa (1950a:iii) found Ulithi "a researcher's paradise" and published extensively, mostly from his early fieldwork. In no attempt to diminish Lessa's ethnographic work, I was told that when Lessa visited Yap in 1947, the old men chose Lessa's chief informant and decided not to divulge certain sensitive information (which is against the culture) to Lessa. Josede Figirliyong (1976), an Ulithian, has since written a Master's thesis on the Ulithian political system.

While conducting fieldwork, I acquired an appreciation for the difficulties and dilemmas involved in creating ethnographies. Different Western Carolinian individuals possess knowledge about different specialized topics. Information concerning land ownership and political history is concealed and imparted to only select persons. Secrecy in matters such as genealogies, information, and land ownership histories prevents fraudulent claims to both land, power, and protects an individual from another's claim that he or she has more rights. One informant frequently followed his replies to me: "listen to my words, but don't take them," intimating that his answer was but one among many.

Carolinian exchange behaviors, specifically *sawei*, changed drastically in the nineteenth and twentieth centuries and were in a state of decline and alteration before twentieth century observers began reporting them. Only a few early foreign observers had witnessed what was left of older *sawei* practice, that is, Outer Islanders on tribute voyages landing on Yap (Tetens 1958:72; Hambruch 1912) and visiting their Gachpar "parents" (Christian 1899:307; Müller 1917). In addition, foreign observers commented on the *sawei* exchange and what they perceived to be Gachpar authority over the Outer Islanders (Christian 1899; Damm 1938; Hambruch 1912; Müller 1917). Arno Senfft (1903:58), the first German colonial government district officer, and Fr. Salesius (1907:82-83, 102-103), a German Capuchin missionary, also mention Gachpar's hegemony over the islands to the east. They also noted the tribute exacted by the chief of Gachpar and add that a few years earlier the chief of Gachpar traveled to his tributary Outer Islands. The supernatural component and sanctions involved in the tributary offerings in Gachpar were not ignored, "a tidal wave would swallow everything if they [Outer Islanders] neglected their duty" (Salesius 1907:83).

Senfft (1903:58) briefly describes the *sawei* exchange system, but did not identify it as such. He adds more details than had previous observers and notes that despite yearly Outer Island tribute "[t]he chief of Gatschbar [Gachpar] had no influence over the internal administration of these tributary islands." Apart from listing the exchange items of the Yapese and the Outer Islanders, Senfft depicts some of the material differences between the low caste (*milingei*) and the chiefly caste (*pi Uap*). The differences included limited access to valuable items such as *Spondylus* shell valuables and stone money (Senfft 1903:50).

Hambruch (1912) published a brief manuscript about Carolinian and Marshallese ocean voyaging. Specific mention is made of a canoeload of Ulithians encountered in August 1909 while attempting a tribute voyage to Yap (Damm 1938:327). The Ulithians were sighted close to Palau (Hambruch 1912:12-13). Important data from this report are the same points mentioned earlier: (1) these voyages were seasonal and (2) long voyages were executed in steps, from one island to the next (Hambruch 1912:25).

In describing, the complex Yapese political system of 1909, Müller explains that the inhabitants of Yap recognized no common supreme chief and that Yap was ruled by eight high chiefs (1917:242). Before European colonization, Teb Village of Tomil District was regarded as the highest village in Yap and maintained its neutrality vis-à-vis Gagil and Rull (Müller 1917:245).

Although his source was not specified, Müller (1917:242) notes:

> The village of Gatsapar [Gachpar], although highly respected, has had a high chief *only in relatively recent times*. It succeeded the now abandoned Ru [Ruu‘], which bordered on the sea between Umun [Amun] and Maki [Makiy]. The reason for the migration of its inhabitants to Gatsapar was a war with Tamil (italics added).

Ushijima (1987b:69) adds that a meeting place called Meilif in Ruu‘ Village, where Outer Islanders stayed when they visited Yap, was burned down. Besides collecting much mytho-history, Müller was also a participant observer of Yangolab cult ceremonies. Müller (1917:326, 328) witnessed Ruepon perform an epidemic prevention ceremony for Outer Island guests on 26 November 1909 at the Filsew (C36-75) *pebaey* and at the Numurui (C36-16) *tabinau*.

Müller's ethnographic inventory of Yap includes illustrations of exotic materials from the Outer Islands in the form of textiles and shell goods. *Gau*, the exotic *Spondylus* shell, was the most valuable (Müller 1917:41, 128). Other materials of importance in symbolizing rank and wealth included stone money (*fei* or *rai*), *Tridacna* pestles for pounding areca nuts (*ma*), banana fiber mats (*mbul*), sperm whale tooth pendants, sennit twine (*auu*), turmeric bundles, coconut oil (*gagip*), and pearl shells or *yar* (*Pinctada margaritafera*) Kubary 1889:3; Müller 1917:127-132).

The division of labor in fabricating exchange objects is not obvious in Müller (1917), however, it can be said with certainty that low caste women fabricated the earthenware pots and that men mined the stone money from Palau. Other activities could be performed by both men and women, but weaving and gardening, for examples, tended to be performed by women, while men tended to build houses, canoes, and helped in the heavy garden work.

The Japanese colonial government took over German Pacific colonies north of the equator in October 1914 (Peattie 1988:43). The Japanese South Seas government's economic and military interests in Micronesia lasted thirty years. Japanese ethnographic texts from this time period are not used in this study because of their inaccessibility.

United States military forces seized Ulithi Atoll (W-day) in September 1944 without opposition. Ulithi Atoll became "a secret advance base for the invasion of Okinawa and the Philippines" (Lessa 1968:353). Japanese military forces on Yap surrendered 2 September 1945 (Poyer 1995:231). In 1947, following World War II, the United States administered the Carolines as a Trust Territory for strategic military purposes. In the same year, the Pacific Science Board of the National Research Council organized the Coordinated Investigation of Micronesian Anthropology (CIMA). Sponsored by the United States Navy and other donors, CIMA sent anthropologists to the Carolines, Marianas, and Marshalls to collect ethnographic information for universities and to aid in the governing of this newly acquired territory.

William Lessa, a CIMA team member, conducted ethnographic fieldwork in Ulithi Atoll, primarily on Mogmog. He empathized, as did Tetens (1958) and Hambruch (Damm 1938), with his Ulithian hosts and disapproved of their subordination to the Yapese in Gagil. His objection is evident in a paper given at an American Association for the Advancement of Science meeting, later published in the applied anthropology journal *Human Organization*:

> In summary, agencies for the breakdown of the Yap empire already exist and operate. The American administration wittingly or not, fosters the accelerated efficacy of these agencies through missions, schools, trade, motorized transportation and democratic ideals. The trend is irreversible and plans to aid it should be made accordingly. This should be done discreetly so as not to cause unpleasant reverberations [from the Yapese; Lessa 1950b:18].

Summary

Ethnohistoric data about Yap-Outer Island interaction events give essential context to the archaeological record post-dating European entry into the area. The shorter time scale of the ethnohistoric data shows much culture change, some genuine, and some probably caused by time gaps and omissions by the texts' authors. The ethnohistoric information introduces a number of different factors which need to be considered when relying on these documents to construct an exchange history between Yap and Ulithi, such as: authors' biases, social and political organization, introduced diseases, population levels, value of introduced exchange goods, interaction intensity, ideological components, and European interaction history. Despite the biases of observers, exchange information can be gleaned from ethnohistoric sources. Ethnohistoric evidence can aid in reconstructing the most recent 400 years of interactive behaviors between Yap and the Outer Islands. We can extract from the rich ethnohistorical record that intensive voyages must have taken place at least from the seventeenth century up through the beginning of the twentieth century.

The extensive Carolinian geographical knowledge displayed in the early maps of Fathers Klein and Cantova suggests considerable antiquity to island interaction. On more than one occasion, Carolinians attempted to initiate a formalized exchange system for new exotic goods sought from Europeans. The investigation of documentary sources alone highlights the numerous changes that inter-island exchange practices underwent.

Chapter V

Archaeology of the Western Carolines and Micronesian Ceramic Provenance Studies

This chapter reviews previous archaeological work in the Western Caroline Islands that bear on ceramic analysis, provenance studies, and island interaction. Particular geographic attention is paid to Yap and Ulithi. Before describing the archaeology of Yap and Ulithi, both islands are placed in the archaeological context of the Northwest Tropical Pacific.

Settlement of the Northwest Tropical Pacific

Yap and Ulithi are situated in what Rainbird (1994) terms the "Northwest Tropical Pacific" of remote Oceania. Remote Oceania, a term coined by Green (1991), refers to an area where islands are not inter-visible and distances between them are relatively large. Inter-visibility is the ability to always see at least one island while inter-island voyaging. The inter-visibility of islands is an important factor for understanding the exploration and colonization of the Pacific (Irwin 1992). Inter-visible islands adjacent to the Asian homeland (Near Oceania) of Pleistocene voyagers and later Austronesian-speaking voyagers were the first to be explored and colonized. The smaller and less accessible islands of Remote Oceania took considerably longer to settle by navigating peoples.

Colonization dates for the Western Carolinian archipelago of Palau (also in Remote Oceania) are expected to be the earliest in Micronesia using the safest exploration and colonization strategy proposed by Irwin (1992). Until the recent work of Fitzpatrick (2002), settlement dates older than 2000 years for Palau were rare. Fitzpatrick (2002:219) reports a human bone date of cal BC 770 (750) 550 at one sigma. The next closest archipelago, Yap, has early dates approximately 2000 years old (AA-21203 in Appendix A; Gifford and Gifford 1959:159; Takayama 1982a:91). The earliest Micronesian dates associated with ceramics are from the Mariana Islands at 3500 years B.P., most likely from Austronesian speaking colonizers from the Philippines region (Bellwood 1985:253; Spoehr 1957).

Paleoenvironmental evidence in Micronesia in the form of microfossil pollen and charcoal particles is pushing dates for early human settlement further back in time. Athens and Ward (2002:165) rely on the presence of *Cyrtosperma* (giant swamp taro) in the pollen record of a Palauan sediment core to suggest human colonization reaching as far back as "the middle 5th or even the 6th millennium B.P." in Palau. Dodson and Intoh (1999) have recently argued for a colonization date of 3300 years B.P. (see also Intoh 1997:28) based on charcoal particle evidence from two taro swamp sediment cores, but, Wickler (2002:189) questions their interpretations. If these indirect dates are accepted, the early colonization dates for Palau, Yap, and the Marianas would support Irwin's (1992) model of safe voyaging strategies against the wind.

Apart from the early Bikini Atoll dates (Streck 1990:255), which may have been contaminated from nuclear bomb tests, the central and eastern Carolines appear to have been settled approximately 2000 years B.P. (Athens 1995:78; Intoh 1997:19; Rainbird 1994:300). Ayres (1990:190, 203, 207) believes the colonization of Pohnpei is as old as 3000 years B.P. and suggests a southeast Melanesia or Fiji-West Polynesia homeland for Pohnpei based on the agricultural complex, linguistics, and early material culture. Davidson (1988:93) also posits a Melanesian homeland in the Santa Cruz region for Nuclear Micronesian populations relying on "shell adzes, slingstones, plain pottery, fishhooks, various kinds of shell peelers and a variety of shell ornaments".

Linguistic evidence also sheds light on the early settlement of the Western Micronesian high islands. Palauan and Chamorro are both non-Oceanic languages. Yapese shares affinities with the Oceanic and the non-Oceanic language sub-groups. The remaining people of the Micronesian geographic area, not including the people of the Polynesian Outliers, speak Nuclear Micronesian, a sub-group of Oceanic. Ross (1996:127) argues that the conservative Yapese language, which sits on the linguistic border between Oceanic and non-Oceanic Micronesian languages, contains five "layers" of Austronesian lexicon. Three Yapese language layers identify its Oceanic group origin while two other layers are non-Oceanic. Suggesting long antiquity of human settlement on Yap, Ross (1996:150) proposes that the Yapese language inherited traits from the Admiralty Islands language group, an early offshoot of Oceanic.

Linguistic and archaeological evidence has led Micronesian researchers to suggest what has been called the "orthodox model" for early settlement in the Northwest Tropical Pacific (Ayres 1990; Bellwood 1978; Craib 1983; Davidson 1988). The "orthodox model" postulates dual origins for the inhabitants of Micronesia, where Palau, the Marianas, and possibly Yap, were settled independently from Island Southeast Asia; eastern Micronesia was settled later during the first millenium B.C. by people with Lapita or Lapita-derived ceramic and shell tool industries (Ayres 1990:207;

Davidson 1988:91). The earlier alternative model has Micronesia simply as a sea-way, through which ancestral Polynesians traveled to get to Polynesia (Buck 1938; Howells 1973). With simulation evidence, Irwin (1992:120-123) has shown that ocean voyaging from Fiji, northern West Polynesia, the Solomons, and the Reef/Santa Cruz Islands to eastern Micronesia is feasible.

Yap

Edward and Delila Gifford's (1959) archaeological project in 1956 represents the first modern archaeological investigation of Yap. The Giffords (1959:151) investigated 26 sites, but chose not to excavate in Gagil Municipality because they did not find any "promising sites." They identified surface features of diverse past human activities, and found cookhouse mounds, house platforms, midden, pottery scatters, stone alignments, paths, and walls. Ceramics and tools made of shell and stone were associated with these features are. Considering the geological resources of Yap, a high island, relatively few stone tools were recovered: one disk, hammerstones, mineral pigments of goethite with traces of hematite, pestles, and whetstones (Gifford and Gifford 1959:194). Many shell tools on the other hand were recorded, such as *Cassis* taro peelers, *Conus* knives, *Tridacna* adzes, bracelets, disks, money, pottery smoothing tools, rings, scrapers, and trumpets. Exotic artifacts located by the Giffords include Chinese and Japanese ceramics and stone money from Palaua and Guam. The Giffords (1959:179) note that samples of the scarcer Unlaminated ware were unhesitatingly identified by Dr. Alexander Spoehr "as the same type as his Marianas Plain ware from Saipan and Tinian [Mariana Islands]."

The Giffords (1959:159) recovered an early Yap settlement date of 1780 ± 250 years B.P. (UC-9) from a four-level composite charcoal sample between a depth of 1.2 - 1.8 m at the Pemrang site in southern Yap. In 1980, Takayama and Intoh revisited the Giffords' Pemrang and Boldanig sites of southern Yap. Takayama (1982a:91; 1982b:107) reports an earlier date of 2310 ± 80 B.P. from a *Trochus* shell (N-034) at a depth of 3 m at the Pemrang site.

Giffords' Ceramic Typology

Ceramics are the most ubiquitous artifacts found in Yap. The Giffords (1959:179) define two ceramic types in their ceramic analysis: Tempered ware, found chiefly in the archaeological investigations of southern Yap, and the common Untempered Laminated ware, found island-wide. Tempered ceramics were found in older archaeological contexts preceding the Untempered ware. Laminated ceramics unearthed in deeper excavation levels are interpreted as possible results of bioturbation from land crabs and hermit crabs (Gifford and Gifford 1959:179).

Nine rim types are defined, five of which are common to both ceramic types and four of which are found only in the older tempered ware. Gifford and Gifford (1959:183-184) report Laminated rim sherds with drilled perforations as well as four Unlaminated ware sherds with incised decorations. Four body sherds with a brick red pigment applied in parallel lines were also found (Gifford and Gifford 1959:184).

Reba W. Benedict, a University of California geology graduate student at the time, conducted petrographic analyses and found that the Laminated sherds contained hornblende and plagioclase feldspar fragments, which appeared to be penetrated by small mineral inclusions. Unlaminated ware is characterized by fresh looking and altered quartz and feldspar inclusions. Benedict (Gifford and Gifford 1959:184-185) also notes organic-tempered sherds with carbonate material from foraminifera. This early study did not recognize iron oxide temper or sherd temper (grog) in the Unlaminated potsherds.

Intoh's Ceramic Typology

Ceramics are the predominant artifacts in Yapese archaeological contexts and are in continuous usage for over 2000 years (Intoh and Leach 1985:146). Intoh creates three types and two sub-types from her archaeological data and the previous typological definitions of Takayama (1982a:84) and the Giffords (1959). The types are based on the technological attributes of the ceramics, "characterized by their tempering material, their texture, and shaping method" (Intoh and Leach 1985:96). All three types are made predominantly of metamorphic montmorillonite clays and open-fired in oxidizing conditions with temperatures between 700° and 800° C.

Calcareous Sand-Tempered (CST) Ware

Calcareous Sand-Tempered ware is pottery made from clay mixed with calcareous sand temper consisting of reef shell, coral, and foraminifera. This composition is common in early Micronesian archaeological contexts, and is found in the ceramic producing islands of Chuuk, Kosrae, the Marianas, Pohnpei, and Yap. CST pottery is presently the oldest cultural material found on Yap, radiocarbon dated from associated materials (mostly shell) to approximately 2000 years ago (Intoh 1988:131). According to Intoh's (1988:97, 100-101) ceramic analyses, CST ware was made into a variety of vessel shapes, probably formed by coils or slabs, and fired under a variety of firing conditions. A terminal date for this ceramic type is less certain, however, Intoh (1988:134; 1990) suggests the ceramic technology persisted 1400 years. Porous sherds are sorted as CST ware ceramics because Intoh (1988:46, 89) discovered that porous sherds had their calcium carbonate temper chemically eroded in acidic archaeological contexts.

Plain Ware

Plain ware consists of a mixture of kaolinite and montmorillonite-rich clays without calcareous sand temper or laminations (Intoh 1988:135). Consequently, this broadly delimited group has much variation. Intoh (1988:43) constructs two sub-types: Iron Oxide Tempered pottery and Quartz Tempered pottery. Iron Oxide Tempered ware has red hematite grains or goethite (hydrated iron oxide), some of which are interpreted as natural inclusions from clay-bearing latosols and others as temper (Intoh 1988:95). Dickinson (1997a:1) observes some Iron Oxide Tempered ware sherds contain silty grog temper.

Quartz Tempered pottery contains inclusions of quartz and feldspar and polycrystalline microgranitic to felsitic quartzo-feldspathic rock fragments set in a clay paste of fine quartz-feldspar and actinolitic amphibole crystals (Dickinson 1997a:1). Intoh (1988:96) suggests that the angularity of quartz grains demonstrates that the potters added temper to the clay. Dickinson (1994:2), on the other hand, submits that the quartzofeldspathic grains are natural inclusions from the weathering of intrusive bodies within residual clays.

The 1400 year duration of Plain ware is roughly contemporaneous with the dated range of CST, that is from 2000 years ago to 600 years ago; the Plain Ware type is dominant in southern Yapese sites between 600 and 800 years ago (Intoh 1988:132, 1990). Like the CST ware, the end is difficult to establish, but with little direct evidence, Intoh (1988:132) estimates that Laminated ware gained prominence over Plain ware 600 years ago.

Intoh and Leach (1985:88) used x-ray photographs to infer that Plain pot manufacture used a coil-building technique. Seventy percent of Plain rim sherds have straight rim courses (Intoh and Leach 1985:81). Examining a Plain sherd under a scanning electron microscope, Intoh (1988:91) identified stick-like sponge spicules in the pores and interprets them as intrusive from the archaeological matrix (Intoh 1988:91). Another possibility is that the fine pores in Plain pottery are remains of lime tempering (Intoh 1988:111).

Laminated Ware

Laminated ware pottery is the youngest and most common ceramic type found on Yap. Prevalent on site surfaces, this pottery type has very hard walls, no temper, laminations in the wall section, and a uniform incurved bowl shape used for cooking or steaming (Intoh and Leach 1985:98). Though untempered, Laminated ceramics contain rounded goethite-rich grains and white feldspar grains from the clay sources (Intoh 1988:96). Yapese Laminated ware is characterized by metavolcanic (plagioclase and actinolitic amphibole) detritus in its paste (Dickinson 1997a:1).

Laminated ware is roughly smoothed and has well smeared joints of coils or slabs (Intoh 1988:99, 100). Intoh (1988:103) perceives the uniform firing conditions and the increasing number of oxidized sherd cores of this type as evidence of more controlled firing conditions. Intoh (1988:121) used an ethnoarchaeological analogy to suggest that the characteristic laminations in the sherd sections are a result of strong steam pressure generated by the wetting of the pots just before firing. Laminated ceramics continued to be manufactured and used on Yap until the Second World War. The earliest appearance of Laminated ware is unclear, but Intoh (1990:44) proposes that this pottery became important about 600 years ago.

Laminated pottery was superior to previous Yapese ceramic types and eventually became the dominant ware across the island. Intoh (1988:134) considers Laminated ware an advanced adaptation to an unusual Yapese natural environment and "closely correlated with the disadvantage of the technology involved in CST pottery making." From Mössbauer spectra analyses, Intoh determines that Laminated pots were fired at higher temperatures. In conjunction with the absence of temper and technological standardization, she considers Laminated pots were stronger than previous wares.

Descantes (2002) has recently proposed a model to explain the relatively recent end of ceramic pot production on Yap. Relying on a historical approach which considers the social dynamics of pots and a combination of archaeological, ethnographic, and ethnohistoric records, I suggest the Yapese gradually replaced their ceramic vessel technology with metal pots due to new conditions encountered during contact and colonialism. Factors contributing to the ease of replacement of ceramic pots in Yap include the form and function of clay vessels in the society, the specialized labor required to produce ceramic containers, and the durability offered by the replacement technology. Despite their technological advantages over their earlier clay counterparts, metal pots today have lost the ability to hold the complex Yapese identities and distinctions. The replacement of clay pots by metal ones symbolizes the weakening of past political prerogatives enjoyed by the high-caste and the blurring of rank distinctions in the household. Whether or not a ceramic pot is a utilitarian tool or a complex symbol of artistic expression when its technology is dismissed by the producing culture, it is indicative of a changed perception of the object.

Gachpar Village

Price (1975), a cultural anthropologist, did a land tenure map of Gachpar in his ethnographic study of Yapese socio-economic changes. The map provides vital information for later archaeological settlement and spatial pattern studies of the stone architectural features. The map does not include the location of architectural features, but it does contain property names and boundaries. Cordy (1986:62-65, 117-118) initiated a settlement pattern study of the Gachpar

Village landscape in 1980 and in a partial survey identified 60 architectural features for a general settlement pattern study investigating the development of social stratification.

Gachpar's architectural features include dayif, *faluw*, *pebaey*, and *wunbey*. *Dayif* are the most common architectural structures in the Yapese archaeological landscape. Made of stone, these structures serve as house foundations. *Dayif* serve as powerful symbols of authority and ownership and are founded by ancestral ghosts. Yap *dayif* are hexagonal-shaped. A *faluw* is a young men's club house often situated near the lagoon shore (Cordy 1986:xii). The foundations of the preserved *faluw* in Gachpar are rectangular. The walkway leading from the *faluw* to the shore is constructed of stone, usually coral boulders and tabular schist. A *pebaey* is a men's house, which is large and often centrally located in the village. A *wunbey* is a low paved sitting platform (Cordy 1986:xii). *Wunbey* are usually constructed of tabular schist and have schist uprights for persons to sit against. These paved sitting areas join *pebaey* and habitation platforms.

Intoh was the first to conduct archaeological excavations in Gachpar Village (Intoh 1988; Intoh and Leach 1985). Interested in the Yapese ceramic tradition, Intoh excavated the sites of Farchee and Garingmog (Intoh and Leach 1985:33-45).

Farchee Site

The Farchee site (C36-31) is located 300 m inland, approximately 2 m above a taro swamp in the Tree-Covered Gradual Slopes zone. Intoh investigated two excavation units (2 by 2 m and 2 by 2.5 m), one on a possible cooking place and the other on a house mound (Intoh and Leach 1985:37). Exotic materials include fragments of historic iron and glass recovered from the top layer. Charcoal and all three types of Yapese pottery, i.e., CST, Laminated, and Plain wares, were found in the unit. Most of the artifacts in the two layered unit were in the top stratum, which contained a charcoal sample radiocarbon dated to 469 ± 66 years B.P. (NZ 6651; Intoh and Leach 1985:38, 174). One Laminated sherd and a few porous paste sherds (CST) were also found in the upper portions of the second layer.

The second unit of 2 by 2.5 m, located on the north side of a house mound, was excavated to a depth of more than 1 m and produced two parallel stone walls (65 cm apart) made of volcanic and coral stones. Intoh and Leach (1985:45) interpret the contemporaneous features as a double wall construction to hold soil fill for the house platform. Three hundred fifty-nine potsherds were recovered, most in the top layer comprising Laminated and porous sherds with a few Plain sherds (Intoh and Leach 1985:43). The top layers also contained historic iron and glass fragments.

Garingmog Site

The Garingmog site is located in the Shore zone of Gachpar in front of a mangrove swamp that extends into the taro swamp. Intoh excavated a 2 by 2 m unit and found sherds in the top two layers of the three-layered site. Two hundred twenty-four Laminated ware potsherds, in addition to beer bottle fragments, midden, a stone file, and a shell artifact were collected (Intoh and Leach 1985:36-37). The top layer produced a charcoal radiocarbon date of less than 250 years B.P. (NZ 6676; Intoh and Leach 1985:35, 174). The excavation was stopped at a depth of 78 cm because of the difficulty in removing water in the excavation unit.

Yapese Ceramic Environment

Intoh interprets the Yapese archaeological ceramic sequence as a gradual adaptation to the environment of Yap with changes primarily in ceramic tempering and firing conditions. CST pottery lasted 1400 years and was the simplest adaptation to Yapese resources where ready access to hard terrigenous sands necessary for tempering pottery was absent (Intoh 1988:131). The Giffords (1959:179) suggest the laminated technology "may represent a degeneration in technique from the earlier [U]nlaminated [type]." Despite a lack in chronometric control, Snyder (1989:1) in his Palauan ceramic research suggests "the physical properties of Palauan pottery [(A.D. 745 – 1920)] did not change through time and that the variability observed in these properties is not explained with a model of adaptational change". Intoh (1988:134) argues the contrary with her Yapese data: Laminated pottery "represents an advanced adaptation by local potters to a highly unusual natural environment" which replaced Plain and CST pottery; "the development of Laminated pottery technology is closely correlated with the disadvantage of the technology involved in CST pottery making" (Intoh 1988:134). In sum, Intoh (1990) concludes that Laminated pottery is an adaptation to the terrigenous-lacking ceramic environment of Yap. While I agree that Laminated ceramics are well adapted to the Yapese ceramic environment, I think cultural causes based on Yapese needs also play a role in explaining why technological changes in pottery-making occurred. I do not believe the ceramic environment or potter's access to ceramic constituents changed appreciably through time, but rather that the cooking demands of the Yapese changed. I discuss this hypothesis in Chapter 7.

Western Caroline Coral Islands

Although it has been demonstrated that Micronesian coral atolls contain substantial archaeological deposits (Davidson 1967; Fujimura and Alkire 1984), they remain under represented in Pacific archaeological investigations. Low coral islands were once believed to be archaeologically unrewarding because of their low elevation, susceptibility to natural disaster damage, late settlement, and meager natural resources (Davidson 1967:363). Atoll sites, however, have shown stratigraphy and substantial subsurface deposits in Micronesia (Davidson 1967) with dates possibly going as far back as 2000 years (e.g., Dye 1987; Shun and Athens 1990). Since the pioneering efforts of Davidson (1971), archaeologists have recovered radiocarbon dates of A.D. 800 ± 100 (charcoal) from And Atoll (Ayres et al. 1981:83), A.D. 1000 (fish, human and turtle bones) for the Faraulep and Woleai Atolls (Fujimura and Alkire 1984:123), and 1760 ± 75 B.P. (*Tridacna* shell) for Ngulu Atoll (Takayama 1982b:107).

When Davidson discovered the first stratified archaeological deposits on a Micronesian coral island, she also found evidence for exchange. Davidson (1971:101-102) notes exotic lithic materials on Nukuoro Islet such as gabbro, particularly nephelinite and nepheline basalt, as evidence for island interactions at various times in the past. Numerous historic Asian and European artifacts recovered by Davidson (1971:83) include buttons, china, clay pipes, coins, concrete bricks, glass, plastic, metal, and nails.

Lamotrek

Fujimura and Alkire (1977, 1984) were the first to conduct archaeological investigations on coral islands within the ancient "Yapese Empire" by investigating between 1975 and 1976 the atolls of Faraulep, Woleai (Falalus Island), and Lamotrek. Fujimura and Alkire (1984:87) unearthed midden, a number of shell artifacts, and four potsherds from the third level of the Sabaig site on Lamotrek. Bolipi, possibly a former house site, 150 m south of Sabaig, was also excavated. They recovered shell artifacts, some of which are pots for cooking and storage, and midden (Levels 7-10) with a radiocarbon date of A.D. 1500 – 1670 (turtle bone; N-3124) in a 1 by 3 m trench. A complete human skeleton in an extended burial was dated to 800 ± 85 B.P. In Bolipi II, a 1 by 1 m perpendicular extension of Bolipi I, midden, shell artifacts, four potsherds, and three historic Asian sherds were found. Twenty-seven ceramic potsherds were excavated: two from Sabaig, eighteen from Bolipi I, and seven from Bolipi II.

From their Lamotrek excavations, Fujimura and Alkire define three ceramic types: A, B, and an unidentified type. Six samples of Type A (thick, reddish and poorly fired) and B (thick, well-fired, finely manufactured) were sent to Dickinson for petrographic analysis. Dickinson observes that Type A sherds contain metavolcanic rocks similar to those found in a Yapese geological province and the Gifford Laminated sherd collection. These sherds were dated to between A.D. 1200 and 1500 on Lamotrek (Fujimura and Alkire 1984:112). According to Dickinson, Type B earthenware contains broken-sherd aggregate temper and silty clay "that probably formed by weathering of volcanic debris" (Fujimura and Alkire 1984:112). Initially, the sherds were interpreted as coming from Palau because of the grog temper, which had only been found on Palau (Dickinson 1984:132-133; Dickinson and Shutler 1979:1690-1691, 1693). Now, however, grog-tempered sherds are also documented from Yap and Pohnpei, and after re-examining the sherds, Dickinson (1994:6) concludes that the Lamotrek sherds are probably from Yap and not Palau.

Exotic stones were found in the Lamotrek archaeological excavations. The petrographic analysis of Professor R. L. Hay of the University of California at Berkeley detected five classes of stone: oceanic volcanic lava, probably oceanic volcanic, pumice, limestone (probably local), and undiagnostic lava (Fujimura and Alkire 1984:114). All of the lithic materials probably originate from islands east of the Andesite Line (Fujimura and Alkire 1984:114).

Fais

Intoh (1996) discusses five excavation units from three sites on the island of Fais, a raised coral island 80 km east of Ulithi Atoll. Intoh (1996:111, 113-114) collected approximately 800 potsherds representing all three Yapese ceramic types and reports a 1900 year habitation history for Fais during which pottery was constantly imported. Through petrographic analysis, sherds from the Faligochol-2 site are interpreted as originating from Palau (Intoh and Dickinson 1994, 2002). Palauan sherds appeared in a layer dated to A.D. 100 - 400 and were found in every subsequent layer. Many other non-local materials were recovered throughout the settlement history of Fais. Metamorphic schist rock, a common geological component of Yap, was found in the oldest layer (Intoh 1996:113).

Intoh (1996:114) suggests Solomon Island influence from an excavated trolling bonito lure fishhook shank and a bone lure point resembling those found in the southeastern Solomon Islands area. She also argues that linguistic similarities between Nuclear Micronesian and languages of the Solomons-Vanuatu region indicate affinity between the two communities. However, trolling bonito lure fishhooks are known to have also existed in eastern Micronesia (Ayres 1990). Finally, an excavated piece of tree gum identified as belonging to the Dipterocarpaceae family, indigenous to the Indo-Malaysian region, implies further island interactions (Intoh 1996:115).

Ngulu Atoll

In 1980 Takayama and Intoh investigated Ngulu Atoll situated between Yap and Palau, approximately 200 km southwest of Yap. Three hundred sherds were retrieved and sorted into four main categories: Yapese Laminated ware, Yapese Unlaminated ware, Yapese CST ware, and Palauan ware (Intoh 1981:75). Dickinson's (1994:7) petrographic report on these sherds argues for Yapese pottery on Ngulu. Grog-tempered sherds resemble those from Yap, while the other grog-tempered sherds resemble Palauan grog-tempered sherds (Dickinson 1994:7). Intoh (1981) concludes Palauan, Yapese, and European contacts based on the archaeological evidence. At Ngulu, Takayama (1982b:107) reports radiocarbon dates of 1760 ± 75 B.P. (N-4052; *Tridacna* shell) to 470 ± 80 B.P. (N-4053; *Tridacna* shell).

Intoh (1992:159) states that contact was maintained with Palau and Yap throughout the 1800-year occupation history of Ngulu. She suggests that pots were essential in the resource-limited environment of Ngulu for two important functions: (1) simmering coconut sap enabled longer preservation; and (2) detoxifying *Alocasia* by cooking it in coconut syrup. Pots may have been essential to Ngulu inhabitants, but I think their function could have also been served by large *Cassis* sp. shell pots (Figure 11). *Cassis* pot fragments and other *Cassis*-made tools (peelers, adzes) were also recovered in Ngulu excavations (Intoh 1981:76).

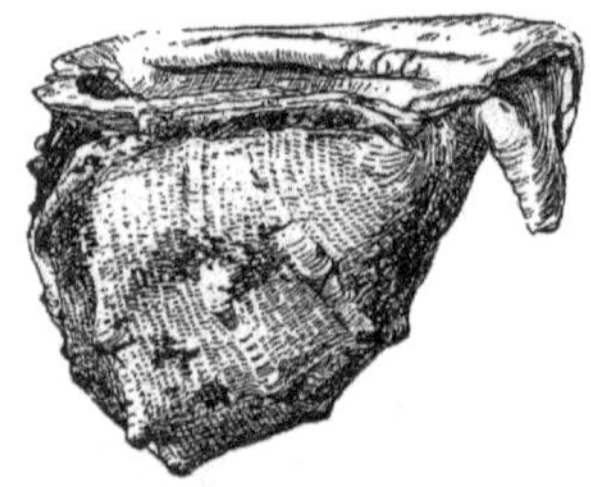

FIGURE 11. *Cassis* sp. pot at a one sixth scale (Damm 1938:316)

Mogmog and Ulithi Atoll

John Craib conducted archaeological surveys and excavations in Ulithi to assess the nature of archaeological remains and investigate how former villages varied from those in the ethnographic pattern (Craib 1980, 1981). Originally, Craib planned to conduct his doctoral dissertation work on Ulithi, but owing to the lack of deep undisturbed archaeological deposits, he chose to work in the Marianas.

Ulithian islets suffered from earth-moving activities and landscape modifications during and after World War II. Mogmog was transformed into the fleet relaxation center by the U.S. Navy and served as a military base from 1944 through 1946 (Wheeler 1979:88). Approximately 300 Ulithians not already forcibly moved to Yap or Palau by the Japanese military temporarily stayed on Fassarai (an islet in Ulithi Atoll) until the end of the war (Craib 1980:42). Mogmog platforms suffered damage during World War II (see Lessa 1987:127), and were not all rebuilt after the war (Craib 1981:51). Craib (1980:83-89; 1981:51) notes the major impact that the U.S. military presence had on the Ulithian landscapes and remarks that only the graves and the men's house platforms on Mogmog survived. However, Lessa (1987) believes that the military impact was not as pervasive as Craib had alleged and that the Navy made an effort to minimize *dayif* and cemetery destruction. From interviews, I learned that much modification to *dayif* occurred while Mogmog was converted into a "Rest & Relaxation" island/military base between 1944 and 1946. Some of these modifications include the building of an officer's kitchen at the site of the Lamrui *errau dayif* (Mog-25); the destruction of the Falol *errau dayif* (Mog-13) for the building of a Navy Quonset hut, and; the shortening of at least two *dayif*, Fal Le Mei *errau* (Mog-22) and Hathiar *errau* (Mog-27), to make space for roads. From FEMA (Federal Emergency Management Agency) assistance, some households have cement typhoon-proof houses over pre-existing *dayif*.

Recent archaeological investigation suggest that the Mogmog Village location fronting the lagoon on the sheltered side of the island has remained unchanged since first settlement (see also Craib 1980; Lessa 1986:28), it is less likely that archaeological deposits have suffered from extensive bioturbation. Smaller hermit crabs, which are found in the village, can inflict minimal disturbance to archaeological deposits (see also Davidson 1967:370). Natural disasters, such as typhoons (e.g., 1907, 1960), have also had an impact on Mogmog's landscape, however, typhoon damage to stone house platforms is minor compared to that endured by habitations.

Surface surveys of Ulithi, where possible, approach one hundred percent (Craib 1980:61). Craib (1980:66) discovered cultural remains on 24 islets in Ulithi Atoll and reports a variety of surface remains on Mogmog including: *Conus* and *Terebra* shell adzes, Japanese glazed ceramics, *Tridacna* knives, Yapese Laminated ware, as well as coral slab uprights, graves, and coral platforms (Craib 1980:83). Other common artifacts included *Conus* shell scrapers and *Cassis* shell bowls (Craib 1981:53).

The most archaeologically productive excavation in Ulithi was dug by the people of Mogmog for a septic tank before Craib's arrival in 1978. Nine stratigraphic layers were discerned in the 1 by 2 m unit. Radiocarbon samples of charcoal and burnt coral from a hearth were dated separately to avoid carbonate contamination (Craib 1983:924). Craib (1983:924) reports uncorrected dates of 1690 ± 100 years B.P. (UCR-174A) for the carbonate component and 1460 ± 90 years B.P. (UCR-174B) for the organic component. Together, the dates produced a mean of A.D. 400 (Craib 1980:198). Other excavation units were placed nearby, but none showed the midden or clear stratigraphy of the septic tank unit (Craib, personal communication, 1994).

Most of Craib's (1980:193) subsurface investigations were shovel tests, some in transects, others randomly distributed, and he discovered that Yapese Laminated ceramic sherds were the most common cultural remains in the archaeological landscape of Ulithian islets. Traditional structures on the Mogmog landscape included canoehouses (*fagil*), men's (*metalefal*) and women's (*imölipöl*) houses, residential platforms (*dayif*), cookhouses (*malum*), stone habitation platforms, and graves. Unlike Yapese *dayif*, Mogmog has rectangular-shaped platforms. According to informants, *dayif* were a historic introduction from the Yapese (Craib 1981:50).

Ceramic Provenance Studies in Micronesia

Much Pacific pottery is undecorated thus hindering efforts to determine manufacturing sources and leaving compositional analysis the primary avenue for addressing provenance issues. This section reviews Micronesian ceramic provenance research based on compositional analyses acquired from mineralogical and chemical analyses (Bryson 1989; Graves et al. 1990; Intoh and Leach 1985; Pavlish et al. 1986).

Petrographic Analyses

As in all provenance studies, successful petrographic examination of ceramic thin-sections depends on the familiarity one has with the potential geological sources (Dickinson and Shutler 1971:191). Due to the varied geotectonic environment of the Pacific Basin, temper analysis of potsherd thin sections allows researchers to identify exotic wares and trace the movement of materials between islands in differing geological contexts. Early petrographic studies addressed issues concerning the peopling of the Pacific Islands. Today, Pacific petrographic analyses also help examine concerns such as ceramic production and exchange.

The Pacific has been divided into major temper provinces for ceramic studies. Calcareous tempers may originate from any island that has reef growth (Dickinson and Shutler 1979:1669). Yap is geologically complex and fits into a tectonic highland temper group containing metamorphic and recycled sedimentary sources (Dickinson and Shulter 1979:1670, 1684). Yapese sherds are described as having plagioclase, hornblende, and epidote traces. Part of an andesitic arc on the west side of the Andesite Line and adjacent to subduction zones, Palau is distinguished by rocks which are commonly andesitic or dacitic (Dickinson and Shulter 1979:1683). Palau's ceramic tempers are exclusively calcareous and volcanic sands. Palauan potsherds are characterized by sherd temper (grog), plagioclase, hornblende, and ferromagnesium silicate (pyroxene) grains (Dickinson and Shulter 1979:1647, 1669, 1683). Carolinian islands east of Yap and Palau make up an intra-oceanic archipelago typified by oceanic basalt (Dickinson and Shutler 1979:1669, 1682). The high islands of Chuuk, Pohnpei, and Kosrae are members of the intra-Oceanic basalt temper group. They are "entirely free of quartz and calcic plagioclase is normally the only feldspar present" (Dickinson and Shutler 1979:1682). Dickinson differentiates Pohnpei and Kosrae by noting that Kosrae ceramics contain phlogopitic mica and oxyhornblende ("kaersutite"; Dickinson 1997b:2).

Constituent Analyses of Palauan Ceramics

In an attempt to seriate Palauan ceramics, Snyder (1989:45) concludes elemental abundances of 12 short-lived radioactive isotopes analyzed via INAA are not stratigraphically significant. Results from 27 Palauan ceramics also indicate that thin-walled and thick-walled ceramics are chemically indistinguishable (Pavlish et al. 1986). Snyder also conducted INAA on four clay sources from three widely separated locations on Babeldoab (Pavlish et al. 1986). Based on chemical similarities, Pavlish et al. (1986) suggest that two of the clay sources are similar to the ceramics and possible source areas for the earthenware. The elemental concentrations of Snyder's clay sources were dissimilar, but not statistically significant, which was most likely a result of his small sample size (n=7).

Constituent Analyses of Mariana Islands' Ceramics

To study issues of ceramic variability and its possible interpretations, Graves et al. (1990) conducted compositional analyses on ceramic potsherds (n=34) and clay sources (n=2) to identify temporal and spatial variability in the Mariana Islands. Using an energy dispersive spectrometer (EDS) integrated with a scanning electron microscope (SEM), they selected clay matrix from the sherd thin sections for chemical characterization. They collected the abundances of 12 major elements and identified four groups using two different statistical algorithms. Combining the elemental characteristics and the macroscopic attributes of their data, the authors suggest stronger inter-island distinctions between Guam, Saipan, and Tinian after the Pre-latte period (after A.D. 1200). Despite the small data set, Graves et al. (1990:227) argue that "Pre-latte pottery was more widely produced from a greater variety of clays than Latte period pottery", but exchange during the Pre-Latte period was more localized. The late prehistoric pottery divergence is explained as a "conscious effort to produce and maintain geographically based social distinctions" (Graves et al. 1990:228). Based on the elemental data of only 2 clay sources and 34 sherds, the authors rely on too small a sample size to interpret 3000 years of ceramic production and exchange in the Marianas. Their interpretations should be considered preliminary until more data can be collected to test statistically the authors' hypotheses and factors known to affect elemental abundances of sherds such as the depositional environments of the potsherds and the intra and inter-source variability of the clay sources.

Constituent Analyses of Pohnpeian Ceramics

Bryson (1989) conducted INAA on Pohnpeian sherds (n=26) and clay sources (n=5) to assess the suitability of the analytical technique and investigate the compositional variability of ceramic data collected at different sites. Unfortunately, the INAA laboratory results are enigmatic

(Bryson 1989:233) and did not allow for a precise evaluation. Bryson, however, cautiously suggests that relative abundances of rare earth elements may be used to separate Awak Valley ceramics from Dauahdpeidak Islet (DPK) ceramics at Nan Madol.

Ceramic compositional and provenance analyses in Micronesia hold much promise for future archaeological studies. Larger data sets of ceramics and raw materials will allow the full potential of this work to be realized in the future, as they have been in other parts of the world. At this stage, it is more important to gather data from well-recorded environmental settings to understand the dynamic between sherd composition and the life of a sherd than make premature interpretations relying on inadequate data sets.

Summary

The Western Caroline Islands in Micronesia have received archaeological investigations crucial to this research. Previous works have shown that coral islands hold archaeological potential and that the settlement histories of Palau, Yap, and the Marianas may extend as far back as 5 to 6 millennia. Untempered Laminated ware, the youngest Yapese ceramic type, predominates on Yap, Ulithi, and the nearby coral islands of Fais and Ngulu. The prevalence of undecorated ceramics in Micronesian sites has led to effective mineralogical and chemical characterization studies to investigate settlement, technological, and provenance issues. The realization of compositional studies' potential in interpretations of the past lies in learning more about the geological nature of Pacific Islands and analyzing larger ceramic data sets.

Chapter VI

Archaeological Investigations: Spatial and Ceramic Analyses

This chapter presents the analyses and results of my archaeological investigation into the past exchange between the people of Yap and Ulithi. I report the archaeological investigations I conducted in Yap and Ulithi, concerned primarily with the ceramic evidence collected beneath *dayif* in Gachpar and Mogmog, historically known (Lessa 1950c; Ushijima 1987b) to be the locations of people who held *sawei* exchange privileges. Ruu' Village, which according to informants and published oral historical information held Outer Island exchange relations before Gachpar (Müller 1917:242; Ushijima 1987b:69), was also briefly explored. A general spatial analysis of the platforms that once practiced exchange with the Outer Islands is presented. Ceramic studies, particularly chemical characterization analyses of the collected clays and ceramics, follow the spatial analysis. Chronological details of different processes are also presented.

Archaeological Investigations

The majority of archaeological investigations were on *dayif* because archaeological deposits beneath them are less susceptible to post-depositional disturbance. The platforms also historically held *sawei* privileges (see Lessa 1950c; Ushijima 1982, 1987b). Where possible, I chose traditional matrilineal head platforms (*imwel hailang*) because their locations tended not to move according to patterns of residence after marriage in ethnographic works. *Dayif*, as mentioned earlier, are raised stone habitation foundations, usually hexagonal in shape in Yap. In Yap, *dayif* symbolize the ownership rights of the patrilineal estate or *tabinaw* while in Ulithi, *dayif* are rectangular in shape and signify matrilineal properties. Some *dayif* could not be investigated because of site destruction. The platform could be replaced by a larger modern structure or completely destroyed. In rare instances, platform owners did not allow excavations on their property.

Spatial Analyses

Spatial characteristics of archaeological features and artifacts in the villages under study provide important chronological and organizational details about Yap-Ulithi exchange. The socioeconomic exchange system paired Yapese patrilineage estates (*tabinaw*) with Outer Island matrilineal sibs (*hailang*; Ushijima 1982:66). The spatial distribution of the *dayif*, and by extension of the potsherds, provides interesting details about the settlement patterns of Gachpar and Mogmog. The following sections present spatial information necessary to understand the provenience and provenance of the data. More detailed analyses concerning the spatial dynamics of the architectural features in relation to the economic, ideological, and political organization of the villages will be pursued in the future.

Before examining the *sawei* landscapes of Gachpar and Mogmog, it is important to bear in mind certain aspects of these maps. First, the maps collapse centuries of *dayif* construction and habitation and second, locations shown on them were probably never contemporaneously occupied. Third, the *sawei* landscape perspective of the maps is a static representation of informant knowledge going back as far as 1947 (Lessa 1950c; Ushijima 1982, 1987b). Because *sawei* canoe fleets stopped sailing before the collection of this information, it is quite possible that much is missing from the representation of the *sawei* landscape in these maps. It is probable that my representation of the *sawei* landscape depicts only the last stage of *sawei*. There are probably numerous more *dayif*, which at one time or another had *sawei* relationships. Only some of the many modern features in both villages are included in the maps.

Mapping in Yap and Ulithi

A Brunton® pocket transit mounted on a tripod measured bearings for mapping architectural features on Yap and Ulithi. Distances were measured by taping from the transit datum to the points of interest. Mogmog Village *dayif* locations are more accurate than those of Gachpar Village because unlike Mogmog, a great many Gachpar foundations are on a landscape with considerable relief and under thick forest canopies.

Feature designations on Mogmog are preceded by "Mog" and followed by a feature number. On Yap, I used Cordy's (1986) archaeological site coding system. His system designates municipalities (also called districts) by letters and villages by numbers. Gagil Municipality, where I excavated, is represented by the letter "C." The seventeen villages in Gagil range from Makiy which is 26 to Ul which is 42 (see Figure 3). Gachpar platform numbers, where possible, resemble those of Cordy (1986:62-65, 117-118).

Gachpar Village Survey

A survey strategy using a line of people walking back and forth on the landscape was not applicable in Gachpar because of the strong Yapese sentiments toward trespassing. Unlike Ulithi, Gachpar sites were not found by a line survey, but rather by informants, who led me to *dayif* locations. The Gachpar map is limited by containing only features known today and may not contain all of the *dayif* in the village. This restriction was alleviated by inspecting around known *dayif* for other possible surface remains of archaeological sites. No attempt to delineate site boundaries in the village was made. Instead, archaeological and modern features on the landscape were assigned numbers following Cordy's (1986) system.

My local assistants and I mapped approximately 170 stone architectural features in heavily forested Gachpar Village, considerably more than previously reported, however, previous *dayif* number estimates are close (Cordy 1986:73; Hunter-Anderson 1983:89). As previously shown by Cordy (1986), the large village of Gachpar is divided into three ranked geo-political sections: Tholang, Ariap, and Galpagal. Tholang section contains the Bulwol *tabinaw* (C36-83), seat of one of the three paramount chiefs in the tri-partite political ruling system of Yap, which beneath it has two complementary sections or villages. The Tholang section was the highest section (*bulce'*) and Ariap the complementary (*ulun*) lower section. The *bulce'* was considered the older sibling of an *ulun* ranked village (Labby 1976:100). The complimentary pair was also a "regional leader of one side of two opposed Yap-wide alliances, groupings of villages of all ranks, which were allied politically, the *bulce* headed the 'side of the chiefs' (*ban pilung*) and the *ulun* headed the 'side of the young men' (*ban pagal*)" (Labby 1976:102). Tholang and Ariap led the Ban pagal alliance or what has also been called "the side of the young men" because it was a less historical center of Yap, but had grown strong by the tribute received from the Outer Islands (Labby 1976:106-107).

Galpagal is the smallest, lowest, and last established section according to oral tradition. It consists of households from the villages of Gachpar and Wanyan and forms a small buffering section between the two villages. Despite its lower rank in Gachpar, a Galpagal *dayif* held the highest *sawei* (*sawei lap*) relationship with Ulithi (Lessa 1950c:33). As observed by others during the ethnographic present, most recently by Ushijima (1987b:65), *sawei* privileges did not correspond to the political structure of Gachpar Village. For example, the Ethow (C36-77) *tabinaw* in Galpagal, held the highest *sawei* (*sawei lap*) relationship with Ulithi (Lessa 1950c:33). Lessa actually records the *sawei lap* relationship belonging to the Märlo *dayif*, which is where the incumbent head of Ethow had moved to following the Second World War.

Sacred and Politically Important Sites Related to *Sawei*

Except for C36-33 (Pebinau), sacred (*taliw*) and politically important platforms in Gachpar tend to be situated inland rather than on the coastal land extensions such as C36-13 (Gapin), C36-16 (Numrui), C36-22 (Togobuy), C36-77 (Ethow), and C36-83 (Bulwol). All of the *taliw dayif* noted above, except for C36-83, are related in one way or another to *sawei* ideology and the hierarchical political structure of Gachpar, e.g., Pebinau was the Tholang section's platform and Togobuy was the platform for the Ariap section chief.

Tholang section also holds the sacred places for Yangolab. *Sawei*-related ceremonies at Numurui, a *taliw* site for Yangolab, the mythical chief and founder of Gagil and the first chief of the Outer Islands, were witnessed by Müller (1917:300) in 1909 of the Südsee-Expedition. He observed Outer Island women spreading orange-red turmeric powder on the high priest of Numurui in order to make the god Yonalav (Yangolab) favorably disposed towards them.

The two *faluw*, Siro' (C36-1) and Faltamol (C36-2), were clubhouses near the boundary of Gachpar and Wanyan where Outer Islander visitors stayed before stepping foot on the shore (Lingenfelter 1975:151; Ushijima 1987b:69). The *faluw* have been added to the Gachpar Village map (Figure 12). Informants showed me their approximate locations because the *faluw* remains are no longer visible. After ritual cleansing ceremonies, Outer Islanders advanced to a *pebaey* for them called Filsew. Müller (1917:326) observed the same high priest Ruepon giving a prayer there to end an Outer Island epidemic.

Ruu' Village Investigations

Ruu' was only briefly investigated because the rainy season was approaching. Wet weather worsens the potential of being infected by the sap of poisonous trees called *changad* (*Semecarpus venenosus*) that infest the area. I visited Ruu' to determine when and to what extent the area was occupied. I surveyed the forest-covered village and excavated two test units: one on a *dayif*, the other in a small shallow shell midden. Seven shovel tests were also dug from the mangrove swamp area up to the elevated reaches of the uninhabited village.

Stone burial mounds, *dayif*, *wunbey*, and extensive raised mound ditch systems (*milay'*) for yam, sweet potato, and turmeric growing were located in the red lateritic volcanic soils of the higher reaches of the village, which appeared to have been in use in the recent past. American beer cans and Japanese beer bottles were also scattered throughout the higher and lower reaches of Ruu'. There were Japanese World War II trenches in the lower reaches. At the bottom reaches of Ruu', on the inland edge of the mangrove swamp, we found one Quartz-Feldspar sherd, a stone alignment, and numerous Laminated ware potsherds. According to one of my informants who guided us in the survey, we may have located the Meilif *pebaey*, 20 m inland from the mangrove swamp, which was burnt down when the village was annihilated. The leveled area also had a complete square-shaped stone money disk on the ground surface close by. Cultural materials in the excavations were relatively shallow, i.e., less than 50 cm below the surface. Historic artifacts and Laminated ceramics were the most common finds. Shovel tests also produced Laminated ceramics.

Based on this preliminary investigation of Ruu', I think that people have continuously visited this area, some for

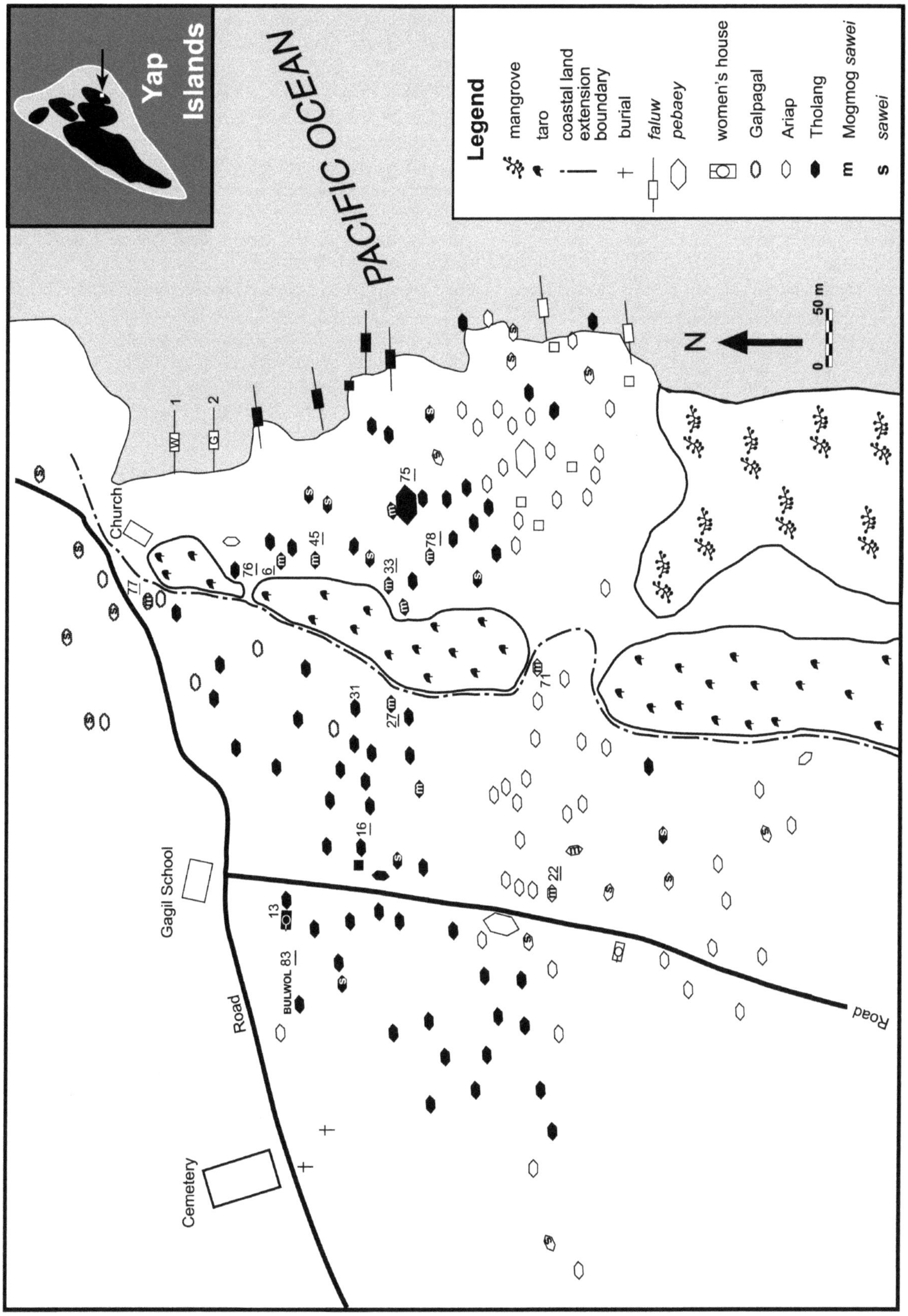

FIGURE 12. Gachpar Village map. Only features discussed in the text numbered. Underlined numbers refer to excavated sites.

gardening, particularly in the upper reaches of the village after the original village was abandoned. No one lives there today, but from informant interviews and a survey, I think there has been limited settlement in the area during the last 100 years. Excavations would be necessary in the lower reaches of the valley to properly evaluate the extent of settlement. Based on small shovel tests with Laminated potsherd evidence, I suggest that if the village supported a large population (for which there is no stone architectural evidence) and was abandoned, it was probably within the most recent 600 years, which is the earliest date of appearance for Laminated ware based on my Gachpar excavations. Margie V. Cushing Falanruw of the U.S. Forest Service examined the vegetation cover of Ruu'. She concludes that the area has been gardened extensively and the forest does not appear to be 600 years old.

Mogmog Village

I conducted a complete survey of Mogmog Islet to familiarize myself with the island, the archaeological landscape, and the people. A three-man crew surveyed the island in less than a week. We followed courses approximately 5 m apart in alternating northerly and southerly paths from the lagoon shore to the ocean shore while local assistants familiarized me with the characteristics and oral history of the Mogmog landscape. During the survey we searched for evidence of stone architecture, ceramics, non-coral lithics, and shell, in addition to evidence for World War II military activities and modern land-use practices.

After the survey, it was evident that the entire island had distributions of archaeological artifacts and features. Delineating site boundaries was difficult, if not impossible. This quandary was noted by Craib (1981) in his earlier Ulithi project. All of the different features, archaeological and modern, are identified by number. Feature designations do not represent site boundaries, but are reference points for the location of archaeological deposits. The Mogmog Village map (Figure 13) includes all the archaeological *dayif* on the island.

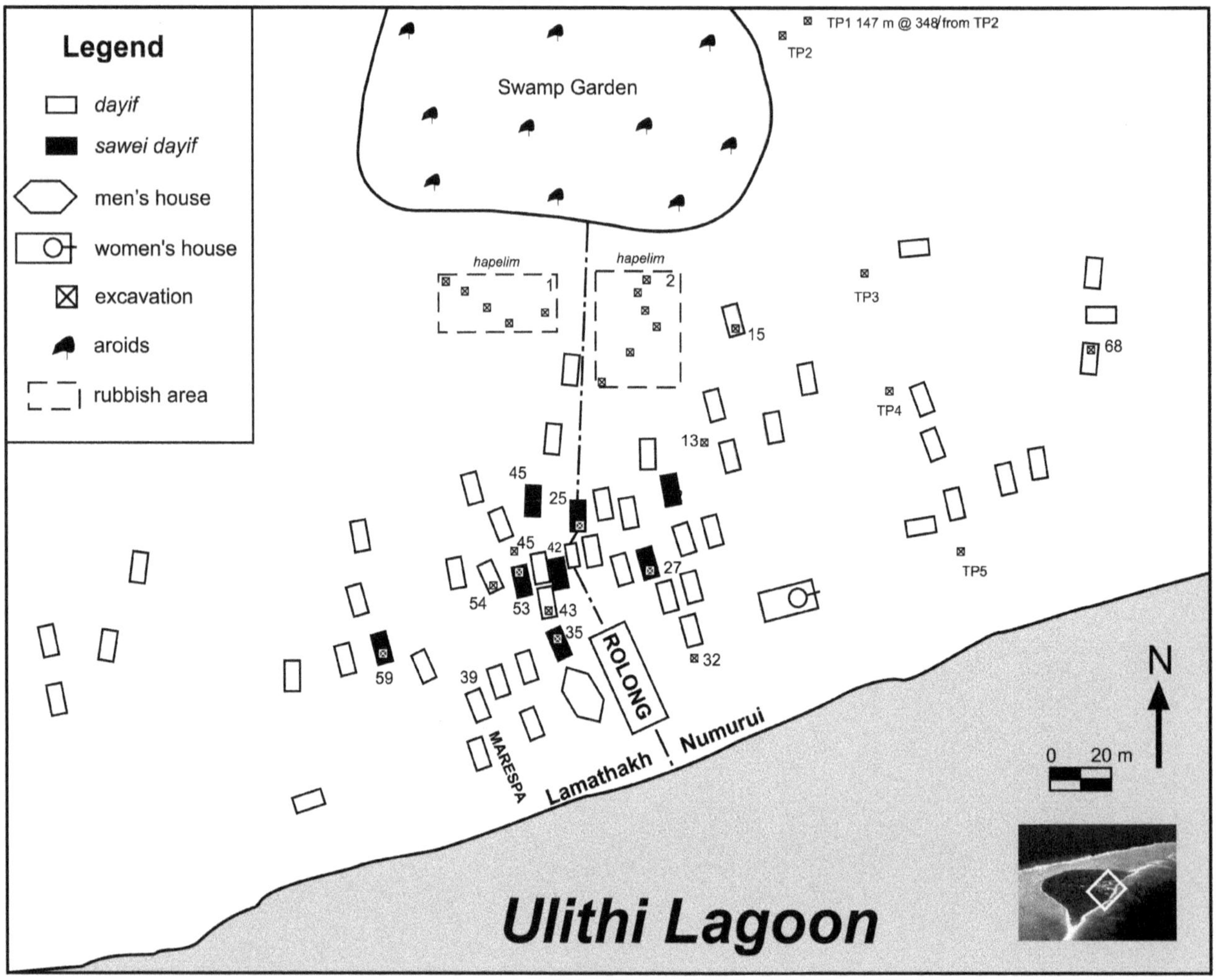

FIGURE 13. Mogmog Village Map. World War II U.S. Navy iron wharves are not shown. Only features discussed in the text are numbered.

Mogmog Village is nucleated and divided into two territorial moieties, one called Lamathakh, the side of the primary moiety chief, and the other Lamrui, the side of the secondary moiety chief (Lessa 1950a:81). The moieties comprise the households of different matrilineages (*hailang*), but are not based on consanguinity. Raised rectangular-shaped stone *dayif* in Mogmog Village are characteristically orientated perpendicular to the lagoon shore and face the lagoon (Craib 1980:28). People sleep in habitations on platforms. Cooking areas and sometimes burial plots are associated with the dwelling platforms.

Mogmog today has a large men's and women's house. The men's house on the lagoon shore is where men greet male visitors and have meetings. The smaller women's house, also on the shore, used to be the only structure with its long axis parallel to the shore (Craib 1981:50). Today, however, there are other habitations oriented this way. Women retreat to the women's house when they want seclusion or when they are giving birth or menstruating. Other noticeable landscape features include the large cemeteries situated on each end of the island. Canoe houses, also male activity areas, where the canoes are kept, are on the lagoon shore.

Rolong is the name of a sacred area on Mogmog. It was the location of the atoll-wide meeting house, where the paramount chief of the Outer Islands was invested and transformed into a sacred individual (Lessa 1950a). The area is avoided, especially by women. Turtles killed by Mogmog islanders are butchered there and distributed to the different lineages. In the past, every turtle captured in the atoll had to be killed on Mogmog and butchered at Rolong.

The large swamp garden in the center of Mogmog is also considered sacred. The large natural depression was converted to a swamp garden by digging to the brackish Ghyben-Herzberg water lens (Lessa 1977). Women grow plants such as taro (*Colocasia esculenta*) and giant swamp taro (*Cyrtosperma chamissonis*) there.

Excavations

Archaeological data were collected by geological strata when possible and arbitrary 20 cm levels on Mogmog and 10 cm levels in Gachpar. Excavation unit sizes were all 1 m by 1 m. Local assistants did most of the excavating under my supervision. I screened the archaeological matrix and recorded information. Archaeological matrix was excavated with a shovel and trowel; screened in a 6 mm (¼") size screen; and immediately collected and bagged on site. A 3 mm (⅛") size screen was initially tried, but later changed to a larger screen size because of the archaeological objectives, archaeological matrix, human resources, and time limitations. Given my archaeological objective of representing the ceramic assemblages associated with the many *dayif* which historically practiced *sawei*, I decided that a 6 mm size screen would allow us to meet our objectives without losing ceramic evidence.

Archaeological matrix from Mogmog was not wet-screened owing to the scarcity of fresh water, the distance from the lagoon shore to the site features, and the blackening effect the screening had on the lagoon water. One Mogmog unit's archaeological matrix, however, was wet-screened in the lagoon. The submerged lower reaches of one Gachpar coastal unit were also wet-screened through a 3 mm size screen. The collection of Mogmog faunal materials would have been larger from the black greasy charcoal matrices (midden) if they had all been wet-screened. Dietary information was not my primary objective so faunal collections should only be considered as representative.

It is worth noting the integrity of the Mogmog archaeological deposits I encountered before using these data for constructions of the past. The interpretations relying on Mogmog archaeological data are contingent on the integrity of the archaeological deposits. All of the 11 platform excavations appeared to be rebuilt after the Second World War because twentieth century historic artifacts, usually small thin pieces of folded iron fragments, were found beneath the platforms. The iron fragments and *dayif* rebuilding was likely the result of the US Navy transforming the entire island into a Rest and Relaxation Island for officers and sailors during the Second World War (see also Craib 1981:51; Lessa 1987:127). Keeping in mind the small excavation unit sizes, it should also be mentioned that there were archaeological layers beneath platforms that did not contain historic artifacts and that appeared undisturbed.

Archaeological Materials

Archaeological materials were divided into seven classes at the site: (1) bone; (2) ceramics; (3) charcoal; (4) historic artifacts; (5) lithics; (6) shell; and (7) sediment samples. Due to the heat and high humidity of the island, archaeological materials in plastic bags collected condensation. In order to prevent the growth of mold and the disintegration of faunal remains, I dried all of the collections in a corrugated iron roofed dwelling for at least 24 hours before sealing the bags. Ceramic sherds were cleaned with water and a soft tooth brush in the field.

Non-Ceramic Artifacts

This study concentrates on the ceramic artifacts, but there are other non-local artifacts found on Yap and Ulithi that can help build exchange models. For example, shell valuables were found in Gachpar. Fragments of broken pearl shell (*yar*) were not uncommon on ground surfaces near *dayif*. Non-local pearl shell fragments were also found in the C36-78 *dayif* excavation. A small green glass bead was also found in the same excavation unit.

There is a paucity of suitable lithic materials for stone tool making on coral islands. Consequently, the people have an extensive shell tool assemblage. Exotic lithic samples found in the Mogmog archaeological landscape include amphibole schist, andesite, aragonite (or calcite), basalt, chert (crypto-crystalline silica), pumice, and quartz. The majority of the metamorphic lithic materials on Mogmog probably originates from Yap, the nearest source for these rocks, but can also derive from other metavolcanic highlands, such as those in Island Southeast Asia and New Guinea. Aragonite and andesitic igneous rocks probably originate from Palau or Guam. Basalt can originate from Palau, Guam, or the intra-oceanic volcanic archipelagoes to the east of Ulithi, such as Chuuk, Pohnpei, and Kosrae. However, wherever the origin of non-Yapese rocks, they may still have been taken to Mogmog via Yap.

Not all non-lithic and shell materials were necessarily transported by people to Ulithi Atoll. Cobble-sized pumice, a common stone on Mogmog, used in the past for sharpening objects, can float to the atoll. Pumice is also used for polishing things like tuba coconut shells or used as a sort of rat trap where you rub copra on the pumice, put it up in a coconut tree and have the rat chew it and grind down its teeth. The *Lipus* sp. shell, also exotic to Ulithi, can also reach Ulithi without human assistance. Ulithians call the shells *giligil* (my spelling) and told me they float on exotic logs. I witnessed a clump of *giligil* shells growing on a floating coconut which had washed up on Mogmog's lagoon shore. Requiring no modification, except separation of the valve at the hinge, people in the past used the shells' sharp edges to cut plant materials, such as pandanus. Damm (1938:322) mentions the use of a shell to split fibers (such as hibiscus), which is probably the same tool.

Ceramics

This research relies primarily on the ceramic evidence of the archaeological record to construct past exchange models between Yap and Ulithi because pottery found on Mogmog is tangible evidence of island interaction. There are other artifacts and ecofacts that can inform queries about inter-island exchange behavior, but only ceramics are used here because they are the most ubiquitous artifacts preserved in Yapese and Ulithian archaeological contexts. Ceramic sherd attributes were quantified to measure the variability of ceramic distributions in different spatio-temporal contexts. I used ceramics and their attributes as a proxy for island interaction between the inhabitants of Yap and Ulithi. Ceramic evidence, of course, cannot possibly represent all of the past interactive behaviors. Nonetheless, I think general comments on the past interactive behaviors between Mogmog and Yap, which must have included *sawei*, can be made using ceramics.

Ceramic Types

Based on my ceramic analysis and petrographic analysis by Dickinson, I have slightly modified Intoh's typology (1988). The ceramic typology I use consists of six types: (1) Calcareous Sand Tempered (CST) ware; (2) Iron Oxide/Grog Tempered ware; (3) Quartz-Feldspar ware; (4) Plain ware; (5) Laminated ware; and (6) Rumé ware. My definitions for CST (Figure 14) and Laminated pottery (Figures 15-17) are the same as those of Intoh (1988).

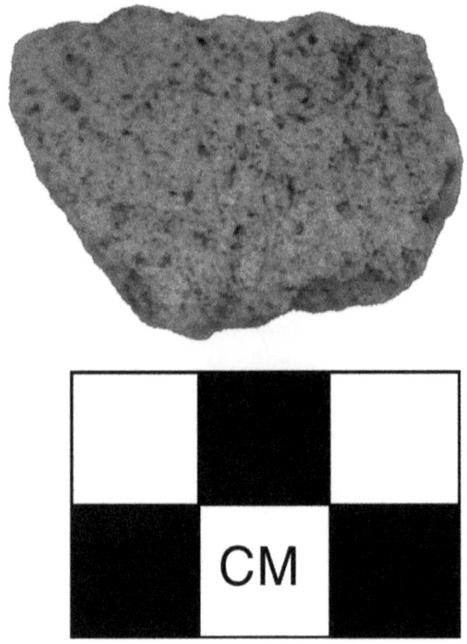

FIGURE 14. CST potsherd from Gachpar site C36-16.

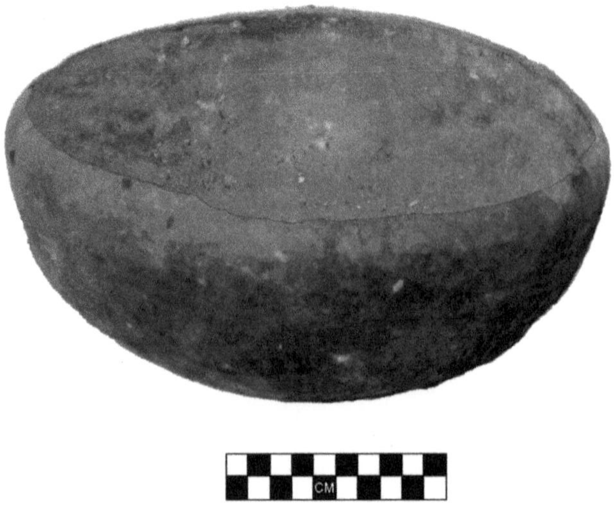

FIGURE 15. Laminated pot from Mogmog.

FIGURE 16. Laminated ware potsherd from Mog-27.

FIGURE 18. Quartz-Feldspar ware potsherd from Mog-1 (Lamathakh *hapelim*).

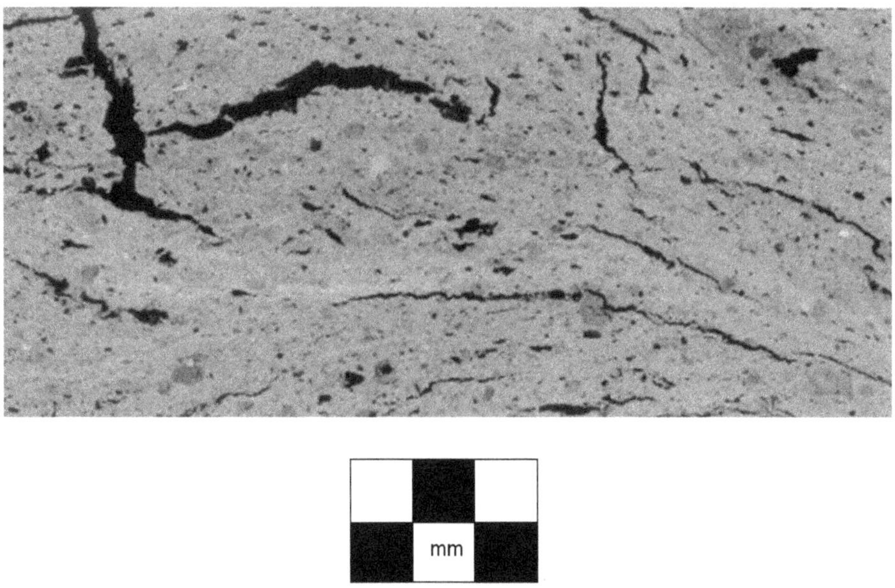

FIGURE 17. Laminated potsherd with black resin-filled laminations.

I upgraded Intoh's two Plain ware sub-types: Iron Oxide Tempered and Quartz Tempered wares to types and changed their names. I have re-labeled "Quartz Tempered" ware to "Quartz-Feldspar" ware (Figure 18) because many feldspathic grains in the ceramic paste appear to be natural inclusions in the paste (Dickinson 1997b:4). My collection of Iron Oxide Tempered ware also has crushed sherd (grog) temper (Dickinson 1994:1-3, 1997a:1, 1997b:4). Similar to the quartz-feldspar grains in the Quartz-Feldspar ware, it is not evident that the iron oxide nodules were added as temper; therefore, I have renamed the "Iron Oxide Tempered" to "Iron Oxide/Grog Tempered" (Figure 19). My upgrading of Iron Oxide/Grog Tempered and Quartz-Feldspar ware sherds has reduced the attribute variability of the Plain ware type. In other words, Plain ware contains earthenware that is not clearly distinguished as CST, Iron Oxide/Grog Tempered, Quartz-Feldspar, or Laminated.

FIGURE 19. Iron Oxide/Grog Tempered ware potsherd from Mog-27.

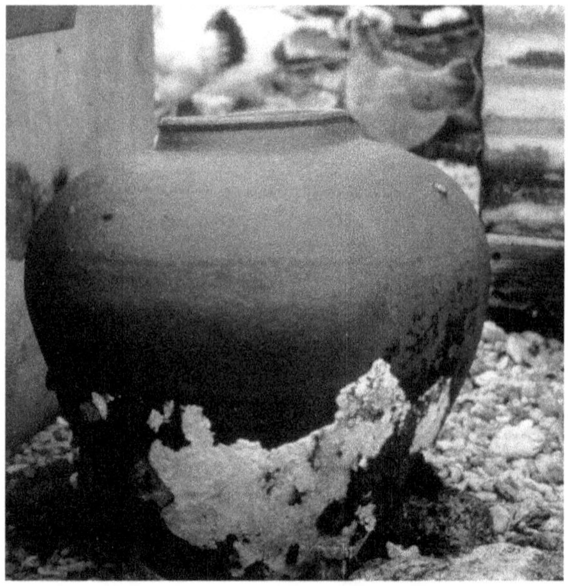

FIGURE 20. Rumé pot from Mogmog.

I have also added a ceramic type called "Rumé" (Figure 20), which is a historic ware found in a number of Mogmog archaeological contexts. Ulithians call large, heavy, shouldered, and undecorated ceramic jars used for water catchment, "Rumé" (my spelling). Intoh and Leach (1985:34; Plate 5) who have found similar jars on Yap suggest they originate from the Philippines. Kubary (1895:Plate 24) illustrates a similar shaped jar found on Yap, noting that it originated from the Philippines.

Professor William R. Dickinson conducted petrographic analyses to determine the provenance of these high-fired ceramic vessels. He suggests the volcaniclastic sand temper component diagnostic of island arc origin and the presence of subordinate argillitic and microgranitic detritus an indication of derivation from an arc of complex geology, such as that found in Japan and the Philippines (Dickinson 1997a:2).

Ceramic Type Variability in Gachpar and Mogmog

I use earthenware sherds from Yapese and Ulithian archaeological contexts to build a diachronic exchange model. Notable similarities and differences exist between the pottery found in Gachpar and Mogmog. An understanding of this variability in terms of spatial and temporal dimensions in these two villages is essential before attempting to address questions about exchange. I use the following variables to investigate ceramic variation: elemental abundances, potsherd counts and weights, potsherd density in the archaeological matrix, rim course, rim shape, rim thickness, and type.

More pottery was recovered from Gachpar than in Mogmog. Approximately three times more pottery by weight was found in Gachpar (25 kg compared to 9 kg) and there was

TABLE 4. Ceramic Type Distributions by Weight (g). Sherd counts are in parentheses

Ceramic Ware	Gachpar		Mogmog	Total
	Coastal	Inland		
Modern Japanese	0	0	92 (6)	92 (6)
Rumé	0	0	143 (10)	143 (10)
Dragon jar	0	25 (4)	0	25 (4)
Laminated	11029 (1457)	10231 (1350)	7580 (1078)	28840 (3875)
Plain	339 (22)	1558 (584)	104 (20)	2001 (626)
Iron Oxide/Grog	13 (1)	550 (47)	215 (37)	778 (85)
Quartz-Feldspar	8 (1)	16 (1)	616 (67)	640 (69)
CST	7 (3)	982 (214)	0	989 (217)
Total	11396 (1484)	13362 (2200)	8750 (1218)	33508 (4892)

four times (4.36) more pottery per excavation unit in Gachpar (1.92 kg/unit) than in Mogmog (.44 kg/unit). Very little Quartz-Feldspar pottery was found in Gachpar. Intoh (1988:96) also did not recover any Quartz tempered (Quartz-Feldspar) sherds in Gachpar.

I excavated only 102 sherds (673 g) or 8.7% of all the Mogmog sherds that were ceramic types older than Laminated ware; another 22 sherds (262 g) were recovered on the surface. However, Mogmog had a greater number of the older, unlaminated ceramics than did the coastal area of Gachpar (Table 4). The oldest Yapese earthenware, CST pottery, was not found. This is not a consequence of Mogmog's preservation environment, which is good, but rather a result of rarer occurrence of ceramic sherds older than Laminated ware. Intoh (1981, 1996) reports of CST pottery from Fais and Ngulu suggest that CST ceramics should also be found on Ulithi.

Gachpar Village Inland and Coastal Sites Ceramic Type Distributions

The Gachpar coastal zone begins at the lagoon shoreline and ends in front of the taro swamps. Archaeological sites behind the taro patches are considered inland (see Figure 12). Unlaminated and tempered ceramic types – such as CST, Iron Oxide/Grog Tempered, Plain, and Quartz-Feldspar – are rare in coastal excavations and make up a larger share of the ceramics collected in inland excavations. The dearth of early potsherds in the coastal area implies that coastal habitation on the coastal land extensions began after the introduction of Laminated pottery. Laminated ceramics predominate in the coastal and inland sites of Gachpar. The few early sherds found on the coast may well be a result of secondary deposition. Although I did not find much evidence for early ceramics, I would not reject the possibility of earthenware from earlier coastal sites beneath the coastal land extensions.

Mogmog Ceramic Type Distributions

Ceramics on Mogmog were recovered from surface contexts and 25 excavations, 14 of which were on sib *hailang dayif*. Most Mogmog excavation units are close to living village habitations, whereas in Gachpar, where I excavated on 13 estates, excavations tended to be much farther from presently occupied areas.

The Quartz-Feldspar ceramic type distribution differs significantly between Gachpar and Mogmog. In Mogmog, Quartz-Feldspar earthenware makes up 7% of the total pottery recovered. In Gachpar, Quartz-Feldspar potsherds only represent .1% of all the ceramics. This suggests that before 600 years B.P., or the time Laminated ceramics appear, the little pottery that did make it to Mogmog was an uncommon type in Gachpar. Similar to Yap, the Mogmog ceramic type distribution includes mostly Laminated ceramics. The predominance of Laminated ware suggests more intense interactions between the people of Yap and Ulithi during the period of Laminated ware production.

Iron Oxide/Grog Tempered pottery was found only in village *dayif* excavations and not behind the present village. Quartz-Feldspar ceramics, on the other hand, were found mostly in surface and subsurface deposits behind the village. Plain ware was found in equal amounts inside and behind the village. Numerous older ceramics – such as Iron Oxide/Grog Tempered, Plain ware, and Quartz-Feldspar (but not CST) pottery – found in the disturbed dumping area surface behind the village is evidence that pots older than Laminated ones were used on Mogmog. Larger excavation unit sizes in the village, though logistically difficult, should produce earlier cultural deposits and associated Yapese CST pottery.

Ulithians did not depend only on pots made of clay in the past. Unlike cooking practices in Yap, Hambruch noted that *Cassis* sp. (*meial*) shells were used in earth ovens as containers (Damm 1938:313). These cooking practices may not have been witnessed by Hambruch who stayed only two weeks in Ulithi Atoll. During my fieldwork, I learned that coconut shells did not burn easily and could also be used to hold food in earth ovens. In addition, Mogmog informants reported that older and less desirable ceramic pots were used to contain food in earth ovens. All of these different pot types were used in the recent past.

Conventions for Rim Measurements

Pottery rim attributes measured include thickness, rim course, rim shape, and lip shape (Figure 21). Thickness is an average metric rim measurement from three locations and is taken with a vernier caliper. Thickness of incurved rim sherds from Laminated pottery was measured at the point where the rim shoulder became the body. The thicknesses of rims are simply measured at the lip.

Rims

The dearth of non-Laminated pottery rims from Mogmog permits inter-site and inter-island comparisons of only Laminated rims. Almost all Yapese Laminated rim sherds found in Gachpar and Mogmog have incurved rim courses and parallel shapes. Rim sherds were not large enough to calculate pot diameters.

However, given the straightness of the rim chords, one can estimate the pots were relatively large, that is 20 – 40 cm, and similar in size to some intact pots Ulithians still own. Three intact Laminated pots had the following average dimensions: rim lip thickness = 7.2 mm, diameter = 31.4 cm, height = 17 cm and weight = 3.7 kg.

The rim thicknesses of Yapese Laminated ceramics from Mogmog are statistically larger than those found in Gachpar with approximately the same variability (standard deviation) of the rim thicknesses (Table 5). The thickest Laminated rim sherd on Mogmog is .3 mm thicker than the thickest rim recovered in Gachpar. A small, non-representative sample of six rims from Ruu' Village is also on average significantly thinner than those found in Mogmog.

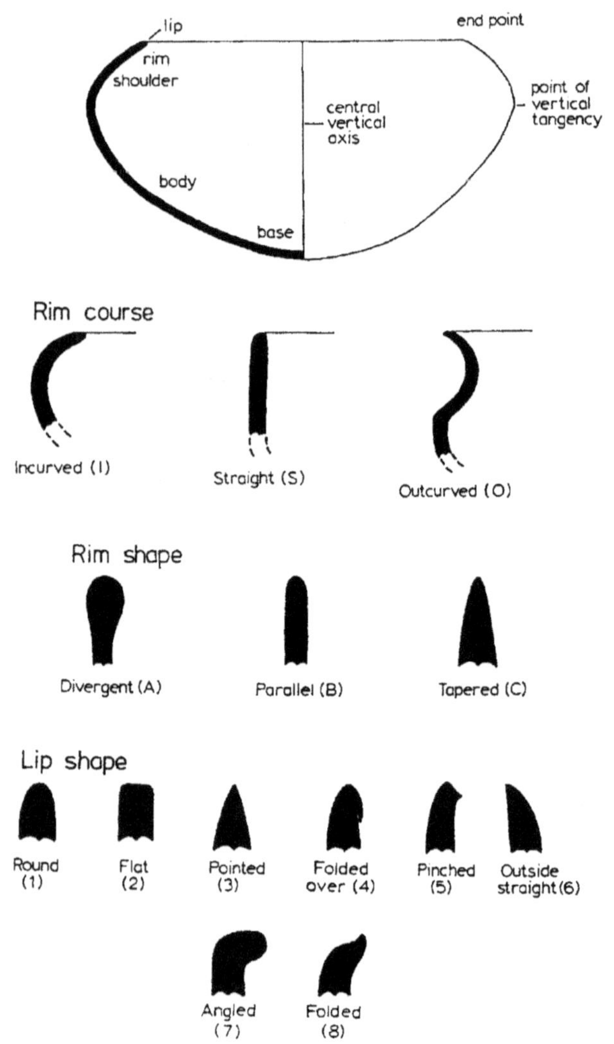

FIGURE 21. Terminology and classification of pottery (Intoh 1988:57).

Thicker rims suggest that the Laminated pots in Mogmog were larger than those found in Gachpar. Possible explanations include: (1) Mogmog people were selecting thicker or stronger pots to withstand sea-voyaging; (2) larger pots were selected by the Outer Islanders in order to carry more materials in the pots when sailing to Ulithi; (3) larger pots were selected for preparing larger quantities of coconut syrup (*lutch*); or (4) during at least the most recent 600 years, the eating group size on Mogmog (if we assume that all the pots were used for cooking) was larger than that in Gachpar, that is more people were fed per pot during each cooking session.

Ethnographic evidence from Walleser (1913) and others (e.g., Labby 1976:87) detail the complex and strict organization of food preparation and consumption in early twentieth century Yap, where different pots were used for cooking the food of different people. A Yapese household during the turn of the twentieth century had at least two earthen cooking pots, one for the male head of the household, and another for the mother and children (Christian 1899:292). Eating sessions on Mogmog, however, could include an extended family made up of two or more nuclear families (Lessa 1950a:61, 63) as opposed to the nuclear household on Yap. But certain Ulithian individuals had their own pots: such as (1) *rewei* - the fortune tellers; (2) *pelu* - the navigators; (3) *rethal* - the magicians who go to the channels and make magic so that there will be plenty of fish; (4) *saruwei* - the typhoon chaser; and (5) the *unga cha* - the paramount chief. From Mogmog informants, I learned a family had three pots at the most: one large one for simmering coconut syrup and smaller ones for cooking food.

Different pot sizes in Gachpar and Mogmog suggest selection pressures based on pot-use. Laminated pots are well suited for the cooking needs of the Yapese who steamed their food in a layered pressure cooking manner (Müller 1917:68). Mogmog, on the other hand, may well have put the Yapese Laminated pots to different uses, such as the cooking of coconut syrup (Intoh 1992).

Provenance

Provenance studies play an important role in Pacific research with numerous techniques used on different artifacts. In the Pacific, provenance of basalt has been determined by energy dispersive x-ray fluorescence (EDXRF) analysis (Weisler and Kirch 1996). Cherts have been characterized by instrumental neutron activation analysis (Sheppard 1997). Chemical abundance data for provenance work on obsidian has been collected from INAA (Beardsley et al. 1992) and particle-induced x-ray emission-particle-induced gamma-ray emission (PIXE-PIGME) analysis (White and Harris 1997). Pottery

TABLE 5. Thickness (mm) of Gachpar and Mogmog Laminated Pottery Rims

Village	N	Min	Max	Mean	*SD	**CV
Gachpar	205	2.90	11.23	5.74	1.37	.24
Mogmog	40	4.53	11.53	7.41	1.53	.21
Separate Variance t=-6.444 df = 52.0 Probability = .000						

*SD standard deviation.
**CV correlation of variation.

has played a large role in Pacific provenance research. Compositional data of ceramics and clays can be collected from microprobe and SEM (scanning electron microscope) analysis (Hunt 1989), INAA (Bryson 1989), petrographic analysis (Dickinson and Shutler 1979), PIXE-PIGME analysis (Summerhayes 1997), and x-ray fluorescence (XRF) analysis (Leach and Intoh 1985).

Petrographic Characterization of Ceramics

A necessary complimentary technique to the chemical characterization analyses, petrographic studies on clay and ceramic samples were conducted by Dickinson (1997a, 1997b). Dickinson's petrographic methods (Dickinson and Shulter 1979), first started in 1965, involve identifying the mineral suites of polished 30 μ thick cross-sections mounted on glass slides with a polarizing microscope. The mineral suite of the sherds is then compared to the known geological traits of the Pacific. Given the distinctive geological provinces in the Pacific, examination of the plastic and non-plastic constituents can lead to the identification of exotic wares and allow them to be sourced to their island of origin. The more we know about the geological details of an island's ceramic environment, the more accurate our conclusions of the geological provenance of the sherd can be.

Ceramic Chemical Characterization

Chemical characterization studies provide a precise method for finding the provenance or "source" of an artifact by matching elemental abundances. "Source" is a complex notion encoding compositional profiles of raw materials and cultural behavior, such as source selection and paste preparation (Arnold et al. 1991:87). Ceramic chemical characterization data can also be influenced by ceramic use and diagenetic changes within the buried contexts. In the absence of decoration, elemental data provided by INAA allow for more attributes to be quantified for the investigation of ceramic diversity issues.

Instrumental Neutron Activation Analysis

Instrumental neutron activation analysis is a precise and accurate analytical technique used on archaeological materials since the 1950s (Neff 1992:2). One of the most sensitive analytical methods, INAA has multi-elemental detection limits at the parts-per-million (ppm) and an accuracy range between 1 and 10 percent of the reported values of known standards (Glascock et al. 1996:10). Briefly, INAA involves activating the nuclei of objects by bombarding them with neutrons generated from a nuclear reactor. After activation, radioactive isotope nuclei emit gamma rays with characteristic energies. Hyperpure or intrinsic germanium (HPGe) detectors operating at liquid nitrogen temperatures count the gamma radiation and measure their energies to determine the concentrations of specific isotopes. Unlike many other chemical characterization techniques, INAA collects rare earth element abundances.

INAA for this project was conducted at the Missouri University Research Reactor Facility (MURR). The Missouri University Research reactor is a 10 megawatt pool-type, light-water moderated and cooled, beryllium-reflected reactor. It is the largest and highest powered university research reactor in the United States. Samples are irradiated by inserting them in the central region of the reactor that acts as a flux trap. The facility also has a pneumatic vacuum tube system that injects samples into the radioactive core for irradiation to measure the abundances of elements with short half-lives.

INAA Ceramic Sampling Strategy

Ceramic sherd samples collected on Yap represent ceramic surface distributions from nine Yapese villages: 'Atliw, Binaw, Guror, Gachpar, Gitam, Ruu', T'enifar, Wanyan, and Wocholab (Figure 22). Non-Gachpar Village ceramics from Yap ceramic samples (n=65) are included for an understanding of the chemical variability of Gachpar and Yap. Analytical identification numbers at MURR are preceded by the initials of the person submitting the samples, in this case "CHD."

The majority of the ceramic samples in this study come from beneath Gachpar and Mogmog stone platforms. Except for the historic (Japanese and Rumé) ceramics, all of the ceramic types are represented.

Most of the chemical compositional data derive from Laminated sherds (n=163) because these ceramics are the most numerous in Yap and Mogmog and they represent a time period when intense interaction is known to have occured.

Yapese Clays

This study has a representation of Yapese raw materials. There are a total of 26 Yapese sediment samples. My study has benefited from Intoh's permission to conduct INAA on her Yapese clay briquettes (n=18). Clay samples collected from the villages of Binaw (C37) and T'enifar (C38) were also not collected by me, but my Yapese field assistant Augustine Gilbeengin. Unlike some of Intoh's clay samples, none of the samples I collected are from known clay sources except for one Gitam Village sample (CHD225). Sample CHD105 is a calcareous sand sample from a coastal Gachpar excavation and samples CHD280 - CHD283 are all clay-like soils from the bottom of excavations.

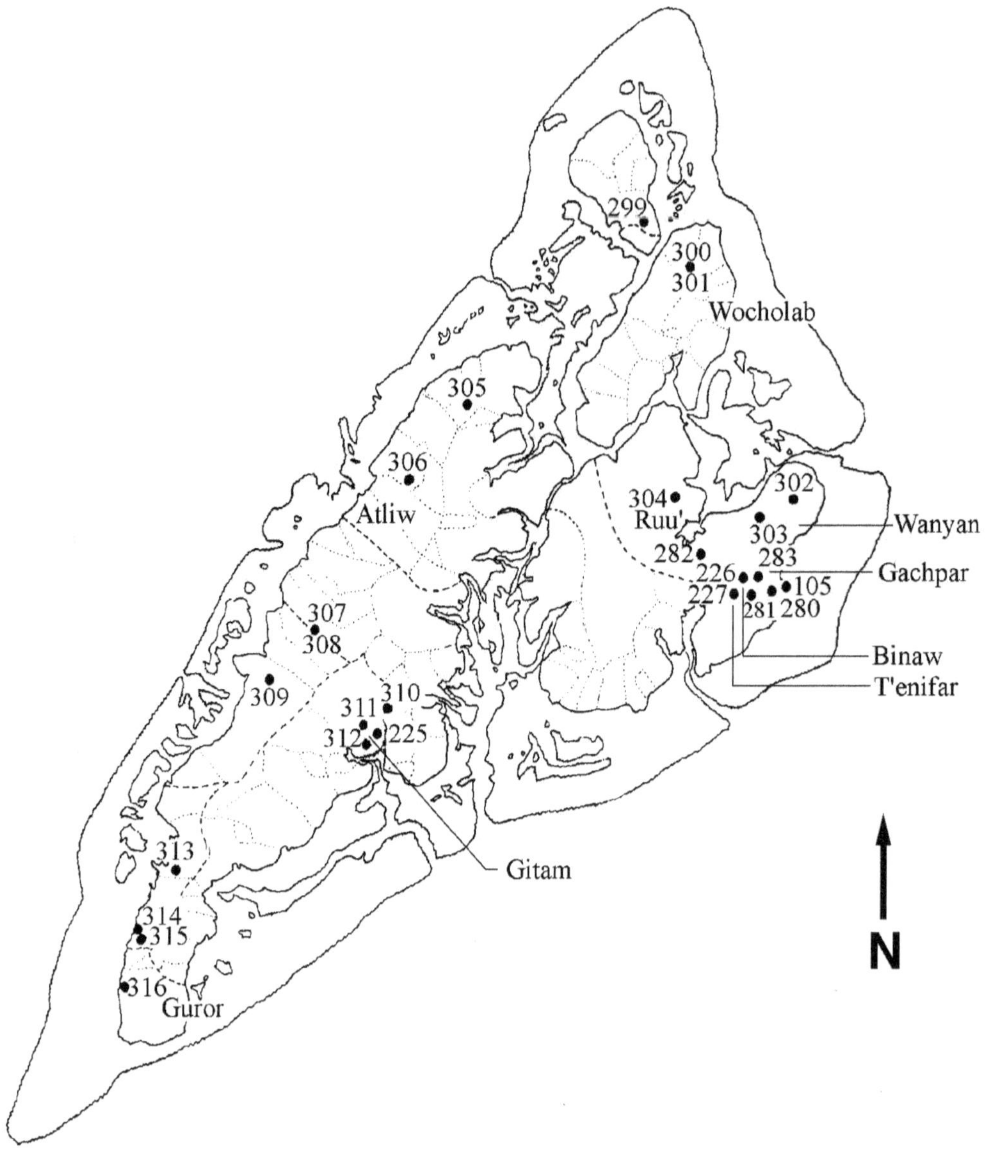

FIGURE 22. Provenience of Yapese clay, sediment, and ceramic samples used in INAA (adapted from Intoh 1988:36). Numbered points indicate clay and sediment sample locations. Ceramic samples were recovered from the listed villages.

INAA Sample Preparation

After INAA sample selection, I burred, washed, and dried the samples overnight. Samples were then ground in an agate mortar and dried in a 100° C oven for at least 48 hours to reduce the water content. Samples were then inserted in vials for short and long neutron irradiation. Bundles of the samples were irradiated with standards. For a full description of the procedures I used in the INAA sample preparation and of irradiation procedures used at MURR (Table 6) see Glascock (1992) and Glascock et al. (1996).

Elemental Abundance Determination

The gamma ray counting system at MURR is automated with Nuclear Data software (today owned by Canberra Nuclear Products) using a software program called PEAK. It accumulates and stores spectra, performs a peak search, a pulse pile-up correction, and calculates elemental abundances correcting for decay time, spectral interferences, and sample weight.

A high dead time adversely affects chemical abundance determination. Dead time is a condition when the gamma-ray detector shuts off because of excessive gamma-ray bombardment. Many ceramics found in the lateritic nickeliferous iron ore rich soils of Gachpar caused the short irradiation gamma-ray detectors to have high dead times. Samples with dead times of 50% or more were repeated with smaller sample weights, i.e., less than 100 mg, instead of the usual 150 mg. Abundances were calculated in relation to the measured radioactivity of the known National Institute for Standards and Technology (NIST) standard constants, which are irradiated at the same time as the unknown samples {[(counts/sec)/mg]/per unit of concentration}.

TABLE 6. INAA Conditions at MURR

Parameters	Short Irradiations	Long Irradiations	
Sample weight	150.00 mg ± 10 mg	200.00 mg ± 10 mg	
Vials	High-density polyethylene	High purity quartz	
Flux	8 x 10^{13} n cm^{-2} s^{-1}	5 x 10^{13} n cm^{-2} s^{-1}	
Irradiation time	5 seconds	24 hours	
Decay time	25 minutes	7 days	3 – 4 weeks
Counting time	720 seconds	30 min	2.5 hours
Elements measured	Al, Ca, Dy, K, Mn, Na, V	As, Ba, La, Lu, Nd, Sm, U Yb	Ce, Co, Cr, Cs, Eu, Fe, Hf, Ni, Rb, Sb, Sc, Sr, Ta, Tb, Th, Zn
NIST Standards	SRM 1633a (Coal Flyash), SRM 688 (Basalt Rock), Ohio Red Clay		
Detectors	HPGe (high purity germanium)		
Resolution	1.9 – 2.0 KeV at 1332 KeV		
Relative efficiency	25% - 30%		

Data Reduction of Elemental Data

Neff's GAUSS® routines are used to reduce the data, that is substitute missing data, generate bivariate plots and biplots, calculate principal components, and calculate probabilities of group membership based on Mahalanobis distances. The first step in the analysis of compositional data was to visually inspect the compositional data for outliers and anomalous specimens (Neff 1992:19). Elements for which too many specimens are zero, or more accurately, below detection limit, are eliminated from the data matrix because the statistical algorithms I used require non-zero matrices.

Elemental Variability

Examination of elemental variability within the ceramic data set is essential before performing complex multivariate statistics required in provenance analysis due to the number of different processes that can affect the ceramics and complicate the provenance exercise. A total of 322 Micronesian ceramic samples and clays underwent INAA, but only the 26 Yapese sediment samples and 242 ceramic samples collected from Faderai (Ulithi), Fais, Mogmog (Ulithi), Satawal, and Yap are detailed in this study. Compositional analyses from ceramics recovered from Palau, Chuuk, Guam, Pohnpei, and Kosrae are discussed only briefly here (but see Descantes et al. 2001). The Archaeometric Laboratory at MURR measured the elemental abundances of 33 elements. Eleven elements (As, Ba, Cs, K, Nd, Rb, Sb, Sr, Tb, U, Zr) were excluded from the analysis because too many samples had concentrations below detection limits. If the concentration of a particular element was below the detection limit, a zero value was recorded for the elemental abundance. The remaining elements used in this analysis include Al, Ca, Ce, Co, Cr, Dy, Eu, Fe, Hf, La, Lu, Mn, Na, Ni, Sc, Sm, Ta, Th, Ti, V, Yb, and Zn.

Ceramic Depositional Contexts

Clearly an understanding of how different ceramic production techniques, ceramic-uses, and archaeological contexts affect particular element abundances is imperative before chemical characterization results can be accurately interpreted. Many have commented that the elemental characterization of ceramics can be influenced by many processes during a pot's "ceramic life history," some of which include clay selection, temper addition, ceramic-use, and post-depositional alterations (Arnold et al. 1991:87-88; Bishop et al. 1982:299; Neff et al. 1988, 1989; Stein et al. 1991). Chemical abundances can be enriched or depleted. Jones (1986:36-37) recorded the absorption of magnesium in Greek and Cypriot ceramics buried in the sea. Intoh (1988:46, 89), on the other hand, noted the depletion of calcareous sand in porous Yapese CST ceramics found in acidic soil contexts (see also Dickinson 1997b:4-5). Cogswell et al. (1996) have shown that firing temperature does not affect elemental abundances, but shell temper and its alteration through leaching can introduce error in provenance studies which need to be mathematically corrected (Cogswell et al. 1998). This is relevant to this study because similar to shell temper, early Yapese CST ceramics contain calcium carbonate, which can undergo leaching in acidic archaeological contexts. If less is known about the particular dynamics between element abundances and the history of the ceramic sample in question, elements less likely to be affected should be relied upon. Rare earth contents (Lanthanide series elements) are informative because their abundances are affected minimally by perturbations, such as weathering and mild metamorphism (Goles 1978:366).

Certain elements within Laminated ceramics are found to significantly differ based on their archaeological contexts. Only Laminated ceramics were used to test the influence of the deposition environment because I had a large sample size from three varying depositional contexts, the ceramics were untempered, and Laminated ceramics existed only in the preceding 600 years, a time when *sawei* is known to have operated. Following exploratory data analyses, I found that calcium (Ca), Sodium (Na), and Nickel (Ni) varied in the different depositional contexts of coastal Gachpar, inland Gachpar, and Mogmog. An analysis of variance (ANOVA) test confirmed significant statistical differences among the elemental abundance means of Laminated ware sherds in the different depositional environments (Table 7). After examining the distribution of element abundances in the Laminated ceramics (the largest sample group) in three different archaeological contexts, and finding that some of the elements were influenced by their depositional surroundings, I decided to remove Ca, Na, and Ni from the provenance analysis, leaving only 19 elements of the original 33 (Figure 23).

TABLE 7. ANOVA of Ca, Na, and Ni in Laminated Sherds from Different Contexts

Element	N	Sum-of-Squares	df	Mean-Square	F-ratio	p
Ca	98	5.98×10^{8}	2	2.99×10^{8}	4.432	.014
Na	98	1.56×10^{8}	2	7.81×10^{7}	4.875	.010
Ni	96	7.57×10^{5}	2	3.79×10^{5}	6.138	.003

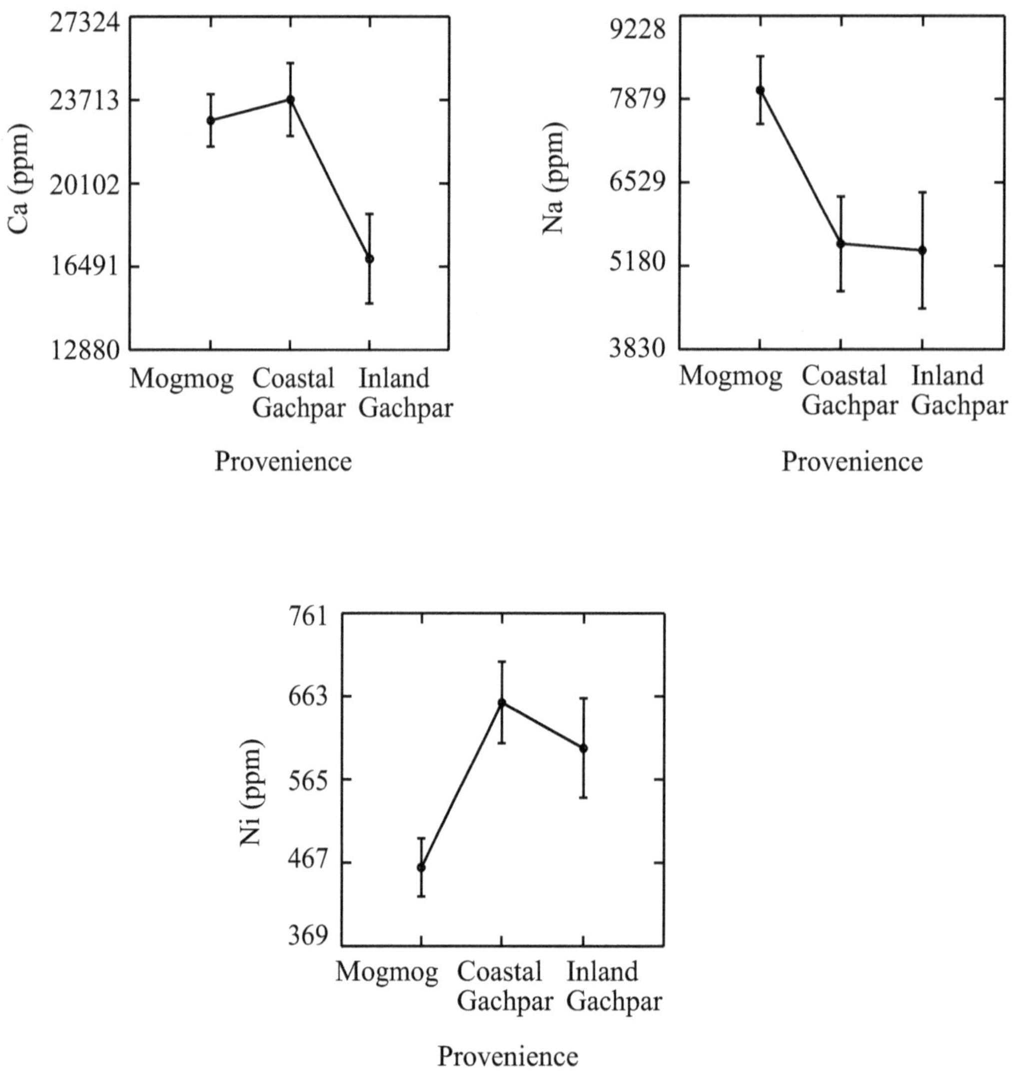

FIGURE 23. ANOVA mean squares means plots for Ca, Na, and Ni of Laminated ceramics in three different depositional contexts.

Calcium concentrations in Laminated sherds recovered from Mogmog and coastal Gachpar sites are significantly greater than those found in inland Gachpar sites (Table 8). Acidic lateritic volcanic loam soils leach Ca from even the non-calcareous tempered Laminated pottery sherds. There is no significant correlation between the provenience depth of the sherds and their Ca abundances. This is unexpected because even though the acidity of inland Gachpar soils does not necessarily increase with depth (see Smith 1983:39-51), deeper sherds can be expected to have undergne leaching for a longer length of time.

Sodium abundances are noteworthy because the Mogmog sherds are conspicuously more enriched in Na than either the coastal or inland Gachpar sherds (note Inland Gachpar is approaching statistical significance). The cause for the enriched Na in Mogmog ceramics or the depletion of Na in the coastal and inland Gachpar ceramics is not known and requires more work. The predominantly Ngedebus Variant soils of Mogmog are enriched in Na (Table 9). In addition, Smith (1983:88) notes that both atoll and coastal Gachpar areas can receive very brief occasional flooding at any time during the year. Flooding from wave inundation during a typhoon introduces salt (NaCl) in the soil.

Sherds from Mogmog have significantly smaller abundances of Ni than do those from coastal Gachpar. In Gachpar, the large Ni concentrations in ceramics recovered from the coast are similar to those found inland (Table 10). Again, an explanation is only suggested because the geochemical dynamics between the archaeological materials and their depositional contexts, while important, is not the focus of this book. Despite trace amounts of nickel in Gachpar village soils, more than anywhere else in Yap, Gachpar Laminated sherds are not more enriched in Ni than are Laminated sherds found in other Yapese villages. Perhaps Gachpar Laminated sherds are enriched with Ni from the surrounding lateritic nickeliferous iron ore deposits derived from the weathering of nickel-bearing serpentine.

TABLE 8. Pairwise Comparison of Bonferroni Adjusted Probabilities for Ca Abundances in Laminated Sherds Recovered in Different Depositional Contexts

Depositional Context	Mogmog	Coastal Gachpar	Inland Gachpar
Mogmog	1.000	------	------
Coastal Gachpar	1.000	1.000	------
Inland Gachpar	**.026**	**.021**	1.000

TABLE 9. Pairwise Comparison of Bonferroni Adjusted Probabilities for Na Abundances in Laminated Sherds Recovered in Different Depositional Contexts

Depositional Context	Mogmog	Coastal Gachpar	Inland Gachpar
Mogmog	1.000	------	------
Coastal Gachpar	**.030**	1.000	
Inland Gachpar	**.058**	1.000	1.000

TABLE 10. Pairwise Comparison of Bonferroni Adjusted Probabilities for Ni Abundances in Laminated Sherds Recovered in Different Depositional Contexts

Depositional Context	Mogmog	Coastal Gachpar	Inland Gachpar
Mogmog	1.000	------	------
Coastal Gachpar	**.004**	1.000	------
Inland Gachpar	.122	1.000	1.000

Gitam Ceramics

Ceramics recovered from Gitam Village, Yap, had uncharacteristically large zinc (Zn) concentrations (Table 11, Figure 24). James W. Cogswell, MURR Research Specialist, conducted a microprobe analysis on these anomalous Laminated ceramic sherds. Upon microprobe analysis, Cogswell detected the large Zn concentrations to be greatest near the exterior of the sherd and to steadily decrease toward the core of the sherd. Cogswell concludes that the Zn was introduced post-depositionally (personal communication 1997). Following further research into the provenience of the sherds, I discovered the samples came from approximately 1 m below a garbage dumping pit "with all kinds of rusted meat cans and bike and auto parts" (John Tharngan, personal communication 1997).

CST Ware

Intoh (1988:46, 89) classified porous sherds as CST ware when she recognized the remains of calcareous sand grains in the pores with a scanning electron microscope (SEM). Upon petrographic analysis, Dickinson (1997b:4-5) also concludes that porous sherds I recovered were also at one time CST pottery. The INAA recorded greater Ca concentrations in porous sherds than in Laminated sherds found in similar acidic contexts (Table 12, Figure 25). This corroborates Intoh's and Dickinson's findings that porous sherds were at one time calcareous sand tempered.

TABLE 11. Zn (Log-base 10 ppm) Abundances in Gitam and Non-Gitam Yapese Laminated Ceramics

Village	N	Mean	SD
Gitam	17	3.245	.337
Non-Gitam	144	2.034	.176

Separate Variance t = 14.571 df = 17.0 Probability = .000

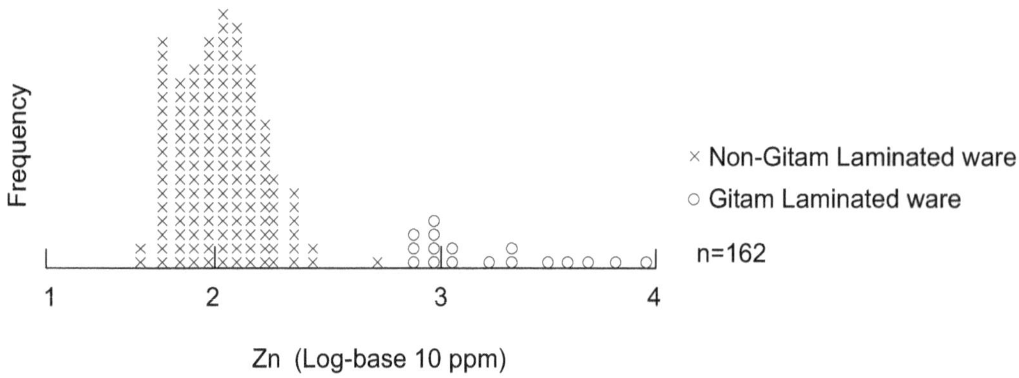

FIGURE 24. Zn (log-base 10 ppm) abundances in Gitam and non-Gitam Yapese Laminated potsherds.

TABLE 12. T-Test of CST and Laminated Pottery Ca Abundances (ppm) from Inland Gachpar Sites

Ceramic Ware	N	Min	Max	Mean	SD	CV
CST	6	14816	36804	26699	8302	.53
Laminated	18	4988	32054	16829	8962	.31

Separate Variance t = -2.471 df = 9.2 Probability = .035

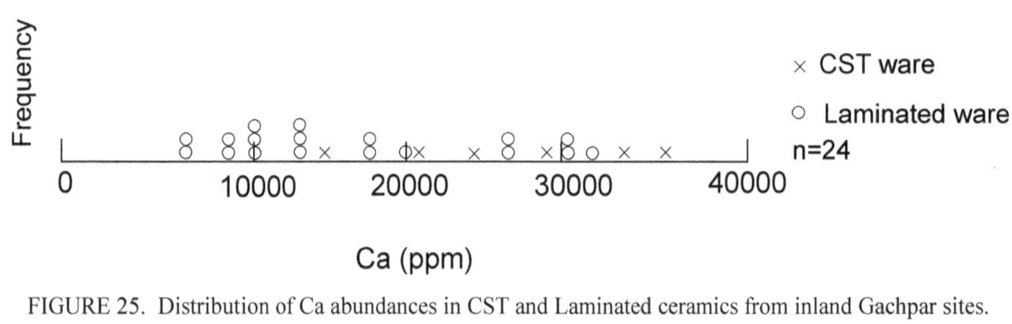

FIGURE 25. Distribution of Ca abundances in CST and Laminated ceramics from inland Gachpar sites.

Ceramic Compositional Group Formation

Hypothetical compositional groups from the Yapese ceramics (n=226) were constructed by quantitative pattern-recognition analysis of the chemical data (see Neff et al. 1997). Principal component analysis (PCA), a dimension-reducing procedure, calculated principal component scores based on either a correlation or a variance-covariance matrix. I used a variance-covariance matrix because with fewer components it accounts for more of the variance. A principal component is a "linear combination of optimally-weighted observed variables"; principal components account for a maximal amount of variance in the data set (Hatcher 1994:5-7). PCA is an attractive statistical technique because unlike cluster analysis, it treats the variables and the cases together and identifies different independent dimensions of variation in the data (Shennan 1997:298). Relative influences of the original elemental variables on the variability of the data are also visible.

Group membership is determined by Mahalanobis distance-derived probabilities. The Mahalanobis distance measure is the "[i]ndex of distance between two multivariate populations, which takes into account the differences in dispersion across variables" (Silva and Stam 1995:315). The percentage of variance criterion used in the PCA is 92.72% of the total variance, which was met by six principal components (Table 13). In order for an observation to be included as a member of a hypothetical compositional group, I used a standard 5% cut-off. Group 3 had more members than variables (elements) so the 19 elements (transformed to log-base 10 elemental abundances) were used to calculate the Mahalanobis distance-derived probabilities for group membership.

At least a four-level compositional structure was revealed with a classification of 161 observations (including the Dragon Jar ceramic sherd; Figure 26). Sixty-four specimens (28%) were unclassified. Element coordinates of the biplot in Figure 26 suggest chemical distinctiveness between the ceramic compositional groups. Groups 2, 3, and 4 are enriched in Ce, Cr, Eu, Fe, La, Sm in relation to Group 1. Groups 3 and 4 are members of a continuum (Figure 26, 27).

In fact, the majority of the unclassified sherds belong in the chemical compositional continuum between Groups 3 and 4, suggesting numerous other compositionally similar groups not yet defined. Group separation can be shown to not be an artifact of PCA by constructing a bivariate plot of the log-base 10 concentrations of Ce and Ti (Figure 27). Dickinson (1997a:2) suggests that the variance in Ti contents of Groups 1, 2, and 3 derives from the Ti abundance in opaque iron oxide grains of Group 2 ceramics and the even greater concentrations of Groups 3 (and Group 4):

> attributable to metavolcanic detritus from titanium-rich oceanic lavas rafted into and metamorphosed within the Yap subduction zone (both ocean-floor and ocean-island mafic lavas typically contain 2%-3% titanium vs 1% or less for island-arc mafic lavas).

TABLE 13. Eigenvalues and Percentages of Variance Explained in the Simultaneous R-Q Factor Analysis Based on Variance-Covariance Matrix

Principal Component	Eigenvalue	Variance (%)	Cumulative Variance (%)
1	.5068	40.72	40.72
2	.3229	25.95	66.67
3	.1599	12.85	79.52
4	.0717	5.76	85.28
5	.0555	4.46	89.74
6	**.0371**	**2.98**	**92.72**
7	.0196	1.57	94.30
8	.0186	1.50	95.79
9	.0132	1.06	96.85
10	.0097	.78	97.63
11	.0071	.57	98.21
12	.0056	.45	98.66
13	.0043	.34	99.00
14	.0037	.29	99.30
15	.0025	.20	99.50
16	.0024	.19	99.69
17	.0021	.17	99.85
18	.0015	.12	99.97
19	.0004	.03	100.00

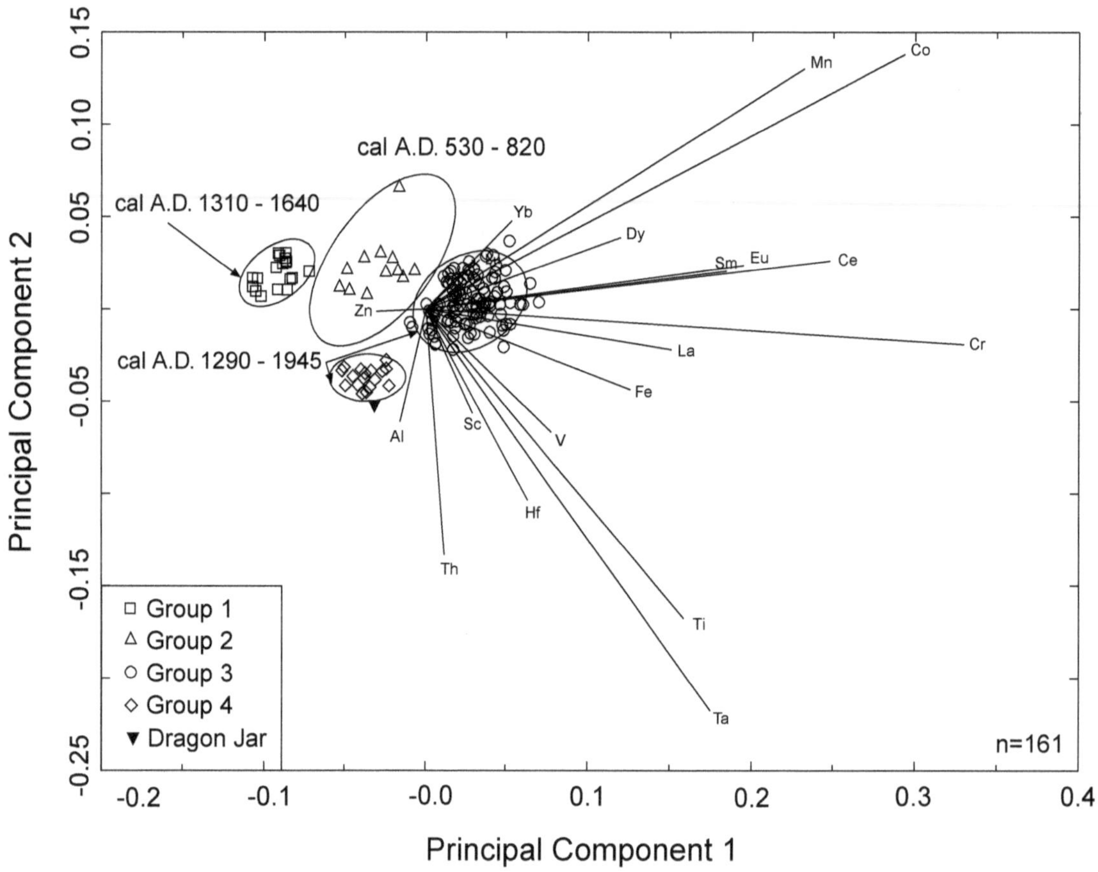

FIGURE 26. PCA plot of four Yapese ceramic groups. Ellipses indicate 90% probability level for membership in the four groups.

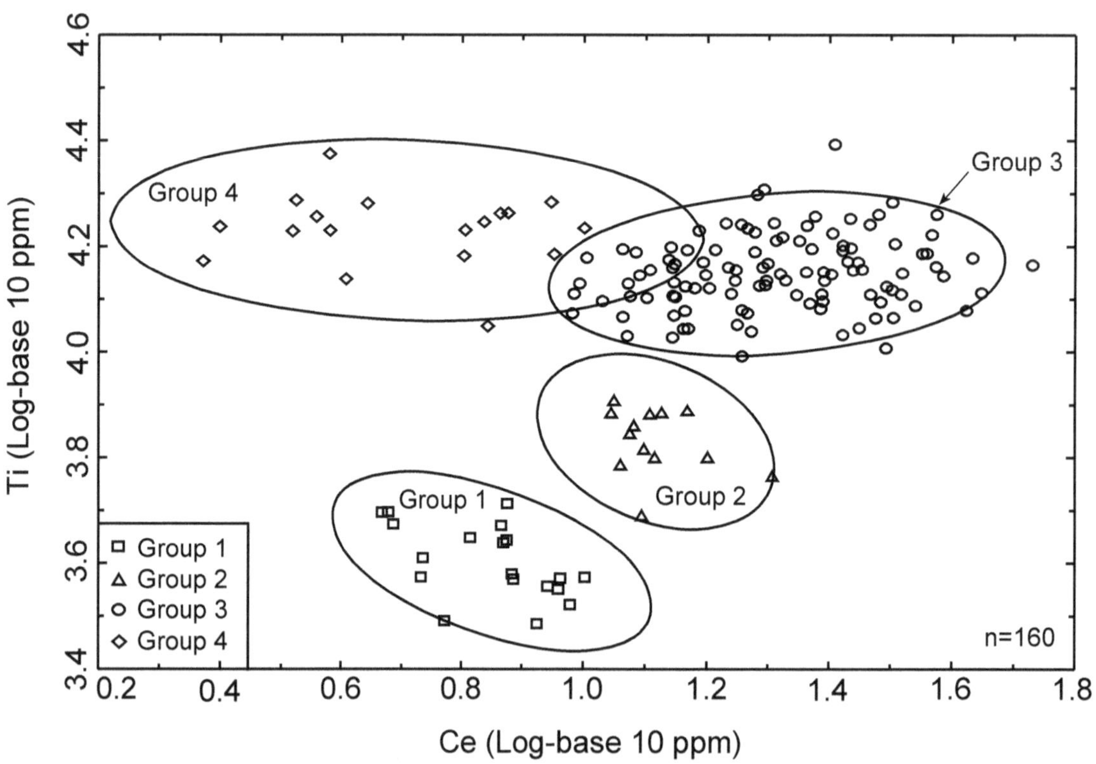

FIGURE 27. Bivariate plot of log-base 10 transformed Ce and Ti abundances distinguishing the four ceramic groups. Ellipses indicate 90% probability level for membership in the four groups.

Group 2 lies intermediary in most of the elemental abundances between Group 1 and Group3. However, Group 2 is not a combination of Group 1 and 3 because it can be shown to have greater concentrations of the rare earth elements Lu and Yb (Figure 28).

The distinct partition of the compositional groups represents the major Yapese typological ware distinctions and their major clay source origins. The typological distinction is evident when the type designations of the ceramics are plotted against the compositional members of the groups (Table 14, Figure 29). All of the sherds in Group 1 are Quartz-Feldspar, except for one Iron Oxide/Grog Tempered sherd. Group 2 contains only Iron Oxide/Grog Tempered sherds. Group 3 and 4 contain predominantly Laminated ceramics in addition to three CST sherds and ten Plain ware sherds.

Plain ware sherds are compositionally more similar to the varied compositional Groups 3 and 4 than to Groups 1 or 2. CST ceramics, which are not well represented in this study because of their conspicuous absence on Mogmog, are more similar to compositional Group 3 than any other group.

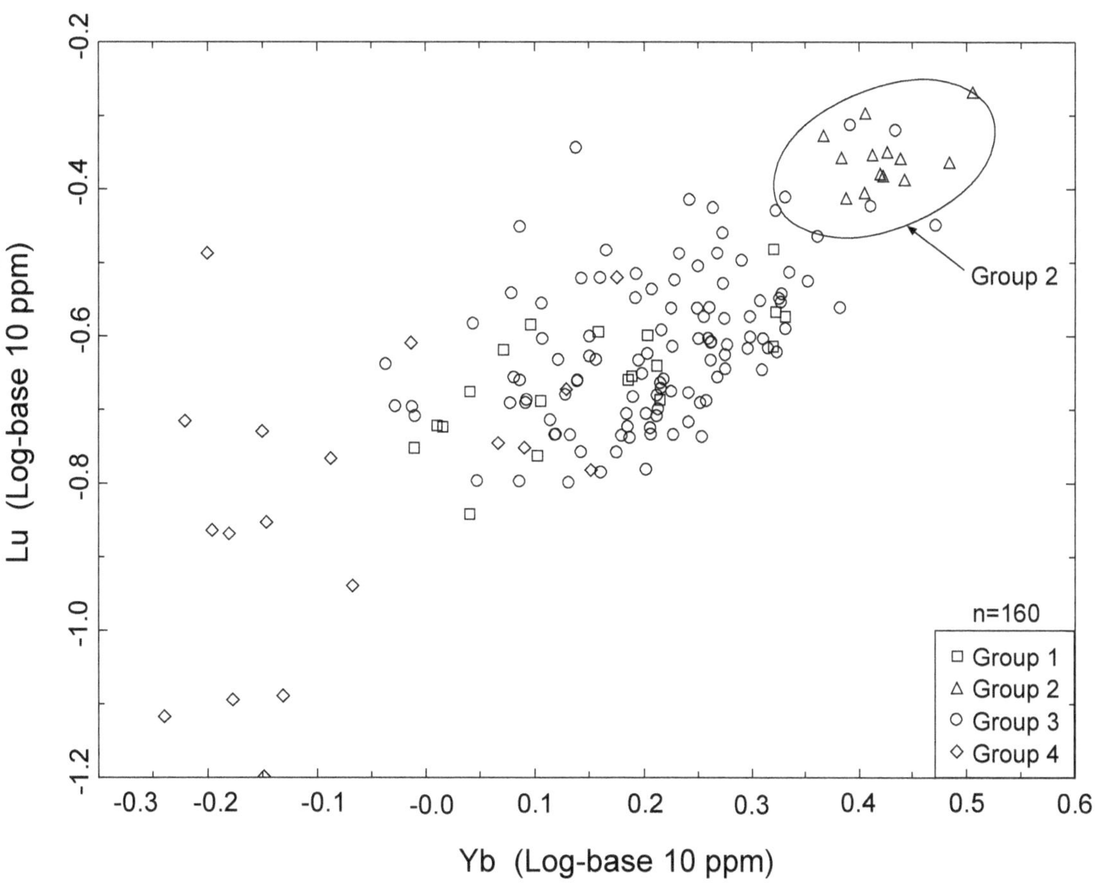

FIGURE 28. Bivariate plot of log-base 10 transformed Yb and Lu abundances distinguishing ceramic Group 2. Ellipse indicates 90% probability level for membership in Group 2.

TABLE 14. Cross-Tabulation of Ceramic Type Designations and Compositional Group Membership

Type	Group 1	Group 2	Group 3	Group 4	Unclass.	Total
CST	0	0	3	0	6	9
Iron Oxide/Grog Tempered	0	13	0	0	2	15
Quartz-Feldspar	18	0	0	0	1	19
Plain ware	1	0	10	1	25	37
Laminated	0	0	97	17	30	144
Total	19	13	110	18	64	224

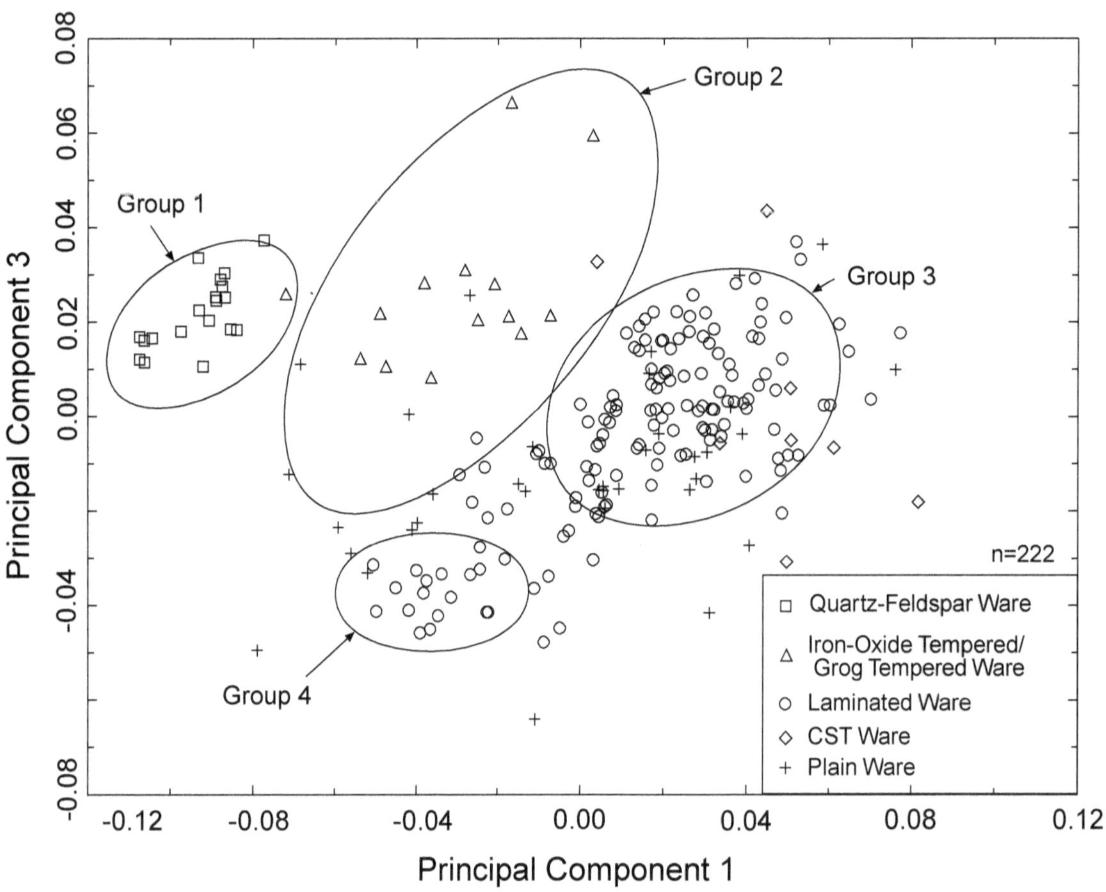

FIGURE 29. Ceramic type designations plotted against the 90% confidence ellipses of the four ceramic compositional groups. Ellipses indicate 90% probability level for membership in the four groups.

Southeast Asian Dragon Jars

Four small greenish-brown glazed Southeast Asian sherds with carinated decorations on the rims were excavated from the inland Gachpar site of Togobuy (C36-22), a politically important site with much surface evidence of prestige goods, such as stone money and shell valuables. A landowner of this site permitted us to excavate only on the *wunbey* (sitting platform pavement abutting the habitation). From a photograph of the sherds, Dr. Carla M. Sinopoli (personal communication 1996) of the University of Michigan Anthropology Museum identified the sherds as fragments of stoneware jars, commonly referred to as the little studied Southeast Asian "Dragon Jars". According to Sinopoli these jars served as heirlooms and were in use for the last few centuries in Southeast Asia. Comparisons of chemical characterization showed one of the sherds (CHD041) to clearly fit into Sinopoli's Group 2, the largest of four chemical compositional groups of Dragon Jars from the Philippines. Group 2 is extremely homogeneous despite its members coming from all over the Philippines and may represent output from a single Southeast Asian mainland production center (Hector Neff, personal communication 1997). A charcoal radiocarbon determination (AA-21214) beneath the archaeological contexts of the Asian sherds indicates the direct or indirect exchange of these artifacts took place at the earliest after cal A.D. 1510 (94.5% probability). Since the writing of this study, Descantes et al. (2002) have published a paper developing the significance of the sherds by discussing how the sherds got to Gachpar as well as how the Yapese incorporated the original jar into their political economy.

Clay Provenance

Intoh's research included a raw source material survey and analysis of clays and tempers (Intoh 1988, 1990; Intoh and Leach 1984, 1985). To examine the ceramic environment on Yap and gain insights into the selection of raw materials, Intoh collected nineteen clay samples, some from known pottery making villages. For a description of the clay source locations, see Intoh and Leach (1985:118-123). Nineteen clay briquettes from 15 villages throughout Yap were made and fired in an electric furnace under identical conditions (Intoh 1988:35). In an oxidized atmosphere, the temperature was ramped at a rate of 100°C per hour increments until 700°C was reached. The briquettes were fired for 30 minutes and then left in the furnace until 100°C (20 hours) was reached. Yosuke Kawachi did the petrographic examinations (Appendix H; Intoh and Leach 1985:199-200) and G. C. Claridge of the New Zealand Soil Bureau determined the approximate mineralogical content, the particle size distribution, and elemental composition through x-ray fluorescence (XRF), x-ray diffraction (XRD), differential thermal analysis (DTA), and infrared absorption (Appendix G; Intoh and Leach 1985:194-198).

From petrographic examinations, Kawachi identified two different source clays in Intoh's fired Yapese clay samples (CHD299-CHD316). One clay source was metamorphic, the other was sedimentary. Metamorphic derived clay samples include CHD299 and CHD302-CHD312. Common minerals include "actinolite, epidote, chlorite and oligoclase along with minor to trace quartz and clinopyroxene" (Kawachi 1985:199). Common minerals in the sedimentary-derived clay samples (CHD300-301, CHD313-CHD316) include ubiquitous quartz (quartzite in some cases and discrete grains in others) with lesser amounts of actinolite, oligoclase, epidote, chlorite, and opaque minerals (Kawachi 1985:200).

Claridge's analysis complemented Kawachi's study; he discovered the Yapese clay samples were from strongly weathered tropical materials and that the principal clay mineral in some of the samples was montmorillonite while in others kaolinite (vermiculite and illite are also present). All of the metamorphic clay samples (except CHD299) identified by Kawachi predominated in montmorillonite clay while four of the six sedimentary clay derived samples (CHD313-CHD316) identified by Kawachi predominated in kaolinite clay. In addition, Claridge (1985:195) identified quartz, oligoclase, magnetite, and amphiboles (actinolite) from the XRD and DTA analyses.

Claridge's (1985:194-195) XRF analysis determined the major element composition of the clay samples. He found,

> ... the samples are all very similar in composition, with relatively high iron oxide contents, and for the most part, relatively low silica contents. ... Extractable iron oxide contents are all low, compared with the total iron present, indicating that much of iron content of the samples is still contained within unweathered primary minerals such as magnetite, amphiboles, etc, and has not been converted into secondary iron oxides, such as goethite.

Despite the clays' similarity in chemical composition, I found that by performing a principal components analysis (PCA) on the elemental XRF data (Al, Ca, Fe, K, Mg, Mn, Na, P, Si, Ti) significant chemical differences could be discerned between the clay samples.

Projection of Clay Samples into Hypothetical Ceramic Compositional Groups

This section projects the clay samples Intoh and I collected against the ceramic compositional groups. Fortuitously, each ceramic compositional group has a clay member based on the Mahalanobis distance-derived probabilities. Table 15 presents the probabilities of the clay samples belonging to compositional Group 3 with Mahalanobis-derived distances calculated from the 19 elemental abundances while Table 16 presents the probabilities of the remaining clay specimens, which fit into ceramic compositional Groups 1, 2, and 4. Ten clay specimens fit into three of the compositional groups with probabilities above the 5% confidence level; if a 1% confidence level is used, four additional clay specimens fit into the ceramic compositional groups. Significantly, the probability that clay specimen CHD300 fits into ceramic Group 2 is more evidence that Group 2 is not a combination of Groups 1 and 3. The fact that each of the Yapese ceramic groups admitted Yapese clay members is an argument for all of the prehistoric ceramic members of the hypothetical groups originating from Yapese clay sources. Unlike previous ceramic analyses from archaeological work on Fais (Dickinson 1994; Intoh and Dickinson 2002) and Ngulu (Dickinson 1982), I did not find any Palauan ceramics in my Mogmog sample.

TABLE 15. Mahalanobis Distance-Derived Probabilities Calculation and Posterior Classification of Clay Specimens into Group 3 Using the Nineteen Elements

Analytical Identification	Group 3	Analytical Identification	Group 3
CHD307	**80.516**	CHD227	.000
CHD306	**59.799**	CHD280	.000
CHD303	**46.744**	CHD281	.000
CHD225	**36.926**	CHD282	.000
CHD304	**26.070**	CHD283	.000
CHD312	**21.686**	CHD299	.000
CHD309	**6.454**	CHD300	.000
CHD310	**2.315**	CHD301	.000
CHD308	**1.463**	CHD302	.000
CHD311	.807	CHD313	.000
CHD305	.001	CHD314	.000
CHD105	.000	CHD315	.000
CHD226	.000	CHD316	.000

TABLE 16. Mahalanobis Distance-Derived Probabilities and Posterior Classification of the Remaining Yapese Clays into the Three Yapese Ceramic Composition Groups Using Six Principal Components

Analytical Identification	Group 1	Group 2	Group 4
CHD301	**38.221**	.007	.001
CHD300	.238	**3.099**	.000
CHD302	.000	.001	**53.950**
CHD299	.000	.001	**13.021**
CHD311	.000	.038	**1.413**
CHD105	.000	.001	.000
CHD226	.000	.000	.009
CHD227	.000	.005	.007
CHD280	.000	.016	.003
CHD281	.000	.000	.000
CHD282	.653	.000	.016
CHD283	.000	.019	.000
CHD305	.000	.033	.003
CHD313	.698	.000	.002
CHD314	.000	.455	.000
CHD315	.051	.000	.000
CHD316	.000	.001	.000

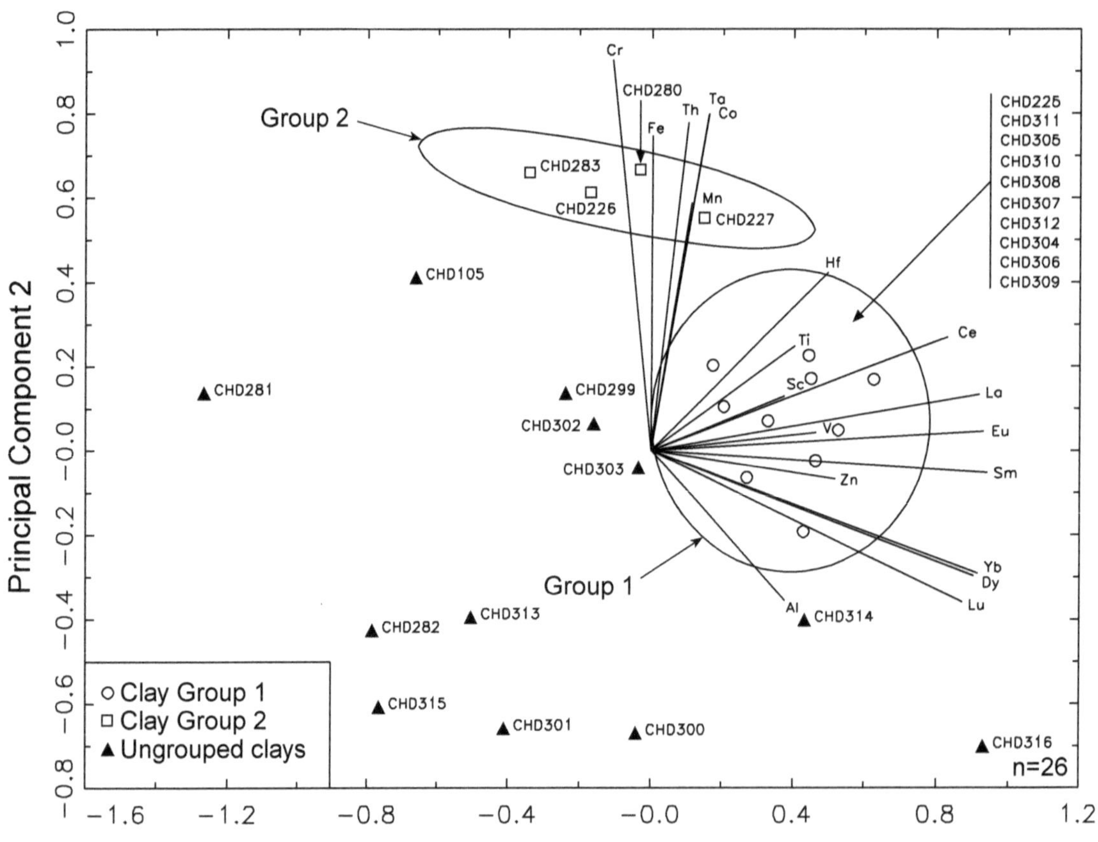

FIGURE 30. PCA biplot of the clay samples with two hypothetical clay compositional groups. Ellipses indicate 90% probability level for membership in the two groups.

Another ceramic provenance distinction of geological source is apparent when comparing the different geological proveniences of the clay specimens (see Figures 4 and 22) with the PCA analysis of the clay samples (Figure 30), the ceramic sherd mineralogies (Dickinson 1997a, 1997b), and the ceramic compositional group memberships of the sherds. One clay specimen from the geological Map Formation (CHD301) fits into Group 1. The sample was collected beneath a taro patch (Intoh and Leach 1984:13). According to Intoh (1988:71) it contains montmorillonite clay with many quartz-feldspar grains. Dickinson (1997b:3) describes Quartz-Feldspar sherds belonging to Group 1

(CHD119, CHD136, CHD138, CHD156, CHD223, CHD284) as containing "very poorly sorted sub-angular to sub-rounded granitic detritus" set in very silty pastes derived from granitic rock rather than metavolcanic rock. Dickinson's description of the mineralogical suite of these sherds corresponds to the mineralogy of the Map Formation, which contains fragmented rock of tectonic and sedimentary breccia.

Another Map Formation clay (CHD300) fits into Group 2. This sample contains montmorillonite clay with quartz-feldspar grains and was also collected beneath a taro patch by Intoh (1988:71; Intoh and Leach 1984:13). Dickinson (1997b:4) reports that Iron Oxide/Grog Tempered ceramics (CHD130, CHD173, CHD184, CHD242, CHD254) of Group 2 contain opaque pedogenic iron oxide fragments and tiny sand-sized inclusions in silty clay pastes; rare quartz-feldspar grains are also found in some sherds (Dickinson 1997a:1). "Some of the iron oxide particles contain tiny crystalline inclusions, suggesting that the iron oxides are reworked pedogenic particles derived from lateritic soil horizons, rather than iron oxides from bedrock" (Dickinson 1997b:20). Grog or sherd temper is identified in Iron Oxide/Grog Tempered ceramics only. Dickinson notes that the association of quartzofeldspathic sand with iron oxide grains, and Yapese metavolcanic temper, is evidence these ceramics originate from Yap. The fact that clays can be matched to ceramic Groups 1 and 2 and that some rare earth abundances differ between these two groups and the other predominantly Yap Formation clays (e.g., see Figure 26) is evidence that the Group 1 and 2 ceramics are not diluted versions of Yap Formation clays.

Nine clay specimens (see Table 15) were matched to compositional ceramic Group 3, which consists mostly of Laminated sherds. These aforementioned clay specimens and three clay specimens fitting into Group 4, another predominantly Laminated ware group, all have geological characteristics in common. All of the clay specimens in these two compositional groups derive from the Yap Formation, except for three clays on the Gagil-Tamil Island of Yap, which derived from the Map Formation (CHD302, CHD303, CHD304). Chemically, CHD304, supposedly a Map Formation clay, can be put into a clay compositional group constructed through PCA (see Figure 30) that is made up of only Yap Formation clay members. Despite deriving from different parent materials, the other two Map Formation clays (CHD302, CHD303) are chemically similar to the Yap Formation clay compositional Group 1. These clay samples in question, however, may be Yap Formation clays because Johnson et al. (1960:74) remark that in this eastern part of Yap the Map Formation is thin and has many serpentine and Yap Formation outcrops. Many Yap Formation clays from varied geographical locales fit into clay Group 1 and ceramic compositional Group 3, implying that a number of different clay sources were used for the fabrication of Laminated ceramics, and probably also Plain ware and CST ceramics. With more clay samples representative of Yap and an understanding of clay source variability, the provenance work may have a higher resolution and identify several distinct clay sources. For the moment, it can be shown that Laminated ceramics, the dominant type for the preceding 600 years of Yapese history, were fabricated with Yap Formation derived clays, predominantly manifested on Yap Island. Quartz-Feldspar and Iron Oxide/Grog Tempered pottery, on the other hand, derive from Map Formation clays.

During the preceding 600 years, Yapese ceramic history was dominated by Laminated ware. We know from ethnohistoric sources that a number of different low caste villages manufactured ceramic vessels. Ceramic compositional Groups 3 and 4, predominantly Laminated ceramics, contain a number of geographically separate metamorphic montmorillonite clay sources. This is apparent when the abundances of 19 elements were used to calculate the Mahalanobis distance-derived probabilities of the clay samples resembling the compositional space of ceramic Group 3 (see Table 15).

Four clays separated into clay Group 2 (CHD226, CHD227, CHD280, CHD283) are from Gagil-Tamil Island of Yap. Their compositional similarity suggests they are serpentinite-derived clays, common in Binaw, Gachpar, and T'enifar. The mid and lower reaches of Gachpar Village are dominated by serpentinite rocks. Dikes, sills, and other bodies of serpentinite intrude the Yap Formation and weather to ferruginous clays (Johnson et al. 1960:66). Dickinson (1997b:3-4) notes that CHD226, a member of clay Group 2, is rich in quartz and feldspars, and appears to be derived from intrusive plutonic sources (Johnson et al. 1960:74). None of these clays have a high probability of fitting into any of the ceramic compositional groups. This is surprising because clay samples CHD226 and CHD227 originate from the two *suon* villages that produced earthenware pots for the people of Gachpar. However, these two poor quality clays are unlikely to have ever been used to make pots and therefore can not be depended upon to test if Binaw or T'enifar ever supplied Gachpar with pots.

None of the five clay specimens from the Tomil "Volcanics" in southern Yap or the clay specimen from Ruu' fit into any of the clay or ceramic compositional groups. Compositionally they are chemically distinct from the montmorillonite Yap Formation and serpentinite ferruginous clays. Interestingly, Dickinson (1997b:3) notes that the paste and temper of sherd CHD172 is atypical for Yap because it lacks granitic and metavolcanic minerals. He suggests it is probably from a Tomil "Volcanics" outcrop in the western Gagil-Tamil Island area where pyroxene andesites and other volcanic rocks can be found. Given the chemical distinction of Tomil "Volcanics"-derived clays (see Figure 30) and the membership of CHD172 in ceramic Group 3 (see Figure 27), a predominantly Yap Formation montmorillonite-derived group, the volcanic clasts observed by Dickinson could also originate from Map Formation-derived clays and tempers

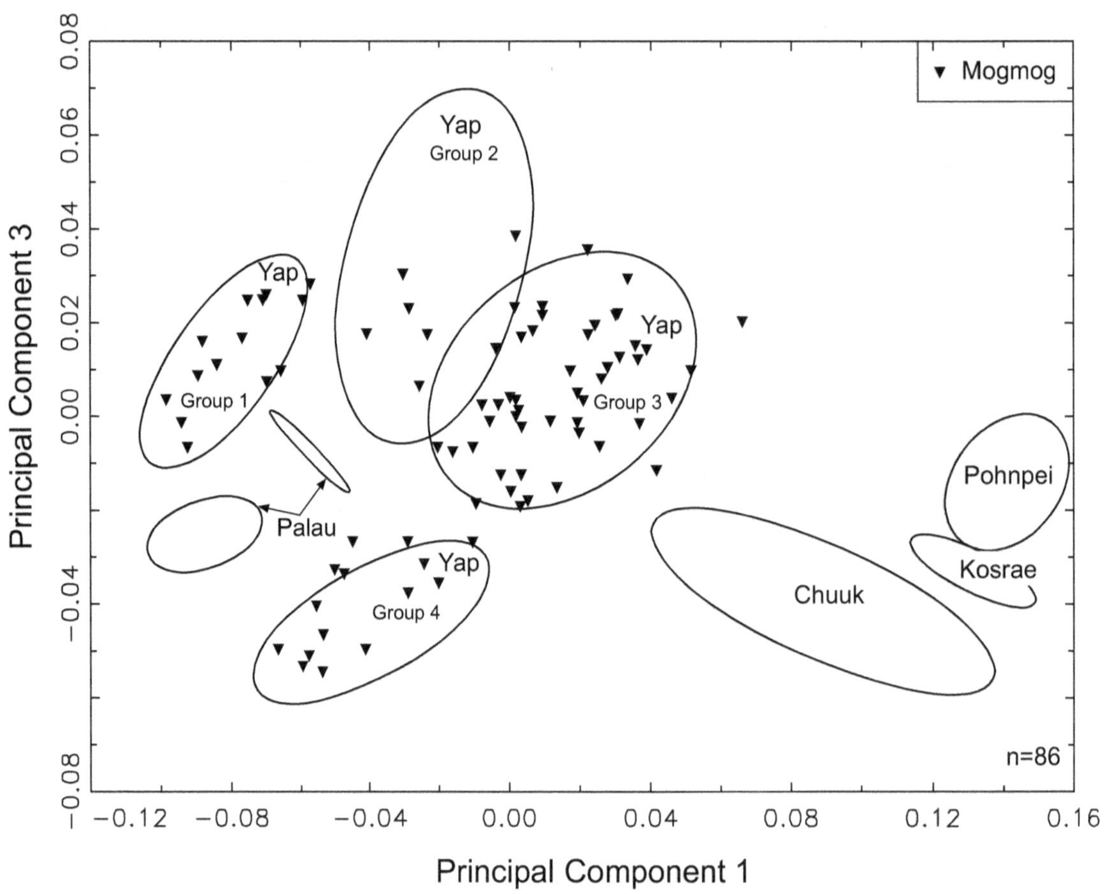

FIGURE 31. Provenance of Outer Island potsherds. Ellipses indicate 90% probability level for membership in the different hypothetical Micronesian island compositional groups. The Guamanian ceramic compositional space is not presented.

that are known to contain fragmented breccias and conglomerates (Johnson et al. 1960:68-69).

Provenance of Mogmog Ceramics

Chemical characterization of prehistoric pottery found on Mogmog confirms Dickinson's (1997a) mineralogical conclusions that all the sherds in my sample originate from Yap. Figure 31, a bivariate plot of the first and third principal components, graphically displays how the chemical characterizations of Mogmog ceramics resemble more those of Yap, than those of any other ceramic-producing Micronesian islands: Palau, Yap, Chuuk, Pohnpei, and Kosrae. It should be noted, however, that my sample sizes were small for the non-Yapese Micronesian islands. Descantes et al. (2001) have recently published these provenance results.

Elemental Variability in Yapese Laminated Ceramics Found in Yap and Mogmog

As expected, the ranges of elemental abundances within Yapese Laminated ware are greater on Yap than they are on Mogmog. There are, however, a few elements for which the ranges are larger in ceramics found on Mogmog. Mogmog has twelve elements (total n=19) with larger elemental ranges than those in Gachpar. Larger ranges from Mogmog could be a result of my Yapese ceramics not being representative of the full elemental variability on Yap (which ultimately supplied Mogmog with ceramics).

Similar inferences can be made after running a principal components analysis (PCA) on these data. PCA implies that the sources of Laminated ceramics found on Mogmog are more varied than those found in Gachpar (Figure 32). The small compositional variability of the Laminated ceramics collected in Non-Gachpar Yapese villages compared to the compositional variability of Laminated ceramics found on Mogmog (which all derive from Yap) is more evidence that the full chemical variability of the Non-Gachpar Laminated ceramics is not represented. In point of fact, if the full elemental variability had been represented, the Non-Gachpar compositional ellipse would be larger than that of Mogmog.

Higher eigenvalues for the first two principal components of separately run PCA analyses of Laminated ceramics from the three proveniences is further evidence that the chemical variability of Laminated ceramics from Mogmog is larger than the chemical variability of Gachpar Laminated ceramics (Table 17). This implies that the clay sources for the Laminated ceramics found in Mogmog are more diverse than the clay sources of Gachpar Laminated ceramics.

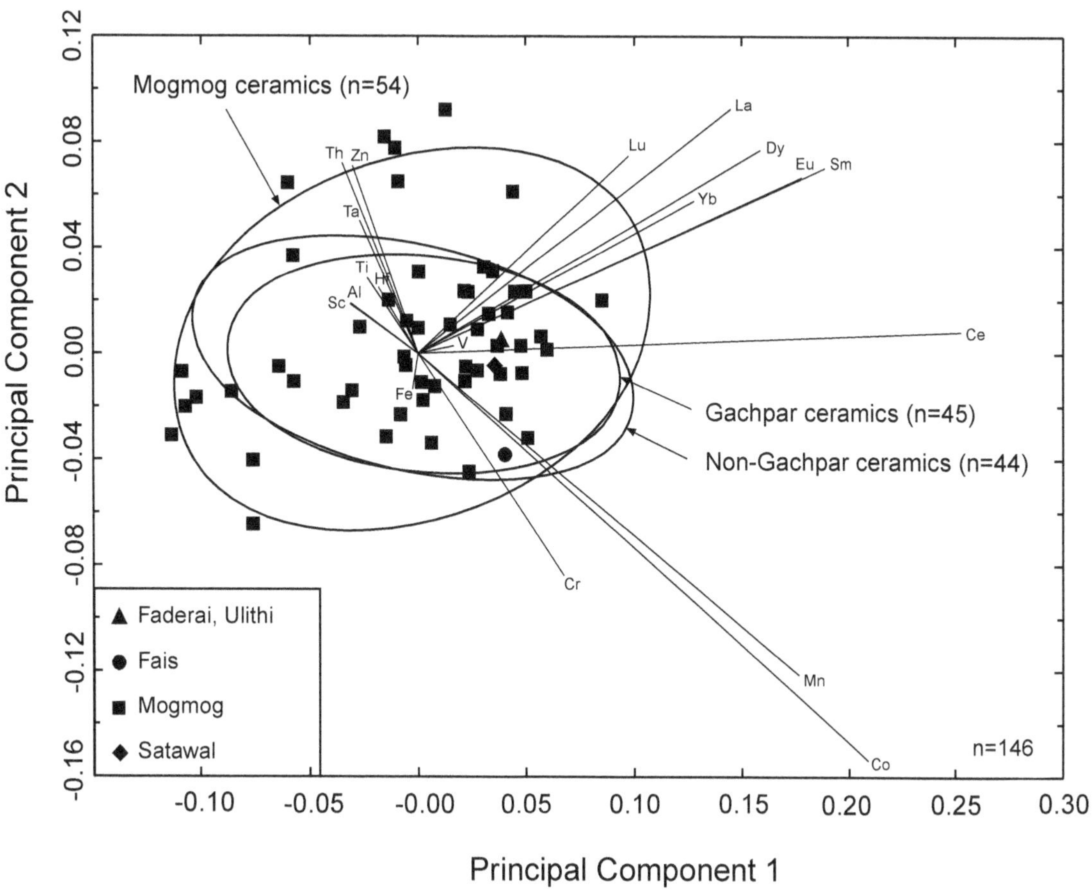

FIGURE 32. Compositional variability of Yapese Laminated ceramics recovered from Gachpar, Mogmog, and non-Gachpar Yapese villages. Ellipses indicate 90% probability level for membership in the three provenience groups. Note the data points of Gachpar and Non-Gachpar ceramics are not shown.

TABLE 17. Eigenvalues and Standard Deviations of PCA for the Laminated Ceramics Recovered in Gachpar, Non-Gachpar, and Mogmog sites

Provenience	Principal Component 1		Principal Component 2	
	Eigenvalue	SD	Eigenvalue	SD
Gachpar (n=45)	.2405	.49	.06503	.26
Non-Gachpar (n=44)	.3053	.55	.06373	.25
Mogmog (n=54)	.3617	.60	.14310	.38

Either people from Mogmog were obtaining some pottery unlike that used in Gachpar from their *sawei* partners or in addition to exchanging with Gachpar people, Mogmog people were acquiring pots from non-Gachpar people.

A posterior classification based on the Mahalanobis distance-derived probabilities of the 19 element concentrations of the 54 Laminated ceramic sherds recovered from Mogmog measured against the 45 Laminated ceramic sherds found in Gachpar provides additional information. Thirty-seven sherds (69%) from Mogmog have a greater than 10% probability of deriving from the Gachpar ceramic chemical compositional space; if a probability cut-off of 5% is used 40 sherds (74%) found in Mogmog resemble chemically those found in Gachpar. I infer from these results that though Laminated ceramics found in Mogmog show more chemical heterogeneity than ceramics from Gachpar, the majority of the ceramics chemically resemble those of Gachpar.

Chemical characterization studies of Laminated ware found in Mogmog and Yap imply that the ceramic sources for people living in Gachpar and Mogmog in the most recent 600 years (if this duration is treated as one synchronic period) were not identical. To reiterate the conclusions of rim thickness of Mogmog and Gachpar potsherds that were found to differ, different geological sources for Gachpar and Mogmog ceramics do not preclude the existence of ceramic vessel exchange or formalized *sawei* relationships between Gachpar and Mogmog.

Radiometric Dating

I report radiometric dates for certain prehistoric events in Yap and Mogmog in this section. The dates allow me to construct a chronological schema and investigate the relation of that scheme to exchange behavior changes between the two islands. Previous reported Yapese marine shell dates can be problematic and over estimate the age of when an artifact was made because shells can ingest carbon from old reefs (Dye 1994). In all but two cases I dated charcoal. Accelerated mass spectrometry (AMS) radiometric dates of organic samples answered the following questions: (1) what is the earliest evidence for occupation in Gachpar and Mogmog; (2) when were Gachpar and Mogmog *dayif* first constructed; (3) what is the earliest evidence for island interaction in Gachpar and Mogmog; (4) what is the date of intensification for exchange practices in Mogmog; (5) when did the Yapese begin reclaiming Gachpar coastal land; and (6) what are the temporal ranges of the different Yapese ceramic types in Gachpar and Mogmog. In all but two cases, I use small amounts of associated charcoal to date these events. A total of 28 organic samples were submitted to the NSF-Arizona AMS Facility for radiometric determinations, 26 charcoal and 2 bone samples. A table of the radiocarbon determinations is given in Appendix A. All the date ranges are reported in 95.4% confidence intervals, i.e., two standard deviations.

Gachpar Settlement

Finding evidence for early sites in Yap is a difficult task because of the acidity of the volcanic loamy soils. However, despite the acidity of these inland Yapese soils, charcoal flecks were numerous and well preserved. The charcoal flecks are probably secondary deposits from extensive swidden agriculture burning activities at higher elevations. Coastal site depositional contexts have a higher pH, which is more conducive to preservation, but are more prone to bioturbation from mangrove crabs. The earliest radiocarbon determination (AA-21203) came from the site of Numurui (C36-16) situated in the interior of Gachpar. Sample AA-21203 has a two standard deviation range of cal A.D. 20 – 380 and Yapese CST pottery associations.

Ulithi Settlement

The earliest charcoal sample associated with Yapese Plain ware ceramics and charcoal is sample AA-21212 at site Mog-39 (Fasilus) with a range beginning at cal A.D. 620. An earlier date range of cal 1530 – 1160 B.C. from a turtle plastron bone (AA-21195) is found at Mog-13 in layer VI/1 at 126 cm below datum (Figure 33), but it is not associated with any cultural material and comes from a unit with questionable integrity. The excavation unit at Mog-13 is behind the present Falol *dayif* and habitation; a U.S. Navy Quonset hut built during the Second World War also once stood in the area. The integrity of the unit is clearly questionable and most likely disturbed for two reasons. First, a charcoal sample (AA-21194; cal A.D. 860 – 1050) stratigraphically higher than the fish bone sample (AA-25707; cal A.D. 1020 – 1260) most likely gives an older radiocarbon date using a two standard deviation range. Second, the fish bone sample (AA-25707), which is found in the same culturally sterile layer as the turtle bone sample (AA-21195) is at least 2200 years younger than the turtle bone (both ages are corrected for the marine reservoir effect). In addition, an insufficient amount of collagen was extracted from the turtle bone sample. The dating of inorganic bone compounds as opposed to that of organic compounds (collagen) also makes the turtle date problematic (see Stafford et al. 1987).

Given the possible early settlement dates from Palau (Athens and Ward 2002), the Marianas (Butler 1995), and Yap (Intoh 1997), it may be premature to rule out the temporary or permanent use of Ulithi by Yapese people before Nuclear Micronesian settlement.

Though the absence of high islands between Yap and Chuuk may have served as a barrier to Western Micronesian high island populations (see Ayres 1990:207), nearby atolls with seasonally rich fish and turtle stocks, such as Ulithi Atoll, only an overnight sail from Yap, conceivably could have served as a temporary hunting site for early Yapese inhabitants. The non-permanence of these particular site types could make finding associated artifacts and ecofacts challenging.

Gachpar Coastal Land Extension

The coastal land extension of Gachpar includes all of the land between the lagoon shore and the taro patches, approximately an area of 11 ha (Figure 12). This monumental landscaping task involved filling the lagoon shore, some of which could have been inhabited by mangrove colonies (particularly at the mouths of silt-transporting streams) that caused shore progradation. The Gachpar coastal land extension is estimated by the radiocarbon determinations of buried charcoal samples and the absence of old Yapese ceramic types. The deepest Gachpar coastal archaeological contexts have predominantly Laminated ceramics if any ceramics at all. The rare older Yapese ceramics found associated with Laminated ceramics in coastal Gachpar sites such as C36-06, C36-33, C36-45, and C36-76 are interpreted as being intrusive and of secondary deposition. Numerous buried charcoal samples may also be secondary depositions from higher elevations; however, the radiocarbon determinations were not in a reverse order on the coast, which would be expected if erosion from higher inland Gachpar ground was depositing older charcoal flecks onto the coast.

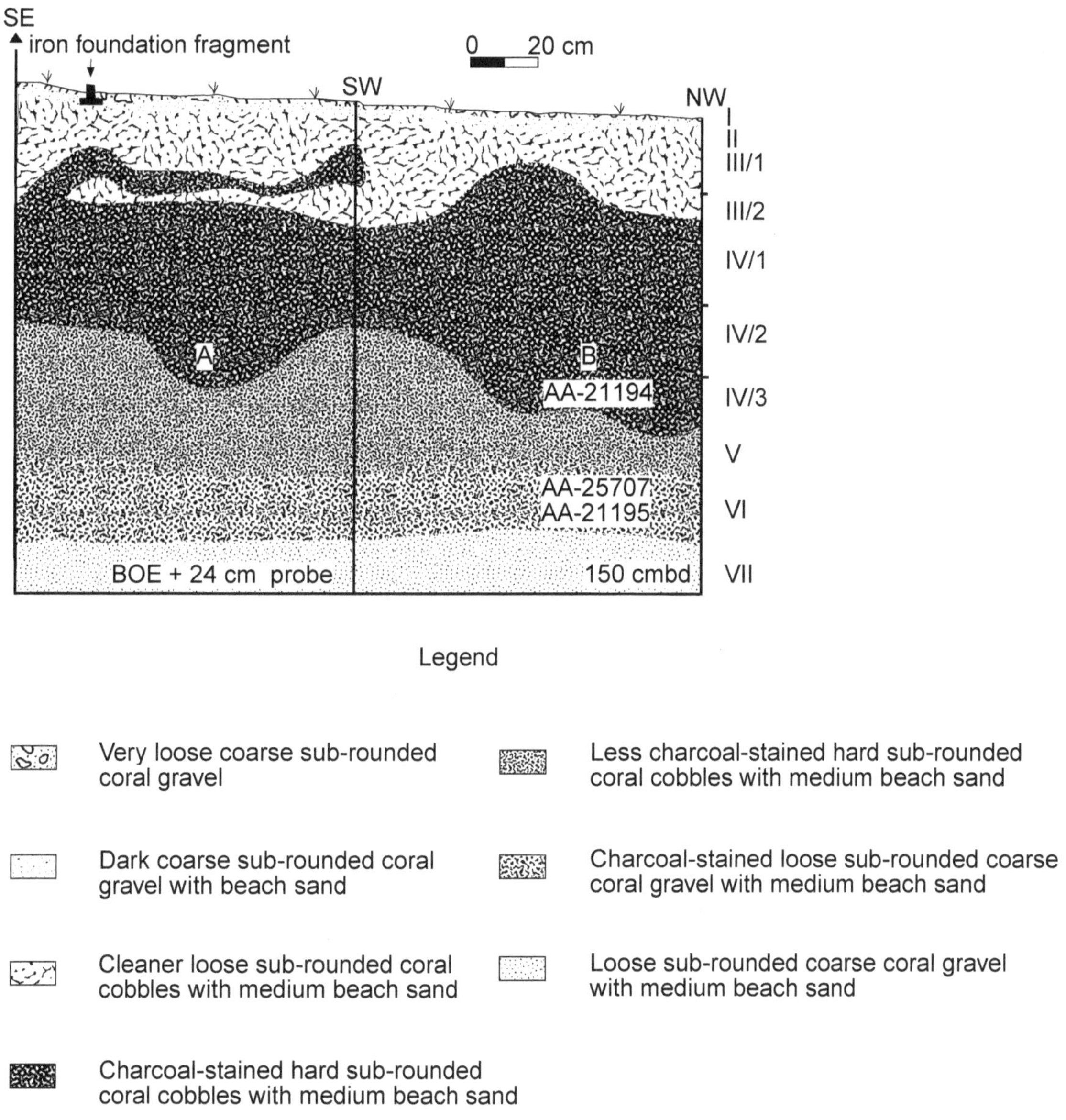

FIGURE 33. Mog-13 (Falol) excavation profile. Note the effect of bulldozing near the top of the unit. The U.S. Navy did much landscaping during World War II in this area.

Land reclamation may have also occurred at different times in different areas. Based on the ceramic associations in the archaeological contexts alone, land extensions behind the taro patches and adjacent to the old shore line were constructed after the introduction of Laminated pottery (at the earliest A.D. 1290). Examining the five radiocarbon dates from the shore contexts, the earliest evidence (AA-21208) of a Gachpar coastal occupation is A.D. 880 from C36-33 (Figure 34), however it is more likely evidence of coastal use rather than of coastal land constructions. Sample AA-21209 is beneath an old buried retaining wall built to protect the adjacent taro patch from salt water before land reclamation in this area. It seems likely that land reclamation started after cal A.D. 1310. In addition, we know that at the earliest cal A.D. 1470, and at the latest cal A.D. 1650, land reclamation had already started at site C36-33. Taking all this information into account then, land reclamation in Gachpar started sometime between the fourteenth and the fifteenth centuries A.D. after the introduction of Laminated ceramics (Figure 35).

From my preliminary inspection of sediment samples recovered beneath excavated coastal *dayif* on the land fill extension (e.g., C36-06, C36-33, C36-45, and C36-78), it appears that there are mangrove swamp sediments beneath some the platforms. This evidence suggests that people land-filled coastal areas already occupied by mangrove colonies (see also Cordy 1986:78). Hunter-Anderson's (1986) find of mangrove soils beneath a taro swamp in an area presently devoid of mangrove (Falanruw 1990:233) is further evidence for land-filling of mangrove swamp for living space and taro patch gardens.

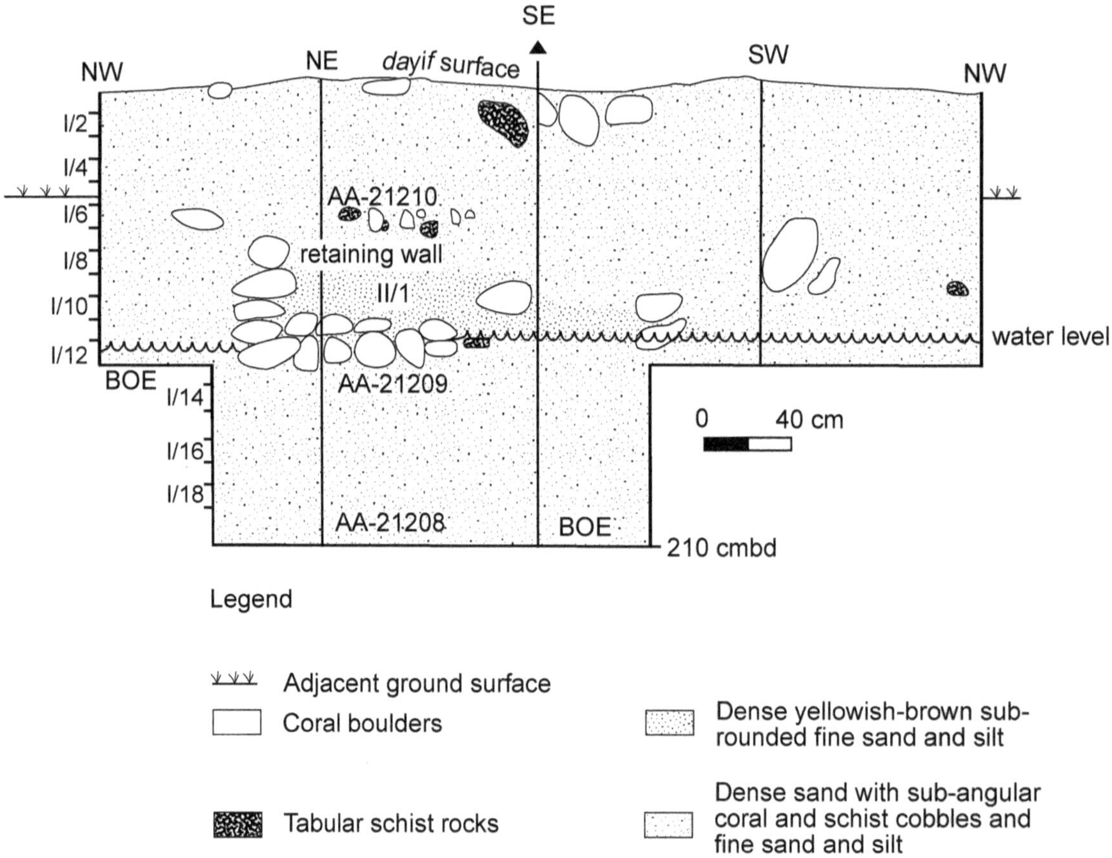

FIGURE 34. C36-33 (Pebinau #1) excavation profile.

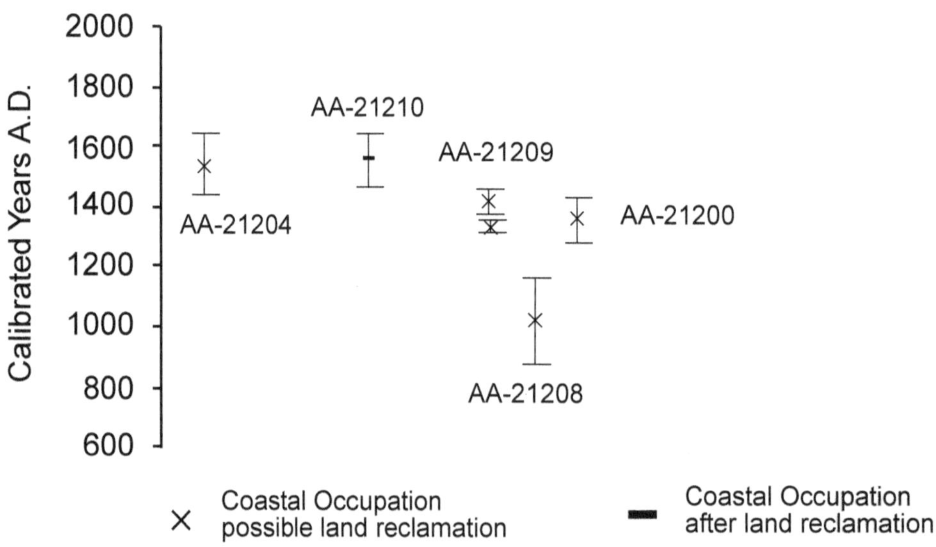

FIGURE 35. Radiocarbon determinations for charcoal samples in Gachpar coastal land extension area.

Dayif Construction

This section attempts to date the first construction of the ubiquitous platform features found in Gachpar and Ulithi. All of the charcoal samples used to determine when *dayif* were first constructed come from beneath the platforms, and therefore before their construction began. Before examining the archaeological evidence, it should be noted that my small excavation unit sizes may have prevented me from finding earlier buried *dayif*.

Gachpar *Dayif* Construction

To address the question of when *dayif* construction began, I used one radiocarbon charcoal sample (AA-21210) from *dayif*-fill and nine others from beneath architectural features (*dayif* and *wunbey*). A charcoal sample within *dayif*-fill likely predates its construction. Sample AA-21210 comes from C36-33. This coastal site, which was situated in an area that had had much crab bioturbation, had historic artifacts well beneath a platform and wall. The two standard deviation chronological range for sample AA-21210 is cal A.D. 1470 - 1650.

Charcoal sample AA-21214 was excavated from a more secure archaeological context at site C36-22 (Togobuy) in the interior of Gachpar Village and produced a two standard deviation chronological range of cal A.D. 1510 - 1800. The archaeological context of the charcoal sample was well below a *wunbey* and its associated *dayif*. With no historic artifact associations, sample AA-21214 has the youngest radiocarbon date beneath *dayif* constructions. Sample AA-21214 also predates the presence of the Southeast Asian Dragon Jar sherds found in this excavation unit. The fact that these artifacts are found beneath a *wunbey* rather than a *dayif* is important because it is less likely that we encountered a *vonod* (a cache beneath a platform where sacred and valued items were stored).

My radiometric data are in accordance with Rainbird's (1994:308-310) conclusion, which he based on Intoh's Gitam Village excavations, that *dayif* construction is "a relatively recent phenomenon, unlikely to have originated more than 500 years ago and, possibly, within the last 250 years." We also know that stone *dayif* architecture predates 1818 because von Chamisso (1835:285) mentioned that "[p]aved paths and square courts in front of the chiefs' houses are found on Eap [Yap]."

Mogmog *Dayif* Construction

Dates for Mogmog *dayif* construction are similar to those found in Gachpar. The identical vocabulary term "*dayif*" (see Damm 1938:332), implies diffusion from Yap at a time when interaction between Yap and Ulithi was already intense. Moreover, the meaning and significance of *dayif* are the same in both societies. *Dayif* symbolize land ownership and other prerogatives of the household. As in Gachpar, *dayif* construction on Mogmog postdates the introduction of Iron Oxide/Grog Tempered, Quartz-Feldspar, Plain, and Laminated ceramics. The youngest two standard deviation chronological range beneath a *dayif*, and therefore before construction, is cal A.D. 1460 - 1650. Similar to Mogmog *dayif* archaeological deposits, coastal Gachpar *dayif* had historic artifacts beneath their stone foundations. Inland Gachpar *dayif*, on the other hand, tended not to have historic artifacts beneath them.

CST Ware

As noted earlier, no CST pottery was found on Mogmog. Three charcoal samples (AA-21203, AA-21204, AA-21211) were associated with Yapese CST pottery found in Gachpar. One sherd from a coastal site was disturbed because it was associated with much Laminated pottery and was the only CST type sherd found in the reclaimed coastal area of Gachpar. Sample AA-21203 comes from a context of only CST sherds in site C36-16 while sample AA-21211 from site C36-27 derives from a deep context with CST, Iron Oxide/Grog Tempered, and Plain ware associations. Incorporating the radiocarbon dates from the two secure contexts gives a date range of cal A.D. 20 to 670. Intoh reports Yapese CST pottery was made from A.D. 1 to 1350 (2000 B.P. to 600 B.P.; Intoh 1990:44). These data fit within Intoh's wider chronological range.

Iron Oxide/Grog Tempered Ware

Only three charcoal samples were associated with Iron Oxide/Grog Tempered ceramics. One Gachpar date (AA-21211) has a range of cal A.D. 530 - 670 while two Mogmog radiocarbon dates from the same archaeological layer, but different levels, give a range of cal A.D. 640 - 820. Together, the two islands extend the Iron Oxide/Grog Tempered ware range to cal A.D. 530 - 820. These chronometric data also fit within Intoh's (1990:44) longer Plain ware (which includes Iron Oxide/Grog Tempered ceramics) range of A.D. 1 and 1350.

Quartz-Feldspar Ware

Only two dated contexts with associated Quartz-Feldspar pottery come from Mogmog. The two radiocarbon determinations have a range of cal A.D. 1310 to 1640. Both contexts also contain younger Laminated ware so it is possible that these contexts are not the earliest for Quartz-Feldspar pottery. Intoh (1990:44) reports older dates for Plain ware (which includes Quartz-Feldspar ware) on Yap, but concludes that Plain ware is no longer found after A.D. 1350.

Plain Ware

Seven dated charcoal samples were associated with Plain ware. Four charcoal samples (AA-21198, AA-21206, AA-21207, AA-21211) with associated Plain ware sherds from Gachpar give a range of cal A.D. 530 – 1440 while three charcoal samples (AA-21193, AA-21194, AA-21212) from

Mogmog give a chronometric range of cal A.D. 620 to 1440. If I use Intoh's typological definition for Plain ware ceramics, my chronological range for Yapese Plain ware becomes cal A.D. 530 - 1440 for Gachpar and A.D. 620 - 1640 for Mogmog. It is peculiar that my chronological duration on Mogmog is longer than that in Gachpar considering Plain ware originates from Yap. Intoh's (1990:44) range of cal A.D. 1 - 1350 begins and ends before my determinations in Gachpar and Mogmog. It is not surprising that my chronometric range for Mogmog begins later because I did not find contexts earlier than cal A.D. 620 (AA-21212).

Laminated Ware

Seven charcoal samples (AA-21204, AA-21205, AA-21206, AA-21209, AA-21210, AA-21214, AA-21216) associated with Laminated pottery in Gachpar (Figure 36) and six charcoal samples (AA-21193, AA-21197, AA-21201, AA-21215, AA-22311, AA-24016) associated with Laminated ceramics in Mogmog (Figure 37) give the same chronometric range: cal A.D. 1290 - 1945 for both islands. Intoh (1990:44) finds that Laminated ceramics became important after A.D. 1350 on Yap.

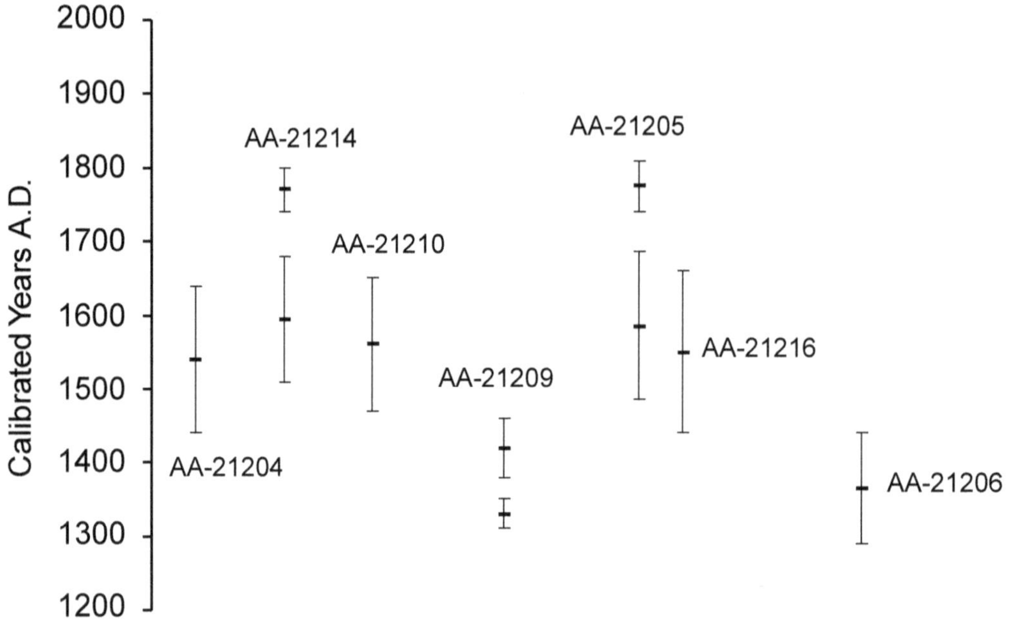

FIGURE 36. Radiocarbon determinations for charcoal samples associated with Laminated ceramics excavated from Gachpar Village.

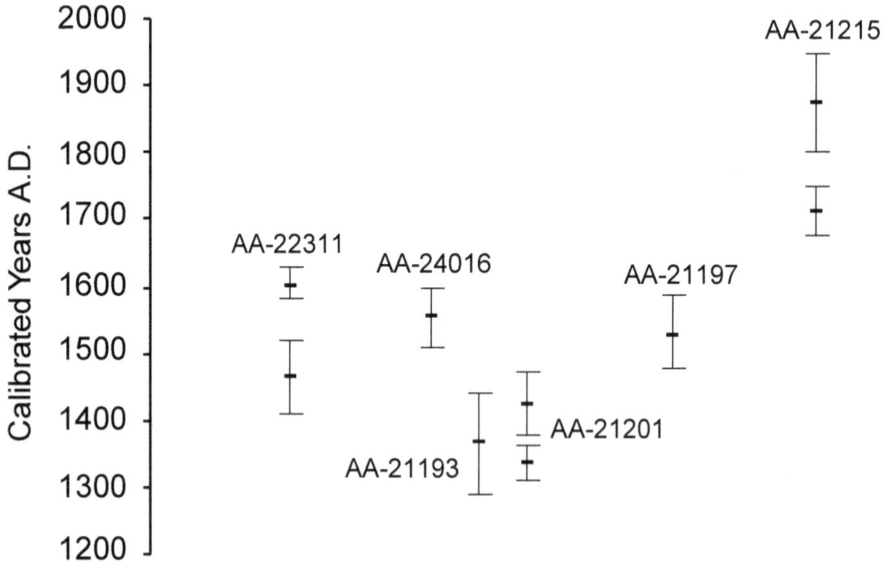

FIGURE 37. Radiocarbon determinations for charcoal samples associated with Laminated ceramics excavated from Mogmog.

Yap-Ulithi Island Interaction

The earliest date for island interaction between Yap and Ulithi on Mogmog is cal A.D. 620 (AA-21212) from site Mog-39. Early Mogmog archaeological contexts have few ceramics. I think this is evidence for what Berg (1992) calls simple trading (or perhaps better called simple exchange). Whether the ideology of exchange in the seventh century is similar to that recorded in ethnohistoric sources is not known, but interaction was probably not as intensive as that of later times when *sawei* voyages were in operation. This cannot be said with absolute certainty because it is possible that early interaction was intensive in materials not visible in the archaeological record.

Yapese Ceramic Density Increases in Mogmog

To quantify and model prehistoric exchange networks, Plog (1977) proposed examining nine variables: (1) content; (2) magnitude; (3) diversity of materials; (4) geographic size; (5) temporal duration; (6) directionality of exchange; (7) symmetry of exchange; (8) centralization; and (9) complexity. This section quantifies the magnitude of exchange and interaction to determine when the interaction between Mogmog and Yap intensified. I use the density of ceramics to measure Plog's (1977) second variable in four different excavations considered representative of the Mogmog archaeological landscape: Mog-22 (Falmei), Mog-27 (Hathiar), Mog-25 (Numurui), and Mog-53 (Ligafalu E Mat). Mog-25 and Mog-53 are situated in the western geographical moiety division called Lamathakh while Mog-22 and Mog-27 are located in the Numurui moiety on the eastern side of the island.

Ceramic density is a measure of the ceramic weight in a particular context divided by the volume of the removed archaeological matrix in that context (g/m^3). I use this measure as representative of interaction intensity between Yapese and Ulithian inhabitants because most of the ceramics originate from Yap. A density increase in ceramics can be somewhat misleading because different archaeological features, such as rubbish pits, can attract more ceramic sherds than other features, such as habitation floors. Comparatively, a probe with a couple of sherds, which has a low archaeological matrix volume, can make the ceramic density misleadingly large. This is significant because I want to compare different ceramic densities at different times. For a better understanding of the densities, I have included the excavation profiles and identified the features when possible. Every layer and level with artifacts or ecofacts is included in the ceramic density graphs.

Besides investigating the densities of ceramics in Mogmog archaeological contexts, I also investigated the density fluctuations of faunal materials. In general, faunal remains included shells and bones. Bird, fish, mammal, and turtle bones provide ubiquitous ecofacts to compare with the ceramic densities. It was found that in general faunal densities mimic the density fluctuations of the ceramics. Beneath Mogmog platform fills, densities for ceramics and faunal materials steadily increase. The increase in animal bones implies a population increase which may explain the presence of more ceramics. A Ulithian population increase requiring more Yapese ceramics and an increase in island interaction between Yapese and Ulithian inhabitants are not mutually exclusive. That is, one can still argue for an increase in island interaction whether there was a population increase or not.

Mog-22 (Falmei)

Mog-22 (Figure 38) has a noticeable increase in ceramic density in layer III/2 (Figure 39). The previous large densities in layers V are ignored because they come from a pit feature. Faunal densities mimic the ceramic density fluctuations. The ceramic density increase in layer III/2 is accompanied by five times (5.09) more bones than in the previous archaeological contexts in the unit. I interpret this increase in the density of foreign ceramics as evidence for an increase in ceramic exchange and island interaction.

Mog-25 (Lamrui)

Mog-25 (Figure 40) has a noticeable increase in ceramic density in its first occupation layer (VII). Layer VII (Figure 41) contains Laminated ceramics and is before the presence of historic artifacts. Animal bone densities also first appear in layer VII; they increase five (5.3) fold in the layer (VI) following layer VII.

Mog-27 (Hathiar)

A sharp increase in ceramic density is visible in layer III of Mog-27 (Figure 42). This layer contains the first presence of Laminated ceramics in the unit and predates the appearance of historic artifacts (Figure 43). Similarly, the animal bones in this layer increase 23 (23.2) fold over layer IV and it is probably part of a midden or cooking oven. As mentioned earlier, ceramic densities removed from probes can be misleading. The one Iron Oxide/Grog Tempered sherd removed from layer V weighs only 40.3 g.

Mog-53 (Ligafalu E Mat)

Layer IV/2 of Mog-53 has a noticeable increase in ceramic density (Figure 44). It is the earliest layer where ceramics appear in the unit and where Laminated ceramics were found (Figure 45). As in the previous units, the ceramic increase takes place before the historic artifacts appear in the deposit. As in Mog-27, there is a huge increase in faunal remains. Layer IV/2 has a 27 (27.1) fold increase in faunal remains over layer V/1. The earliest archaeological context of layer V/2 has only charcoal (2.7 g) evidence.

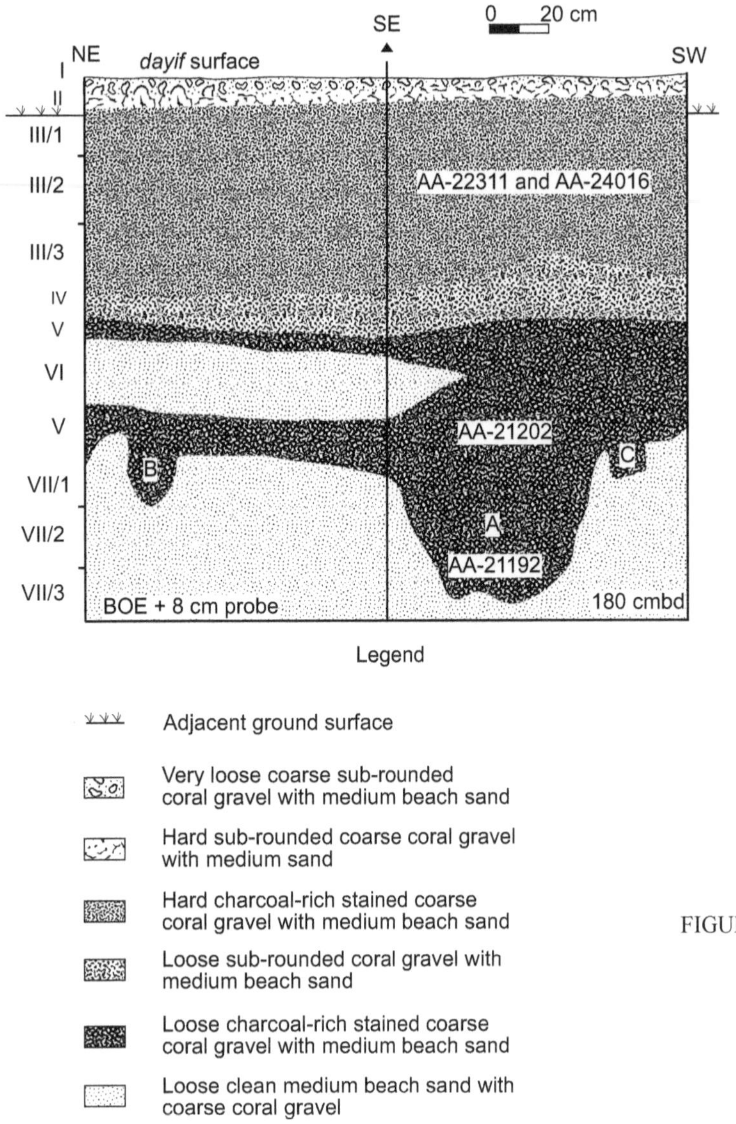

FIGURE 38. Mog-22 (Falmei) excavation profile.

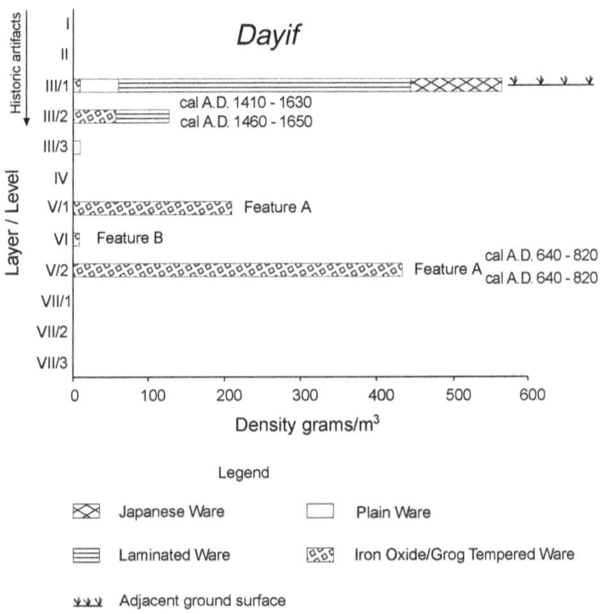

FIGURE 39. Graph of ceramic densities in Mog-22 (Falmei).

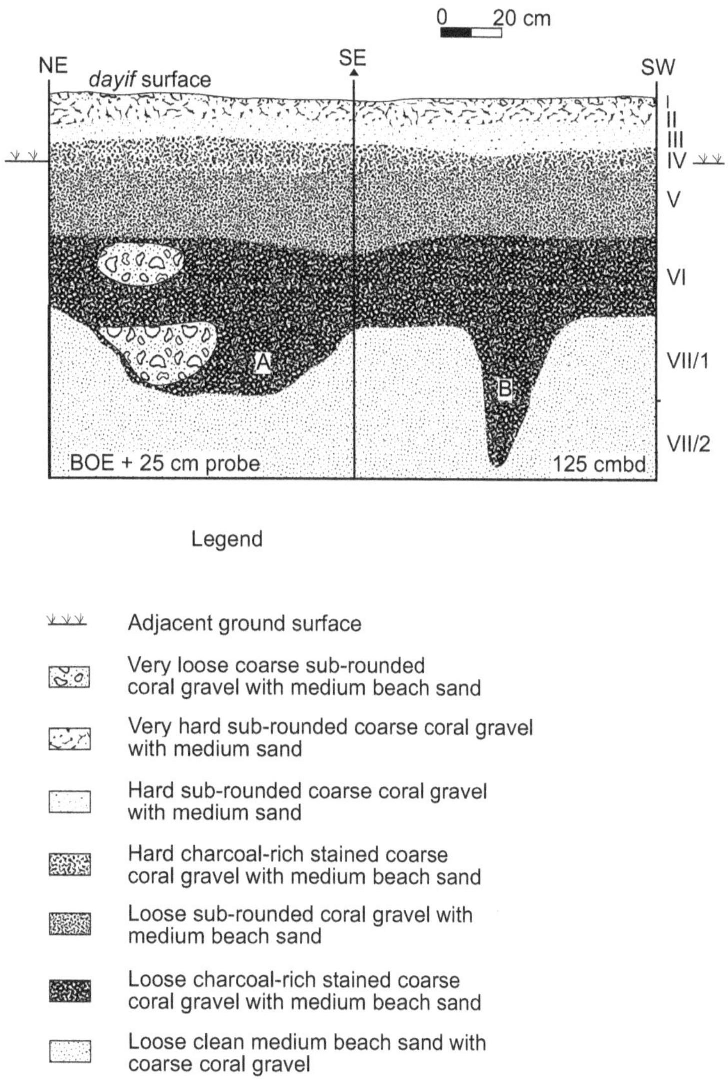

FIGURE 40. Mog-25 (Lamrui) excavation profile.

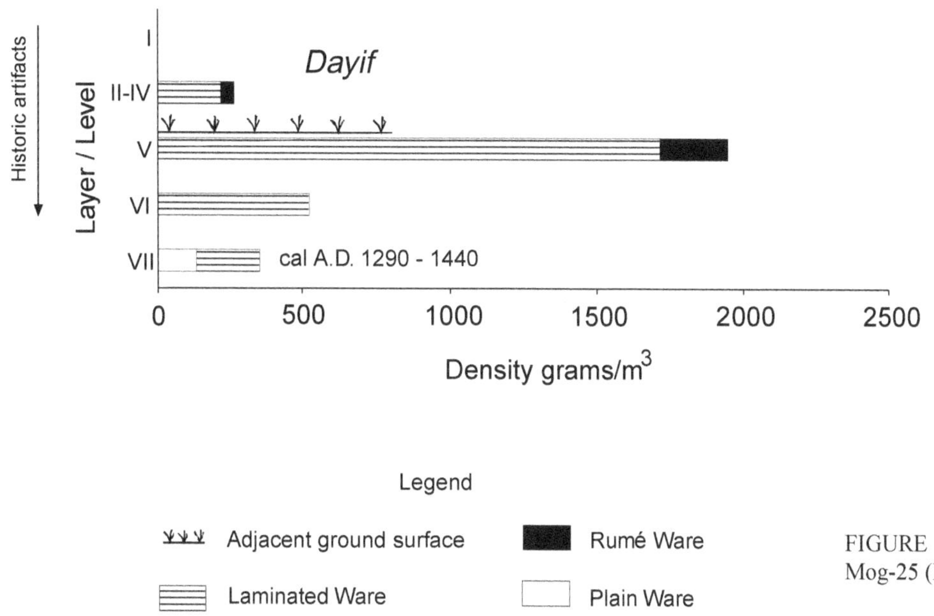

FIGURE 41. Graph of ceramic densities in Mog-25 (Lamrui).

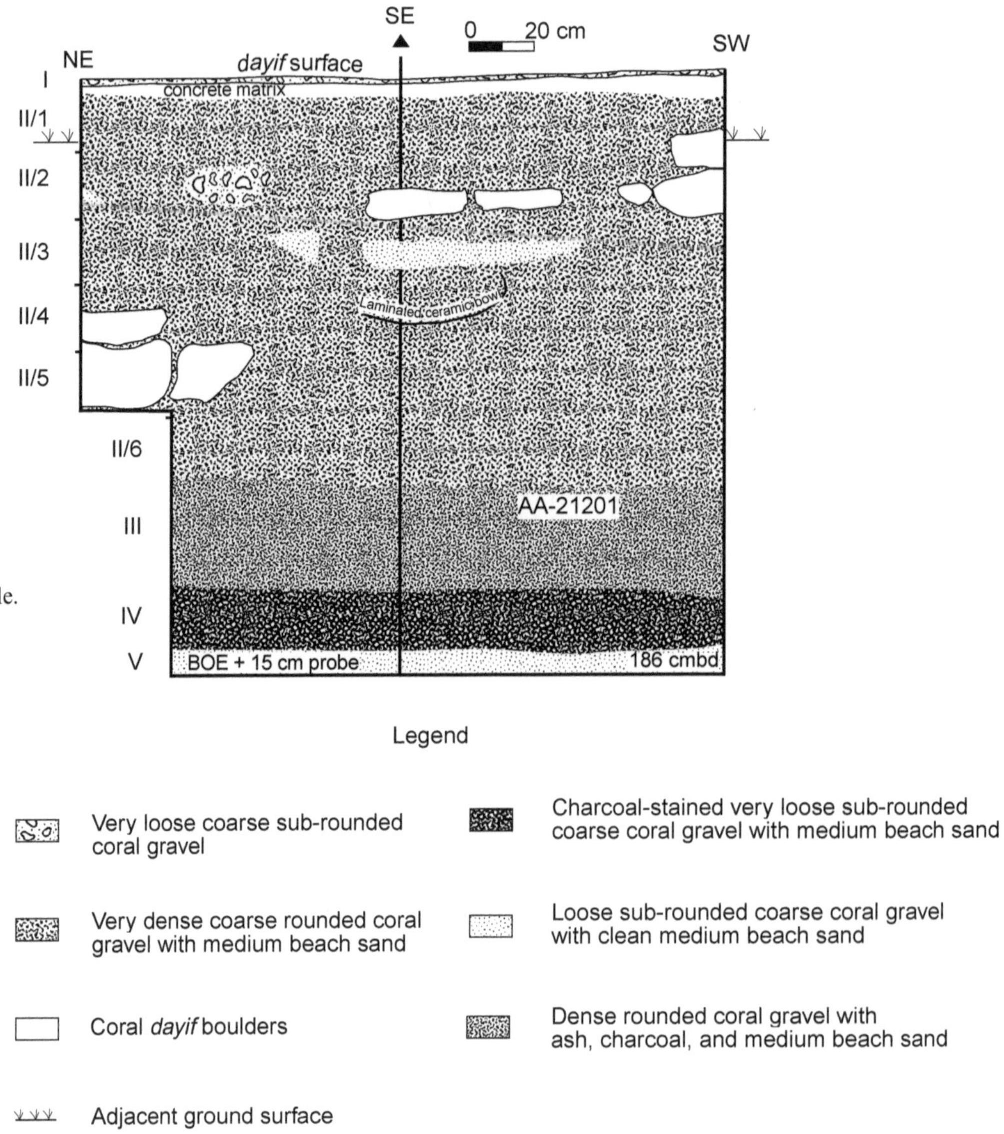

FIGURE 42. Mog-27 (Hathiar) excavation profile.

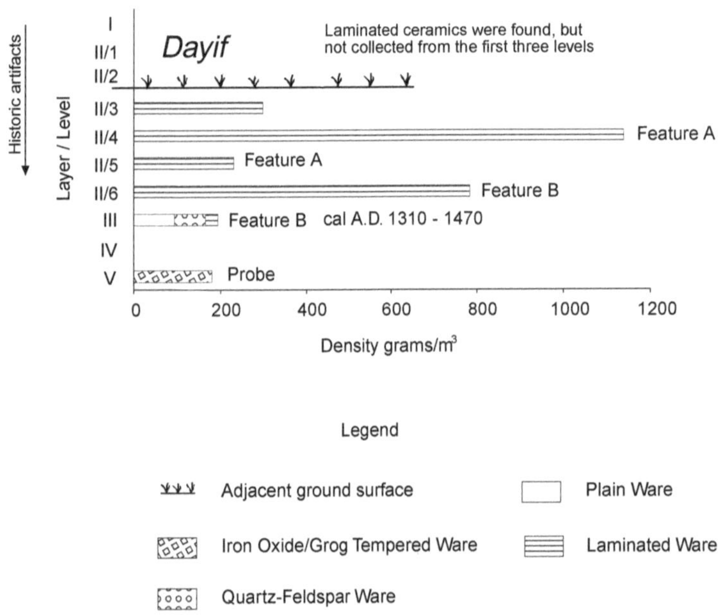

FIGURE 43. Graph of ceramic densities of Mog-27 (Hathiar).

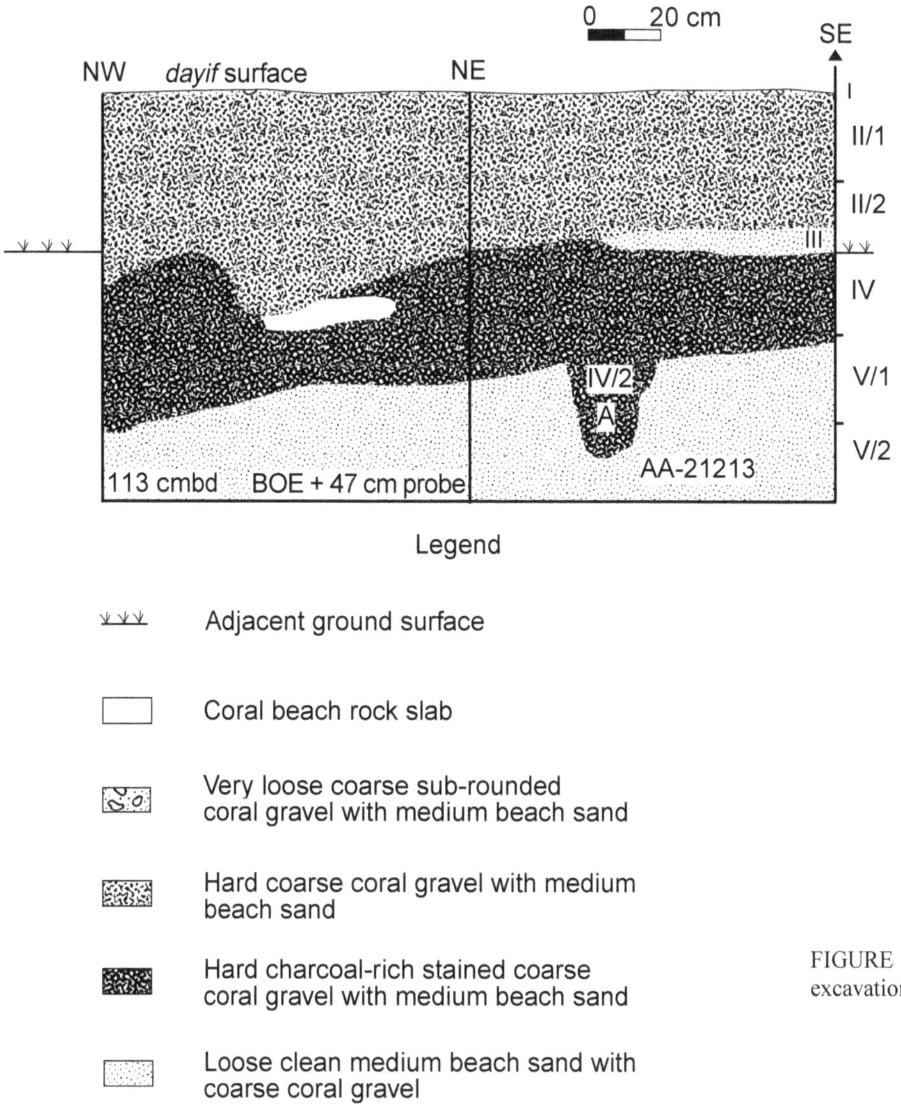

FIGURE 44. Mog-53 (Ligafalu E Mat) excavation profile.

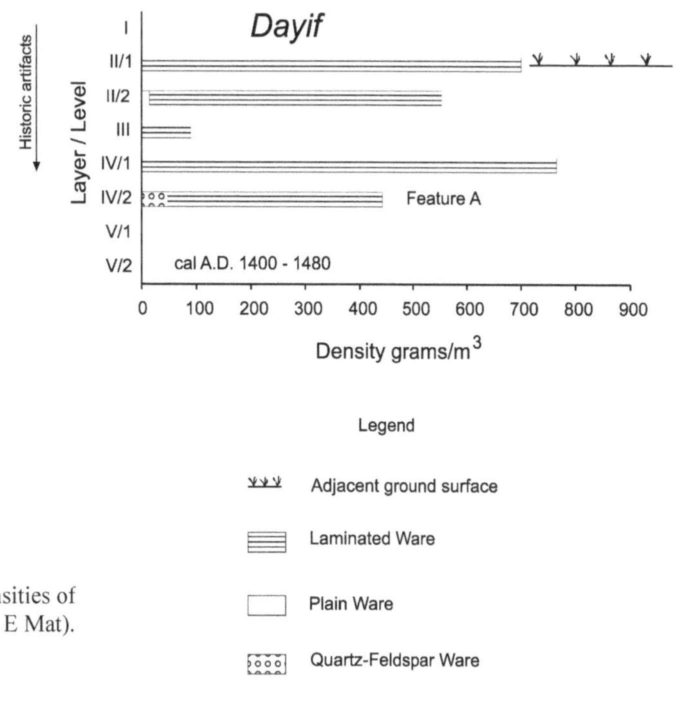

FIGURE 45. Graph of ceramic densities of Mog-53 (Ligafalu E Mat).

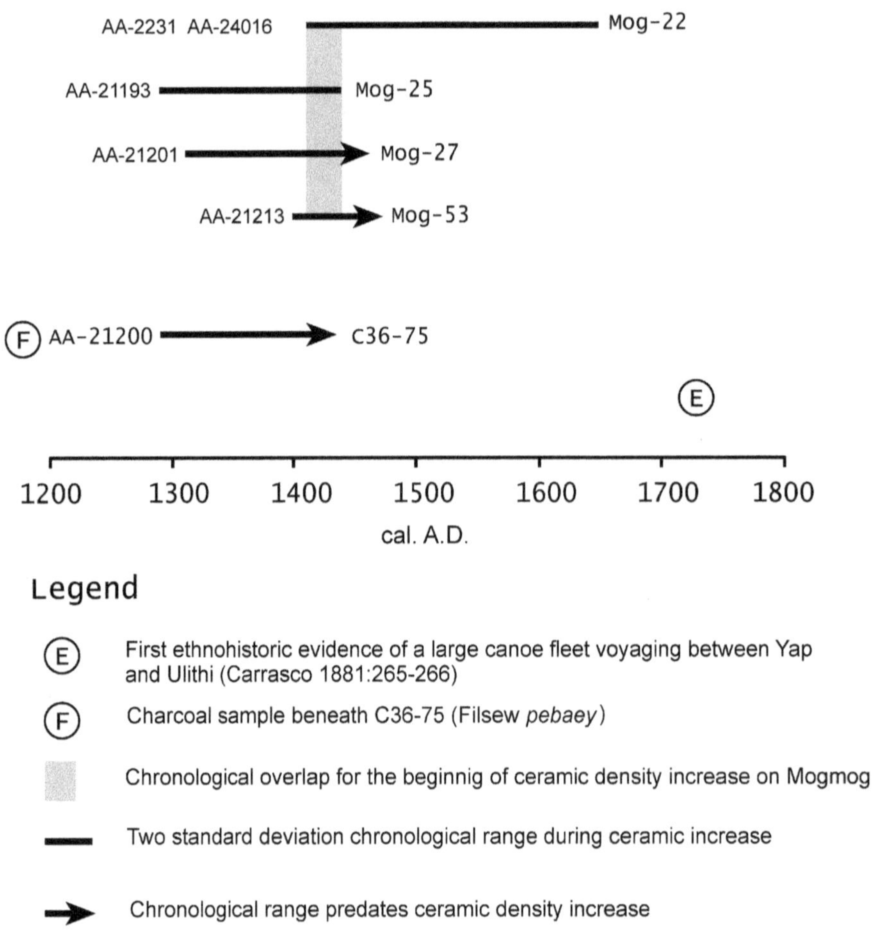

FIGURE 46. Date for the beginning of ceramic density increases in four Mogmog excavations. Dates for the first ethnohistoric evidence for intense interaction and the date before the Gachpar's Filsew *pebaey* construction are also given.

Date for the Beginning of *Sawei*

Four excavations in Mogmog can supply evidence for indicating when a sharp ceramic density increase took place. The ceramic increase is more or less contemporaneous in the different units on the island. Chronological overlap (Figure 46) implies that the ceramic increase occurred in the fifteenth century. Archaeological data firmly indicate that the ceramic density increase is associated with the first appearance of Yapese Laminated ceramics and preceded the appearance of European artifacts.

Filsew

Indigenous oral history collected in the twentieth century from Gachpar and Mogmog claims that Gachpar did not always head the *sawei* system nor did Outer Islanders always visit Gachpar Village. The village of Ruu', also in the Gagil Municipality (Müller 1917:302), is said to have hosted Outer Islanders before Gachpar. According to oral history, when in Yap, Outer Island peoples visited Ruu' and stayed in a meeting house called Meilif. Ruu' Village later outraged another high ranking village and was subsequently annihilated (Ushijima 1987b:69). Thereafter, Outer Island peoples were compelled to visit Gachpar and stay in a new meeting house built for them called Filsew (Figure 47). Filsew is the name of a *pebaey* found in the reclaimed land area of Gachpar. According to Lessa (1950c:43) Falaso (Filsew) *pebaey* "was destroyed by the Japanese during the war for fear it might serve as a landmark for enemy planes." While I was in Gachpar the Filsew meeting house was being rebuilt. I examined two-day old house post holes beneath the foundations of the meeting house and removed an *in situ* charcoal sample. Sample AA-21200, which is well beneath the coral foundation of the Filsew *pebaey* was dated to cal A.D. 1290 – 1440 at two standard deviations. If the mytho-history is accurate, evidence of Quartz-Feldspar and Laminated pottery in Ruu' implies that Ruu' was conquered at the earliest in the fourteenth century. Integrating the oral history, the archaeology in Ruu', and the calibrated radiometric determination beneath the Filsew meeting house, at the earliest, Gachpar headed the *sawei* system only after A.D. 1290.

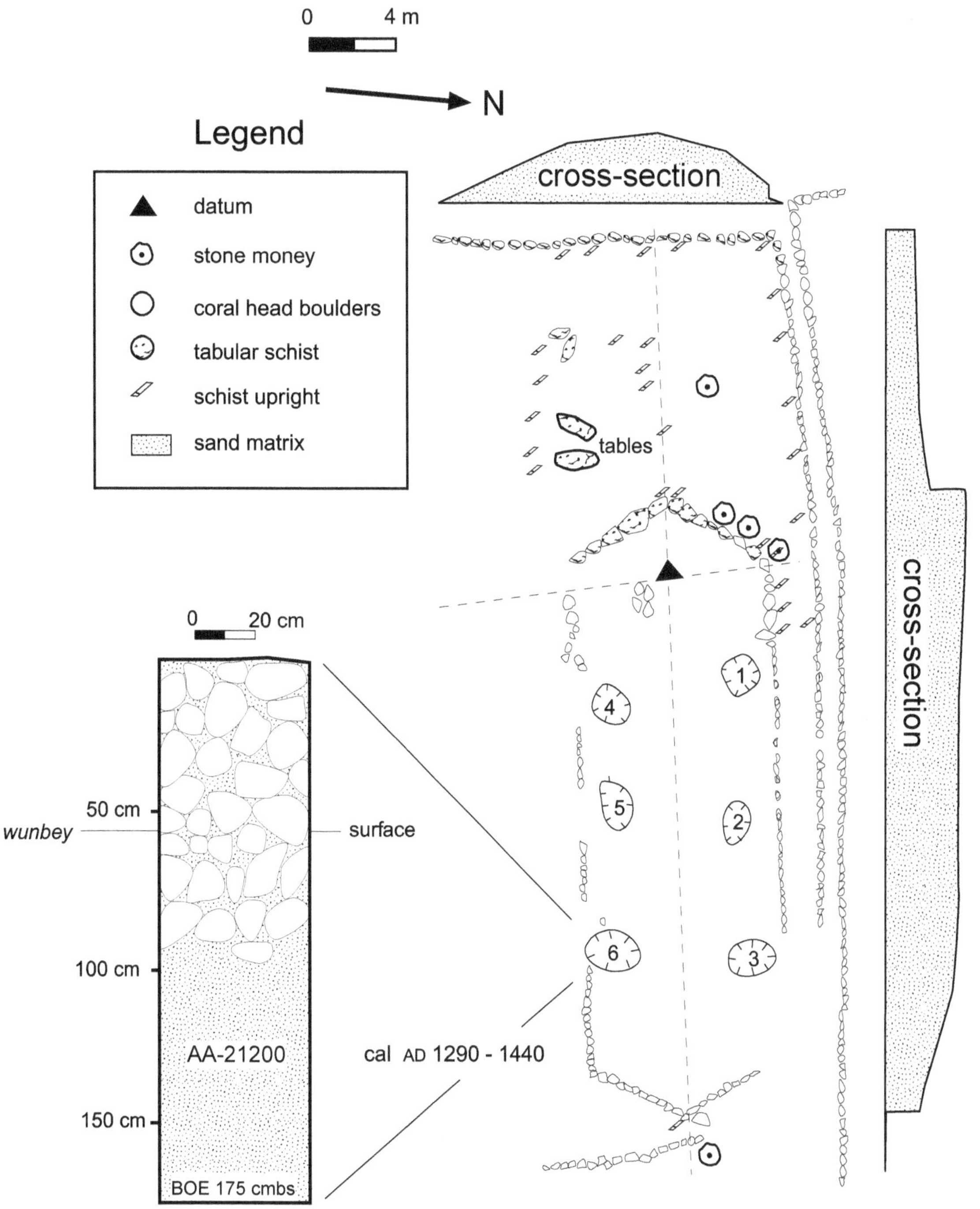

FIGURE 47. Filsew (C36-75) *pebaey* plan view and post hole excavation profile.

Summary

Chemical and mineralogical characterizations of prehistoric pottery all indicate that the sherds recovered from Ulithi originated from Yap, unlike Fais and Ngulu ceramic assemblages, where Palauan earthenware was found (Figure 31). Potsherds are not inert and interact with their depositional environments. Despite the post-depositional alterations of sherd elemental abundances, the provenance exercise is not hindered using a 19 dimensional concentration space (Descantes et al. 2001). Nevertheless, element abundances need to be examined univariately in order to identify chemical anomalies and appreciate the complex geochemical dynamics potsherds can undergo. The contaminated Gitam Laminated pottery is a case in point. Unlike the other Yapese ceramics, Gitam ceramics were ten to hundred times more enriched in Zn than non-Gitam Yapese Laminated sherds. Their enrichment was concluded to have been caused by their post-depositional environment beneath a refuse dump containing metals.

Constructing hypothetical ceramic compositional groups and then determining the probability that Yapese clays resemble the ceramic groups produced interesting results. All four ceramic compositional groups had at least one clay sample resembling its chemical characterization implying that all of the ceramics originated from Yap. Tomil "Volcanics" and serpentinite ferruginous clays were found to not resemble any ceramic compositional group. Map Formation clays resembled Quartz-Feldspar and Iron Oxide/Grog Tempered pottery.

Twelve clays fit into the Laminated ware continuum of ceramic Groups 3 and 4. I infer from these results that a number of Yap Formation montmorillonite clay sources on Yap Island contributed to the Laminated ware ceramic variety. These data corroborate ethnohistoric data (Intoh 1988) which mention that women from various low caste villages produced pottery for high caste villages. Intra-source variability could not be examined in this study, so a full appreciation of the ceramic environment will only be had when a larger raw material analysis is undertaken.

Even though the Binaw and T'enifar clay samples did not resemble any of the hypothetical ceramic groups, I do not think this is sufficient reason to reject the hypothesis that these two low caste villages supplied pots to Gachpar as mentioned by informants. I am not satisfied with the test because the sediment samples I analyzed from these villages were not good quality clay samples. Not until good quality clays can be found in these two *suon* villages, possibly from exposed Yap Formation clays under the thin Map Formation, will this hypothesis be adequately tested. (If no suitable clay sources are found in Gagil, it is also possible that raw clay was also exchanged).

Numerous radiometric determinations were made to investigate dates for the settlement Gachpar and Mogmog, the reclamation of Gachpar lagoonal land, the construction of *dayif* in Gachpar and Mogmog, and the intensification of Yap-Ulithi interaction from a sample of four *dayif* excavations (see Appendix 1). The comparison of date ranges for the different Yapese ceramic types from this study with those of Intoh are found to differ slightly. Through the integration of different records, it is hypothesized that the formalization of *sawei* began in the early fifteenth century. Discussion of the exchange intensification is presented in the next chapter.

Chapter VII

Discussion

In this chapter, an exchange history model between Yap and Ulithi is presented. I use the analytical results of my research to build an exchange model leading up to European entry into the Pacific. I stress again, however, the integrity issues of the archaeological deposits, particularly those of Mogmog. I integrate ethnohistoric data to present a richer diachronic explanation of the interaction between Yap and Ulithi for the most recent 400 years. Unlike previous treatments of the development of Yap-Outer Island interaction, the general concept of "traditional exchange", which obscures the transformative nature of the exchange behaviors, is broken down into more discrete chronological units. These units serve as reference points to compare the timing of events and to facilitate the discussion of different cultural processes.

The centrality of exchange demands a discussion of cultural processes that led to and arose from intense island interaction. Factors involved in the increase and maintenance of interaction include geographic location, ideologies, politics, population pressure, and resource limitations. Some of these elements, which leave archaeological traces, have been detailed in Chapter II and discussed by one or another researcher for the *sawei* exchange phenomenon (e.g., Alkire 1989; Berg 1992; Hage and Harary 1991, 1996; Helms 1993; Hunter-Anderson and Zan 1996; Labby 1976; Lingenfelter 1975; Small 1995). These factors are revisited in light of archaeological and ethnohistorical evidence.

Origins of Exchange Between Yap and Ulithi

Before dealing with the origins of Yap-Ulithi island interaction, an examination of the earliest archaeological indication for exchange is in order. Presently, the earliest archaeological evidence for exchange is Yapese Plain earthenware sherds on Mogmog (Mog-39-VI/2). The potsherds are associated with charcoal radiocarbon dated to cal A.D. 620 – 770 (AA-21212). Two other early contexts with Iron Oxide/Grog Tempered sherds in Mog-22-V/2 are associated with identical charcoal dates of cal A.D. 640 – 820 (AA-21192 and AA-21202). It is unlikely these archaeological contexts represent the earliest Yap-Ulithi interactions because Intoh (1996:111) argues for a Yap-Fais exchange history extending 1900 years based on charcoal dates associated with Yapese CST potsherds and lithic materials. The only possible earlier Mogmog archaeological context at Mog-13 was rejected based on its poor integrity and the absence of cultural associations.

I offer two possible hypotheses: (1) Mogmog settlement coincided with Yapese interactions and (2) Ulithi's earliest colonizers were people from Yap. More archaeological investigations of early Ulithian sites are needed to fully test the offered hypotheses. Lingenfelter (1975:154) suggests that the Yapese may have claimed the Outer Islands as their own from periodic turtle hunting visits before the present Ulithian Nuclear Micronesian speakers arrived. In Gachpar mytho-history, Ulithi was created and first inhabited by a Gachpar woman called Liomarar disgruntled at being cheated out of her fair share of turtle (*Chelonia mydas*) meat (Müller 1918:630). She stayed on Mogmog where she could eat all the turtle she wanted. The Yapese claim to having created and first colonized the atoll before the Ulithians is part of the Yapese justification for Ulithian subjugation.

Radiocarbon data suggest that Mogmog inhabitants continually received Yapese pottery from at least the seventh century A.D. Based on small ceramic densities in Mogmog excavations (Figures 33, 35, 37, 39), I propose that exchange between Yap and Ulithi was simple and not intensive 1300 years ago. Of course, numerous interactions between a small Mogmog population and Yap cannot be rejected because they would be difficult to detect. Nonetheless, the absolute number of exchange interactions is related to the frequency of voyages, the number of canoes in a fleet, and the number of persons per canoe. In other words, interactions would have had to increase through time if the population of Mogmog grew. However, non-materialist factors could also increase exchange interactions. Early pottery from Mogmog is unlike Yapese non-Laminated earthenware found in early Gachpar contexts (see Table 4). While CST pottery is apparently absent on Mogmog, Gachpar exhibits limited amounts of Quartz-Feldspar sherds. Comparing the chemical variability of Plain and Iron Oxide/Grog Tempered wares in both islands is less informative because of small sample sizes, but the non-Laminated pottery from Mogmog appears to be more variable than that found in Gachpar. The data imply the same two possibilities presented in Chapter VI for explaining the disparity between rim thickness and elemental variability of the Laminated ceramics in both villages, that is: (1) Gachpar provided Mogmog with ceramics unlike those it used and/or (2) Mogmog interacted with and acquired pots from non-Gachpar Yapese villages. Gachpar and Ulithian mytho-history place the origins of Yap-Ulithi interaction with personages from Gachpar Village (Damm 1938:353; Lessa 1962a:154; Müller 1918). My interview data from Yap and Mogmog and Müller's (1917:242) Yapese oral history favor the second possibility because they mention that Outer Island peoples visited the village of Ruu' before Gachpar Village headed the *sawei* exchange system. Even though the contradicting mytho-histories were recorded almost a millennium and a half after the practice to which the archaeological data refer, I think the second possibility is more likely: early exchange between Yap and Mogmog involved interactions with non-Gachpar people because the ceramic types are so different in the two villages. Of course, the first possibility cannot be entirely rejected, so it is still possible that interactions with Gachpar people coexisted with those from people in other Yapese villages during the earliest period of Yap-Ulithi exchange. More ceramic analyses from early archaeological contexts could test this further.

Berg's (1992:160) suggestion that simple inter-island trading between Yap and the Outer Islands began in the twelfth and thirteenth centuries, based on disparate elements of legendary and genealogical evidence from Polowat and Satawal collected by the Südsee-Expedition, does not bear out for Ulithi. Moreover, the island of Fais has Yapese archaeological evidence a millennium earlier than Berg's date for simple exchange between Yap and the Outer Islands (see Intoh 1997:21). This exemplifies the limitations of using early twentieth century oral historical data for interpreting the remote past. However, it should be noted that Berg's reliance on oral history from the Central Carolines, found much further east than Fais and Ulithi, might explain his late estimate for simple trading. His estimate is consistent with Fujimura and Alkire's (1984:112) earliest archaeological evidence of Yap-Lamotrek interaction at A.D. 1200.

Previous explanations for the origin of *sawei*-like interactions depend on coral island resource limitations (Alkire 1989; Lingenfelter 1975:28) and the economic material advantages of Yap (Hage and Harary 1991; Lessa 1950c, 1956). No doubt a large resource disparity existed between Yap and the Outer islands with the balance of material exchange in favor of the Outer Islanders during protohistoric interactions (Lessa 1950c:43). Yet, despite the survival advantages for a coral island in a high island-coral island relationship (see Hage and Harary 1991:113), I submit that the paucity of early Yapese ceramics and lithics in Mogmog suggests that Ulithian populations were not in a reliant relationship with Yap until after the fourteenth century.

Factors That Led to the Intensification of Exchange Between Yap and Ulithi: A.D. 600 to 1400

Given the list of exchange items (see Table 1) between Yap and Ulithi and the preservation environment in Yap, it is difficult to find Outer Island goods in the archaeological record. The most likely preserved Outer Island material evidence on Yap are shells, particularly *Spondylus* shell valuables and shell belts. Unlike ubiquitous ceramics, these artifacts are rare, and less likely to be found. Less rare pearl shell valuable fragments were found at C36-78 in the less acidic archaeological contexts of the Gachpar shore. Despite the difficulty in finding archaeological Outer Island exchange goods in Yap, I believe Gachpar holds evidence of what caused the intensification of exchange between Yap and Mogmog.

In my examination of the factors that led to an intensification of exchange, I am not giving primacy to any one factor, but simply discussing the factors that I believe played a role in the formation of intensive exchange between Yap and Ulithi. There has to be causes and circumstances on both islands for the increase in interaction. At the same time, it should be noted that evidence for materialist factors and conditions are more visible in the archaeological record than non-materialist factors. Whatever the prime impetuses for intensifying exchange, whether it is Yapese population pressure or Yapese competition to raise rank, the contributing factors were initiated before Spanish explorer Vasco Núñez de Balboa re-discovered the Pacific in 1513.

Population Pressure

Population pressure as a cause for culture change on resource limited islands is a common occurrence in Oceania (e.g., Gumerman 1986; Kirch 1984, 1991; Ueki 1990). Some researchers have noted that social change involves more than just population pressures (e.g., Cowgill 1975; Earle 1991; Plog 1986). Population density is an important factor in the complex development of Yapese society whether one labels the resulting societies hierarchical (e.g., Lingenfelter 1975; Small 1995) or heterarchical. Lessa (1950c:50-51) postulates that the "Yapese Empire" was predicated on a large population and Hunter-Anderson and Zan (1996:28) suggest "a system of shifting alliances evolved as an adaptive strategy in response to an increase in population density" in Yap, eventually incorporating the Outer Islands into the Yapese alliance system. Expanding populations burden natural resources (Dumond 1965:320). I propose that a growing population on Yap stressed their agricultural resources and led to a number of cultural changes initiated by the Yapese people: agricultural intensification, coastal land extensions, a rise in cooperation (e.g., alliance) and competition (e.g., warfare), an increase in social complexity with an emphasis on alliances, and the display of prestige-goods. I think the formulation and the maintenance of a *sawei*-like exchange system satisfied the political needs of an increasingly complex Yapese political system by providing additional alliance support and prestige-goods while allowing the economic and political needs of a growing Ulithian population to be realized. Manifestations of these varied phenomena are visible in the archaeological record and play a role in my explanation for the origins of intensive exchange between Yap and Ulithi. Population pressure on the islands can be accommodated in a number of ways. Disregarding island emigration, people can either expand household sizes or increase the number of households. I believe there is evidence for both processes in Mogmog. Evidence for increasing household size is evident in the faunal material density increases found in Mogmog excavations. The rising faunal material densities beneath Mogmog *dayif* mimic the ceramic density increases. Yapese Laminated ceramic densities are greater than any other ceramic type and increase in the fifteenth century at Mog-22, Mog-25, Mog-27, Mog-35, and Mog-53. Mog-25 *sawei* exchange system believe that Yap simply extended its political principles to the Outer Islands and that Gagil's political power was enhanced by incorporating the Outer Island communities into its political realm (Berg 1991:408; Labby 1976:106; Lessa 1950c:45, 1986:36; Lingenfelter 1975:133). Views differ, however, on exactly how Gagil benefited.

Hunter-Anderson and Zan (1996) question the previous conjecture that the Yapese political organization was centralized and stratified and argue more for a heterarchical society, placing more importance on rank. Borrowed from Fried (1967), for Hunter-Anderson and Zan (1996:27), in a "rank society", "kinship is a sine qua non of the social structure; in stratified societies and in states, kinship authority is limited to a narrow social sphere." I agree with their proposal for a more heterarchical political organization during pre-contact times. However, while Outer Island navigation knowledge, *lavalavas*, and shell valuables from *sawei* voyages may not have played a large role in the sociopolitical economy of Yap, I think it is erroneous to discount the ideological (Helms 1993) and political worth of the exchange goods. Valuables that Outer Islanders brought to Yap, which did not all necessarily originate from the Outer Islands, were important artifacts for communicating what Hunter-Anderson and Zan call "alliance worthiness." Outer Island prestige-goods may have included textiles and shell goods early on with the later addition of new goods and services, such as Outer Island labor, important for quarrying and transporting aragonite stone money from Palau (Berg 1992).

Ulithi's Anomalous High Political Position

Ulithi's high intermediary position in the *sawei* exchange system gave it more economic benefits than any other coral island in the "Yapese Alliance System." Ulithi's high rank vis-à-vis its eastern coral island kinsmen is anomalous when one considers that Ulithians are at the western periphery of the Nuclear Micronesian language group dispersal and junior descendants of older pan-Micronesian clans in the east. Lessa (1950a:75-78) recognizes that Ulithi's sibs were intrusive and predominantly from the east (Central Carolines), belonging to what he called macro-sibs, such as Hofalu, Mangolfach, Sawol, and Soflachikh. Mason (1968:318) detects Ulithi's high rank and political posts as a "superficial overlay" derived from its role in the historically-derived chain of command in the "Yapese Empire." In fact, the investiture of a new Outer Island paramount chief (*unga cha*) had to be approved by Gagil chiefs. How then did Ulithians become higher ranked than their ancestors to the east or a "lower status segment of the center" and a "long-distance transformational agent" of Yap (Helms 1993:191)?

Lessa (1986:38) considers that "Ulithi's right to *sawei* from the eastern islands seems to be compensation for its administrative services" resulting from its proximity to Yap and geographical position between Yap and the other Outer Islands. Helms (1993:191) concentrated on the ideological component of the *sawei* system contending that Ulithi's participation in the manufacturing of religious offerings (*lavalavas*) heightened its political position and made it a long-distance transformational agent for Yap. I propose that Ulithi's anomalous high position is also largely a result of its geographical position between Yap and the Outer Islands (see Hage and Harary 1991). Today, these high standings of Gachpar and Ulithi are jokingly downplayed by non-Gachpar Yapese and non-Ulithian Outer Islanders where Gachpar is called "*Hatchepar*," translated to "a lie" in Ulithian and Mogmog is labeled "the island of lies." Without making too much of this, it may refer to the relatively recent imposition of Outer Islanders being told to bring *sawei* to Gachpar, not Ruu', via Mogmog.

Emergence of Laminated Pottery

The emergence of Laminated pottery is significant to Yapese culture history. Laminated ware densities are greater than all the earlier types in Yap and Mogmog excavations. The presence of Laminated pottery is a useful marker for an increase in island interaction on Mogmog. I include the emergence of Laminated pottery in my exchange model because I think it signals an important process in Yap – the intensification of wet-land taro cultivation.

Intoh (1988:123) suggests that the change in Yapese ceramic technology is an adaptive transformation,

> . . . the pottery technology used for the Yapese Laminated ware is well *adapted* to the available resource and environmental conditions. Instead of modifying the clay itself to increase its workability, the whole technology involved in pottery making was altered to *adapt* to the characteristics of the raw clay [emphasis added].

While adapting to an environment is imperative for any society, an adaptive explanation in this particular instance lacks explanatory power by omitting the human motive for relying on a new pot type after using non-laminated Yapese ceramic types for hundreds of years (see Giddens 1995). Intoh (1992), however, does rely on cultural reasons for the importation of Yapese ceramics to Ngulu, an atoll 110 km southwest of Yap. She proposes pots were essential for simmering coconut sap (*lutch*) and detoxifying *Alocasia* taro.

Ceramic pots must have always been adapted to the ceramic environment and Yapese needs. Indeed, unlaminated Yapese ceramic types survived for hundreds of years before the appearance of Laminated pottery. I do not believe access to the necessary ceramic ingredients explains the technological shift to Laminated pottery. I propose that Laminated pots satisfied a new Yapese need that could not be met by the previous pot types. My explanation is similar to that of Butler (1990), who recognized pots as "tools," designed to achieve specific functions in the subsistence pattern changes of the prehistoric peoples of the Mariana

Islands. Examining the physical attributes of Marianas pots, Butler (1990) suggests that the shift from shallow bowls and pans to thicker-walled pots and jars indicates a change in food-processing and cooking practices. Thicker-walled Latte Period pots were more durable and suited for the tasks of "prolonged heating of liquids (boiling and stewing) as well as storage" (Butler 1990:41). Ultimately, the ceramic transition reflected the increasing importance of starchy tubers in the diet of a growing population (Butler 1990:43).

I submit a similar scenario for the emergence of Yapese Laminated earthenware and propose that Laminated pots replaced previous ceramic types because of an intensification in wet-land taro cropping. A growing population intensifying taro cultivation along the coastal fringes of Yap would have required stronger, more durable (thermal resistant) pots than previously required to handle the longer cooking, boiling, and steaming times required to soften taro. The fact that Yapese meals consisted of different foods layered in a single pot may explain why Laminated pots replaced the previous types all over Yap, i.e., there does not appear to be any existing ceramic pot types with specific functions. Intoh (1988, 1990) has shown in her research of Yapese pottery that Laminated pottery is a stronger ware than its predecessors. If indeed thicker-walled Plain ware pots were from an experimental stage before the emergence of Laminated pottery as Intoh (1988:135) suggests, then they may well represent the search for more durable pots necessary in the cooking of taro. In addition, Yapese informants conceded that taro needed more cooking than any of the other traditional foodstuffs. Earth ovens were effective in cooking many Pacific Island starchy vegetables, such as taro (Pollock 1992), but do not appear to have ever been used in Yap (Müller 1917:68). If the intensification of taro cultivation and the adoption of Laminated pottery were the results of a growing population, then Yapese society experienced demographic pressures before intensifying exchange with Ulithi.

Yapese Laminated ceramics found in Mogmog and Gachpar differ significantly. Mogmog pots are larger and their compositional variability considerably greater than those found in Gachpar. These results imply two possibilities: (1) Ulithians requested and received earthenware pots from Gachpar unlike those used by the people of Gachpar and/or (2) Ulithians received pots from exchange partners in other Yapese villages. Ethnohistory from the turn of the twentieth century favors the first possibility. According to Hambruch, Outer Islanders requested and received famous Gitam Village pots from their Gachpar "parents" (Damm 1938:313). Despite the differences in ceramic assemblages between Mogmog and Gachpar, 38 (70%) of the Yapese Laminated potsherds recovered from Mogmog (n=54) have a greater than 10% probability of resembling Laminated ceramics recovered in Gachpar (n=45), implying that a significant number of Mogmog potsherds were likely from Mogmog-Gachpar exchanges.

It is likely the second possibility also had a role in Yap-Ulithi exchange because biological kin ties between the islanders also necessitated exchange. Naturally, these people would also interact and participate in exchanges. Gachpar informants tended to relate *sawei* exchange as exclusive between themselves and the Outer Islanders. However, I was told that a *sawei* relationship could be divided into smaller parts. The more divisions in a relationship, the easier it was to amass items to give to the Outer Islanders when they were ready to return to their islands. On the other hand, Ulithian informants tended to describe interactions as less exclusive and involving people from other villages once *sawei* obligations had been met. Mogmog informants told me they had heard from relatives that several months of coordinated preparations were necessary for *sawei* voyages to Yap, even if you or a close relative were not going to Yap. In other words, despite the prescribed exchange relationships of historic *sawei* practice, many non-*sawei* people were involved and benefited.

> [I]nformal trading is carried on between individuals, in food, turmeric, purses, and combs, even if they do not live in Gagil. All in all, then, the great voyages undertaken to Yap [were] the occasions for much interchange of goods [Lessa 1950c:43].

Sawei halibag (concealed *sawei*) between Outer Islanders and Gagil people undoubtedly took place between Outer Islanders and non-Gagil villages. Determining the role of each possibility in Yap-Ulithi exchange is not a straightforward question primarily because Gachpar obtained its protohistoric pots from other villages. Gachpar's two *suon* villages of Binaw and T'enifar were obligated to manufacture Laminated pots for them during the protohistoric period.

Four hypotheses were offered to account for the demand of larger Yapese Laminated pots on Mogmog in the previous chapter. Larger pot sizes are assumed from thicker rim measurements. If larger rims do indeed signify pots with larger volumes, then the most parsimonious explanation is that besides using the pots to cook for more people, pots had a specialized function in cooking coconut syrup (*lutch*). Unlike previous *Cassis* shell pots, larger clay pots would have allowed for larger batch processing of *lutch*. It would be interesting to compare the size of Ulithian pots with that found in other Yapese villages and Outer Islands and see if the same pattern of larger pots holds in the Outer Islands.

Intensive Island Interaction: A.D. 1400

Seven hundred years after the first recorded appearance of Yapese earthenware in Mogmog, a new ceramic type with greater potsherd densities is recorded. I consider large Yapese ceramic densities in Mogmog archaeological deposits indicative of intense interactions between the people of Yap and Ulithi. Whether the clear rise in the density of Laminated ceramics is attributable to *sawei* exchange is not clear, but my archaeological evidence for the date of intensive interactions supports Berg's (1992:160) fourteenth and fifteenth century estimate for tribute voyages. However, differentiating *sawei*-type

Cantova describes a monarchistic political system for the Western Carolines. Yap heads the entire system and Mogmog leads the other Outer islands:

> It is at Mogmog that there resides the ruler of all these islands. He is called Caschattel. When the boats (Barques) navigate in this gulf, as soon as they come within sight of Mogmog, they lower their sails – these islanders' way of showing their respect for and submission to their ruler [Cantova 1728:214-215].

This clearly resembles the ethnographic literature describing the protocol for a *sawei* fleet when it arrives to Ulithi, just before the final leg to Yap. *Sawei* gifts to Ulithi and later Yap is a classic example of Outer Islanders in a gift (Mauss 1967) or debt (Gosden 1989) economy. In such an economy, Gachpar attempts to acquire as many gift debtors as possible, while the Outer Islanders, despite the *sawei* gifts, are debtors and left in a subordinate position. According to Gregory (1982:19), "gift exchange is a means by which the relations of domination and control are established in a clan-based economy." This sort of exchange establishes a relationship or alliance between the subjects (people) rather than the objects, as seen in commodity exchange of a class-based economy (Gregory 1982:19). It follows that Gachpar's position vis-à-vis the other villages in Yap was high due to its many gift debtors, not only in the Outer Islands, but also within Yap from gift giving Outer Island gifts. This proposal does not contradict Hunter-Anderson and Zan's (1996) argument that the Yap-Outer Island system was ranked, but not stratified; complex, but not centralized.

Emergence of Yapese *Dayif* in Mogmog

As discussed in Chapter VI, Mogmog *dayif* share a similar name, function, and meaning as those in Yap. Mogmog archaeological evidence implies platforms were introduced to Mogmog after the intensification of exchange, post-European contact, and probably no earlier than the seventeenth century. It must be noted, however, that locating buried or re-modeled *dayif* from 1 by 1 m excavation units is difficult, and that as already mentioned disturbed or rebuilt *dayif* after the Second World War complicates answering when *dayif* appeared on Mogmog.

Dayif were powerful symbols indicating the *materialization* of Yapese sociopolitical ideology (see DeMarrais *et al.* 1996). The adoption of these imposing architectural platforms that displayed Yapese power and beliefs indicates the extent to which Ulithi was a lower status segment of the center (Yap) and unlike its culturally immediate neighbors to the east. As mentioned earlier, *dayif* symbolized ownership of property and privileges. One inherited powers invested in the *dayif*. I interpret their construction as a manifestation of competition for power and resources. These features also add meaning to early missionary texts that include commentaries on political and ideological issues within Ulithian society. As mentioned already in Chapter IV, Cantova (1728) was told about the venerated lizard, the evil magicians, and the tyranny on Yap. Myths and legends collected two centuries after Cantova by Müller (1917, 1918) and Lessa (1956, 1962a) on Yap and Ulithi are not contradictory. Lessa (1962b:362) believes that certain myths and especially the threat of magic maintained Outer Island subjugation (see also Alkire 1989:168).

Stone Money

Stone money (*rai* or *fei*) are large discs which served as prestige-goods on Yap and like the *dayif* were materializations of Yapese ideology. Though *dayif* were part of the cultural landscape on both islands, stone money is really only found on Yap. Mogmog has only one Yapese stone money disc; the small disc lies at the gravesite of a Yapese person. Researchers have hypothesized that the inception of stone money from Palau probably dates to the eighteenth century (Gillilland 1975; Hunter-Anderson and Zan 1996; Müller 1917). The Yapese mined stone discs predominantly from Palau, 400 km from Yap; small amounts were also quarried from Guam. As symbols of prestige, stone money cannot be considered currency, or even primitive money. Stone money were valuables used in *mitmit* village exchanges. Gillilland (1975:21) notes, "[t]he growth of the custom of stone money on Yap is a story of a society in transition." This research does not investigate the changing relationship between the Yapese and the Palauans. Fitzpatrick (2001) has recently archaeologically investigated Omis Cave, site of a major Yapese stone money quarry in Palau. Based on three test excavations at Omis Cave, Fitzpatrick suggests that the Yapese workers were subsisting on local shellfish resources, and using architectural features and carbonate debitage to move the stones. The antiquity of Yapese stone quarrying in Palau is not yet known.

Berg (1992:155) suggests that Gachpar's recent acquirement of the exclusive Outer Island tribute forced the two municipalities of Rull and Tomil to unite. Unlike Gagil, the other two municipalities eagerly welcomed European visitors and their new prestige-goods to counterbalance the relatively recent political and economic advantages of Gachpar. Berg (1992:155) adds that stone money from the islands of Palau was introduced to compensate for the shell money (*Spondylus*) monopoly of Gachpar. There is no archaeological or ethnohistoric evidence that I know of to support Berg's suggestion.

Nineteenth Century

In the nineteenth century, a Woleaian native called Kadu supplied much ethnohistoric information while accompanying the Russian Romanzov expedition (1815-1818). Kadu described a complex exchange system in the Carolines, where the principal objects of trade were canoes, cloth, glass, pieces of iron, stones, and turmeric powder. Later in the century, anthropologists, colonial officers, missionaries, and traders also remarked on the presence of a tribute system between the village of Gachpar and the Outer

Islands. War raged between the petty chiefs of several territories in Yap (Lessa 1962b:354).

Yap had a burgeoning population, internecine warfare, and a young trilateral paramount political system, comprising Gagil, Rull, and Tomil. According to Kadu and others, stone money was exclusively for chiefs in the early part of the nineteenth century (Gillilland 1975:21). Even in the 1840s, large stone discs were still rare, and chiefs strove for them, but they became more accessible because iron tools replaced shell tools in the mining and shaping of the disks, and non-Micronesian ships transported the discs to Yap instead of rafts pulled by outrigger canoes. The initial desire for iron developed into the quarrying of monumental stone disks using iron tools.

After the first European traders settled on Yap in 1843 their materials began to play a larger role in Western Carolinian island life and, as Gillilland (1975:5) notes, this "altered the [Yapese] trade and economy in a most dramatic way." Before 1843, European ships were generally met with hostility in Yap and Ulithi. Crews were often killed and ships looted. German trader Alfred Tetens (1958:84) noted in 1867 that the furnishings of dwellings included "earthen jars, wooden bowls, iron pots, fishing nets, weapons, finely woven baskets and mats". One of Cheyne's sailors introduced the first documented epidemic in 1843 (Shineberg 1971:271). From at least this point in time, the population of Yap decreased by more than 90% over the next 100 years (see also Schneider 1974:96-97). Kadu mentions the presence of a European disease on Woleai approximately 30 years earlier (von Chamisso 1986:284).

Traditionally, land gave prestige, power, wealth, and status to the Yapese (Price 1975:9). Following the catastrophic depopulation, prestige-goods, such as stone money from Palau, gained prominence in the reproduction and dynamics of the hierarchical Yapese sociopolitical system. Nicholas Thomas (1996:89) claims that in a prestige-goods system: "[t]he basis for dominance changes from genealogical rank to control over foreign exchange, which is very frequently a source of valuables rather than (or as well as) mundane things." Pearl shells procured from Europeans powered a revitalization of Rull's alliance network and led to a civil war with Gagil in 1867 (Tetens 1958:97).

Depopulation does not appear to have restrained Yap-Ulithi exchange. In fact, it may well have increased it by providing open social positions. With power contentions, rare exotic goods may have supported or replaced part of the genealogical legitimization. Gachpar Village's ability to monopolize locally unavailable prestige-goods enhanced their political position (alliance formation and maintenance) on Yap while the need for exotic prestige items enforced high levels of interregional interaction (see Schortman 1989:59). Hunter-Anderson and Zan (1996:1) argue that Gagil "communicated their worthiness as alliance partners" by "assuming *sawei* obligations" of the Outer Islanders. I think this worthiness was in part communicated by Outer Island prestige-goods early on and later by the addition of other things, such as Outer Island labor for quarrying and transporting stone money from Palau. I suggest that the role of the prestige-good system of Yap increased after German colonization in 1899 when inter-village fighting was arrested. Before that time, Yap was well known for its inter-village warfare. I do not think the massive depopulation created the Yapese prestige-goods system, but it would have been a factor in emphasizing exotic prestige-goods. The permanence of *dayif* were integral in reproducing Yapese society because the process of hereditary transmission was irreparably upset by massive depopulation.

Dalton (1977:201) recognizes a change to fighting with property when colonial powers enforced colonial peace, citing the *moka* and potlatch exchanges as examples.

> With colonial peace lethal fighting stopped, but nonlethal fighting, contests, and rivalries, which aboriginally were confined exclusively to clansmen, affines, trade partners, and other allies, were now extended to former major enemies, whom one killed before the European colonial peacemakers came and with whom, traditionally, one did *not* conduct ceremonial exchanges. ... They were indeed 'fighting with property' because the colonial authorities would no longer allow them to kill enemies [Dalton 1977:201, emphasis in text].

Referring to *kula* exchange, he mentions another point that may be relevant to Yap and the *sawei* exchange system. Dalton (1977:201) adds that colonial peace displaced reciprocity and introduced market trade where people could now travel without the need of aboriginal alliances for protection. A commodity or market-type economic system shifted the emphasis of the subject from gift giving to the objects.

Gachpar Village's ability to control locally unavailable prestige-goods enhanced their political position on Yap while the need for exotic prestige items enforced high levels of interregional interaction (see Schortman 1989:59). Apart from the introduction of new exchange items, European entry in the Pacific did not have a major influence on western Carolinian societies until the nineteenth century when European visits increased. I agree with Berg that a pre-existing Yapese prestige-goods economy took a new form and became more prevalent after European entry in the Pacific. In 1882, Kubary witnessed four hundred Yapese quarrying aragonite to shape into stone money near Koror and noted that important settlements on Yap were provided with stone money. In the nineteenth and twentieth centuries, the tribute became intensive and oppressive with *corvée* labor for gathering copra, quarrying stone disks, and mining phosphate. The command of the fear is exemplified in the following:

> The trader Evan Lewis, who had many dealings with the Yapese and the low islanders since he had a station on

> Lamotrek and had had one on Yap, witnessed these overbearing tactics. He complained about them to Vogilrou, one of the 'landowners' of islands in the low-island region, most particularly Eauripik, and a leader in the Gagil war alliance:
> When the trader Lewis approached Vogilrou and reproached him by asking why he was driving his island children into the ground, Vogilrou replied, "We aren't doing this. Their own deities are ruining them because they have broken the old taboo" [Krämer 1937:83].

The introduction of European iron tools greatly facilitated the quarrying and shaping of stone money. Irish-American trader O'Keefe affected the Yapese prestige-good system by monopolizing the transportation of workers and stone money between Palau and Yap in exchange for copra (dried coconut meat).

Initially, hegemony, power, and force then may have served only limited roles in initiating and maintaining inter-societal exchange relations. Later, when populations in the area began to decline drastically and island cultures underwent unprecedented transformations, ideological hegemony may have played a larger role in maintaining alliance networks and inter-island exchange. Yap had a reputation for its magical arts in controlling weather at least by 1818; "[t]o them is ascribed the destruction of so many boats from Feis [Fais] and Mogemug [Mogmog], nay, even the gradual depopulation of these islands" (von Kotzebue 1821:205). *Youmaching* is the name of the epidemics which struck Ulithi. The Yapese interpreted deaths, canoewrecks, typhoons, and epidemics as their doing because of missed Outer Island payments. Ironically, increased Yapese-Carolinian interaction may have alleviated population pressure problems, quickening the decimation of the island populations through diseases. Intensive ocean voyaging for materials and forming alliances may have helped distribute the new widespread diseases and made the Yapese threat of epidemics for Carolinians who failed to bring tribute more credible.

Much led to the dénouement or demise of the formalized exchange system near the end of the nineteenth century before detailed anthropological descriptions could be made. Lessa (1950b) lists the introduction of Christianity, foreign involvement in natural disaster relief for the Outer Islands, education of Outer Islanders, the shift from native to modern transportation, and increased foreign contact as the major reasons for the disintegration of the empire and the end of tribute voyages. In 1899, the German colonial government forbade the quarrying of stone money in order to enlarge the work-force of German-endorsed labor projects and eliminate island voyaging and O'Keefe's monopoly.

Epistemological Challenge: Integrating Archaeology and Ethnohistory

This section discusses the integration of the archaeological and ethnohistoric records involved in my exchange model. European contact is an important boundary point because not only major cultural transformations ensued, but also because this is when Western Carolinian cultures entered the European ethnohistoric record. The latter did not have a profound effect on the sedimentation of the archaeological record, but it did influence the ethnohistoric record and my methodology for integrating both records. The last 400 years of the exchange history model is a combination of both records. My construction of the pre-contact period relied, but for a few cases, on the archaeological record alone. I did this for the obvious reasons that the European-made ethnohistoric record was more accessible and understandable to me. While I relied little on indigenous oral histories for explaining the archaeological patterns, I did use it to frame the research. In other words, it is the indigenous oral history that led me to investigate Ruu' Village, archaeological deposits beneath the Filsew *pebaey*, and archaeological deposits beneath Mogmog and Gachpar *dayif*.

Protohistoric period interpretations, which depended upon archaeological and European-produced ethnohistoric data, were richer than either record alone. I used both records in a complementary fashion to focus on the problem of change (see La Lone 1982:309). The ethnohistoric record offered context and insights into underlying processes associated with archaeological patterns which could have been interpreted in any number of ways. In addition, the ethnohistoric data from overlapping archaeological times added details of practice and the *mentalités* of the people.

Combining records of processes of different time duration is challenging. Adopting the time duration concept of the *Annales* paradigm allowed for the incorporation of conflicting data interpretations. *Événements* (events) in historic records can be integrated into the longer-termed cultural structures of the archaeological record, such as agricultural and exchange intensification. Wilson (1993:22) calls these macroprocesses. They can operate across a number of generations before visible in the archaeological record. Conflicting ethnohistoric events and archaeological structures need not necessarily be contradictory for two reasons: (1) contrasting events could be those of a longer archaeological time-duration and (2) a contrasting event could be representative of a contemporaneous structure not yet identified in the archaeological record. Therefore, because the units of archaeological moments are larger than the resolution of ethnohistoric units, testing is not possible.

In the absence of contemporaneous ethnohistories, I relied mostly on the archaeological record for interpreting the past. Similar to Gosden (1996:165), I consider myths, histories, genealogies,

> . . . partial and distorted accounts of the past made to shore up particular interests and undermine others, in exactly the same way as other histories are, but they also contain information about past events and the cultural schemes through which events were appreciated.

The integration of mytho-history in my interpretations about the past is only as accurate as my understanding of the texts. Despite these challenges, I believe this rich data set of ideology is a potential source worthy of closer investigation by archaeologists in collaboration with ethnohistorians and native peoples.

The materialization of Yapese ideology in the Mogmog stone platforms was crucial in identifying the subsequent *mentalité* that followed the increased interaction between Yap and Ulithi. The general meaning of *dayif* and their prerogatives are not found in the archaeological record, but found in the oral historic record concerning the prerogatives invested in these architectural features. However, despite the obvious presence of Yapese ideology on Mogmog, a distinctively Ulithian ideology also coexisted, as evidenced by its varying mytho-history and twentieth century ethnographic record.

In general, the themes of the mytho-histories (Lessa 1961, 1962a, 1980) about Yap-Ulithi relationships are about the unequal relationships between the two peoples. Gachpar is a high place where Ulithians were meant to bring tribute to affirm their alliance bonds, ones as strong as that between parents and their children. To fail to do so, bid the wrath of powerful Yapese magicians and ancestral spirits who could harm the island and its people. To this day, mishaps, such as sudden deaths, are often explained as results of transgressions by Outer Islanders against their Yapese "parents".

I have integrated archaeology and mytho-history to investigate if exchange was always an exclusive practice of the people of Gachpar. I integrated mytho-history with archaeology to determine the timing for when Gachpar Village began heading the *sawei* exchange system (see Figures 46 and 47). The construction of the Filsew *pebaey* supposedly coincided with the annihilation of Ruu' Village and the beginning of Gachpar hosting Outer Island visitors to Yap. The interpretation of the myth is vital in determining if Gachpar took over a formalized exchange system or if they turned it into one. I suggest Gachpar appropriated the system at a time when interactions between Yap and Ulithi were already intensive. The mytho-historical record implied Ruu' threatened the ancestral sanctity of a high ranking village. Perhaps Ruu''s prestige-good economy and alliances with the Outer Islands allowed it to do so. More archaeological investigations and detailed comparisons of chemical characterizations of ceramic sherds found in Ruu' and the Outer Islands might give a clearer picture.

Summary

The role of exchange between Yap and Ulithi evolved in both societies. Initially, at 1300 years B.P., exchange between both island societies was probably reciprocal and infrequent. Ulithians benefited more in economic ways given their islands' relative resource limitations. In addition, they counted on Yap to serve as a source of relief after unpredictable natural disasters disturbed their environment. Ulithian exchange had minor and peripheral implications for Yap at this time. Early chemical and typological attributes of ceramics in Gachpar Village and Mogmog are dissimilar and suggest a pattern unlike the formalized Gachpar-held exchange pattern recorded from the ethnographic and ethnohistoric records. My pre-contact interpretations rely mostly on the archaeological record.

Early unlaminated ceramics found in Mogmog were not common in Gachpar. Given that the early ware is before the intense Yap-Ulithi interactions with Laminated ware, it is likely that Mogmog obtained its pots from villages other than Gachpar. The greater variability in the Mogmog Laminated ceramics compositional space differed from that in Gachpar. This suggests that even in the last 600 years of Laminated ware production Mogmog was likely obtaining pots from more than just its Gachpar "parents".

In the fifteenth century A.D., however, exchange practices between both islands became remarkably different. Exchange between Yap, Ulithi, and the other Outer Islands now played a significant role in the sociopolitical economy of both Yap and Ulithi. Ironically, the Yapese threatened their Outer Island "children" with typhoons and other disasters if they did not bring tribute. In addition, Ulithi became the intermediary between Yap and the other Outer Islands; in so doing, it received an increase in political rank and became recognized as a sacred island. A number of factors were probably involved to bring about this particular historical trajectory, but I depend primarily on Yapese population pressures because of the data on hand. I agree with Hunter-Anderson and Zan's (1996) proposal that Outer Island support was significant in displaying alliance worthiness, however, I do not dismiss the considerable role that shell and other valuables played in legitimating rank and prestige distinctions, regardless of whether the Yapese middle-range society was hierarchical or heterarchical.

Ruu' Village sites and ceramics require more investigation to examine the Gachpar and Mogmog oral historical contention that it held an exchange system with visiting Outer Islanders before Gachpar. If the charcoal sample beneath the Gachpar stone *dayif* of Filsew, the ancient site of where a meeting house was built for the Outer Islanders, predates Gachpar's take-over of the exchange system, it is likely that the system was already intense before Gachpar headed it based on the timing of the large Yapese Laminated ceramic densities on Mogmog.

Despite the difficulty in identifying a more exact date for the initial intensification of exchange, it appears associated with the presence of Yapese Laminated pottery on Mogmog. On Yap, I suggest the emergence of Yapese Laminated pottery signals the intensification of wetland taro cultivation. These more durable pots were neede for cooking taro.

Chapter VIII

Conclusions

This study heeded the call for a *rapprochement* of anthropology and history (e.g., Biersack 1991; Thomas 1995, 1996) by integrating archaeology and ethnohistory to construct a diachronic model of exchange between Yap and Ulithi. Like other archaeological works before it (e.g., Egloff 1978; Irwin 1985; Kirch 1986; Lilley 1988), this research investigated the archaeological past of a historically well known exchange system in the Pacific, and confirmed Biersack's (1991:13, emphasis in text) contention:

> Given the existence of long-distance trade and *kula*-like "rings," barter across cultural borders (Thomas [1992]), and interethnic marriages prior to contact, the possibility that Pacific societies have *always* participated in regional systems, surviving "only by changing in interaction with one another through time" (Gewertz 1983:2), should be considered (Trigger 1984:284-86)."

This research depended on archaeological data to explore the development of inter-island relations before European contact and recorded observations of this so-called "traditional" exchange system. Previous research depended on ethnographic works with informant recollections about the formalized and intensive *sawei* practice, treating the inter-island exchange relations as if they had been detached from time (see also Thomas 1996). As other present and past exchange systems, interactions between Yap and Ulithi were dynamic, not static or timeless.

This research integrated archaeology and ethnohistory to construct an exchange history model of the Western Caroline Islands. Despite the antiquity of relations between Yap and Ulithi and the decline of their past interactive behaviors, the combination of archaeology and history supplied essential quantifiable evidence and contextual information crucial for richer constructions of how people lived in the past (but see Alkire 1989:6; Lessa 1962b:335). I relied primarily upon Yapese earthenware potsherds from Gachpar and Mogmog archaeological contexts to signify interaction between Yap and Ulithi for tracking the intensity of interaction through time. In addition, chemical characterization analysis of ceramic potsherds allowed me to investigate the variability between the undecorated Laminated earthenware assemblages that were made for approximately 600 years, and were prevalent in the archaeological Yap-Ulithi exchange record.

Archaeological investigations suggest a 1300 year interaction history between Yap and Ulithi. Exchange interactions between these two islands are undoubtedly hundreds of years older given the Yapese artifacts in earlier contexts on Fais. Based on typological mineralogical and chemical attributes, I conclude that the majority of the ceramics and lithics found on Mogmog originate from Yap. Early Yapese earthenware in Mogmog was unlike that found in Gachpar. In addition, clay provenance work suggested that for the most recent 600 years of Laminated earthenware production, clay sources originated from non-Gachpar clay sources because they contain Yap Formation montmorillonite clays.

I propose that Yapese population pressures, resource limitations, and history played significant roles in the development of Yap-Ulithi exchange relations. Exchange between Yap and Ulithi existed at least seven centuries before the population and exchange increases were detected on Mogmog. Taro intensification, the emergence of Laminated earthenware, and the beginning of extensive coastal land-fill extensions preceded the intensification of Yap-Ulithi exchange. Before European contact, the emergence of a stronger new Laminated earthenware technology is suggested as an adaptive response to the additional cooking demands of taro after the food production strategy was intensified.

I submit that Ulithian population growth followed the intensification of relations with the Yapese, i.e., unlike the Yapese population, it grew when it had the means to do so. After the intensification of exchange and the emergence of Yapese Laminated pottery in Mogmog, assemblages resembled more those of Gachpar. There was considerable overlap in the chemical variability of Laminated earthenware from both villages. Nonetheless, compositional and rim thickness differences were recognized between the potsherd assemblages of Gachpar and Ulithi. Variance between contemporaneous Yapese ceramic assemblages of Gachpar and Mogmog do not necessarily indicate the existence of non-Gachpar exchange partners. Still, the most parsimonious explanation is that Ulithians had exchange relations with non-Gachpar Yapese people before and during *sawei* practice despite oral history to the contrary. Despite cultural dissimilarities, the one night sailing distance enabled Ulithian society to not only be part of the Yapese sphere of influence, but also to act as intermediary between Yap and coral islands extending 1300 km to the east. The Yap-Ulithi exchange relationship benefited the political economy of both islands in important ways.

The post-contact period is a time fraught with change due to European-Western Carolinian interactions. Contact-induced transformations affected both sides and Western Carolinians were not "passive objects of their own history" (Sahlins 1988:2; Thomas 1991:124; Wilson 1993). Nevertheless,

European-induced circumstances did force the Yapese and Carolinians to react to the massive depopulation and subsequent colonization of their islands in the nineteenth century. Dalton (1977) noted that a common response to colonial-imposed peace was fighting with property and the intensification of prestige-goods economies. Thomas (1996:89) also maintains that in a prestige-goods economy "[t]he basis for dominance changes from genealogical rank to control over foreign exchange." I believe European presence and incorporation in the intensive exchange system between Yap and the Outer Islands added new exotic items to a pre-existing (*sawei*) clan-based gift giving economy. Massive depopulation on Yap and elsewhere did not apparently halt the exchange, instead it became a vehicle for maintaining and creating alliances in the politically competitive environment of Yap. The materialization of Yapese ideology, in the form of stone *dayif* and money, increased in importance when Yapese population was reduced by approximately 90 percent.

Gachpar Village's ability to monopolize control of locally unavailable prestige-goods enhanced their political position on Yap while the need for exotic prestige items enforced high levels of interregional interaction (see Schortman 1989:59). Hunter-Anderson and Zan (1996) have recently argued that Gagil "communicated their worthiness as alliance partners" by "assuming *sawei* obligations" of the Outer Islanders. I think this worthiness was in part communicated by Outer Island gift debts early on and later by the addition of new items, such as Outer Island labor for quarrying and transporting stone money from Palau.

The ideology of the exchange relations that played a role in maintaining exchange relations during the protohistoric is manifested in the archaeological record, notably in the form of *dayif*. Early twentieth century Yapese oral history was useful as structural context (*mentalité*) of inter-island relations for archaeological remains from more or less contemporaneous times. Relations then that had once begun as infrequent gift giving were developed by the Yapese and Ulithians into a formal and intensive exchange system. In the face of depopulation, the Yap-Outer Island interactions persisted and associated *sawei* rituals and behavior continued. The formal and intensive island interactions system satisfied ritual and the socio-political alliance needs in the unstable nineteenth century competitive Yapese political scene. The interactive system may well have done so for some time before also.

In the research of the interaction history between Yap and Ulithi, other related discoveries have also been offered. Settlement for Gachpar Village has been pushed back to cal A.D. 20 – 380. The earliest settlement date for Mogmog was found to be cal A.D. 620 – 770 from charcoal associated with Yapese Plain earthenware sherds. An early date of cal 1530 – 1160 B.C. was rejected because the turtle bone was recovered from a culturally sterile context in a disturbed unit and only the inorganic carbon of the bone was dated.

I used an Annales-type paradigm that relied on events and structures of different duration to integrate ethnohistoric events into archaeological patterns. The transformation of cultural structures and events originated from the dialectic between structure and agency (Bourdieu 1977; Giddens 1979). The archaeological record contained evidence of medium-term processes of ideologies, ceramic technology innovation, crop intensification, demographic pressure, and interaction increases. The ethnohistoric record provided the richest source for events and structures in the post-contact period ranging from Carolinian voyages to ritual performances. Multiple structures were found to coexist and operate simultaneously in the practice and transformation of Western Carolinian culture. The different synchronicities of the two different data sets call for cautious integration. Regarding the combination of indigenous oral history and archaeological remains, I think oral history serves well for formulating questions, rather than testing the validity of indigenous history.

Prehistoric Pacific Exchange Systems

Archaeologists in other regions of the Pacific have argued for major discontinuities between past and present exchange behaviors (e.g., Egloff 1978; Kirch 1991; Lauer1971; Lilley 1988). If the relatively recent archaeological work into Melanesian exchange systems (Kirch 1988; Lilley 1988) teaches us anything, it is that the ethnographically documented patterns are but the latest episodes in long trajectories of exchange histories. This lesson also applies to the exchange between Yap and Ulithi. In fact, the equivalence of the date of Mogmog settlement and the appearance of exotic pottery presents a difficulty in not knowing if the exotic sherds belonged to Ulithians. I am inclined to believe the latter because of the earlier exchange evidence in Fais. But the question remains: what was the ethnicity of the people using 1400 year old Yapese ceramics on Mogmog?

Despite showing that the archaeological record has much to contribute to the exchange history of regional systems, comparing exchange systems from other parts of the Pacific is insightful. Graves et al. (1990) suggest early dispersed populations practiced much interaction for economic reasons in the Mariana Islands. Of course, the water distances between the islands of the Mariana Archipelago are considerably closer than those of the Caroline Islands. Later, when the population was higher and the settlements were more contiguous, exchange became more regional and inter-island exchange decreased. Instead, Yap-Ulithi exchange relations appear to be one of simple and infrequent exchange. Yapese ceramic densities indicate the Yap-Ulithi exchange system only intensified in the fifteenth century.

Kirch (1991:151) argues the *kula* exchange system is a relatively recent development. Kirch (1991:155-156) maintains:

> Throughout the last 2000 years of Melanesian prehistory, there is evidence of gradual or episodic retraction or reduction in the geographic scale of exchange networks, accompanied by subsequent increases in the magnitude or intensity of exchange within these progressively smaller systems.

Without more archaeological evidence from the other Carolinian coral islands, it is too early to say whether this is a trend in the Caroline Islands. However, unlike Melanesia, specialist potters, traders or middlemen and the abandonment of pottery-making did not ensue in the Western Carolines. Indeed, through time the archaeological and ethnohistoric records appear to suggest intensification in inter-island exchange. This work has only investigated island societies separated by 170 km. More research into the exchange histories of islands surrounding Yap is required.

When discussing the prestige-goods system of western Polynesia, Thomas (1996:94) rejects the supposition that Tonga, Samoa, and Fiji participated in such an exchange system for some 2000 years based on archaeological and traditional evidence. Kirch (1984) has shown that the Tonga-Samoa-Fiji prestige-good network is a late development associated with the militaristic expansion of the protohistoric Tongan chiefdom. Without more exchange magnitude data from other coral islands within the ethnohistoric interaction sphere of Yap, not much more can be said about the regional exchange characteristics and their change through time. At this stage in the research, it appears that the intensification and formalization of exchange behaviors between Yap and its neighboring Caroline Islands also appear to be late developments.

Future Work

While this research contributed answers to questions about the history of exchange between Gachpar and Mogmog, many questions remain on the regional aspect of exchange between Yap and its neighboring islands. Much archaeological work is necessary on the islands in the Pacific region that interacted with Yap for a better understanding of the development of exchange not only in the region, but also of Yap and Ulithi. This section ties together some of the suggestions I have made throughout this work and addresses future directions for research in this area.

Ulithi's archaeological record is replete with evidence from Yapese interactions. Future work will involve investigating the role of other Yapese villages and their effect on the exchange system. Specifically, the characterizations of different Yapese village ceramic assemblages need to be compared with that of Ulithi and other coral islands to examine variability and exchange issues. From the preliminary survey of Yapese clays, we know that the production of ceramics and other goods did not simply involve Gachpar Village. More work on the Yapese raw materials and their distribution in the ceramics of the archaeological record will allow for a larger perspective on exchange relations between Yap and its neighboring islands and tie more securely ceramics to their Yapese clay sources. Additional work in the archaeological deposits of other Micronesian islands, particularly Carolinian atolls, is necessary not only to contribute to historical models of island interaction, but also to add to the culture history of these understudied islands. In addition, long-term histories of exchange relations will be available for comparisons with other Oceanic systems.

Research methodologies and laboratory procedures in chemical characterization studies need to be comparable in order to match exchange magnitudes and chemical characterizations. The potential of matching different data sets was illustrated in our tying a glazed corrugated sherd recovered from Gachpar to Dr. Sinopoli's Filipino Dragon Jar data set. I have shown that ceramics were not inert in their different Western Carolinian island depositional contexts. More geochemical work into the relationship between chemical abundances and the manufacture, use, and burial of ceramics will lead to more accurate data and archaeological interpretations. Ceramics represent only a part of past exchange practice in the Caroline Islands. Research into other artifact types such as lithics, shell, and glass will provide other data sets for comparison and integration into models of exchange.

Indigenous mytho-histories make up an abundant untapped source of past processes and events. Much oral history has been collected by previous anthropologists. I have used such information sparingly because of the nature of the data and my unfamiliarity with Yapese and Ulithian language. I think indigenous oral histories can contribute invaluable hypotheses for investigation. General insights about the present and the past can be gained from comparative analyses of myths and legends. Collaborative efforts between archaeologists, ethnohistorians, and native peoples to explore and analyze these texts would contribute to our understanding of the historical trajectories of exchange systems and societies in the recent past.

The primary research goal of this study was to construct a diachronic model integrating archaeology and ethnohistory. Interaction between Yap and Ulithi, members of a larger system which once extended 1300 km, was found to be dynamic. A conjunctive approach integrating history and archaeology is not new in the Pacific. Sahlins (1992:1), for example, has called the overlap of archaeology and history "a privileged intellectual space." In conclusion, the combination of archaeology and history supplies essential quantifiable evidence and contextual information crucial for richer constructions of the past. Used in a dialectical fashion, these partial records contribute significant elements to understanding how historic Yap-Ulithi exchange fits into the long-term context of exchange.

Exchange is central and vital in the lifeways of island peoples and permeates all aspects of island life. This research into the past inter-cultural exchange relations between Yap and Ulithi has shown how island interaction is as old as the island settlements themselves. Regardless of population sizes, cultures, and the distance between islands, interaction and exchange persisted. In describing the 1300 year exchange history of the Western Carolines before the ethnographic present, I have shown that the interactive behaviors between Yap and Ulithi changed through time and were never static or in a "traditional state." Yap-Ulithi exchange as Thomas and others have argued for other cultural practices was not detached from time.

Appendix A: AMS Radiocarbon Determinations

Anid	Location	$\delta^{13}C$ (‰)	^{14}C age (year B.P.)	68.2% cal B.C./A.D.	95.4% cal B.C./A.D.
AA-21194	Mog-13-IV/3	-26.3	1,059±51	890 (0.17) 920 940 (0.83) 1020	860 (1.00) 1050
♣AA-25707	Mog-13-VI	-4.8	❖ 887±70 ☆ 1,429±54	1040 (1.00) 1220	1020 (1.00) 1260
♦AA-21195	Mog-13-VI	-23.1	❖ 3,103±71 ☆ 3,645±55	1500 (0.02) 1490 B.C. 1450 (0.98) 1260 B.C.	1530 (1.00) 1160 B.C.
✶AA-22311	Mog-22-III/2	-26.5	420±37	1430 (1.00) 1485	1410 (0.92) 1520 1580 (0.08) 1630
✶AA-24016	Mog-22-III/2	-26.3	334±43	1480 (0.34) 1530 1550 (0.66) 1640	1460 (1.00) 1650
AA-21202	Mog-22-V/2	-26.1	1,302±46	660 (1.00) 770	640 (1.00) 820
AA-21192	Mog-22-V/2	-27.6	1,305±45	660 (1.00) 770	640 (1.00) 820
AA-21193	Mog-25-VII	-29.8	546±46	1310 (0.43) 1350 1380 (0.57) 1430	1290 (1.00) 1440
AA-21201	Mog-27-III	-26.1	505±45	1398 (1.00) 1442	1310 (0.17) 1360 1380 (0.83) 1470
AA-21199	Mog-32-IV/4	-27.6	1,054±47	890 (0.12) 920 950 (0.88) 1020	880 (1.00) 1040
✶AA-21197	Mog-35-XVI/2	-27.3	404±50	1430 (0.87) 1520 1600 (0.13) 1620	1420 (1.00) 1640
AA-21196	Mog-35-XVII	-26.4	742±46	1235 (1.00) 1283	1180 (0.97) 1310 1360 (0.03) 1380
AA-21212	Mog-39-VI/2	-26.3	1,345±40	640 (0.99) 710 750 (0.01) 760	620 (1.00) 770
✧AA-21215	Mog-45-III/5	-25.0	100±38	1690 (0.27) 1730 1810 (0.73) 1930	1675 (0.31) 1750 1800 (0.69) modern
AA-21213	Mog-53-V/2	-26.0	470±38	1414 (1.00) 1447	1400 (1.00) 1480
✶AA-21204	C36-06-I/5	-26.4	362±45	1460 (0.56) 1520 1570 (0.44) 1630	1440 (1.00) 1640
AA-21203	C36-16-II	-26.6	1,825±66	90 (0.97) 250 300 (0.03) 320	20 (1.00) 380
✶AA-21214	C36-22.1-II/2	-25.1	257±38	1520 (0.35) 1570 1630 (0.53) 1670 1770 (0.12) 1800	1510 (0.81) 1680 1740 (0.19) 1800
AA-21211	C36-27-III/12	-26.7	1,456±40	560 (1.00) 640	530 (1.00) 670
✶AA-21210	C36-33-I/5	-27.5	317±38	1510 (1.00) 1640	1470 (1.00) 1650
AA-21209	C36-33-I/13	-25.1	504±38	1405 (1.00) 1436	1310 (0.10) 1350 1380 (0.90) 1460
AA-21208	C36-33-I/19	-28.7	1,037±59	890 (0.14) 920 940 (0.86) 1040	880 (1.00) 1160
AA-21200	C36-75.6-III	-25.7	542±46	1310 (0.38) 1350 1390 (0.62) 1430	1290 (1.00) 1440
✶AA-21205	C36-77-I/9	-27.9	258±44	1520 (0.41) 1580 1620 (0.45) 1670 1770 (0.14) 1800	1490 (0.80) 1680 1740 (0.20) 1810
✶AA-21216	C36-77-I/10	-26.7	335±62	1480 (1.00) 1640	1440 (1.00) 1660
AA-21207	C36-83.1-I/7	-26.1	842±54	1060 (0.05) 1080 1120 (0.95) 1260	1040 (1.00) 1270
AA-21198	C36-83.1-I/14	-27.0	658±46	1270 (0.52) 1320 1350 (0.48) 1390	1270 (1.00) 1400
AA-21206	C36-83.2-II	-27.3	550±45	1310 (0.46) 1350 1380 (0.54) 1430	1290 (1.00) 1440

Symbol Legend: ♣ Parrot fish palette. ♦ Turtle plastron bone fragment. ☆ Atmospheric radiocarbon date calibration based on Stuiver and Brazuinas (1993). ❖ Marine radiocarbon age. ✶ Warning: Calibrated date may extend out of range. ✧ Warning: Calibrated date probably out of range.

All of the sample materials were analyzed at the NSF Arizona AMS Facility at the University of Arizona. The dates are calibrated with the OxCal v2.18 software program using the Gröningen (van der Plicht 1993) 1986 calibration curve.

Appendix B: Instrumental Neutron Activation Analysis Data

ANID	MATERIAL	ISLAND	LOCATION	AS	LA	LU	ND	SM	U	YB	CE	CO	CR	CS	EU	FE	HF	NI	RB	SB
CHD001	POTTERY	YAP	C28-ST3.03 (40-44)	0.0000	[illegible].1626	0.2235	12.7626	3.3457	0.0000	1.5778	11.8856	78.1341	2144.5806	2.3212	1.1949	134982.0	3.3112	911.25	10.00	0.0000
CHD002	POTTERY	CHUUK	TKFE-1-TP3	86.2822	3[illegible].7498	0.2256	45.9333	12.2806	51.6474	1.7811	70.7458	27.5536	585.6464	0.0000	2.8408	62271.5	10.5427	103.04	0.00	10.8662
CHD003	POTTERY	CHUUK	TKFE-2-W4	75.0803	2[illegible].8128	0.6746	35.5820	9.8467	38.1788	2.3323	65.5591	47.9771	1347.5042	0.0000	2.4365	93649.5	8.9001	195.92	0.00	4.1838
CHD004	POTTERY	POHNPEI	POC3-1-DPK-227.41	29.1272	[illegible].3438	0.5439	55.5020	14.4094	8.7354	3.1460	116.5944	106.1348	876.7119	0.0000	4.6389	130924.4	10.0066	237.85	14.66	1.6419
CHD005	POTTERY	POHNPEI	POC3-1-DPK-227.26	46.6617	[illegible].6996	0.4491	92.2354	21.1692	16.7100	3.0764	205.0295	26.7264	148.7214	0.0000	6.7710	81232.7	17.5315	137.55	0.00	3.4338
CHD006	POTTERY	POHNPEI	POC3-1-DPK-227.210	75.7527	164.6054	0.7540	81.7643	17.0023	34.1693	2.3017	129.6257	29.4010	1714.7116	0.0000	4.6993	86248.6	10.1790	157.70	0.00	3.5919
CHD007	POTTERY	POHNPEI	POC3-1-DPK-227.229	37.3484	1[illegible]1.9610	0.2590	165.1516	31.2615	12.6598	2.6710	328.7215	36.6707	402.5815	0.0000	9.3139	47475.8	11.4549	153.13	0.00	0.9747
CHD008	POTTERY	POHNPEI	POC3-1-DPK-215.30	45.7080	[illegible]4.5411	0.7291	59.1575	13.9258	4.0024	4.2145	119.8196	90.5912	460.8252	0.0000	4.7425	199793.4	11.1423	195.85	0.00	0.0000
CHD009	POTTERY	POHNPEI	POC3-1-DPK-211.16	0.0000	[illegible]7.7076	0.9282	62.6935	14.7504	3.2948	6.0052	103.4707	70.6067	369.9533	0.0000	5.1622	173704.3	10.5089	201.91	0.00	0.0000
CHD010	POTTERY	POHNPEI	WASAU-8-I/1	0.0000	[illegible]9.5766	0.4726	76.7957	18.1182	4.1246	3.1629	156.8458	80.0101	672.7627	0.0000	6.2357	178033.3	12.0011	140.01	0.00	0.0000
CHD011	POTTERY	POHNPEI	WASAU-9-I/1	0.0000	48.1440	0.8200	58.8430	16.5993	3.4833	5.9222	130.4334	93.1530	521.5046	0.0000	6.1573	197768.4	11.5403	161.63	0.00	0.0000
CHD012	POTTERY	POHNPEI	WASAU-10-I/1	15.2847	53.4775	0.8131	65.4021	14.5437	5.0155	4.8019	118.8343	90.4773	451.3074	0.0000	5.0058	197708.9	11.3932	166.55	0.00	0.0000
CHD013	POTTERY	PALAU	AIRAI VIEW HOTEL 40-70CM	6.6578	1.4205	0.1685	0.0000	1.1039	1.8570	1.1542	2.7900	11.2640	490.6477	0.0000	0.3108	38698.7	2.1545	0.00	0.00	0.0000
CHD014	POTTERY	PALAU	AIRAI VIEW HOTEL 40-70CM	9.2047	1.7394	0.2796	0.0000	1.3973	3.9703	1.4320	3.0179	9.5630	507.7573	0.0000	0.2769	51670.5	2.3185	0.00	0.00	0.0000
CHD015	POTTERY	PALAU	AIRAI VIEW HOTEL 40-70CM	3.3911	1.4424	0.1810	0.0000	1.1054	2.5595	1.4076	3.4864	11.2642	485.2768	0.0000	0.3689	37857.0	2.4388	0.00	0.00	0.0000
CHD016	POTTERY	PALAU	AIRAI VIEW HOTEL 40-70CM	6.6634	1.7037	0.2051	0.0000	1.3494	4.5041	1.4253	4.2475	9.3360	488.2059	0.0000	0.3925	52243.6	2.3791	0.00	0.00	0.0000
CHD017	POTTERY	PALAU	AIRAI VIEW HOTEL 40-70CM	9.3529	1.8282	0.2436	0.0000	1.3231	4.6206	1.3861	3.6701	8.9143	489.0665	0.0000	0.3750	58449.8	2.6169	0.00	0.00	0.0000
CHD018	POTTERY	PALAU	AIRAI VIEW HOTEL 40-70CM	11.3777	1.6712	0.1572	0.0000	0.7588	2.0250	1.0014	4.1919	16.0117	449.0801	0.9318	0.2357	54568.6	2.6198	0.00	0.00	0.0000
CHD019	POTTERY	PALAU	AIRAI VIEW HOTEL 40-70CM	0.0000	3.6457	0.4747	5.5603	2.1845	0.0000	3.1875	8.8763	19.0476	205.5829	0.0000	0.8306	34357.1	2.4389	0.00	0.00	0.0000
CHD020	POTTERY	PALAU	AIRAI VIEW HOTEL 40-70CM	7.9022	2.7372	0.4838	8.0351	2.4899	1.5671	3.1154	7.8533	19.4015	426.4617	0.6976	0.8834	39418.1	2.5889	0.00	0.00	0.0000
CHD021	POTTERY	PALAU	AIRAI VIEW HOTEL 40-70CM	5.9719	3.1893	0.4034	0.0000	2.4845	5.9211	2.3413	4.9594	11.6291	429.1047	0.6912	0.7202	33989.4	2.4443	55.47	0.00	0.0000
CHD022	POTTERY	PALAU	AIRAI VIEW HOTEL 40-70CM	5.9900	3.1044	0.3857	9.7858	2.4420	6.4910	2.4276	6.4404	11.9608	418.1910	0.5780	0.7294	35391.8	2.4372	43.71	0.00	0.0000
CHD023	POTTERY	PALAU	AIRAI VIEW HOTEL 40-70CM	0.0000	3.2323	0.4177	5.5919	2.7855	7.8688	2.2787	7.6081	8.6400	525.8109	0.5118	0.7626	40759.7	2.7709	0.00	0.00	0.0000
CHD024	POTTERY	PALAU	AIRAI VIEW HOTEL 40-70CM	4.5189	3.0849	0.5056	8.8813	2.7874	9.3640	2.5183	8.3461	7.6505	518.9342	0.0000	0.6979	40835.0	2.6224	0.00	0.00	0.0000
CHD025	POTTERY	PALAU	AIRAI VIEW HOTEL 40-70CM	6.4021	1.4940	0.2364	0.0000	1.3326	3.8172	1.5739	4.6609	11.0599	484.0018	0.0000	0.4572	49315.9	2.2872	0.00	0.00	0.0000
CHD026	POTTERY	GUAM	GUAM, BARA-TUMON T-1@200CMBS	21.3440	4.5388	0.3563	6.3673	2.0948	3.9314	1.9969	10.5283	12.3601	208.9940	4.4749	0.6875	54313.4	2.2816	0.00	5.07	0.7236
CHD027	POTTERY	GUAM	GUAM, BARA-TUMON T-1@200CMBS	14.9351	5.2850	0.2930	9.1183	2.5092	3.4422	1.9031	9.2276	7.9318	108.9742	3.7273	0.7547	35633.4	2.0909	0.00	0.00	0.6079
CHD028	POTTERY	GUAM	GUAM, TOMEN MALESSO SURFACE	0.0000	5.3463	0.5389	9.0111	2.9486	0.7870	3.0700	11.0483	58.8061	929.8217	0.4085	0.9910	73986.8	2.0880	154.38	15.50	0.2437
CHD029	POTTERY	GUAM	GUAM, TOMEN MALESSO SURFACE	0.0000	4.5915	0.3677	6.9275	1.8858	0.0000	2.3794	6.6720	20.2181	238.6626	1.3794	0.6671	56745.8	4.4874	0.00	19.35	0.3019
CHD030	POTTERY	GUAM	GUAM, TOMEN MALESSO SURFACE	4.6247	10.1819	0.5889	12.0908	4.5286	1.5659	4.2977	20.0448	42.7937	895.9977	0.8513	1.5468	76829.9	3.1031	67.83	15.38	0.0000
CHD031	POTTERY	GUAM	GUAM, TOMEN MALESSO SURFACE	0.0000	6.5138	0.2426	9.9045	2.5687	0.0000	1.6417	13.8545	31.7011	233.8165	0.6958	0.9081	79826.0	1.9050	50.25	44.83	0.0000
CHD032	POTTERY	GUAM	GUAM, TOMEN MALESSO SURFACE	0.0000	13.7529	1.0146	21.5092	7.4604	1.3750	6.6682	21.2041	50.1792	412.1739	1.0357	2.3282	60211.1	2.2102	0.00	11.13	0.0000
CHD033	POTTERY	GUAM	GUAM, TOMEN MALESSO SURFACE	0.0000	10.5968	0.5389	13.7546	4.5383	2.0822	3.7015	18.4489	49.4990	620.1386	1.5489	1.4295	71494.9	3.0909	0.00	21.08	0.5259
CHD034	POTTERY	GUAM	GUAM, TOMEN MALESSO SURFACE	0.0000	22.7648	1.8660	31.5403	11.6523	1.4172	12.7753	21.5045	41.0942	330.9974	0.8125	4.2692	67853.3	2.2099	87.67	27.65	0.3191
CHD035	POTTERY	GUAM	GUAM, TOMEN MALESSO SURFACE	8.1008	8.9756	0.3091	10.9887	2.6119	2.0837	1.7985	13.1198	27.1213	493.6343	0.5637	0.7822	84306.5	2.9393	0.00	26.70	0.4342
CHD036	POTTERY	GUAM	GUAM, TARAGUE BEACH I/I 0-2.5CMB	7.6400	7.3594	0.4823	9.3614	2.7008	2.0541	2.6485	11.6242	22.9732	411.3127	9.2016	0.8806	92194.6	2.5824	0.00	0.00	0.9750
CHD037	POTTERY	GUAM	GUAM, TARAGUE BEACH I/I 0-2.5CMB	0.0000	14.4347	0.6776	17.2592	5.5889	1.8183	4.7991	28.5860	31.7269	418.8463	10.3041	1.8364	92974.1	3.1857	0.00	0.00	0.0000
CHD038	POTTERY	GUAM	GUAM, 1992, SURFACE COLLECTION	0.0000	13.3293	0.4764	15.5569	4.9148	2.0796	3.6093	27.9257	55.4631	559.1609	1.5914	1.6029	79883.0	2.1602	0.00	17.94	0.5150
CHD039	POTTERY	GUAM	GUAM-3, 1992, SURFACE COLLECTION	0.0000	6.4793	0.3438	9.6047	2.5394	0.0000	2.3637	16.4895	53.7102	859.5365	0.0000	0.8677	93687.4	2.0022	0.00	0.00	0.0000
CHD040	POTTERY	GUAM	GUAM-1, 1992, SURFACE COLLECTION	0.0000	4.6759	0.2540	0.0000	1.6443	1.7190	1.7283	11.8740	27.6254	558.4099	1.4019	0.5233	104208.7	2.8966	0.00	0.00	0.5949
CHD041	POTTERY	YAP	C36-22.1 I/5	0.0000	78.0613	1.1456	61.4562	13.4702	24.3926	6.3372	132.7278	4.4492	13.8034	5.0586	1.5639	14064.8	8.9187	0.00	227.68	0.1942
CHD042	POTTERY	YAP	PEMRANG, INTOH-1	10.1592	6.4352	0.2293	17.2803	3.5317	1.1878	1.7606	23.0619	94.2740	1768.2803	0.0000	1.2760	144877.3	2.3915	292.71	0.00	0.0000
CHD043	POTTERY	YAP	PEMRANG, INTOH-2	0.0000	6.5683	0.2240	12.9387	4.0347	0.0000	1.9387	19.7649	36.0558	663.4599	0.0000	1.4269	117523.4	4.2946	0.00	24.27	0.0000
CHD044	POTTERY	YAP	ATLIW SURFACE	0.0000	4.4773	0.1958	7.8814	2.1210	0.0000	0.9766	12.1341	56.1741	1660.9099	0.0000	0.8081	136930.4	3.7762	372.67	0.00	0.0000
CHD045	POTTERY	YAP	ATLIW, MEN'S HOUSE SURFACE	0.0000	5.9424	0.2191	9.8123	3.0678	0.0000	1.3784	18.9552	61.6708	1645.1290	0.0000	1.0048	124770.1	3.7227	286.33	0.00	0.0000
CHD046	POTTERY	YAP	ATLIW SURFACE	0.0000	12.6879	0.2088	18.6924	5.2410	0.0000	1.6277	37.5146	126.1723	2048.4927	0.0000	1.6988	139297.7	3.6188	627.58	0.00	0.0000
CHD047	POTTERY	YAP	ATLIW SURFACE	0.0000	6.0046	0.2371	10.8340	3.6375	0.0000	1.8819	17.9982	64.4454	1854.8785	0.4212	1.3195	136061.3	3.8500	357.14	14.03	0.0000
CHD048	POTTERY	YAP	ATLIW SURFACE	0.0000	6.5906	0.1848	12.6948	2.8593	0.0000	1.3159	23.5014	94.3081	1377.5833	0.0000	0.9425	125599.0	4.0942	358.84	0.00	0.0000
CHD049	POTTERY	YAP	MAAP VILLAGE SURFACE	0.0000	4.3052	0.2015	7.0296	1.8667	0.0000	0.9712	11.7826	77.1933	1810.6465	0.0000	0.7028	150530.5	3.6120	604.20	0.00	0.0000
CHD050	POTTERY	YAP	BINAW	0.0000	9.3847	0.4716	12.8072	5.8778	0.0000	2.2943	48.9755	278.7263	1704.9497	0.6633	2.0524	147439.3	4.3202	304.23	0.00	0.0000
CHD051	POTTERY	YAP	BINAW	0.0000	5.1206	0.2869	12.7718	4.0477	0.0000	2.1281	35.6145	136.8648	2362.3257	0.4926	1.4522	152891.9	4.3560	1008.43	0.00	0.3371
CHD052	POTTERY	YAP	BINAW	0.0000	2.9340	0.1651	0.0000	1.6251	0.0000	1.4187	3.3375	18.7286	1172.2661	0.5720	0.6654	128534.6	5.4650	264.75	0.00	0.0000
CHD053	POTTERY	YAP	RUU', LAGOON SHORE, SURFACE	0.0000	3.9132	0.4307	0.0000	1.9512	0.0000	1.2527	54.4842	615.8640	1434.1150	0.0000	0.8606	145785.6	3.4667	854.70	0.00	0.0000
CHD054	POTTERY	YAP	BINAW	0.0000	6.5120	0.3260	13.2315	4.1455	0.0000	1.8510	27.2534	109.4914	1724.4425	0.0000	1.5677	151390.2	4.5839	599.18	0.00	0.0000
CHD055	POTTERY	YAP	BINAW	7.1826	6.6756	0.2464	12.4486	4.1494	0.0000	1.8253	13.7427	53.8174	1461.9240	0.8907	1.4537	127109.7	4.4276	666.45	20.78	0.0000
CHD056	POTTERY	YAP	BINAW	0.0000	4.3747	0.2127	5.4347	1.9163	0.0000	1.3465	8.8556	19.3585	1184.2570	0.0000	0.7780	129811.2	5.5714	236.33	0.00	0.0000
CHD057	POTTERY	YAP	BINAW	0.0000	3.5095	0.2020	8.2031	2.1012	0.0000	1.1733	12.5737	45.4319	1150.3191	0.6732	0.7650	126454.1	3.5542	220.13	0.00	0.0000
CHD058	POTTERY	YAP	GITAM	0.0000	6.6464	0.3511	11.8386	3.0157	0.0000	1.4761	40.7754	123.5545	1546.0005	0.0000	1.0432	162180.9	3.8212	551.75	0.00	0.0000
CHD059	POTTERY	YAP	BINAW	0.0000	2.3640	0.1981	0.0000	1.1238	0.0000	0.6908	5.3049	41.5730	1647.1229	0.4256	0.4430	136450.5	3.6529	609.31	0.00	78.2296
CHD060	POTTERY	YAP	GITAM	0.0000	5.5915	0.3339	10.2368	3.8601	0.0000	2.0262	13.7222	36.8133	1502.1199	0.0000	1.4119	132010.8	3.8632	565.99	0.00	0.0000
CHD061	POTTERY	YAP	GITAM	0.0000	6.0797	0.4344	9.3292	3.7468	2.1716	1.7490	13.3983	42.6038	1589.3577	0.0000	1.3601	140833.3	3.7706	516.58	0.00	0.0000
CHD062	POTTERY	YAP	GITAM	0.0000	5.3967	0.3810	12.4732	3.6942	0.0000	1.6401	13.1603	37.6088	1591.2836	0.0000	1.3197	138084.7	3.6790	579.09	0.00	0.0000
CHD063	POTTERY	YAP	GITAM	0.0000	5.7843	0.2564	15.0632	3.6687	0.0000	1.7988	15.2572	42.9134	1562.6704	0.0000	1.3165	137914.8	4.0330	543.36	0.00	0.0000
CHD064	POTTERY	YAP	GITAM	0.0000	4.9144	0.3631	10.4716	3.0013	0.0000	1.8355	12.3981	41.1974	1484.5743	0.0000	1.0574	137205.6	3.6152	540.28	0.00	0.0000
CHD065	POTTERY	YAP	GITAM	0.0000	4.1829	0.2884	0.0000	2.5066	0.0000	1.4984	14.4426	52.4683	1538.8472	0.0000	0.8738	135617.4	4.0949	482.05	0.00	0.0000
CHD066	POTTERY	YAP	GITAM	0.0000	4.4801	0.2780	9.1161	3.0330	0.0000	1.6608	10.0590	35.7568	1591.8970	0.0000	1.0434	146779.3	3.9526	530.31	0.00	0.0000
CHD067	POTTERY	YAP	GITAM	0.0000	5.0872	0.2426	7.9504	2.5018	0.0000	1.4442	14.2892	37.9305	1496.2549	0.0000	0.8540	134188.1	3.6999	508.24	0.00	0.0000
CHD068	POTTERY	YAP	GITAM	0.0000	5.0764	0.3267	12.2094	3.2186	0.0000	1.7239	12.3111	36.7475	1547.2572	0.0000	1.1448	138946.1	3.5889	558.87	0.00	0.0000
CHD069	POTTERY	YAP	GITAM	0.0000	6.3099	0.4283	13.7905	4.0342	0.0000	1.8099	30.1044	131.4341	1524.6178	0.0000	1.4083	134365.0	3.8064	569.91	0.00	0.0000
CHD070	POTTERY	YAP	GITAM	0.0000	5.5881	0.3344	7.5025	3.3126	0.0000	1.7202	25.6163	95.6049	1525.4767	0.0000	1.1636	132620.1	3.8686	482.40	0.00	0.0000
CHD071	POTTERY	YAP	GITAM	0.0000	6.2590	0.3010	11.9609	3.5486	0.0000	2.0900	12.2990	36.9063	1544.9739	0.0000	1.2452	136353.8	4.1162	588.79	0.00	0.0000
CHD072	POTTERY	YAP	GITAM	0.0000	4.6718	0.2434	7.9729	2.6192	0.0000	1.3784	18.1764	47.1639	1538.1681	0.0000	0.9319	135887.0	3.8409	517.58	0.00	0.0000
CHD073	POTTERY	YAP	GITAM	0.0000	6.1729	0.3014	8.9379	3.6396	0.0000	1.7903	22.2805	115.4420	1504.2044	0.0000	1.2712	139742.4	3.5454	633.08	0.00	0.0000
CHD074	POTTERY	YAP	GITAM	0.0000	4.4214	0.2768	7.0258	2.7970	0.0000	1.3719	11.1320	34.0993	1626.5953	0.0000	1.0663	141288.3	3.6788	634.65	0.00	0.0000
CHD075	POTTERY	YAP	GITAM	0.0000	4.3209	0.3073	6.9647	2.2258	0.0000	1.3289	12.1323	38.9637	1503.2186	0.0000	0.8396	135458.5	3.8426	504.13	0.00	0.0000
CHD076	POTTERY	YAP	THENFAAR	0.0000	3.2882	0.1404	4.9392	1.4584	0.0000	0.7136	7.5222	25.9294	966.7147	0.0000	0.5512	148782.8	4.6540	258.12	16.08	0.0000
CHD077	POTTERY	YAP	THENFAAR	0.0000	2.3639	0.1369	0.0000	1.0245	0.0000	0.6364	3.6109	33.1878	941.2510	0.7013	0.4060	146590.6	4.8648	277.18	0.00	0.0000
CHD078	POTTERY	YAP	THENFAAR	0.0000	5.9754	0.3128	10.4479	2.8310	0.0000	1.4562	13.2342	32.6686	740.9466	0.7389	1.0478	128127.2	4.4860	267.84	16.65	0.0000
CHD079	POTTERY	YAP	THENFAAR	0.0000	3.4812	0.1797	0.0000	1.4888	0.0000	1.1671	8.9631	23.2640	1124.1305	0.4808	0.5533	126930.9	4.0935	200.83	18.48	0.5315
CHD080	POTTERY	YAP	THENFAAR	0.0000	3.2253	0.3131	10.1928	2.6450	0.0000	1.7769	13.9327	40.5941	1854.8705	0.0000	1.0237	138983.2	3.7606	494.42	0.00	0.0000
CHD081	POTTERY	YAP	THENFAAR	0.0000	4.7185	0.3726	9.9836	3.9838	0.0000	2.0999	28.4112	133.3966	1717.9473	1.2677	1.3663	135246.0	3.3606	761.80	38.50	0.0000
CHD082	POTTERY	YAP	THENFAAR	0.0000	2.4049	0.1150	6.4402	1.1619	0.0000	0.8562	4.3966	27.9709	943.5222	0.0000	0.4915	151238.5	4.8738	208.22	16.83	0.0000

ANID	MATERIAL	ISLAND	LOCATION	AS	LA	LU	ND	SM	U	YB	CE	CO	CR	CS	EU	FE	HF	NI	RB	SB
CHD083	POTTERY	YAP	THENFAAR	0.0000	3.1194	0.3461	9.5823	2.8951	0.0000	1.6508	6.7192	30.2128	1711.3600	0.9574	1.0883	146662.2	4.5403	421.09	0.00	0.0000
CHD084	POTTERY	YAP	THENFAAR	0.0000	2.5832	0.1865	5.5490	1.2008	3.2884	0.7074	3.8010	30.3806	1357.2849	0.3681	0.4846	158270.8	5.4028	372.17	0.00	0.0000
CHD085	POTTERY	YAP	THENFAAR	0.0000	4.7264	0.2669	12.3929	2.5875	0.0000	1.7987	14.7140	37.3415	1337.8057	0.0000	1.0175	140461.6	4.4000	227.47	0.00	0.0000
CHD086	POTTERY	YAP	C28- LAGOON SHORE, SURFACE	0.0000	4.2220	0.2336	13.9239	3.2596	0.0000	1.4330	18.0600	72.4947	1943.9476	0.5213	1.1912	122850.3	3.1183	1182.69	0.00	0.0000
CHD087	POTTERY	YAP	C28- LAGOON SHORE, SURFACE	0.0000	4.4515	0.2192	5.2872	1.6171	1.6541	1.5328	9.1738	18.1932	234.2011	0.0000	0.4896	16619.8	2.6033	91.62	0.00	0.1480
CHD088	POTTERY	YAP	C28- LAGOON SHORE, SURFACE	0.0000	4.9106	0.2748	8.6099	3.5653	0.0000	1.8205	18.4421	70.7903	2045.0903	0.9969	1.2683	124066.6	2.5949	1037.99	0.00	0.0000
CHD089	POTTERY	YAP	C28-ST-3 (0-30)	0.0000	5.1703	0.2827	17.3004	4.1323	0.0000	2.1167	33.0608	75.3719	2832.7529	0.0000	1.4961	167200.8	4.6375	966.59	0.00	0.0000
CHD090	POTTERY	YAP	C28-1.01.200 I/1	0.0000	4.9046	0.1939	5.4983	1.0896	0.0000	1.1535	8.9284	16.7977	799.5156	1.2448	0.4003	98969.7	2.7500	158.42	0.00	0.0000
CHD091	POTTERY	YAP	C28-ST5.1 (28-40)	0.0000	4.8719	0.2360	10.5312	2.7264	0.0000	1.4139	31.0929	137.8751	2043.8153	1.4164	1.0084	141332.4	3.6403	1071.42	0.00	0.0000
CHD092	POTTERY	YAP	C28- LAGOON SHORE, SURFACE	0.0000	2.9225	0.1791	3.1047	1.2557	0.0000	0.9651	9.1854	63.6929	1838.9258	0.0000	0.5684	174077.8	4.1163	962.14	0.00	0.0000
CHD093	POTTERY	YAP	C28-2.1.1.1	0.0000	3.7344	0.2040	8.1697	2.2769	0.0000	1.2355	19.2971	85.0106	1858.9827	1.7077	0.8630	132133.9	3.7286	672.73	19.99	0.0000
CHD094	POTTERY	YAP	C28- LAGOON SHORE, SURFACE	0.0000	4.1931	0.3758	9.2871	3.3983	0.0000	1.8336	14.0100	60.2046	2052.8540	0.8838	1.2404	132690.0	3.1175	993.99	0.00	0.0000
CHD095	POTTERY	YAP	C28- LAGOON SHORE, SURFACE	0.0000	4.8324	0.2909	10.0457	3.3941	0.0000	1.6097	14.6260	56.6527	2048.7605	0.4744	1.2538	132655.9	3.1172	784.25	0.00	0.0000
CHD096	POTTERY	YAP	C28- LAGOON SHORE, SURFACE	0.0000	6.0866	0.3328	10.8480	3.3891	0.0000	1.6960	15.8664	64.9659	712.9295	0.0000	1.2184	120509.2	3.9234	436.83	0.00	0.0000
CHD097	POTTERY	YAP	C28- LAGOON SHORE, SURFACE	0.0000	4.9896	0.2115	7.9960	3.2053	0.0000	1.6778	15.3633	69.4308	2012.1879	1.3624	1.2494	131371.2	2.9377	1271.27	0.00	0.0000
CHD098	POTTERY	YAP	C28-2.1.1.2 I/1	0.0000	5.6095	0.1655	7.1317	2.8692	0.0000	1.4658	73.2974	116.5698	1672.4161	0.0000	1.1118	141721.5	4.2481	711.71	0.00	0.0000
CHD099	POTTERY	YAP	C28-2.1.1.3 I/1	0.0000	3.5444	0.1848	7.7119	2.9557	0.0000	1.6063	25.2908	91.6185	2016.3257	0.0000	1.1323	140094.3	3.5468	912.34	0.00	0.0000
CHD100	POTTERY	YAP	C28-2.1.1.4 I/1	0.0000	3.7258	0.1846	6.7816	2.3317	0.0000	1.3123	12.3180	43.6022	1551.9558	0.3580	0.8656	120541.8	3.9236	722.72	0.00	0.0000
CHD101	POTTERY	YAP	C36-77, SURFACE	6.4530	2.5875	0.2056	3.4785	1.4614	0.9934	1.6376	7.5174	23.9830	262.8121	0.0000	0.5522	88248.8	1.7660	0.00	0.00	0.2481
CHD102	POTTERY	YAP	C36-77-I/12	0.0000	21.5550	0.1735	19.8885	3.3561	0.0000	1.0824	46.3433	49.8573	777.9363	0.1563	1.0204	80120.4	5.5544	1051.26	0.00	0.0000
CHD103	POTTERY	YAP	C36-78-I/5	25.0891	2.8837	0.1908	8.5077	2.1132	3.0447	1.4231	8.0133	49.0594	325.6668	0.6084	0.7053	118038.7	3.6274	224.60	0.00	0.4675
CHD104	POTTERY	YAP	C36-78-I/9	19.9984	3.5948	0.2331	8.6698	3.2875	0.0000	1.5660	17.7419	122.3283	1907.4858	0.9124	1.2393	141311.0	2.9169	927.98	0.00	0.0000
CHD105	CLAY	YAP	C36-78-I/1	64.2940	2.9057	0.0753	0.0000	1.5572	3.3860	0.6976	5.6517	260.8807	4874.4575	0.0000	0.5345	266467.9	0.7619	971.97	0.00	0.9880
CHD106	POTTERY	YAP	C36-78-I/4	40.8464	4.3765	0.2093	10.0065	3.0678	1.5845	1.3433	17.6440	62.5737	1849.1133	0.0000	1.1461	129270.3	3.8892	697.68	0.00	0.2290
CHD107	POTTERY	YAP	C36-78-I/7	15.2563	3.5079	0.1590	11.6262	2.5530	0.0000	1.3520	14.7759	121.0272	1762.2809	0.7935	1.0185	138243.9	2.9443	956.56	0.00	0.0000
CHD108	POTTERY	YAP	C36-45-SURFACE	7.7316	5.2217	0.2336	9.7273	3.1823	1.8962	1.3226	14.0879	80.1808	2352.1204	0.6001	1.0091	130665.8	2.8587	873.57	0.00	0.0000
CHD109	POTTERY	YAP	C36-45-SURFACE	60.0794	2.4346	0.2604	0.0000	1.4409	4.3995	1.2487	7.3417	24.5580	246.4224	0.0000	0.3757	55107.4	2.4040	167.71	0.00	0.3024
CHD110	POTTERY	YAP	WONYAAN SURFACE	0.0000	5.7124	0.2039	6.9684	3.9018	0.0000	1.7855	22.1990	72.1811	1776.8995	0.0000	1.4429	125873.7	3.4115	885.39	0.00	0.0000
CHD111	POTTERY	YAP	WONYAAN SURFACE	0.0000	7.6959	0.2781	8.0094	2.0500	0.0000	1.3607	15.1667	39.5686	517.4048	1.8209	0.6826	123535.3	5.6578	248.02	29.02	0.0000
CHD112	POTTERY	YAP	WONYAAN SURFACE	2.7837	5.8547	0.2508	10.5928	3.9411	0.0000	1.9866	18.7272	79.4787	1714.0806	0.5723	1.4175	131429.4	3.2657	801.21	0.00	0.0000
CHD113	POTTERY	YAP	WONYAAN SURFACE	0.0000	4.9314	0.2672	8.7709	3.8524	0.0000	1.9862	21.2179	81.7160	1681.7186	0.4680	1.4599	128202.8	3.2311	770.42	0.00	0.0000
CHD114	POTTERY	YAP	WONYAAN SURFACE	0.0000	5.5796	0.2573	11.9794	4.1372	0.0000	2.1455	23.0673	85.2953	1412.7194	0.0000	1.5924	128816.1	4.0973	503.53	0.00	0.0000
CHD115	POTTERY	YAP	C36-45-II/1	7.4156	3.2379	0.4251	0.0000	2.0080	4.4161	1.4418	8.3699	30.5674	188.3654	1.5838	0.6097	162901.5	3.8541	218.10	0.00	0.0000
CHD116	POTTERY	YAP	C36-45-I/4	40.3440	5.1664	0.1910	1.2194	1.1844	0.0000	1.0303	8.6629	46.5370	107.6687	0.0000	0.3992	153081.0	3.2549	462.71	0.00	0.0000
CHD117	POTTERY	YAP	C36-45-I/4	0.0000	5.3968	0.2332	9.5095	3.6730	0.0000	1.8254	25.4123	82.9368	1417.5796	0.0000	1.3520	137105.7	4.5580	744.55	0.00	0.0000
CHD118	POTTERY	YAP	C36-76-I/8	0.0000	12.5879	0.2212	17.1760	5.4048	0.0000	1.8520	44.4287	149.5522	1815.2479	0.0000	1.8202	127035.0	3.6967	951.36	0.00	0.0000
CHD119	POTTERY	YAP	C36-76-I/4	3.3432	3.3339	0.2519	4.1407	1.3935	0.5994	1.5957	7.4028	13.0088	195.3693	0.0000	0.4701	27046.9	2.3133	0.00	0.00	0.0000
CHD120	POTTERY	YAP	C36-76-I/5	11.5160	4.7319	0.4457	13.4042	3.0954	5.2007	2.6730	12.5315	29.6067	192.4509	0.7121	0.8598	79683.2	2.6836	157.80	0.00	0.0000
CHD121	POTTERY	YAP	C36-76-I/7	0.0000	5.1620	0.2795	10.0569	4.2247	0.0000	2.1237	24.5079	160.3589	2066.3560	0.0000	1.5529	135353.1	3.5603	1052.51	0.00	0.0000
CHD122	POTTERY	YAP	C36-76-I/6	0.0000	7.9676	0.2136	13.0589	4.0663	0.0000	1.6414	24.6542	55.4792	1598.6381	0.6774	1.3250	117815.2	3.3923	684.88	0.00	0.0000
CHD123	POTTERY	FAIS	FAIS SURFACE	0.0000	4.8580	0.1893	12.9626	3.2226	0.0000	1.5311	29.9223	168.7892	1792.8870	0.0000	1.2165	116159.9	3.2510	1023.55	0.00	0.0000
CHD124	POTTERY	FADERAI	FADERAI, ULITHI, SURFACE	0.0000	9.7118	0.3011	15.7623	3.6929	0.0000	1.3896	37.5927	96.7974	1958.7752	0.0000	1.2682	154031.4	4.9751	852.12	0.00	0.0000
CHD125	POTTERY	SATAWAL	SATAWAL SURFACE	8.5062	5.3288	0.2447	14.9459	4.0089	0.0000	1.8916	23.3348	88.4770	1826.5979	0.0000	1.5211	131414.1	3.1345	822.87	0.00	0.0000
CHD126	POTTERY	YAP	C36-77-I/9	0.0000	9.6541	0.2053	18.3036	4.3991	0.0000	1.8088	31.8092	79.1969	2216.1404	1.1702	1.4978	160442.9	4.4746	1589.02	0.00	0.0000
CHD127	POTTERY	YAP	C36-77-I/9	8.4945	4.5537	0.1582	9.4693	2.4800	0.0000	1.1839	16.1663	86.5804	2773.4805	0.9786	0.7882	152580.8	2.9227	1545.30	0.00	0.0000
CHD128	POTTERY	YAP	C36-77-I/12	0.0000	5.6346	0.1780	12.3113	3.0764	0.0000	1.3264	19.5714	57.9639	2113.6228	0.0000	1.0566	152596.7	3.8659	971.11	0.00	0.0000
CHD129	POTTERY	YAP	C36-27-III/13	0.0000	4.9327	0.1308	7.7288	2.0404	0.0000	0.9124	21.8005	245.0634	1868.6985	0.7162	0.7373	117955.9	2.3910	1234.03	0.00	0.0000
CHD130	POTTERY	YAP	C36-27-III/12	6.0544	3.8591	0.3925	6.9083	2.3732	1.2091	2.5411	12.4295	172.1183	228.0253	0.6274	0.7561	79578.6	2.4244	613.65	0.00	0.0000
CHD131	POTTERY	YAP	C36-27-III/3	0.0000	10.5208	0.1841	18.8097	3.7644	0.0000	1.5108	26.9156	70.4423	1510.5159	0.0000	1.2751	132838.9	3.7911	589.01	3.92	0.0000
CHD132	POTTERY	YAP	C36-27-I/4	0.0000	7.5637	0.1847	11.4346	3.5032	0.0000	1.6845	21.0429	162.1907	2759.6294	0.5964	1.2367	154847.5	3.6672	1462.59	0.00	0.0000
CHD133	POTTERY	YAP	C36-27-III/10	9.8623	4.8411	0.1540	8.9675	2.1957	0.0000	0.9432	14.7680	182.8500	862.3674	0.4325	0.7755	147635.4	2.9665	955.00	0.00	0.0000
CHD134	POTTERY	MOGMOG	MOG-1-G4-S	0.0000	3.8816	0.2290	4.4751	1.6942	0.0000	1.6270	8.4257	11.0138	236.3238	0.0000	0.6047	31015.2	2.3558	0.00	0.00	0.2506
CHD135	POTTERY	MOGMOG	MOG-1-L3-II/1	3.2129	3.6162	0.2218	7.6902	1.7808	0.0000	1.5450	7.6982	8.0112	210.4488	0.0000	0.5832	31026.2	2.1369	0.00	0.00	1.1865
CHD136	POTTERY	MOGMOG	MOG-1-A6-S	3.4047	3.8084	0.2048	6.2762	1.3804	0.0000	1.2755	9.5209	12.5683	201.2871	0.0000	0.4968	35963.1	2.1938	0.00	0.00	0.0000
CHD137	POTTERY	MOGMOG	MOG-1-A6-S	0.0000	3.8090	0.2433	7.2063	1.8343	0.0000	2.0894	9.1127	6.2566	105.2161	0.0000	0.5997	21694.0	2.5553	0.00	0.00	0.1220
CHD138	POTTERY	MOGMOG	MOG-1-I4-S	7.5528	2.0981	0.1890	0.0000	0.9873	0.4800	1.0370	5.4420	11.7057	130.6519	0.0000	0.3094	51668.3	1.8540	0.00	0.00	0.5780
CHD139	POTTERY	MOGMOG	MOG-1-L3-II/1	0.0000	13.0132	0.2424	20.2799	5.5445	0.0000	2.0645	36.2279	77.4276	1765.5386	0.0000	1.8268	143350.2	4.3356	861.53	0.00	0.6864
CHD140	POTTERY	MOGMOG	MOG-1-L3-II/2	0.0000	2.4874	0.0764	5.7858	1.1017	0.0000	0.5761	3.2971	23.0462	569.0836	0.0000	0.4332	142174.3	4.6373	174.31	0.00	0.0000
CHD141	POTTERY	MOGMOG	MOG-1-L3-II/2	3.6689	1.9076	0.1898	0.0000	1.0923	0.0000	1.0243	4.7658	9.4874	161.4264	0.0000	0.3840	28159.2	1.7591	0.00	0.00	0.3967
CHD142	POTTERY	MOGMOG	MOG-2-D9-II/1	0.0000	2.3749	0.1438	6.8479	1.1760	0.0000	1.0980	5.9169	18.8214	153.2845	0.0000	0.4363	44568.0	1.8447	0.00	0.00	0.3998
CHD143	POTTERY	MOGMOG	MOG-2-K4-S	0.0000	9.6504	0.3390	19.8555	6.0919	0.0000	2.6490	30.9915	49.8337	583.5422	0.0000	2.2345	106462.5	3.9924	172.52	0.00	1.8541
CHD144	POTTERY	MOGMOG	MOG-2-L1-II/2	34.8651	3.9758	0.1787	6.4548	1.9080	0.0000	0.7663	10.4665	53.8336	1597.2011	0.0000	0.6970	167700.9	4.1489	331.21	0.00	1.6887
CHD145	POTTERY	MOGMOG	MOG-2-L1-II/2	32.8151	2.5641	0.2130	0.0000	1.3836	0.0000	0.8501	8.0615	38.0019	1703.6429	0.5966	0.5267	142930.5	3.7627	465.46	15.50	3.2251
CHD146	POTTERY	MOGMOG	MOG-2-I4-IV/2	25.7959	3.2712	0.2017	7.7650	1.6944	0.0000	0.9369	14.0457	49.9937	2051.7874	0.3443	0.6341	135614.6	3.7214	505.98	0.00	111.3149
CHD147	POTTERY	MOGMOG	MOG-2-I4-IV/3	38.6504	5.7618	0.2211	5.3946	2.8381	2.0862	1.2054	16.9885	43.4671	1517.2844	0.0000	1.0026	128544.6	3.8868	295.71	0.00	193.4381
CHD148	POTTERY	YAP	C36-33-I/16	24.8888	2.3101	0.1933	0.0000	1.5728	1.1419	1.3005	10.1072	59.1863	1847.3619	0.4016	0.5749	148826.2	4.4726	520.02	0.00	0.0000
CHD149	POTTERY	YAP	C36-33-I/5	0.0000	2.6572	0.2305	3.3303	1.7338	0.0000	0.9182	10.7116	71.1649	1782.0300	0.6634	0.6309	129646.8	3.7771	593.67	0.00	0.0000
CHD150	POTTERY	YAP	C36-33-I/18	19.8910	2.6339	0.2518	6.5986	1.7184	0.9522	1.3129	12.9324	80.4295	1957.3003	0.0000	0.6195	145697.5	4.4969	549.70	0.00	0.0000
CHD151	POTTERY	YAP	C36-33-I/13	16.3840	4.2829	0.2470	8.9118	3.4880	0.0000	1.8278	13.9302	105.6406	1868.9343	0.4586	1.2192	143410.9	3.5786	675.80	0.00	0.0000
CHD152	POTTERY	YAP	C36-33-I/12	4.8566	7.6196	0.2538	0.0000	1.5047	0.0000	0.7684	16.5556	26.3390	1574.8750	0.5674	0.5765	126779.9	3.3390	259.93	0.00	0.0000
CHD153	POTTERY	YAP	C36-33-I/2	37.1604	6.0472	0.3056	8.3497	3.4439	1.6188	1.5576	18.4420	119.6984	1612.4479	1.6618	1.2216	167934.7	3.7720	483.96	0.00	0.0000
CHD154	POTTERY	YAP	C36-33-I/11	4.2776	1.6259	0.1770	0.0000	0.8636	1.4116	0.9757	4.8593	25.2015	145.7804	0.0000	0.2983	57469.9	2.1923	0.00	0.00	0.0000
CHD155	POTTERY	YAP	C36-33-I/9	7.5727	3.6235	0.2900	8.5084	1.9946	0.0000	1.0964	10.0890	62.5465	1156.1471	1.0733	0.7202	139079.1	3.7932	348.70	0.00	0.0000
CHD156	POTTERY	YAP	C36-32-S	3.5739	2.5147	0.2407	0.0000	1.0066	0.0000	1.1800	4.6553	17.0707	209.9039	0.4336	0.3431	80276.4	2.1287	275.55	0.00	0.0000
CHD157	POTTERY	YAP	C36-34-S	5.1317	7.7505	0.3436	14.3973	5.2126	1.5536	2.2974	27.9985	115.7329	1964.5234	0.5652	1.7300	151371.1	3.6176	511.27	0.00	0.0000
CHD158	POTTERY	YAP	C36-34-S	0.0000	8.2408	0.3887	13.4013	4.3432	0.0000	2.1449	23.0281	75.9408	1535.4627	0.0000	1.6525	140098.9	3.6557	413.67	0.00	0.0000
CHD159	POTTERY	YAP	C36-32-S	0.0000	4.7773	0.3287	10.6781	2.8680	0.0000	1.4638	19.5363	49.6380	1822.4633	0.4906	0.9708	133508.7	4.1151	471.78	0.00	0.0000
CHD160	POTTERY	YAP	C36-06-I/5	3.8800	6.3493	0.3016	10.2041	2.9902	1.9108	1.4451	32.1457	85.8461	1814.9988	0.0000	0.9378	139474.0	3.6203	408.86	0.00	0.0000
CHD161	POTTERY	YAP	C36-06-I/5	44.5396	6.7019	0.3190	16.3483	4.4590	5.4456	1.7998	24.5016	69.3341	1636.5461	0.0000	1.4395	138011.7	3.9489	398.98	0.00	0.3850
CHD162	POTTERY	YAP	C36-06-I/5	4.0823	3.8788	0.1713	0.0000	1.0181	0.0000	0.8172	6.3618	21.7432	1043.1776	0.0000	0.3684	120029.5	4.1586	670.39	0.00	0.0000
CHD163	POTTERY	YAP	C36-06-S	0.0000	7.9338	0.5834	11.5500	3.2491	0.0000	2.9482	17.0241	48.7157	105.2761	0.7450	1.2114	125455.6	3.6357	117.11	0.00	0.0000
CHD164	POTTERY	YAP	C36-06-I/3	29.1898	5.6698	0.2785	7.8105	2.7394	1.9555	1.2765	18.9469	40.3546	1328.1487	0.8228	0.9690	151537.4	3.6539	263.08	0.00	0.5874

ANID	MATERIAL	ISLAND	LOCATION	AS	LA	LU	ND	SM	U	YB	CE	CO	CR	CS	EU	FE	HF	NI	RB	SB
CHD165	POTTERY	YAP	C36-06-I/1	0.0000	5.1885	0.2847	9.4806	2.5720	0.0000	1.5311	14.6138	70.5369	1049.5111	0.0000	0.9021	116276.4	3.4475	1435.38	0.00	0.0000
CHD166	POTTERY	YAP	C36-06-I/4	7.4728	3.1555	0.2545	7.3993	1.4626	3.3901	1.4406	7.6526	8.3268	134.8609	0.0000	0.4173	29474.3	2.4226	50.80	0.00	0.1716
CHD167	POTTERY	MOGMOG	MOG-22-V/2	86.8081	6.1437	0.5378	8.7729	3.2770	2.1180	3.2034	15.8809	21.5732	186.3239	0.2208	1.1037	101586.0	2.9332	0.00	0.00	24.2876
CHD168	POTTERY	MOGMOG	MOG-22-V/1	41.3361	3.0094	0.3134	7.0972	1.8105	1.5020	2.0425	8.1047	20.2451	117.8218	0.2097	0.6050	81071.7	2.6811	0.00	0.00	12.8485
CHD169	POTTERY	MOGMOG	MOG-22-III/2	78.1567	2.5594	0.3781	0.0000	1.3886	0.0000	1.1777	3.3246	36.9740	532.8915	0.0000	0.5417	161199.4	3.9134	167.56	0.00	30.7570
CHD170	POTTERY	MOGMOG	MOG-22-III/2	0.0000	9.4206	0.2495	9.6407	4.1094	0.0000	1.7784	34.7099	127.0748	1877.7748	0.5247	1.3766	123410.7	3.2692	589.20	0.00	2.8611
CHD171	POTTERY	MOGMOG	MOG-22-III/1	4.5507	11.3784	0.3846	15.7957	4.0099	0.6747	2.5837	26.7239	30.4704	89.9689	1.8057	1.2444	66857.1	3.0334	71.09	28.22	3.0500
CHD172	POTTERY	MOGMOG	MOG-22-III/2	6.4189	5.8134	0.2994	12.9055	3.3444	0.0000	1.6903	22.4275	101.7257	2067.1252	0.0000	1.1474	142401.1	4.0035	514.86	0.00	3.9930
CHD173	POTTERY	MOGMOG	MOG-13-IV/2	20.6103	5.0876	0.3857	11.4206	2.7808	1.5681	2.4424	13.0611	22.5607	350.4255	0.0000	0.9201	57950.0	2.9209	0.00	0.00	5.6857
CHD174	POTTERY	MOGMOG	MOG-13-IV/3	14.3276	5.0913	0.3184	12.0051	2.3410	0.0000	1.6094	19.3229	48.9728	1728.2024	0.0000	0.8427	140255.9	3.6371	433.44	0.00	6.9313
CHD175	POTTERY	MOGMOG	MOG-13-IV/1	6.1971	1.9607	0.2461	0.0000	1.0486	0.0000	0.9693	3.8109	26.0144	534.9744	0.0000	0.3713	159532.9	3.8180	137.13	0.00	4.7731
CHD176	POTTERY	MOGMOG	MOG-13-IV/2	4.4192	3.3031	0.1753	0.0000	1.1371	0.0000	0.8662	9.7909	39.5673	1744.3702	0.3291	0.3935	134346.3	4.3523	385.88	0.00	6.6003
CHD177	POTTERY	MOGMOG	MOG-13-IV/1	2.6352	3.8407	0.3298	6.8298	1.9852	0.4152	2.0915	10.0517	11.4653	130.9549	0.0000	0.6338	32438.3	2.9642	0.00	0.00	0.8331
CHD178	POTTERY	MOGMOG	MOG-13-IV/1	0.0000	4.1079	0.1470	7.9824	2.1083	0.0000	0.9180	16.2532	67.3492	1718.8221	0.0000	0.7621	126017.9	3.5122	621.89	0.00	0.3253
CHD179	POTTERY	MOGMOG	MOG-27-III/1	4.5092	3.9869	0.2669	7.5500	2.0077	0.0000	2.1450	8.7617	10.7639	134.4578	0.0000	0.6462	26562.4	2.6904	0.00	0.00	0.2444
CHD180	POTTERY	MOGMOG	MOG-27-III/1	16.5718	10.7594	0.7922	20.3823	5.4845	0.0000	4.8338	12.6642	26.6068	105.6622	0.0000	1.9952	127851.8	3.6341	0.00	15.29	1.4025
CHD181	POTTERY	MOGMOG	MOG-27-II/6	5.7271	6.9931	0.2495	16.4713	4.9394	0.0000	2.0424	27.1626	76.1610	1508.4790	0.0000	1.8683	115006.0	4.6028	355.51	0.00	0.7428
CHD182	POTTERY	MOGMOG	MOG-27-II/5	0.0000	6.1816	0.4534	9.8270	3.5331	0.0000	1.3747	15.9639	52.2516	1272.0596	0.0000	1.1661	125092.5	4.0036	275.59	0.00	0.7461
CHD183	POTTERY	MOGMOG	MOG-27-II/4	0.0000	3.9536	0.2172	7.9383	3.0542	0.0000	1.6389	19.7293	43.1508	2019.7623	0.0000	1.1602	138800.5	3.6944	516.30	16.48	1.7151
CHD184	POTTERY	MOGMOG	MOG-27-V/1	15.3864	5.0681	0.4367	13.4954	2.8846	1.3834	2.7504	12.8115	22.9875	286.2705	0.0000	1.0238	88657.2	3.3459	0.00	10.80	1.7458
CHD185	POTTERY	MOGMOG	MOG-25-VII/1	10.7658	3.3534	0.2903	0.0000	0.8251	0.0000	0.9952	4.6613	22.3394	118.0107	0.0000	0.3377	139907.0	3.7104	0.00	0.00	6.6815
CHD186	POTTERY	MOGMOG	MOG-25-VII/1	6.8921	4.3697	0.2615	8.7989	2.4397	0.0000	1.1059	9.8403	39.2472	1002.6760	0.0000	0.8564	123504.6	3.3616	156.49	0.00	12.3348
CHD187	POTTERY	MOGMOG	MOG-25-VI/1	5.7866	5.3456	0.2962	12.3135	4.4101	0.0000	1.8741	24.2944	82.7195	2133.4946	0.0000	1.6273	131497.4	3.8827	628.09	0.00	3.7296
CHD188	POTTERY	MOGMOG	MOG-25-VII/1	6.6028	8.0246	0.2435	12.7960	3.4418	0.0000	1.6823	32.9078	104.6469	2392.0007	0.0000	1.3324	148626.0	3.5627	428.32	0.00	5.3841
CHD189	POTTERY	MOGMOG	MOG-25-VI/1	6.2499	12.1236	0.4950	44.2334	5.2645	0.0000	2.3717	24.3760	17.4453	581.2760	0.0000	1.9760	107880.2	4.0925	86.76	0.00	3.7374
CHD190	POTTERY	MOGMOG	MOG-53-IV/2	0.0000	9.6693	0.3856	18.9424	4.6044	0.0000	1.7446	31.1637	83.4548	1572.4802	0.0000	1.7156	129784.8	3.5171	389.61	0.00	4.6146
CHD191	POTTERY	MOGMOG	MOG-53-IV/2	8.0273	2.1059	0.2110	3.6801	1.0270	0.0000	1.0990	5.4059	17.7045	218.7198	0.0000	0.3599	43297.4	2.0808	0.00	9.51	1.7581
CHD192	POTTERY	MOGMOG	MOG-53-III/1	0.0000	4.9377	0.2744	8.4942	3.3561	0.0000	1.6778	9.5783	45.2628	1553.7358	0.0000	1.2169	127444.0	3.3558	451.48	28.05	4.5324
CHD193	POTTERY	MOGMOG	MOG-53-IV/1	0.0000	5.8267	0.3778	9.9154	4.1901	0.0000	2.5749	14.5939	64.4379	1339.6475	0.0000	1.5010	111390.0	3.0621	482.55	0.00	2.3746
CHD194	POTTERY	MOGMOG	MOG-2-L1-II/1	51.3534	3.6618	0.2642	8.2971	3.2397	0.0000	2.0563	9.4760	19.3120	136.6351	0.4134	1.2612	113964.9	3.7520	0.00	0.00	7.9988
CHD195	POTTERY	YAP	C36-34-S	0.0000	8.4966	0.2287	15.2916	4.8686	0.0000	2.0181	24.8838	243.0077	1596.2131	0.6000	1.7089	139487.4	4.2607	822.23	0.00	0.0000
CHD196	POTTERY	YAP	C36-32-S	0.0000	4.3967	0.1346	0.0000	1.4823	0.0000	1.1924	10.2388	77.8609	833.6980	0.7400	0.5940	128567.9	5.8303	356.06	0.00	0.0000
CHD197	POTTERY	MOGMOG	MOG-54-III/2	0.0000	1.0167	0.1972	17.3318	4.2183	0.0000	1.5270	29.3525	50.5518	2022.9122	0.0000	1.4093	143630.1	3.2967	460.35	0.00	9.6650
CHD198	POTTERY	MOGMOG	MOG-54-II/2	0.0000	9.9651	0.4614	13.1980	3.2878	0.9428	3.3866	23.0883	9.7545	62.8076	0.0000	1.0346	15445.5	4.8336	0.00	10.90	1.6758
CHD199	POTTERY	MOGMOG	MOG-54-III/1	0.0000	4.7419	0.1772	0.0000	2.1688	0.0000	1.2328	6.8691	15.3178	826.2938	0.0000	0.7720	116913.6	4.1216	172.01	0.00	1.4988
CHD200	POTTERY	MOGMOG	MOG-54-III/1	0.0000	8.7714	0.1958	14.4688	3.5575	0.0000	1.6261	38.5611	139.7231	2204.4370	0.0000	1.2307	134854.8	3.0783	786.82	0.00	24.7135
CHD201	POTTERY	MOGMOG	MOG-59-II/2	0.0000	5.5429	0.2420	13.2626	4.2078	0.0000	1.9763	15.1410	72.5230	1812.3372	0.0000	1.5417	128428.5	3.1844	636.98	15.52	0.9712
CHD202	POTTERY	MOGMOG	MOG-59-II/3	0.0000	4.2856	0.2270	14.1835	3.7329	0.0000	1.8830	17.6064	62.0911	1458.4596	0.0000	1.3630	118535.8	3.2831	477.76	15.11	0.3796
CHD203	POTTERY	MOGMOG	MOG-59-II/2	0.0000	2.4617	0.0805	2.8625	1.0563	0.0000	0.6650	2.5076	21.4201	1280.6984	0.0000	0.4442	140496.9	3.5676	193.78	8.84	1.0839
CHD204	POTTERY	MOGMOG	MOG-59-II/2	0.0000	2.9976	0.0815	0.0000	1.2536	0.0000	0.7388	6.3879	21.5861	1284.6545	0.0000	0.5168	144535.6	3.4196	164.80	0.00	0.5121
CHD205	POTTERY	MOGMOG	MOG-32-IV/1	0.0000	4.4232	0.2380	10.4571	3.3754	0.0000	1.5948	11.5520	63.1112	1726.5304	0.0000	1.2098	113945.1	3.0107	619.81	13.23	0.6187
CHD206	POTTERY	MOGMOG	MOG-32-IV/1	0.0000	3.0445	0.1656	9.0352	2.6605	0.0000	1.5901	26.4098	162.0391	1960.9751	0.0000	0.9944	143889.3	3.3833	667.15	0.00	2.7596
CHD207	POTTERY	MOGMOG	MOG-32-III/1	0.0000	8.0885	0.1971	11.9754	3.7518	0.0000	1.5916	19.9127	34.8345	1964.9127	0.0000	1.2843	150668.1	3.4558	560.48	0.00	2.6387
CHD208	POTTERY	MOGMOG	MOG-32-III/1	0.0000	4.2750	0.2078	7.2501	3.1980	0.0000	1.5476	11.5358	67.7173	1791.7759	0.0000	1.1554	129882.5	3.4315	673.27	5.97	0.9570
CHD209	POTTERY	MOGMOG	MOG-39-VI/2	12.1783	5.6673	0.2808	15.1503	4.6176	0.0000	2.0295	31.9595	100.5100	1649.8760	0.7611	1.7017	128007.6	3.4843	636.16	0.00	4.7120
CHD210	POTTERY	MOGMOG	MOG-39-V/1	0.0000	2.2992	0.0956	0.0000	1.3726	0.0000	0.6880	5.9594	41.7071	1565.2155	0.0000	0.4319	144168.7	3.2987	397.55	0.00	4.1099
CHD211	POTTERY	MOGMOG	MOG-39-V/1	7.9939	[illegible].2284	0.1921	16.3502	3.9510	0.0000	1.7420	36.9377	73.0697	2601.6140	0.0000	1.4082	183420.8	4.5938	763.80	0.00	8.2174
CHD212	POTTERY	MOGMOG	MOG-39-III/1	0.0000	[illegible].2476	0.3563	27.2187	6.5809	0.0000	2.9606	53.6920	165.1129	1698.2501	0.0000	2.2208	130167.7	4.2049	523.70	0.00	1.8096
CHD213	POTTERY	MOGMOG	MOG-39-III/1	0.0000	[illegible].3207	0.1597	0.0000	2.1134	0.0000	1.2185	16.3151	82.7606	1737.8676	0.6047	0.7924	145945.8	4.6576	597.43	0.00	1.8369
CHD214	POTTERY	MOGMOG	MOG-35-XVI/2	0.0000	[illegible].0094	0.2787	9.1271	2.2636	0.0000	2.1755	10.5523	13.6933	122.5989	0.0000	0.7786	32771.7	2.1697	0.00	0.00	1.3286
CHD215	POTTERY	MOGMOG	MOG-35-XVI/2	0.0000	[illegible].7632	0.1830	12.1285	3.3779	0.0000	1.5367	9.6386	53.1457	1713.6069	0.0000	1.2140	129389.4	3.1576	630.24	0.00	0.5404
CHD216	POTTERY	MOGMOG	MOG-35-XIV/1	0.0000	1[illegible].5805	0.2263	18.8923	5.1194	0.0000	2.0381	26.4221	54.0601	2259.0676	0.0000	1.7593	145859.9	4.1622	846.46	0.00	0.7469
CHD217	POTTERY	MOGMOG	MOG-35-XVI/1	0.0000	[illegible].9943	0.3648	13.2130	4.7387	0.0000	2.3924	16.7597	14.5033	566.9367	0.0000	1.6346	111637.2	4.6524	78.49	0.00	0.9619
CHD218	POTTERY	MOGMOG	MOG-35-X, XII, XIII	0.0000	[illegible].1033	0.1835	13.2076	3.8052	0.0000	1.7917	18.0867	71.8650	1659.9514	0.0000	1.3943	116240.8	2.9817	598.09	0.00	0.2400
CHD219	POTTERY	MOGMOG	MOG-35-VII TO XI	8.7829	[illegible].0992	0.1845	8.3133	3.0779	0.0000	1.3563	13.9696	48.0978	1791.8192	0.4308	1.0986	114740.1	3.5790	587.90	15.66	1.3584
CHD220	POTTERY	MOGMOG	MOG-43-III/3	0.0000	[illegible].2162	0.2496	13.3455	3.4307	0.0000	1.8156	24.5680	114.8873	1727.9131	0.0000	1.2277	129306.5	3.5052	518.98	0.00	3.2668
CHD221	POTTERY	MOGMOG	MOG-43-III/4	8.8237	[illegible].2309	0.2596	18.3087	4.9181	0.0000	2.3831	18.5906	17.9234	552.8008	0.4913	1.7530	105472.3	4.6260	141.43	12.80	15.3892
CHD222	POTTERY	MOGMOG	MOG-43-III/4	8.5184	[illegible].3645	0.0407	0.0000	0.8527	0.0000	0.7316	10.1358	56.0580	2351.9146	0.0000	0.3405	115361.1	3.7840	700.73	0.00	1.8888
CHD223	POTTERY	MOGMOG	MOG-45-III/3	11.1810	[illegible].2461	0.1727	0.0000	1.0839	0.0000	1.2665	6.5223	11.8449	164.6463	0.0000	0.3457	41547.3	2.5619	0.00	0.00	1.2032
CHD224	POTTERY	MOGMOG	MOG-45-III/5	0.0000	[illegible].4519	0.1641	0.0000	2.4704	0.0000	1.4474	20.5457	77.9029	1827.9047	0.3742	0.9637	127958.8	3.3662	727.76	20.10	0.8889
CHD225	CLAY	YAP	GITAM VILLAGE	0.0000	1[illegible].2602	0.2299	17.1036	4.3819	0.0000	1.7429	59.3791	119.9336	2603.9832	0.0000	1.5127	154952.6	3.6188	1086.91	0.00	0.0000
CHD226	CLAY	YAP	BINAW VILLAGE	0.0000	2.1756	0.0688	0.0000	0.8925	0.0000	0.7404	11.5490	104.2488	7181.7769	0.0000	0.3143	208701.5	7.0340	370.73	0.00	0.4496
CHD227	CLAY	YAP	THENFAAR VILLAGE	12.9169	[illegible].9022	0.2060	0.0000	1.6715	0.0000	1.2211	11.8497	101.5515	7642.4370	0.0000	0.6088	256191.6	7.6449	456.06	0.00	0.8225
CHD228	POTTERY	MOGMOG	MOG-45-III/4	0.0000	[illegible].5843	0.2513	11.5537	3.5600	0.0000	1.4135	27.4858	59.3731	1469.4780	0.0000	1.2240	113131.5	3.7345	422.13	0.00	1.0636
CHD229	POTTERY	MOGMOG	MOG-45-III/3	0.0000	[illegible].8301	0.0633	0.0000	0.8221	0.0000	0.7100	4.0515	22.2450	1671.1686	0.0000	0.2877	129128.0	3.7845	258.45	0.00	1.2956
CHD230	POTTERY	YAP	C36-83.1-I/15	0.0000	5[illegible]6278	0.1351	8.9244	1.7806	0.0000	1.0863	21.4971	65.4142	1655.1013	2.4612	0.5717	114130.6	3.3627	388.35	0.00	0.0000
CHD231	POTTERY	YAP	C36-83.1-I/14	0.0000	7[illegible]8763	0.2271	17.4603	4.3443	0.0000	1.6677	28.6300	55.1193	650.3237	1.5306	1.4552	104257.5	5.0767	190.77	0.00	0.0000
CHD232	POTTERY	YAP	C36-83.1-I/15	11.9569	8[illegible]2092	0.3068	14.2349	4.5905	1.5001	2.1633	23.7798	41.9141	1474.3392	1.2780	1.5889	144911.3	4.2463	235.03	12.04	0.0000
CHD233	POTTERY	YAP	C36-83.1-I/14	0.0000	5[illegible]4488	0.1532	10.0823	1.9667	0.0000	1.1092	20.9722	85.3331	2501.1194	2.0996	0.7683	141876.9	3.5372	413.97	0.00	0.0000
CHD234	POTTERY	YAP	C36-75-3.10 (+100)	0.0000	2[illegible]5737	0.0997	0.0000	1.5545	0.0000	1.0697	8.4423	25.1814	1513.4117	1.9868	0.6155	132080.9	3.6359	253.14	0.00	0.0000
CHD235	POTTERY	YAP	C36-75-1.03 (+130)	0.0000	5.4526	0.1885	9.9295	3.4586	0.0000	1.6044	42.0057	225.9012	1738.6176	0.0000	1.2162	126449.2	3.1313	851.39	0.00	0.0000
CHD236	POTTERY	YAP	C36-75-0.01	0.0000	23[illegible]5254	0.0642	15.6967	2.0359	0.0000	0.4570	41.1180	15.5707	409.4528	0.9282	0.5880	92935.8	5.1307	121.34	13.20	0.0000
CHD237	POTTERY	YAP	C36-16-II/1	0.0000	6[illegible]3461	0.1598	7.6246	3.1059	0.0000	1.1152	25.6165	126.0907	2092.9968	0.9971	1.0940	143074.7	3.4577	610.94	0.00	0.0000
CHD238	POTTERY	YAP	C36-16-I/7	0.0000	7[illegible]4457	0.1503	11.3700	3.0587	0.0000	1.0978	32.4119	637.1309	2729.2659	5.6137	0.9852	133758.9	2.8785	1593.81	0.00	0.0000
CHD239	POTTERY	YAP	C36-16-I/7	0.0000	5[illegible]3276	0.1749	12.7260	3.0879	0.0000	1.3886	19.1397	65.6362	1766.2664	1.1096	1.1369	172262.8	3.4242	421.05	0.00	0.0000
CHD240	POTTERY	YAP	C36-16-I/6	5.2691	5[illegible]0343	0.4165	9.3275	2.6335	0.0000	2.6314	11.1940	40.3127	388.9835	1.2340	0.8773	94174.8	2.8464	186.77	8.94	0.0000
CHD241	POTTERY	YAP	C36-16-I/2	0.0000	4[illegible]9587	0.2742	8.6968	3.1835	0.0000	1.7739	12.8086	49.8223	1860.1935	1.3138	1.2233	135610.8	3.8544	736.30	0.00	0.0000
CHD242	POTTERY	YAP	C36-13-S	10.6076	5[illegible]7809	0.4091	12.4905	3.1775	0.0000	2.7741	14.7500	33.6054	584.7097	1.2473	1.0695	81346.7	2.8246	183.97	14.80	0.0000
CHD243	POTTERY	YAP	C36-13-S	4.6630	5[illegible]030	0.4138	16.3128	2.6610	0.0000	2.6508	13.4070	50.7143	824.3771	1.3341	0.8577	98503.5	3.2342	120.03	9.92	0.0000
CHD244	POTTERY	YAP	C36-80-S	0.0000	4[illegible]853	0.2876	8.9571	3.2564	0.0000	1.1991	19.6139	88.4930	1701.8263	0.5547	1.1612	131777.5	4.3224	594.84	0.00	0.0000
CHD245	POTTERY	YAP	C36-80-S	0.0000	6[illegible]027	0.4789	15.5887	5.2361	0.0000	2.7190	17.1485	53.0869	1701.1930	0.3591	1.9720	135350.0	4.2231	443.75	0.00	0.0000
CHD246	POTTERY	YAP	C36-81-S	0.0000	4[illegible]333	0.3255	11.0124	3.5547	0.0000	1.7069	14.0135	77.4925	1377.3732	0.4196	1.2919	113853.4	3.1851	489.06	0.00	0.0000

ANID	MATERIAL	ISLAND	LOCATION	AS	LA	LU	ND	SM	U	YB	CE	CO	CR	CS	EU	FE	HF	NI	RB	SB
CHD247	POTTERY	YAP	C36-81-S	0.0000	5.1979	0.4869	10.2606	3.6844	0.0000	2.4622	12.6618	61.0142	1733.3206	0.6654	1.3953	133655.3	3.3987	546.51	14.32	0.0000
CHD248	POTTERY	YAP	C36-84-S	0.0000	5.6146	0.2192	14.8303	2.5505	0.0000	1.2203	15.7439	60.4086	1430.8168	1.4052	0.8740	119544.2	3.4717	362.17	15.98	0.0000
CHD249	POTTERY	YAP	C36-84-S	0.0000	3.8507	0.1624	0.0000	2.0243	2.3617	1.0250	29.7550	61.9052	3518.5098	1.1151	0.7392	140164.5	2.8044	285.33	7.53	0.0000
CHD250	POTTERY	YAP	C36-72-S	8.1644	10.1735	0.3543	13.9168	4.1613	0.0000	1.2203	30.2285	79.8190	1353.2955	0.6053	1.3631	125281.3	3.3768	809.53	0.00	0.4678
CHD251	POTTERY	YAP	C36-72-S	0.0000	1.6949	0.1675	6.4018	1.4804	0.0000	1.0652	8.5197	57.2245	1714.2863	0.0000	0.5161	153809.4	4.3358	459.83	0.00	0.0000
CHD252	POTTERY	YAP	C36-71-II/9	0.0000	4.2038	0.3472	9.6283	2.9469	0.0000	1.8726	24.3941	142.3530	1486.9235	0.6433	1.0099	132076.8	3.5729	708.34	0.00	0.0000
CHD253	POTTERY	YAP	C36-71-II/8	4.4687	5.3539	0.4693	6.5940	2.5282	2.0821	2.3265	20.2997	153.5763	236.3325	0.9278	0.8467	96224.8	2.7853	1085.16	0.00	0.0000
CHD254	POTTERY	YAP	C36-71-II/5	3.9750	4.8973	0.5031	7.1900	2.6681	0.0000	2.5479	12.0654	60.2493	290.1454	0.5167	0.8747	92634.9	2.8928	505.12	0.00	0.0000
CHD255	POTTERY	YAP	C36-83.1-I/12	0.0000	3.8200	0.4374	7.9834	2.3738	0.0000	2.4174	11.4706	41.8010	366.8637	1.3420	0.7787	95029.0	2.6162	135.74	0.00	0.0000
CHD256	POTTERY	YAP	C36-22.1-II/2	0.0000	5.4854	0.2495	7.1818	3.4353	0.0000	1.2789	26.4523	67.3066	2141.8650	0.8013	1.2375	135304.1	4.0871	680.47	0.00	0.0000
CHD257	POTTERY	YAP	C36-22.1-I/6	4.9350	2.7295	0.1291	0.0000	1.2512	1.1818	0.7716	13.5102	46.1273	1967.6047	0.6369	0.4694	162107.4	3.9194	584.94	0.00	0.0000
CHD258	POTTERY	YAP	C36-22.1-I/6	0.0000	3.5800	0.2185	0.0000	2.5314	0.0000	1.3776	15.6021	81.5279	2334.8687	1.6526	0.9479	158263.4	3.8909	781.82	0.00	0.0000
CHD259	POTTERY	YAP	C36-33-I/2	0.0000	4.6326	0.3187	9.1270	3.5572	0.0000	1.9506	21.2856	58.8441	1817.6918	1.5936	1.2214	109909.0	3.5805	599.87	0.00	0.0000
CHD260	POTTERY	YAP	C36-27-I/2	0.0000	4.1151	0.3258	0.0000	0.9850	0.0000	0.6303	6.9714	26.7016	697.1317	0.3323	0.3787	113329.7	3.0225	165.10	0.00	0.0000
CHD261	POTTERY	YAP	C36-27-I/2	5.8877	5.6047	0.2834	11.2752	2.8103	0.0000	1.5559	20.3646	76.1815	1820.4799	1.2645	1.0323	162460.3	3.5125	435.55	0.00	0.0000
CHD262	POTTERY	YAP	C36-06-I/3	0.0000	4.8221	0.2563	14.9861	3.2200	0.0000	1.6424	14.5098	68.9839	1382.2408	0.5512	1.0602	111203.2	2.8473	447.06	0.00	0.0000
CHD263	POTTERY	MOGMOG	MOG-54-III/2	0.0000	2.5152	0.1926	0.0000	0.9036	0.0000	0.6014	2.3558	45.6928	1659.2242	0.0000	0.3823	158388.8	3.9850	497.31	0.00	3.2750
CHD264	POTTERY	YAP	C36-76-I/3	0.0000	11.9356	0.5439	19.4466	6.1801	0.0000	2.5471	70.4559	165.2125	790.3105	0.4907	2.1772	130886.6	4.5870	193.97	0.00	0.0000
CHD265	POTTERY	YAP	C36-76-I/9	12.2042	4.6041	0.2059	9.0674	1.8607	0.0000	1.2377	17.3505	75.5877	1699.4083	0.0000	0.6462	122023.5	3.4173	602.15	0.00	0.0000
CHD266	POTTERY	MOGMOG	MOG-22-III/1	0.0000	7.4338	0.2656	11.5634	4.0785	0.0000	1.8804	30.4897	115.0384	1682.4008	0.0000	1.5043	123175.9	3.6606	525.04	0.00	12.4737
CHD267	POTTERY	MOGMOG	MOG-22-V/2	67.1339	5.6497	0.4317	10.3630	2.6706	2.7631	3.0505	11.8873	24.6846	117.4210	0.3877	0.8600	86723.0	3.3623	0.00	15.88	17.1192
CHD268	POTTERY	MOGMOG	MOG-22-III/1	0.0000	12.9797	0.1999	16.2689	4.6727	0.0000	1.6309	42.9887	130.4259	2066.7649	0.0000	1.6389	135808.7	4.0365	680.18	0.00	4.1129
CHD269	POTTERY	MOGMOG	MOG-25-V/1	0.0000	10.6037	0.2676	16.2166	4.1265	0.0000	1.5096	25.7029	61.9440	1053.8832	0.0000	1.4205	110571.7	3.1345	226.82	44.38	1.6178
CHD270	POTTERY	MOGMOG	MOG-25-II/1	0.0000	5.0179	0.3019	4.2846	1.9770	0.0000	1.4968	10.0202	14.5268	480.0189	0.0000	0.7428	119127.7	4.5260	173.54	0.00	0.0000
CHD271	POTTERY	MOGMOG	MOG-53-IV/2	0.0000	9.2907	0.2748	19.3934	4.8582	0.0000	2.4087	19.8041	50.9506	1645.1637	0.3607	1.7733	123876.6	3.8836	478.25	0.00	1.5379
CHD272	POTTERY	YAP	C36-78-I/7	16.6987	4.1717	0.2037	10.8104	2.6053	0.0000	1.1963	11.7535	125.1082	1719.5703	1.0467	0.9499	133217.8	3.1070	663.20	0.00	0.0000
CHD273	POTTERY	YAP	C36-77-I/3	0.0000	3.5396	0.1354	0.0000	1.1542	0.0000	0.6598	7.3043	16.5485	644.0224	0.4084	0.4274	129732.0	4.7340	224.18	0.00	0.0000
CHD274	POTTERY	YAP	C36-77-I/3	0.0000	4.4603	0.4417	6.9544	2.4584	0.0000	2.5868	11.0820	50.0244	539.1613	1.4332	0.8228	78617.6	3.1687	397.52	0.00	0.0000
CHD275	POTTERY	MOGMOG	MOG-43-III/4	0.0000	3.9428	0.1748	5.0564	2.9023	0.0000	1.4951	13.8532	76.6611	1836.1356	0.7070	1.0410	130107.2	3.3206	597.71	31.20	1.0892
CHD276	POTTERY	MOGMOG	MOG-43-III/2	0.0000	6.3444	0.3709	12.0936	4.0287	0.0000	2.0116	19.1312	24.4335	653.3561	0.0000	1.4896	117709.7	4.4407	166.59	0.00	7.2182
CHD277	POTTERY	MOGMOG	MOG-27-II/3	0.0000	7.5547	0.2985	14.8138	5.1491	0.0000	2.2493	31.8131	96.4664	1603.4782	0.4133	1.8099	122305.2	3.2964	567.47	0.00	0.8898
CHD278	POTTERY	YAP	C36-16-I/5	0.0000	7.0642	0.4221	13.2082	3.0535	1.4581	2.7373	18.8434	17.1924	663.5131	1.5513	1.0544	30181.5	4.0319	284.66	12.41	0.0000
CHD279	POTTERY	YAP	C36-16-I/5	0.0000	9.3858	0.2198	15.1500	4.0637	0.0000	1.6505	28.1355	93.3685	1664.8721	0.6679	1.4925	114084.8	3.0102	642.08	0.00	0.0000
CHD280	CLAY	YAP	C36-27-I/3	6.9601	6.8090	0.1797	0.0000	0.9072	0.0000	0.7098	7.2541	339.1569	10966.6800	0.0000	0.2870	252133.5	5.0981	1579.87	0.00	0.0000
CHD281	CLAY	YAP	C36-22.1-PROBE	0.0000	0.7544	0.0348	0.0000	0.1498	0.0000	0.2042	0.0000	138.0638	7235.5800	0.0000	0.0661	54759.2	0.0000	3548.65	0.00	0.0000
CHD282	CLAY	YAP	C28-2-I/1	0.0000	0.7496	0.0606	0.0000	0.2388	0.0000	0.4278	2.3981	10.0179	280.4600	0.0000	0.0616	129786.7	1.5293	0.00	0.00	0.0000
CHD283	CLAY	YAP	C36-16-II/3	0.0000	1.7486	0.0000	0.0000	0.4249	0.0000	0.0000	0.0000	857.6342	22801.3900	0.0000	0.0000	545260.4	0.0000	6146.08	0.00	0.0000
CHD284	POTTERY	MOGMOG	MOG-2.A6-I/1	0.0000	3.5875	0.2709	5.4683	2.0148	0.0000	2.1018	7.5015	12.9038	201.2500	0.0000	0.6672	28276.6	2.1705	0.00	0.00	0.4071
CHD285	POTTERY	YAP	C36-77-I/2	0.0000	11.1598	0.2104	16.8275	4.8761	0.0000	1.7412	29.2595	102.4668	2263.4500	1.2862	1.6378	147420.9	4.1026	903.44	0.00	0.0000
CHD286	POTTERY	MOGMOG	MOG-27-III/1	11.1083	7.7630	0.3656	8.2822	3.0976	0.0000	2.7814	14.9837	26.5702	231.5000	0.0000	1.2037	122648.9	3.7971	0.00	0.00	1.5053
CHD287	POTTERY	YAP	C36-22.2-II/3	0.0000	5.2588	0.3259	12.0429	3.3624	0.0000	3.1574	17.2193	55.7670	337.8100	0.0000	1.2951	169442.2	3.8300	47.49	0.00	0.0000
CHD288	POTTERY	YAP	C36-83.1-I/4	0.0000	7.8980	0.2392	16.1192	4.3144	0.0000	2.1053	20.8614	67.0292	1966.2600	0.0000	1.5603	125949.0	3.8233	535.18	0.00	0.0000
CHD289	POTTERY	YAP	C36-27-III/12	10.8481	4.5840	0.1726	8.9694	2.9371	0.0000	1.5071	22.4974	577.6903	1756.4100	0.0000	1.1196	186964.8	3.1414	1317.74	0.00	0.0000
CHD290	130 IO	YAP	C36-27-III/12	6.6614	6.3573	0.3608	6.4637	2.7565	1.6723	2.6563	16.8522	202.8347	194.7354	0.5370	0.9305	106953.9	2.5960	549.12	0.00	0.0000
CHD291	130 PASTE	YAP	C36-27-III/12	5.5799	8.9195	0.5422	10.1367	2.3330	0.9925	2.1048	20.5197	239.9689	191.0563	0.7973	0.7844	85162.4	2.6713	625.46	0.00	0.0000
CHD292	130 GROG	YAP	C36-27-III/12	4.6055	5.1148	0.5343	5.6132	2.2095	1.8936	2.2278	11.5019	123.0465	195.5418	0.7446	0.7301	67282.9	2.4571	398.16	0.00	0.0000
CHD293	254 IO	YAP	C36-71-II/5	9.7173	6.7309	0.4529	10.9570	3.3103	1.5954	3.0092	18.0940	61.3789	264.2365	0.3221	1.1274	151926.6	2.5243	590.67	9.02	0.0000
CHD294	254 PASTE	YAP	C36-71-II/5	6.8155	3.9758	0.4513	7.8293	2.1015	1.1772	2.1152	9.9186	64.0701	342.1773	0.6110	0.7027	90684.8	2.9397	839.53	0.00	0.0000
CHD295	254 GROG	YAP	C36-71-II/5	6.0225	6.6701	0.4515	10.7548	2.3369	1.5394	2.3262	14.7741	49.0771	239.4665	0.4258	0.7900	74446.0	2.8650	578.32	0.00	0.0000
CHD296	184 IO	MOGMOG	MOG-27-II/3	15.4474	7.1763	0.5753	10.3294	3.7169	1.0857	3.4956	18.8382	35.2913	336.5994	0.0000	1.2500	207027.7	2.5115	0.00	0.00	1.7214
CHD297	184 PASTE	MOGMOG	MOG-27-II/3	15.0573	5.0333	0.4136	8.9697	2.5891	1.5762	2.7567	11.3925	18.7809	126.2794	0.2933	0.8733	54395.0	3.4138	0.00	12.47	1.6781
CHD298	184 GROG	MOGMOG	MOG-27-II/3	13.0139	5.2274	0.4112	8.9509	2.6582	1.3282	2.6956	13.0065	16.5817	143.7185	0.2347	0.9116	63967.3	3.3771	0.00	13.11	1.7976
CHD299	CLAY	YAP	WENTARA	0.0000	1.3871	0.1429	3.7068	0.9529	0.0000	0.6845	8.2296	39.3767	1626.8767	0.0000	0.3125	180247.2	5.0772	210.21	0.00	0.0000
CHD300	CLAY	YAP	NLUL	0.0000	3.0992	0.2726	4.9930	2.0072	0.0000	1.7092	7.0909	40.7516	238.4262	0.0000	0.7611	83900.4	1.2583	0.00	17.11	0.0000
CHD301	CLAY	YAP	NLUL	6.8233	1.8502	0.1667	0.0000	0.9332	0.0000	1.0728	3.9766	10.9279	115.8854	0.2032	0.2788	92100.0	1.0227	0.00	26.11	0.3315
CHD302	CLAY	YAP	GOOCHOL	0.0000	2.9990	0.1763	4.6123	1.2105	0.0000	0.9036	5.5485	23.0887	629.8721	0.0000	0.3940	135297.5	3.4093	123.76	0.00	0.0000
CHD303	CLAY	YAP	MUYUB	0.0000	3.3232	0.1731	8.8543	2.1399	0.0000	1.1815	6.1907	48.5904	2133.7517	0.0000	0.7767	147188.6	3.7152	601.81	0.00	0.0000
CHD304	CLAY	YAP	MAKI	0.0000	7.4667	0.4587	13.6208	4.6765	0.0000	2.2958	12.1169	50.0884	1602.8107	0.0000	1.6388	149840.6	4.5771	540.73	0.00	0.0000
CHD305	CLAY	YAP	AYRECH	0.0000	11.0260	0.3643	13.0568	4.3781	0.0000	1.6623	43.7600	150.0805	1340.2076	0.0000	1.4685	162588.5	3.6557	384.50	0.00	0.0000
CHD306	CLAY	YAP	TABELANG	0.0000	6.9037	0.2398	13.9691	4.3014	0.0000	1.9760	22.2688	73.2605	1456.5341	0.0000	1.5226	103244.8	3.2052	558.35	0.00	0.0000
CHD307	CLAY	YAP	KADAY	0.0000	7.4849	0.2717	8.9918	3.8074	0.0000	1.8216	33.9768	162.7846	2241.5632	0.0000	1.3240	139411.4	3.4980	965.96	0.00	0.0000
CHD308	CLAY	YAP	KADAY	0.0000	4.5032	0.2113	6.9783	2.2286	0.0000	1.3451	19.3515	45.0283	2734.4153	0.0000	0.7437	184473.4	4.4904	539.33	0.00	0.0000
CHD309	CLAY	YAP	ARINGEL	0.0000	7.8478	0.3975	15.3911	5.1327	0.0000	2.5375	15.0252	48.4731	1665.3709	0.0000	1.8842	117426.4	3.8346	572.14	0.00	0.0000
CHD310	CLAY	YAP	DACHANGER	0.0000	12.6294	0.4966	25.9885	6.1706	0.0000	2.4270	38.0757	108.8437	2038.6950	0.0000	2.3454	139700.7	4.5638	771.48	0.00	0.0000
CHD311	CLAY	YAP	GITAM	0.0000	5.6550	0.2665	6.3719	1.8699	0.0000	1.1036	13.5238	82.1014	2292.2073	0.0000	0.6200	155553.4	4.8991	550.58	0.00	0.0000
CHD312	CLAY	YAP	BAANIMAUT	0.0000	12.3595	0.3945	19.6852	6.2205	0.0000	2.3934	31.3954	72.5886	1778.5931	0.0000	1.9151	130074.0	3.8767	684.79	0.00	0.0000
CHD313	CLAY	YAP	NEL	3.6975	0.6144	0.1850	0.0000	0.3484	0.7998	0.7826	1.1414	27.9441	169.3758	0.0000	0.1045	131130.6	1.9498	0.00	0.00	0.0000
CHD314	CLAY	YAP	FUNECHU	4.0724	5.3188	0.7745	8.8479	3.5577	0.0000	3.4153	14.6183	49.0447	73.2602	0.0000	1.2868	118419.1	2.0932	0.00	0.00	0.0000
CHD315	CLAY	YAP	BURUDEMIC	6.4369	0.8810	0.1921	0.0000	0.2716	1.7463	0.5621	0.6536	9.0111	84.4177	0.0000	0.0565	113497.7	2.5289	0.00	0.00	0.2484
CHD316	CLAY	YAP	ARIMOW	0.0000	21.2095	1.4757	37.9887	13.2368	0.0000	10.8947	42.4995	41.4730	18.4663	0.0000	4.3122	71679.9	3.2998	71.49	25.58	0.0000
CHD317	POTTERY	CHUUK	TKFE-1-TP4	101.3877	20.4642	0.5162	22.0197	7.8941	43.2394	1.0746	48.6456	56.0402	541.4243	0.0000	1.3465	92371.4	6.4792	199.72	0.00	12.1900
CHD318	POTTERY	CHUUK	TKFE-4-4	87.4717	38.3083	0.7600	48.9663	13.8160	65.4229	1.3551	75.6545	30.8885	522.8937	0.3701	2.8909	77727.3	12.2198	193.94	0.00	6.7730
CHD319	POTTERY	KOSRAE	LELU	17.9289	59.0154	0.3991	51.7437	12.3938	5.1607	3.1712	130.9406	79.4500	1404.0968	0.0000	4.1684	142446.8	12.0194	279.77	20.68	1.0232
CHD320	POTTERY	KOSRAE	LELU	37.6919	57.2993	0.5081	59.7382	13.9894	10.2944	2.7321	126.1936	68.8680	456.9099	0.2337	4.2655	94354.7	12.1894	175.98	18.49	1.1644
CHD321	POTTERY	KOSRAE	LELU 210-230	12.0985	63.8806	0.6178	67.9278	14.3293	11.2176	2.9533	145.1906	62.7548	454.6316	0.5685	4.6487	90269.7	12.1400	181.75	28.10	0.9705
CHD322	POTTERY	KOSRAE	LELU 210-230	10.3976	67.7668	0.4773	70.9422	15.0940	7.0101	2.9303	149.8392	73.8212	808.8908	0.0000	4.7505	89689.4	14.0313	273.16	0.00	2.5229

ANID	MATERIAL	ISLAND	LOCATION	SC	SR	TA	TB	TH	ZN	ZR	AL	BA	CA	DY	K	MN	NA	TI	V
CHD001	POTTERY	YAP	C28-ST3.03 (40-44)	13.8637	0.00	0.3690	0.6247	0.3930	97.79	0.00	83302.1	85.6	18447.0	3.0698	2293.9	2094.4	3152.9	12747.6	368.0
CHD002	POTTERY	CHUUK	TKFE-1-TP3	36.4506	1128.61	4.6542	1.3855	3.1426	93.02	600.59	118737.2	82.4	68137.0	5.7910	1913.2	638.7	1483.7	48474.8	537.5
CHD003	POTTERY	CHUUK	TKFE-2-W4	37.7268	86.24	3.8683	1.2309	2.9245	109.26	509.26	125754.9	0.0	3403.0	5.9997	2381.9	633.9	7266.5	45287.0	674.1
CHD004	POTTERY	POHNPEI	POC3-1-DPK-227.41	34.2525	527.32	5.1029	2.1791	8.1478	238.69	311.36	98291.5	0.0	23764.2	10.7174	1915.3	880.1	6575.6	31680.8	372.3
CHD005	POTTERY	POHNPEI	POC3-1-DPK-227.26	32.3242	872.78	8.4124	3.0488	11.1115	118.34	593.32	130612.8	0.0	60952.0	13.3852	2253.3	244.5	6332.9	46303.9	500.3
CHD006	POTTERY	POHNPEI	POC3-1-DPK-227.210	29.9903	1420.85	4.4560	1.9580	5.7058	119.58	515.64	95830.4	0.0	105944.2	9.2374	3548.1	408.3	5029.4	30253.2	415.3
CHD007	POTTERY	POHNPEI	POC3-1-DPK-227.229	34.4814	1870.56	6.4247	3.3356	13.4113	90.70	553.22	99449.5	0.0	138874.0	13.5325	1541.4	197.5	6156.1	28287.7	229.0
CHD008	POTTERY	POHNPEI	POC3-1-DPK-215.30	44.9746	1348.77	4.8792	1.9701	5.6634	507.52	342.58	118501.6	61.8	6475.0	11.3144	2393.9	1588.6	5183.5	43519.1	484.2
CHD009	POTTERY	POHNPEI	POC3-1-DPK-211.16	43.8977	428.10	4.9540	2.4339	5.5077	224.16	248.19	118292.8	47.6	5026.0	13.3262	779.7	1697.3	7581.7	39086.3	484.2
CHD010	POTTERY	POHNPEI	WASAU-8-I/1	42.5809	0.00	5.4262	2.6271	6.6501	291.64	360.86	118476.1	100.2	7134.0	11.0261	3548.9	2014.7	6259.8	38742.4	449.6
CHD011	POTTERY	POHNPEI	WASAU-9-I/1	45.1817	0.00	5.0958	3.2596	5.6793	362.36	377.89	115881.5	56.7	5219.0	15.6636	1150.2	2021.4	5523.4	43563.3	491.6
CHD012	POTTERY	POHNPEI	WASAU-10-I/1	45.0624	923.59	5.2577	2.3657	5.6762	581.02	384.53	119709.2	0.0	4900.0	11.3617	2072.6	1846.2	5582.3	42478.3	480.0
CHD013	POTTERY	PALAU	AIRAI VIEW HOTEL 40-70CM	65.0562	0.00	0.0000	0.0000	0.5322	69.20	0.00	163512.9	38.9	11466.7	1.5611	1277.7	147.1	748.3	5686.6	377.4
CHD014	POTTERY	PALAU	AIRAI VIEW HOTEL 40-70CM	65.0723	0.00	0.0000	0.0000	0.3926	76.15	0.00	173998.1	45.1	9756.1	2.0089	299.0	164.6	375.8	6191.2	430.3
CHD015	POTTERY	PALAU	AIRAI VIEW HOTEL 40-70CM	67.0340	0.00	0.0000	0.0000	0.4077	91.10	0.00	169930.3	48.2	10427.0	1.6980	0.0	142.7	595.1	6337.1	360.3
CHD016	POTTERY	PALAU	AIRAI VIEW HOTEL 40-70CM	62.8214	0.00	0.0000	0.0000	0.5706	59.23	0.00	171030.8	36.5	9960.7	1.8366	0.0	146.4	372.5	6065.0	411.9
CHD017	POTTERY	PALAU	AIRAI VIEW HOTEL 40-70CM	64.0590	0.00	0.0000	0.2299	0.4251	60.02	0.00	171037.9	0.0	9591.0	1.8058	0.0	162.6	349.9	6655.1	464.4
CHD018	POTTERY	PALAU	AIRAI VIEW HOTEL 40-70CM	61.9707	0.00	0.0000	0.7401	0.5084	83.58	0.00	163707.8	36.7	10270.0	0.9784	1725.4	555.0	549.5	7024.9	457.3
CHD019	POTTERY	PALAU	AIRAI VIEW HOTEL 40-70CM	65.1423	0.00	0.0000	0.5235	0.3764	70.30	0.00	153030.1	0.0	10020.3	3.9084	0.0	164.0	872.8	4900.8	355.4
CHD020	POTTERY	PALAU	AIRAI VIEW HOTEL 40-70CM	66.6041	0.00	0.0000	0.6606	0.5298	60.71	0.00	159668.0	52.2	9432.0	4.2817	2198.5	519.0	761.2	6590.2	376.8
CHD021	POTTERY	PALAU	AIRAI VIEW HOTEL 40-70CM	58.3365	0.00	0.0000	0.5627	0.4495	70.36	0.00	157592.5	53.7	11160.0	3.3521	538.4	134.2	627.5	6031.5	385.7
CHD022	POTTERY	PALAU	AIRAI VIEW HOTEL 40-70CM	58.7618	119.85	0.0000	0.4113	0.6086	68.91	0.00	152798.3	83.9	10089.0	3.1115	1425.6	120.2	651.1	6175.6	404.8
CHD023	POTTERY	PALAU	AIRAI VIEW HOTEL 40-70CM	58.0111	0.00	0.0000	0.4885	0.5222	51.39	0.00	162629.0	0.0	11668.0	3.3992	0.0	129.0	406.8	6752.7	335.8
CHD024	POTTERY	PALAU	AIRAI VIEW HOTEL 40-70CM	48.9605	0.00	0.0000	0.4519	0.5280	58.49	109.59	166489.9	35.4	11198.0	3.5354	0.0	117.0	431.6	7281.9	355.6
CHD025	POTTERY	PALAU	AIRAI VIEW HOTEL 40-70CM	61.2535	0.00	0.0000	0.0000	0.6059	85.22	0.00	166552.8	39.2	11004.0	1.6872	0.0	194.5	449.2	6026.7	406.6
CHD026	POTTERY	GUAM	GUAM, BARA-TUMON T-1@200CMBS	25.8319	3010.93	0.0000	0.4212	0.5285	74.18	52.86	85644.7	0.0	166030.0	2.5976	2775.3	223.6	2493.5	3405.0	133.6
CHD027	POTTERY	GUAM	GUAM, BARA-TUMON T-1@200CMBS	19.8896	4000.81	0.0000	0.5120	0.4168	54.25	0.00	67204.1	0.0	208358.0	2.6264	1395.5	155.8	1627.6	2748.7	80.8
CHD028	POTTERY	GUAM	GUAM, TOMEN MALESSO SURFACE	4[illegible].9076	585.37	0.0000	0.6894	0.7334	127.78	0.00	95917.7	196.1	13098.0	3.3968	9822.9	1824.5	9206.8	2811.5	237.2
CHD029	POTTERY	GUAM	GUAM, TOMEN MALESSO SURFACE	35.0061	878.51	0.0000	0.4716	0.9558	107.58	0.00	115445.4	175.9	15508.0	2.8970	14098.6	531.9	13122.4	4738.0	146.3
CHD030	POTTERY	GUAM	GUAM, TOMEN MALESSO SURFACE	41.9484	636.55	0.0000	0.7843	1.1216	139.71	0.00	123378.4	97.6	14775.1	6.0814	6372.4	588.0	4056.4	4766.1	286.4
CHD031	POTTERY	GUAM	GUAM, TOMEN MALESSO SURFACE	31.4773	832.56	0.0000	0.4118	0.6514	106.32	0.00	97136.8	188.8	24270.0	2.2498	12524.9	863.7	10832.6	3981.1	219.2
CHD032	POTTERY	GUAM	GUAM, TOMEN MALESSO SURFACE	34.5789	667.34	0.0000	1.8954	0.5655	107.28	0.00	94178.5	180.4	17016.9	9.8842	2850.6	771.3	20138.3	2357.9	180.1
CHD033	POTTERY	GUAM	GUAM, TOMEN MALESSO SURFACE	47.4879	878.48	0.1006	1.0609	1.2721	125.81	0.00	124098.1	179.9	16978.0	5.9303	12036.0	1298.9	6968.3	4960.8	210.4
CHD034	POTTERY	GUAM	GUAM, TOMEN MALESSO SURFACE	36.0511	773.84	0.1091	3.4220	0.6065	184.39	176.26	106846.9	204.8	20430.1	20.4369	13465.6	662.8	14689.4	2610.7	176.6
CHD035	POTTERY	GUAM	GUAM, TOMEN MALESSO SURFACE	42.0204	888.42	0.0000	0.5495	1.5635	119.36	0.00	121201.4	98.3	16732.6	3.2151	9951.7	465.1	8071.1	5207.7	248.2
CHD036	POTTERY	GUAM	GUAM, TARAGUE BEACH I/1 0-2.5CMB	57.3829	0.00	0.0000	0.5463	1.1716	67.95	0.00	146816.6	0.0	20566.3	4.0426	3584.1	511.0	2468.6	5316.5	272.0
CHD037	POTTERY	GUAM	GUAM, TARAGUE BEACH I/1 0-2.5CMB	48.1177	0.00	0.0000	1.1772	1.8070	115.51	0.00	136185.9	65.7	17796.0	7.5155	5288.9	366.0	3913.9	5167.9	264.6
CHD038	POTTERY	GUAM	GUAM, 1992, SURFACE COLLECTION	45.3485	869.03	0.0000	0.8948	0.5786	114.28	0.00	108672.1	0.0	17096.0	5.9115	7804.2	983.6	13662.7	5104.1	295.6
CHD039	POTTERY	GUAM	GUAM-3, 1992, SURFACE COLLECTION	46.2475	0.00	0.2154	0.6414	0.8540	66.07	0.00	117613.5	0.0	28706.6	3.4319	0.0	964.2	7429.5	4429.6	265.2
CHD040	POTTERY	GUAM	GUAM-1, 1992, SURFACE COLLECTION	48.9781	302.85	0.0000	0.0000	1.0812	59.29	0.00	141967.5	0.0	11163.0	2.6043	10489.2	754.2	8578.3	5241.8	260.8
CHD041	POTTERY	YAP	C36-22.1 I/5	11.1139	0.00	3.8955	1.7579	46.6172	121.44	306.69	135705.7	504.1	1477.0	9.8989	38080.2	945.3	5304.5	2900.6	45.9
CHD042	POTTERY	YAP	PEMRANG, INTOH-1	36.8659	1375.43	0.7258	0.5769	0.4703	72.68	0.00	73695.5	0.0	90318.6	3.0034	0.0	1755.2	5777.4	16646.0	474.3
CHD043	POTTERY	YAP	PEMRANG, INTOH-2	51.3173	301.69	0.6674	0.5580	0.5825	82.73	0.00	96199.3	0.0	30531.4	3.7004	11401.6	557.6	14220.0	18400.4	493.8
CHD044	POTTERY	YAP	ATLIW SURFACE	49.3450	0.00	0.4871	0.0000	0.0000	103.84	0.00	95753.5	0.0	9069.2	2.2153	7374.9	678.0	11309.9	15450.9	506.0
CHD045	POTTERY	YAP	ATLIW, MEN'S HOUSE SURFACE	53.7068	281.96	0.5869	0.4719	0.3253	80.25	92.08	102613.8	0.0	19718.7	2.7276	0.0	882.4	12250.0	16858.7	619.9
CHD046	POTTERY	YAP	ATLIW SURFACE	41.7877	0.00	0.8211	0.7560	0.7690	100.25	0.00	80261.9	540.1	24412.2	4.0651	2724.9	1999.4	4796.7	14518.6	453.4
CHD047	POTTERY	YAP	ATLIW SURFACE	46.2314	396.69	0.6399	0.6964	0.4555	85.59	92.32	84153.5	0.0	13485.6	3.9660	6770.6	747.5	13134.3	17428.7	495.1
CHD048	POTTERY	YAP	ATLIW SURFACE	45.3786	0.00	0.5311	0.5070	0.4016	71.27	139.60	90133.3	0.0	20704.9	2.5616	3575.1	1393.9	11842.7	15686.4	567.5
CHD049	POTTERY	YAP	MAAP VILLAGE SURFACE	49.1509	0.00	0.4924	1.2002	0.3868	147.35	0.00	96680.5	0.0	7199.0	2.5897	0.0	669.4	2622.2	13469.7	596.2
CHD050	POTTERY	YAP	BINAW	44.9166	0.00	0.8115	0.0000	0.5214	128.99	0.00	84042.7	0.0	21470.4	4.5582	0.0	3368.0	3540.6	17369.0	572.0
CHD051	POTTERY	YAP	BINAW	54.3951	0.00	0.4886	1.5497	0.4015	145.12	0.00	103714.5	0.0	11841.4	4.5539	1915.5	1485.3	1511.3	15363.8	438.4
CHD052	POTTERY	YAP	BINAW	61.2422	0.00	0.7103	1.6577	0.6808	184.93	0.00	115828.1	0.0	5292.0	2.3432	2423.3	236.6	2130.4	19359.9	322.1
CHD053	POTTERY	YAP	RUU', LAGOON SHORE, SURFACE	59.5665	0.00	0.3937	1.5833	0.0000	113.33	0.00	107759.6	0.0	6894.6	1.9466	0.0	3137.0	2884.2	13784.7	550.6
CHD054	POTTERY	YAP	BINAW	46.7634	0.00	0.7703	2.0913	0.8003	142.86	132.24	87464.0	0.0	23976.8	4.2947	0.0	1708.3	3995.5	15723.7	546.5
CHD055	POTTERY	YAP	BINAW	44.3605	0.00	0.4751	1.4876	0.3595	141.57	79.68	98373.4	0.0	23002.7	4.4114	6535.9	1206.7	6068.7	14966.5	505.8
CHD056	POTTERY	YAP	BINAW	61.0337	0.00	0.6905	1.2086	0.7147	264.98	116.65	112996.7	0.0	6558.9	2.4471	1577.3	298.5	2251.1	19209.0	325.9
CHD057	POTTERY	YAP	BINAW	52.2607	0.00	0.4897	1.2393	0.6175	0.00	0.00	104065.0	0.0	12917.7	2.2452	1247.2	807.1	10929.6	13534.9	365.3
CHD058	POTTERY	YAP	GITAM	48.0581	0.00	0.4948	1.0282	0.5034	1164.69	0.00	91332.3	279.6	10357.9	2.7817	0.0	3291.5	12084.9	15929.3	627.2
CHD059	POTTERY	YAP	BINAW	48.2531	0.00	0.5116	0.0000	0.3276	245.44	0.00	96235.5	0.0	9851.0	1.6232	1343.6	604.1	2252.1	12756.9	298.3
CHD060	POTTERY	YAP	GITAM	55.4528	0.00	0.6262	0.0000	0.2648	3788.70	131.41	92733.6	0.0	12256.1	4.6819	0.0	387.2	12917.8	16369.0	541.0
CHD061	POTTERY	YAP	GITAM	50.8836	0.00	0.6241	1.6311	0.4489	923.10	0.00	93345.3	0.0	7847.0	4.3573	0.0	447.6	13017.2	17089.5	551.5
CHD062	POTTERY	YAP	GITAM	49.7694	0.00	0.6951	1.7901	0.4675	934.28	0.00	93453.5	0.0	8397.0	4.0202	0.0	377.9	13247.5	17942.5	567.7
CHD063	POTTERY	YAP	GITAM	51.6436	0.00	0.5627	1.4989	0.4045	804.02	0.00	91551.9	0.0	8100.0	3.9589	0.0	390.9	12943.9	16597.0	549.6
CHD064	POTTERY	YAP	GITAM	50.2716	0.00	0.6661	1.3315	0.4041	4670.37	0.00	90244.3	0.0	10122.6	3.1955	0.0	421.3	13339.6	16628.2	553.2
CHD065	POTTERY	YAP	GITAM	50.5761	0.00	0.7353	0.9244	0.4299	1037.50	0.00	91556.4	0.0	9718.0	2.7736	0.0	432.2	12750.7	16814.9	555.7
CHD066	POTTERY	YAP	GITAM	51.9130	0.00	0.6042	1.2645	0.6056	1698.20	0.00	94499.5	0.0	8845.3	3.2874	0.0	408.6	13210.3	17863.8	593.2
CHD067	POTTERY	YAP	GITAM	58.6812	0.00	0.5409	1.3679	0.4716	1221.23	123.72	92214.9	0.0	8536.0	2.4484	0.0	352.5	13460.9	17005.5	566.2
CHD068	POTTERY	YAP	GITAM	50.5705	0.00	0.6159	1.5748	0.6094	2143.86	0.00	90819.6	0.0	9253.0	3.0485	0.0	449.5	12920.2	17144.0	559.3
CHD069	POTTERY	YAP	GITAM	50.4727	0.00	0.5578	1.7539	0.2172	831.40	0.00	90661.8	0.0	7349.0	4.0631	0.0	1132.4	13274.3	16504.8	574.7
CHD070	POTTERY	YAP	GITAM	54.4417	0.00	0.5719	1.7297	0.4003	6207.92	0.00	91428.9	0.0	9438.1	2.8456	0.0	941.8	12763.2	16159.3	552.2
CHD071	POTTERY	YAP	GITAM	49.9261	0.00	0.5839	1.5748	0.4393	783.63	0.00	89231.6	0.0	9022.3	3.5690	0.0	361.4	13060.8	16659.0	558.4
CHD072	POTTERY	YAP	GITAM	56.1014	0.00	0.5335	1.1034	0.5286	3105.17	0.00	89065.0	0.0	9938.0	2.5154	0.0	547.1	12949.0	16476.6	542.9
CHD073	POTTERY	YAP	GITAM	53.2252	0.00	0.6978	1.4356	0.3487	8516.36	0.00	87562.7	0.0	8171.0	3.6914	0.0	1248.3	12533.5	17256.7	551.3
CHD074	POTTERY	YAP	GITAM	52.8637	0.00	0.5942	1.2562	0.4997	2213.94	0.00	89868.6	0.0	9982.0	3.0295	0.0	296.5	12220.9	16920.7	556.8
CHD075	POTTERY	YAP	GITAM	58.8673	0.00	0.5710	0.9740	0.6508	945.67	0.00	90428.9	0.0	10607.6	2.2104	0.0	354.3	12684.4	17001.6	576.3
CHD076	POTTERY	YAP	THENFAAR	55.0294	0.00	0.5908	0.0000	0.7600	175.91	142.95	106475.1	0.0	13439.2	1.7677	2667.8	753.1	4854.0	18323.9	463.3
CHD077	POTTERY	YAP	THENFAAR	54.8967	0.00	0.6682	0.0000	0.6662	182.95	0.00	109465.7	0.0	10846.5	1.1882	1260.4	710.6	3851.9	18045.2	474.7
CHD078	POTTERY	YAP	THENFAAR	54.0103	0.00	0.6821	1.3721	0.7134	180.23	125.25	103221.1	0.0	11094.7	3.4511	4449.8	644.9	6322.8	18828.5	418.1
CHD079	POTTERY	YAP	THENFAAR	55.8046	0.00	0.5930	0.0000	0.6973	217.00	0.00	101784.2	0.0	9062.0	1.9587	5046.7	622.7	11840.2	15319.1	387.0
CHD080	POTTERY	YAP	THENFAAR	57.9109	0.00	0.5149	1.7709	0.4708	183.60	0.00	100030.6	0.0	6255.0	3.2291	935.7	591.7	4907.6	14442.6	462.5
CHD081	POTTERY	YAP	THENFAAR	47.6383	0.00	0.4003	2.0537	0.2524	153.83	0.00	84958.5	0.0	11951.0	4.1948	16407.0	2519.1	4935.8	14332.5	364.1
CHD082	POTTERY	YAP	THENFAAR	55.2513	0.00	0.6833	1.1307	0.5206	164.55	127.54	105710.5	0.0	12039.0	1.3109	1081.1	702.6	4217.3	19100.3	467.3

ANID	MATERIAL	ISLAND	LOCATION	SC	SR	TA	TB	TH	ZN	ZR	AL	BA	CA	DY	K	MN	NA	TI	V
CHD083	POTTERY	YAP	THENFAAR	57.6466	0.00	0.6375	1.8130	0.2731	174.46	166.18	109215.2	0.0	10978.0	3.6219	3719.3	679.5	3202.6	17803.1	609.4
CHD084	POTTERY	YAP	THENFAAR	60.7731	0.00	1.0438	0.9250	0.6982	189.55	126.76	111716.0	0.0	6459.0	1.2654	3984.1	999.3	3755.4	23704.8	324.5
CHD085	POTTERY	YAP	THENFAAR	56.8607	0.00	0.6228	1.3757	0.8000	153.31	0.00	102109.8	0.0	17329.0	2.9196	0.0	826.5	5921.5	15590.7	434.2
CHD086	POTTERY	YAP	C28- LAGOON SHORE, SURFACE	41.1591	0.00	0.4525	0.9870	0.4555	107.34	0.00	79095.1	0.0	25512.3	3.3967	0.0	1061.1	3856.2	12002.2	388.1
CHD087	POTTERY	YAP	C28- LAGOON SHORE, SURFACE	25.3976	0.00	0.1082	0.4815	0.5394	83.66	43.68	80984.1	0.0	10201.2	2.2909	0.0	219.5	11983.5	3729.2	165.4
CHD088	POTTERY	YAP	C28- LAGOON SHORE, SURFACE	42.0871	0.00	0.3752	1.5376	0.0000	125.11	0.00	83690.4	0.0	15921.0	3.7871	0.0	957.1	3516.8	11840.9	359.5
CHD089	POTTERY	YAP	C28-ST-3 (0-30)	55.4557	0.00	0.4077	1.6197	0.4479	158.94	0.00	100647.9	0.0	15931.7	4.8750	0.0	1001.8	2573.6	14104.0	573.0
CHD090	POTTERY	YAP	C28-1.01.200 I/1	54.5775	0.00	0.0000	1.7857	0.6244	137.23	0.00	117996.7	35.1	1790.0	1.4619	0.0	152.8	1098.4	6748.4	461.1
CHD091	POTTERY	YAP	C28-ST5.1 (28-40)	45.5206	0.00	0.3951	1.3252	0.4409	160.14	0.00	86679.9	0.0	14917.6	2.3412	1776.7	1698.3	3287.2	10167.7	473.7
CHD092	POTTERY	YAP	C28- LAGOON SHORE, SURFACE	58.2594	0.00	0.6217	1.7745	0.6749	185.10	100.97	102470.8	0.0	5080.2	1.5533	0.0	1108.4	2224.4	16618.6	567.9
CHD093	POTTERY	YAP	C28-2.1.1.1	42.2350	0.00	0.4602	1.4709	0.4539	132.98	80.20	80684.7	117.0	17531.0	2.1947	0.0	1482.9	3003.6	13352.8	395.4
CHD094	POTTERY	YAP	C28- LAGOON SHORE, SURFACE	44.6502	0.00	0.4010	1.3445	0.0000	131.39	0.00	87247.2	0.0	15240.0	3.7001	0.0	1057.8	2950.8	13545.9	383.7
CHD095	POTTERY	YAP	C28- LAGOON SHORE, SURFACE	44.5315	0.00	0.6353	1.6830	0.3952	120.15	0.00	85018.6	0.0	16160.0	3.9658	0.0	959.0	3013.7	13309.3	385.1
CHD096	POTTERY	YAP	C28- LAGOON SHORE, SURFACE	42.4651	0.00	0.4268	1.4870	0.5345	137.34	0.00	84667.5	0.0	36960.0	3.3260	3648.6	1059.8	13869.3	13416.3	433.0
CHD097	POTTERY	YAP	C28- LAGOON SHORE, SURFACE	37.4233	0.00	0.6159	0.5715	0.2160	75.12	97.31	72517.6	0.0	15570.9	2.7679	2468.4	1420.9	3335.0	16973.1	408.9
CHD098	POTTERY	YAP	C28-2.1.1.2 I/1	49.6920	0.00	0.6438	1.1131	0.5339	73.48	0.00	95283.4	0.0	16334.0	2.5553	0.0	2202.8	4445.6	15856.0	405.5
CHD099	POTTERY	YAP	C28-2.1.1.3 I/1	47.5999	0.00	0.4968	0.3574	0.3640	58.06	0.00	90745.7	0.0	11919.0	2.9322	0.0	1468.2	1801.7	14023.5	455.5
CHD100	POTTERY	YAP	C28-2.1.1.4 I/1	47.8184	0.00	0.5009	0.4129	0.3117	66.74	0.00	87647.0	140.4	26436.4	2.6018	0.0	1074.3	5163.7	13967.0	358.2
CHD101	POTTERY	YAP	C36-77, SURFACE	40.6761	0.00	0.0000	0.2246	0.3617	254.59	0.00	102557.3	0.0	3243.0	2.1089	0.0	317.1	2208.2	5163.9	387.2
CHD102	POTTERY	YAP	C36-77-I/12	23.9030	857.73	2.5681	0.3857	2.5985	50.62	152.85	99034.7	161.9	30308.3	2.1729	0.0	1194.3	25356.2	15740.2	265.4
CHD103	POTTERY	YAP	C36-78-I/5	53.7870	502.09	0.4302	0.3277	0.5166	58.36	0.00	117148.6	0.0	19293.6	2.3013	0.0	1009.4	15098.5	14268.5	501.1
CHD104	POTTERY	YAP	C36-78-I/9	43.3373	0.00	0.3480	0.6045	0.2895	55.78	86.86	84690.4	0.0	17731.8	3.6162	0.0	1050.2	3264.6	11256.9	384.0
CHD105	CLAY	YAP	C36-78-I/1	11.0791	1696.47	0.0000	0.3447	0.0000	53.11	0.00	16501.5	313.0	107115.8	0.6534	0.0	7936.0	3166.7	2712.5	168.5
CHD106	POTTERY	YAP	C36-78-I/4	40.6996	249.11	0.4730	0.4877	0.3744	77.12	92.14	88251.4	0.0	37489.8	3.2718	0.0	1010.3	6150.5	14295.1	491.8
CHD107	POTTERY	YAP	C36-78-I/7	38.7760	0.00	0.3556	0.4461	0.2765	61.49	0.00	70018.2	0.0	25959.8	2.4996	0.0	1144.2	4136.6	11068.6	450.8
CHD108	POTTERY	YAP	C36-45-SURFACE	38.4066	152.13	0.4544	0.4613	0.4131	110.69	0.00	71656.2	0.0	35074.0	3.2263	3980.9	1187.6	3851.7	12708.0	386.1
CHD109	POTTERY	YAP	C36-45-SURFACE	27.8241	123.20	0.0000	0.3073	0.4454	88.61	94.29	89729.3	0.0	13086.7	1.5388	1718.2	229.9	4256.5	4697.4	239.3
CHD110	POTTERY	YAP	WONYAAN SURFACE	41.6876	168.56	0.4066	0.6974	0.2848	73.26	66.03	81924.0	0.0	26089.6	4.2115	0.0	1563.4	4607.4	12824.2	429.5
CHD111	POTTERY	YAP	WONYAAN SURFACE	51.5862	476.54	1.2080	0.9140	1.0772	80.85	0.00	93493.1	0.0	22718.8	2.1579	10223.0	1573.7	9878.6	21227.1	335.1
CHD112	POTTERY	YAP	WONYAAN SURFACE	40.7942	265.79	0.3254	0.8647	0.4138	96.11	0.00	79754.3	47.4	26703.8	3.9869	0.0	1637.2	4145.9	10937.0	382.1
CHD113	POTTERY	YAP	WONYAAN SURFACE	40.2484	206.70	0.3173	0.6831	0.2997	100.88	118.03	85496.5	0.0	24618.4	3.7601	0.0	1816.0	4026.1	11294.5	379.9
CHD114	POTTERY	YAP	WONYAAN SURFACE	44.3702	337.59	0.6201	0.5135	0.5004	78.53	117.08	88537.2	0.0	36757.7	4.5784	0.0	1446.6	7374.9	17351.5	397.8
CHD115	POTTERY	YAP	C36-45-II/1	55.2336	195.13	0.5045	0.4141	0.9845	69.57	163.83	97761.8	82.2	34482.0	2.0702	5775.8	538.2	10645.5	14060.9	545.7
CHD116	POTTERY	YAP	C36-45-I/4	56.0375	369.62	0.7455	0.2722	1.0108	74.52	0.00	89932.7	72.1	18198.6	1.2995	0.0	287.0	19543.0	10426.0	432.2
CHD117	POTTERY	YAP	C36-45-I/4	48.2706	187.81	0.4630	0.6186	0.4696	105.14	0.00	97466.6	72.3	26962.3	4.1667	0.0	1128.7	5708.9	16780.6	490.4
CHD118	POTTERY	YAP	C36-76-I/8	37.3906	443.01	0.8035	0.6693	0.6154	91.09	94.97	75506.3	0.0	40795.0	4.0021	0.0	3214.1	5513.7	12945.4	463.8
CHD119	POTTERY	YAP	C36-76-I/4	25.7167	472.65	0.0000	0.3627	0.2627	83.47	0.00	81984.4	0.0	15249.8	2.0288	2361.0	350.5	9210.7	4352.6	173.5
CHD120	POTTERY	YAP	C36-76-I/5	37.1635	222.77	0.1551	0.4919	0.5908	105.12	0.00	105829.7	0.0	12467.0	3.6449	0.0	1070.3	4860.8	6526.4	291.4
CHD121	POTTERY	YAP	C36-76-I/7	45.8900	0.00	0.3767	0.6506	0.3939	63.13	0.00	90207.1	0.0	20879.0	4.4642	2379.4	1654.7	3767.6	12464.5	431.3
CHD122	POTTERY	YAP	C36-76-I/6	44.2164	204.92	0.6013	0.6522	0.4780	86.55	0.00	80625.1	0.0	31174.5	4.1814	0.0	1274.4	9080.2	13650.2	404.8
CHD123	POTTERY	FAIS	FAIS SURFACE	39.7060	0.00	0.3912	0.4949	0.0000	74.09	0.00	78168.7	0.0	30793.0	3.0021	0.0	2021.6	5285.4	11591.8	406.3
CHD124	POTTERY	FADERAI	FADERAI, ULITHI, SURFACE	44.4340	0.00	0.8099	0.4651	0.6372	103.70	0.00	96157.3	0.0	17743.3	3.0076	0.0	1456.1	4638.1	18214.4	511.0
CHD125	POTTERY	SATAWAL	SATAWAL SURFACE	44.9012	223.84	0.4573	0.6331	0.4438	70.68	126.80	87089.7	75.7	25433.0	4.7882	0.0	1344.4	3333.3	12352.0	414.6
CHD126	POTTERY	YAP	C36-77-I/9	52.2895	623.15	0.8211	0.6614	0.5620	96.07	133.25	103252.3	0.0	12409.0	3.6460	0.0	1272.8	10154.0	19200.7	543.0
CHD127	POTTERY	YAP	C36-77-I/9	38.5719	0.00	0.8198	0.3365	0.5212	168.88	0.00	75337.6	0.0	21252.7	2.2866	2610.8	1811.0	3642.2	26381.7	314.8
CHD128	POTTERY	YAP	C36-77-I/12	45.5111	0.00	1.6143	0.4415	0.4315	97.55	73.02	83362.3	0.0	24909.7	2.8417	0.0	1836.5	7939.4	38786.8	549.9
CHD129	POTTERY	YAP	C36-27-III/13	36.1707	0.00	0.4281	0.3119	0.2984	137.73	0.00	68576.3	0.0	36804.3	1.5097	0.0	4386.2	3334.7	12657.8	268.6
CHD130	POTTERY	YAP	C36-27-III/12	39.6910	0.00	0.1198	0.5338	0.3385	83.69	0.00	98189.3	0.0	6104.0	2.9552	0.0	2937.7	5050.2	4889.4	237.3
CHD131	POTTERY	YAP	C36-27-III/3	44.3202	0.00	0.6063	0.5660	0.6306	96.80	0.00	89435.9	0.0	19996.4	3.4636	0.0	1357.5	5960.9	14833.6	587.3
CHD132	POTTERY	YAP	C36-27-I/4	46.8679	0.00	0.7181	0.3349	0.3273	140.52	0.00	91064.5	0.0	20720.8	3.3897	0.0	1959.4	6282.1	16494.1	441.5
CHD133	POTTERY	YAP	C36-27-III/10	39.3330	316.99	0.6278	0.2771	0.4132	62.67	0.00	84219.3	0.0	24434.0	1.2108	490.6	3576.1	10320.5	18758.9	293.5
CHD134	POTTERY	MOGMOG	MOG-1-G4-S	30.5310	244.34	0.0935	0.3175	0.4041	338.48	0.00	83569.1	0.0	20003.9	2.2411	4310.4	400.0	16015.3	3061.2	210.0
CHD135	POTTERY	MOGMOG	MOG-1-L3-II/1	34.6874	373.49	0.0000	0.3518	0.4970	354.37	0.00	87232.2	66.3	20785.0	2.2167	1795.2	413.3	15357.6	3713.5	200.1
CHD136	POTTERY	MOGMOG	MOG-1-A6-S	32.0850	339.68	0.0000	0.3051	0.2800	380.06	0.00	82165.2	0.0	16716.0	1.5907	3062.5	447.4	14849.0	3323.3	231.5
CHD137	POTTERY	MOGMOG	MOG-1-A6-S	26.1282	599.38	0.1435	0.3988	0.3805	99.86	0.00	78209.3	0.0	15957.0	2.4330	1665.3	139.8	11497.1	3555.1	207.0
CHD138	POTTERY	MOGMOG	MOG-1-I4-S	29.6024	232.92	0.1245	0.2141	0.4072	135.13	0.00	79653.1	0.0	15479.9	1.5342	1816.8	327.1	5642.2	4076.9	293.8
CHD139	POTTERY	MOGMOG	MOG-1-L3-II/1	47.4378	343.86	0.7885	0.7375	0.6907	95.01	0.00	93571.0	0.0	17734.0	3.8575	0.0	1254.9	9581.2	15377.2	626.3
CHD140	POTTERY	MOGMOG	MOG-1-L3-II/2	57.9475	0.00	0.7583	2.3170	0.6465	126.35	143.94	106779.0	67.1	12525.0	0.9850	0.0	622.1	9318.9	16941.2	489.3
CHD141	POTTERY	MOGMOG	MOG-1-L3-II/2	33.2606	236.62	0.0000	0.2627	0.3093	131.02	0.00	86978.8	33.4	13812.0	1.5595	0.0	381.0	7091.1	4980.5	264.9
CHD142	POTTERY	MOGMOG	MOG-2-D9-II/1	33.7539	516.59	0.0000	0.2528	0.3141	164.48	0.00	87348.9	0.0	26699.0	1.3506	1889.3	623.2	15231.3	3097.9	248.1
CHD143	POTTERY	MOGMOG	MOG-2-K4-S	49.7627	334.03	0.7607	0.9804	0.5640	537.24	0.00	89875.3	21.5	40769.0	5.9680	1277.1	1392.1	11564.9	15947.4	486.0
CHD144	POTTERY	MOGMOG	MOG-2-L1-II/2	46.3505	273.58	0.7733	0.3728	0.4147	89.65	0.00	94427.4	0.0	15407.0	1.5562	2741.4	1001.5	7229.7	19550.9	633.9
CHD145	POTTERY	MOGMOG	MOG-2-L1-II/2	46.9101	159.15	0.5747	0.4503	0.6508	115.60	0.00	86199.0	0.0	12523.0	1.7842	8181.5	666.4	4210.7	14418.0	325.4
CHD146	POTTERY	MOGMOG	MOG-2-I4-IV/2	44.6481	499.85	0.6303	0.5369	0.7680	144.39	101.76	88984.0	104.9	21023.9	1.8473	3498.0	1105.8	2164.6	14678.5	295.3
CHD147	POTTERY	MOGMOG	MOG-2-I4-IV/3	43.7619	266.50	0.5943	0.5991	0.4685	125.42	100.88	92534.9	0.0	24550.0	2.9612	0.0	465.7	9640.1	17530.9	550.4
CHD148	POTTERY	YAP	C36-33-I/16	45.7084	198.55	0.4717	0.6645	0.4354	126.25	174.35	92590.2	98.8	13471.5	1.6252	6682.6	657.1	4493.7	15099.8	382.9
CHD149	POTTERY	YAP	C36-33-I/5	43.6082	103.36	0.4846	0.6486	0.3658	96.86	113.28	75650.5	77.2	18135.0	2.0328	1764.7	1175.8	1655.4	12484.7	416.8
CHD150	POTTERY	YAP	C36-33-I/18	45.7333	0.00	0.8019	0.3862	0.5529	128.95	0.00	96728.8	65.6	12621.9	2.1237	4945.5	966.8	4486.4	15264.9	388.3
CHD151	POTTERY	YAP	C36-33-I/13	42.9459	254.87	0.3705	0.6277	0.4868	98.23	92.69	81887.9	0.0	17880.0	2.9689	0.0	1208.6	2645.5	10662.4	454.6
CHD152	POTTERY	YAP	C36-33-I/12	61.7707	332.81	1.3740	0.8153	1.3797	154.16	0.00	105928.5	53.3	11996.0	1.3268	1359.7	429.5	7128.1	14136.6	298.3
CHD153	POTTERY	YAP	C36-33-I/2	46.1526	428.47	0.6682	0.6474	0.5728	135.17	0.00	88757.9	81.6	28794.0	2.2755	1597.1	1935.0	8234.2	17134.9	430.9
CHD154	POTTERY	YAP	C36-33-I/11	39.6895	0.00	0.0000	0.4034	0.4737	171.00	0.00	112298.6	0.0	6542.0	1.3180	0.0	441.2	6735.5	4721.0	291.8
CHD155	POTTERY	YAP	C36-33-I/9	49.3579	509.22	0.7513	0.0000	0.6539	134.77	154.64	88311.3	67.2	21787.0	1.3265	0.0	1588.3	7464.7	20808.5	486.6
CHD156	POTTERY	YAP	C36-32-S	35.9619	0.00	0.1646	0.4073	0.3205	106.90	0.00	93901.8	0.0	5697.0	1.3181	1864.1	288.1	6225.4	4967.6	301.1
CHD157	POTTERY	YAP	C36-34-S	57.4373	362.15	0.7333	0.8905	0.7321	176.13	146.00	100862.3	56.3	22548.0	4.2372	977.2	2020.3	3910.7	14787.3	463.3
CHD158	POTTERY	YAP	C36-34-S	44.3261	0.00	0.5880	0.7319	0.5963	125.46	150.39	82171.2	0.0	23543.0	4.1126	0.0	1442.9	7546.3	14167.2	517.4
CHD159	POTTERY	YAP	C36-32-S	43.3851	0.00	0.8617	0.6782	0.7446	134.33	0.00	80026.7	0.0	16699.8	2.1267	3597.4	1055.4	3202.6	14469.5	325.8
CHD160	POTTERY	YAP	C36-06-I/5	48.3623	0.00	0.6217	0.4415	0.6958	181.33	102.07	91303.5	0.0	23474.0	2.6747	0.0	1223.0	5190.6	16027.6	493.3
CHD161	POTTERY	YAP	C36-06-I/5	36.4078	921.91	0.7930	0.6610	0.3599	119.64	120.68	78436.0	0.0	82527.0	2.9782	0.0	1819.9	8113.4	26386.4	368.0
CHD162	POTTERY	YAP	C36-06-I/5	57.0861	0.00	0.9054	0.6042	0.8367	159.17	0.00	104739.0	0.0	6624.0	1.5025	2380.3	404.1	1963.1	15205.6	487.2
CHD163	POTTERY	YAP	C36-06-S	62.1958	301.24	0.8071	0.9913	0.9079	175.93	0.00	87469.5	129.0	25668.0	3.7656	4153.4	1101.7	20993.4	11343.7	438.1
CHD164	POTTERY	YAP	C36-06-I/3	45.7098	445.29	0.4974	0.4271	0.6019	108.16	0.00	92482.2	0.0	18885.0	2.4309	0.0	633.0	11415.0	15470.5	562.1

ANID	MATERIAL	ISLAND	LOCATION	SC	SR	TA	TB	TH	ZN	ZR	AL	BA	CA	DY	K	MN	NA	TI	V
CHD165	POTTERY	YAP	C36-06-I/1	48.0423	455.82	0.7290	0.5877	0.5681	148.58	0.00	92595.3	0.0	17814.2	2.5126	2821.3	773.7	11218.5	11561.6	333.5
CHD166	POTTERY	YAP	C36-06-I/4	22.2154	114.78	0.1262	0.4629	0.5165	106.47	126.71	73648.5	0.0	12570.5	1.8485	0.0	255.6	6424.4	3801.0	171.9
CHD167	POTTERY	MOGMOG	MOG-22-V/2	41.6662	114.08	0.1657	0.7526	0.5973	134.15	87.32	108875.6	40.8	16578.4	5.1205	3054.3	205.6	4910.6	6294.9	272.7
CHD168	POTTERY	MOGMOG	MOG-22-V/1	30.0102	141.00	0.1337	0.7843	0.6171	95.28	62.63	81985.5	25.4	10879.3	2.7524	2313.3	667.7	4218.3	5241.8	177.5
CHD169	POTTERY	MOGMOG	MOG-22-III/2	61.5557	454.38	0.5202	0.5381	0.4731	116.72	0.00	102772.3	0.0	21693.6	1.9402	0.0	405.8	6721.8	15907.6	604.0
CHD170	POTTERY	MOGMOG	MOG-22-III/2	42.9969	147.53	0.6397	0.8893	0.6110	130.96	173.22	83976.2	0.0	21527.8	4.2313	4474.2	1356.8	5441.6	12228.8	366.1
CHD171	POTTERY	MOGMOG	MOG-22-III/1	31.1886	346.11	0.2389	0.6889	1.9491	137.61	116.55	102815.4	320.3	21538.3	4.3805	10925.7	1812.3	13945.6	3674.3	243.8
CHD172	POTTERY	MOGMOG	MOG-22-III/2	46.9561	135.43	0.5678	0.7373	0.0000	135.41	126.35	83432.6	0.0	22300.8	2.6785	1681.4	1133.7	12604.6	16234.4	390.6
CHD173	POTTERY	MOGMOG	MOG-13-IV/2	35.7946	222.48	0.1359	0.6341	0.6010	169.25	0.00	85859.5	53.2	9952.0	3.6955	2600.9	164.4	3763.4	6294.4	228.6
CHD174	POTTERY	MOGMOG	MOG-13-IV/3	43.6339	629.75	0.5839	0.6287	0.4452	86.02	0.00	85290.1	0.0	18479.7	2.9080	0.0	360.0	9160.3	14989.5	568.8
CHD175	POTTERY	MOGMOG	MOG-13-IV/1	60.3933	622.73	0.5471	0.0000	0.5566	132.56	0.00	103282.9	0.0	18855.3	1.3406	2567.5	405.1	4936.9	16980.5	660.0
CHD176	POTTERY	MOGMOG	MOG-13-IV/2	56.3900	446.63	0.7099	0.0000	0.4863	159.34	97.02	104782.7	0.0	17113.7	1.7513	2702.2	434.4	3181.8	15782.8	515.5
CHD177	POTTERY	MOGMOG	MOG-13-IV/1	27.8603	189.33	0.1013	0.4504	0.4859	94.51	134.48	79037.7	0.0	13087.3	2.8442	0.0	258.9	9006.8	3743.5	190.0
CHD178	POTTERY	MOGMOG	MOG-13-IV/1	42.2987	0.00	0.4852	0.6065	0.3374	101.70	119.11	77066.4	0.0	11922.0	1.4825	22817.5	1312.9	14677.1	11263.4	885.1
CHD179	POTTERY	MOGMOG	MOG-27-III/1	25.9929	280.48	0.1406	0.4554	0.3565	195.81	81.05	74386.4	0.0	17774.3	2.8120	2118.9	385.3	12111.8	3597.6	171.5
CHD180	POTTERY	MOGMOG	MOG-27-III/1	67.5454	469.24	0.7682	1.3159	0.9833	194.78	0.00	95096.1	105.7	23463.0	7.9265	5666.9	532.6	16648.8	12438.9	455.5
CHD181	POTTERY	MOGMOG	MOG-27-II/6	43.0550	440.38	0.5954	1.0068	0.4195	115.43	130.18	82882.2	82.9	37370.3	4.9829	0.0	1313.0	8408.1	17887.9	447.9
CHD182	POTTERY	MOGMOG	MOG-27-II/5	44.0713	415.64	0.6422	0.7841	0.6053	121.20	0.00	80924.1	0.0	37846.8	2.8994	1599.3	1049.7	10008.0	13205.8	523.3
CHD183	POTTERY	MOGMOG	MOG-27-II/4	50.3646	0.00	0.5037	0.4622	0.5164	127.54	0.00	91070.6	0.0	18108.4	3.4997	4098.1	825.0	2937.7	13378.3	427.6
CHD184	POTTERY	MOGMOG	MOG-27-V/1	40.4058	532.66	0.2534	0.6428	0.7101	127.24	119.11	118612.5	0.0	17478.7	3.8651	0.0	547.4	5546.2	7611.7	186.2
CHD185	POTTERY	MOGMOG	MOG-25-VII/1	70.1692	0.00	0.8021	0.0000	0.9236	180.89	157.27	107756.2	92.5	19680.8	1.1660	2379.4	155.9	10040.4	13136.8	626.1
CHD186	POTTERY	MOGMOG	MOG-25-VII/1	44.2793	529.52	0.4738	0.4804	0.4677	108.29	72.33	91020.2	0.0	32709.4	2.7645	1880.8	730.5	9331.0	13472.3	397.3
CHD187	POTTERY	MOGMOG	MOG-25-VI/1	43.3247	364.67	0.5173	0.9124	0.3875	118.57	134.13	82281.7	0.0	21465.4	4.5699	5220.6	1252.9	5550.6	12061.2	399.7
CHD188	POTTERY	MOGMOG	MOG-25-VII/1	44.8365	690.00	0.6218	0.6401	0.3755	114.22	0.00	88285.1	0.0	29530.6	3.0513	0.0	1336.1	14128.8	12860.7	513.3
CHD189	POTTERY	MOGMOG	MOG-25-VI/1	50.1321	498.31	0.6227	0.8936	0.4694	298.54	85.51	98014.6	43.6	41732.7	5.6611	0.0	428.7	13029.2	17525.3	460.7
CHD190	POTTERY	MOGMOG	MOG-53-IV/2	43.3400	0.00	0.6722	0.6787	0.6704	127.58	73.05	81870.6	0.0	25336.0	4.6666	5171.2	1145.8	9253.0	13307.0	375.1
CHD191	POTTERY	MOGMOG	MOG-53-IV/2	32.9940	418.43	0.1589	0.0000	0.3400	185.25	0.00	83960.0	0.0	17004.3	1.5210	4503.8	424.1	7765.2	3749.3	214.1
CHD192	POTTERY	MOGMOG	MOG-53-III/1	44.6540	574.99	0.4868	0.6788	0.4866	119.89	0.00	82537.7	0.0	26286.0	3.3864	9836.5	914.8	6743.6	11825.6	392.8
CHD193	POTTERY	MOGMOG	MOG-53-IV/1	39.7399	186.59	0.4273	0.7370	0.3650	72.93	0.00	73167.4	0.0	37294.2	4.4373	2727.9	1229.1	7047.5	11968.9	368.6
CHD194	POTTERY	MOGMOG	MOG-2-L1-II/1	47.9935	516.42	0.6079	0.5577	0.6034	68.53	92.73	102648.1	49.8	29824.2	3.7779	1766.5	627.1	18582.4	13993.4	396.7
CHD195	POTTERY	YAP	C36-34-S	41.7717	214.82	0.6955	0.7100	0.6030	68.89	0.00	85640.9	0.0	27955.4	4.2503	0.0	3944.6	3833.6	13820.9	456.5
CHD196	POTTERY	YAP	C36-32-S	51.3065	386.35	1.4253	0.3552	1.2084	71.23	0.00	100839.9	0.0	20501.3	1.7600	4004.5	420.6	8102.6	21572.3	448.3
CHD197	POTTERY	MOGMOG	MOG-54-III/2	49.3428	253.18	0.7147	0.6325	0.6435	80.99	0.00	93798.3	0.0	21193.3	3.4205	0.0	670.8	5648.9	12849.6	509.6
CHD198	POTTERY	MOGMOG	MOG-54-II/2	28.4650	310.53	0.3390	0.6205	1.9510	52.62	132.85	142818.6	36.2	10897.4	4.5820	13140.0	170.9	8714.3	5086.8	169.7
CHD199	POTTERY	MOGMOG	MOG-54-III/1	53.9033	325.71	0.8179	0.4469	0.4989	107.86	0.00	105626.9	0.0	20510.1	2.8510	7598.6	490.7	13707.4	17616.1	271.0
CHD200	POTTERY	MOGMOG	MOG-54-III/1	40.0930	151.40	0.4473	0.4678	0.4366	74.13	0.00	79315.8	0.0	29206.0	2.3219	2218.5	2903.3	3828.5	13926.0	431.7
CHD201	POTTERY	MOGMOG	MOG-59-II/2	39.9281	0.00	0.4088	0.7187	0.2751	77.72	0.00	76007.4	60.2	25466.0	4.2009	22534.1	1432.3	9907.3	13209.5	363.8
CHD202	POTTERY	MOGMOG	MOG-59-II/3	42.3526	0.00	0.3694	0.7758	0.3884	63.24	114.55	71358.7	0.0	29400.0	3.8007	19138.2	1209.4	11519.3	13644.3	314.4
CHD203	POTTERY	MOGMOG	MOG-59-II/2	47.7309	203.25	0.6479	0.0000	0.5847	58.07	0.00	95715.4	0.0	14266.9	1.0707	7528.3	558.2	5688.2	17270.8	378.6
CHD204	POTTERY	MOGMOG	MOG-59-II/2	45.4031	127.21	0.7888	0.0000	0.6446	44.82	0.00	93801.1	58.5	13674.8	0.9713	4098.8	527.1	4693.1	17018.4	407.5
CHD205	POTTERY	MOGMOG	MOG-32-IV/1	38.1806	0.00	0.4441	0.5234	0.3001	62.52	0.00	73787.8	0.0	36169.3	3.4731	11268.9	1241.4	8637.6	11646.1	306.9
CHD206	POTTERY	MOGMOG	MOG-32-IV/1	45.2960	0.00	0.4007	0.5628	0.4090	67.08	0.00	85507.2	0.0	17546.0	2.6296	1510.9	1711.1	3949.3	10768.3	391.0
CHD207	POTTERY	MOGMOG	MOG-32-III/1	48.1913	195.91	0.7617	0.5683	0.6220	90.67	0.00	96494.7	0.0	16320.0	3.4150	2232.7	509.9	4768.2	14707.8	422.8
CHD208	POTTERY	MOGMOG	MOG-32-III/1	36.8601	0.00	0.5372	0.5993	0.5178	75.77	0.00	71984.4	0.0	25162.2	2.7250	7772.1	1284.2	8788.8	15662.7	370.0
CHD209	POTTERY	MOGMOG	MOG-39-VI/2	41.0265	238.26	0.2982	0.9713	0.3568	76.79	0.00	75257.9	0.0	36403.1	4.2071	1638.2	2081.6	5787.7	11610.9	336.4
CHD210	POTTERY	MOGMOG	MOG-39-V/1	48.4832	130.82	0.5521	0.0000	0.3092	56.26	0.00	96122.5	0.0	14363.0	0.9365	0.0	622.4	1824.7	14293.5	538.6
CHD211	POTTERY	MOGMOG	MOG-39-V/1	54.4778	184.07	0.9813	0.4070	0.8480	92.90	99.07	98415.0	26.2	21815.3	3.3044	2592.6	1006.5	5365.4	16676.4	545.4
CHD212	POTTERY	MOGMOG	MOG-39-III/1	48.5963	292.98	0.9767	1.0644	0.8002	69.51	0.00	88337.6	0.0	19107.0	5.7938	3102.4	1582.5	13597.4	14628.5	420.0
CHD213	POTTERY	MOGMOG	MOG-39-III/1	48.3865	189.12	0.7155	0.3599	0.6394	71.36	0.00	90960.1	0.0	16344.0	2.5445	5584.3	1330.7	3725.1	15609.2	511.9
CHD214	POTTERY	MOGMOG	MOG-35-XVI/2	32.6196	289.27	0.0000	0.5317	0.3668	166.10	0.00	84831.1	0.0	28704.4	3.0292	0.0	614.3	16315.0	3834.2	232.5
CHD215	POTTERY	MOGMOG	MOG-35-XVI/2	45.2464	149.93	0.4073	0.4164	0.3821	50.17	0.00	84519.8	45.5	28363.8	3.2365	0.0	786.7	3883.5	12890.1	450.3
CHD216	POTTERY	MOGMOG	MOG-35-XIV/1	43.7724	0.00	0.7500	0.7217	0.7844	84.99	104.01	82717.1	0.0	16604.6	4.3153	4629.1	830.9	3124.4	15565.1	326.3
CHD217	POTTERY	MOGMOG	MOG-35-XVI/1	53.7770	528.40	0.6371	0.8025	0.7979	62.10	0.00	103828.2	0.0	21178.0	4.1515	0.0	245.8	20492.1	18613.0	484.2
CHD218	POTTERY	MOGMOG	MOG-35-X, XII, XIII	37.6256	113.02	0.3236	0.4789	0.3152	62.77	0.00	75656.8	64.3	27350.7	4.1386	9307.6	1094.5	8834.6	9825.2	320.1
CHD219	POTTERY	MOGMOG	MOG-35-VII TO XI	45.3336	204.93	0.4212	0.5487	0.4246	62.05	0.00	86115.1	0.0	21239.9	2.8327	1561.7	742.6	3279.8	12774.1	385.9
CHD220	POTTERY	MOGMOG	MOG-43-III/3	42.3941	122.09	0.6095	0.5476	0.3273	74.47	132.71	79036.1	0.0	20719.8	2.9139	1928.4	2698.7	7075.6	14182.0	380.9
CHD221	POTTERY	MOGMOG	MOG-43-III/4	53.4356	410.90	0.7103	0.8536	0.5994	58.31	135.27	104827.7	0.0	26278.6	4.3219	990.9	219.4	20407.0	17952.4	454.0
CHD222	POTTERY	MOGMOG	MOG-43-III/4	48.2322	0.00	0.4401	0.0000	0.2799	62.13	0.00	85912.8	0.0	8045.4	0.7981	1630.8	623.1	2805.4	13157.6	388.8
CHD223	POTTERY	MOGMOG	MOG-45-III/3	28.1582	109.23	0.0000	0.2483	0.4978	74.18	0.00	81882.2	34.6	8518.0	1.5992	3938.3	185.1	5086.9	4455.7	170.8
CHD224	POTTERY	MOGMOG	MOG-45-III/5	38.1351	97.46	0.5904	0.6106	0.2599	57.16	0.00	73929.8	0.0	22838.3	2.1838	5923.2	1605.3	6132.6	16265.0	441.1
CHD225	CLAY	YAP	GITAM VILLAGE	51.9532	0.00	0.7234	0.7663	0.7664	107.44	0.00	97337.3	0.0	6817.9	3.3929	0.0	1782.3	2027.9	14658.1	550.7
CHD226	CLAY	YAP	BINAW VILLAGE	51.5323	0.00	1.6149	0.0000	1.2389	85.60	0.00	102886.7	21.8	964.9	0.7702	1304.4	2216.4	269.8	35849.8	592.9
CHD227	CLAY	YAP	THENFAAR VILLAGE	57.9207	0.00	1.2449	0.4077	1.2650	93.42	206.57	92006.3	0.0	0.0	1.5773	0.0	2273.9	207.7	30677.0	685.8
CHD228	POTTERY	MOGMOG	MOG-45-III/4	41.6763	0.00	0.8462	0.6780	0.7135	95.85	0.00	76359.0	0.0	30065.5	3.0142	3040.2	1079.9	4036.9	14263.8	304.2
CHD229	POTTERY	MOGMOG	MOG-45-III/3	52.8975	0.00	0.6109	0.0000	0.4543	57.55	0.00	97904.7	0.0	12692.8	1.0878	5716.2	391.0	3670.9	13731.2	206.1
CHD230	POTTERY	YAP	C36-83.1-I/15	40.7393	0.00	0.6848	0.2130	0.6707	73.97	0.00	74826.1	29.3	6377.0	1.6118	3594.5	647.5	2762.7	14851.3	459.0
CHD231	POTTERY	YAP	C36-83.1-I/14	44.0555	227.39	0.5343	0.7243	0.6227	43.10	139.26	84176.1	0.0	22652.0	3.7129	0.0	1072.1	23022.5	14244.5	512.3
CHD232	POTTERY	YAP	C36-83.1-I/15	50.7802	143.75	0.6080	0.7599	0.6175	65.32	0.00	106225.1	0.0	14344.0	4.6155	0.0	670.6	13705.5	18056.7	504.5
CHD233	POTTERY	YAP	C36-83.1-I/14	52.9603	0.00	0.2590	0.3312	0.2992	69.97	0.00	101057.7	0.0	6768.0	2.4433	0.0	946.7	2240.7	15271.8	517.9
CHD234	POTTERY	YAP	C36-75-3.10 (+100)	50.4507	355.57	0.5865	0.0000	0.4520	101.35	0.00	93769.0	97.1	23877.0	1.4564	0.0	681.1	3701.7	14873.9	346.2
CHD235	POTTERY	YAP	C36-75-1.03 (+130)	40.1089	0.00	0.4181	0.8580	0.2703	58.97	0.00	72518.6	0.0	27412.6	3.5697	0.0	3580.3	4660.9	11975.8	437.9
CHD236	POTTERY	YAP	C36-75-0.01	30.3613	1047.00	2.2075	0.0000	2.6252	38.90	135.12	110641.1	99.5	17413.0	0.9442	11672.8	675.5	23662.8	17552.5	183.6
CHD237	POTTERY	YAP	C36-16-II/1	45.4656	138.80	0.6728	0.3869	0.4614	98.03	0.00	86650.4	0.0	29443.2	2.9498	0.0	2585.7	10290.5	24707.8	416.7
CHD238	POTTERY	YAP	C36-16-I/7	41.9122	0.00	0.6511	0.5343	0.7359	182.83	0.00	77028.2	0.0	33974.0	1.6187	0.0	4791.9	7763.0	15923.6	271.5
CHD239	POTTERY	YAP	C36-16-I/7	46.5181	151.30	0.7394	0.0000	0.4328	74.11	0.00	91012.9	0.0	18926.2	2.8123	0.0	1260.1	5851.3	19855.2	419.0
CHD240	POTTERY	YAP	C36-16-I/6	36.5885	0.00	0.2171	1.2941	0.6241	141.09	121.01	97903.4	0.0	7313.0	3.5132	0.0	947.9	5231.0	8075.8	259.3
CHD241	POTTERY	YAP	C36-16-I/2	47.9422	0.00	0.5410	1.4850	0.5159	161.22	81.17	90388.4	0.0	7739.0	3.8348	0.0	790.5	2289.4	14297.5	417.4
CHD242	POTTERY	YAP	C36-13-S	39.9193	0.00	0.2713	1.4723	0.5852	160.51	0.00	94146.9	0.0	5503.0	4.1700	3223.2	935.4	6200.9	7723.6	262.3
CHD243	POTTERY	YAP	C36-13-S	40.2816	0.00	0.2207	1.5360	0.8296	160.17	70.21	115194.0	114.8	6240.0	3.2971	0.0	1450.0	5204.4	7652.8	247.8
CHD244	POTTERY	YAP	C36-80-S	37.3044	0.00	0.8902	1.3991	0.3997	115.93	117.20	68480.5	82.3	25961.2	3.1832	0.0	1930.9	4779.7	20325.2	414.0
CHD245	POTTERY	YAP	C36-80-S	48.1033	0.00	0.4859	1.8381	0.5314	141.40	162.46	87845.2	0.0	27844.8	5.4701	1947.3	1138.6	5274.6	14464.2	545.8
CHD246	POTTERY	YAP	C36-81-S	37.7209	0.00	0.4381	1.4125	0.3298	119.44	0.00	69365.8	0.0	31382.4	3.8999	3193.8	1152.3	5093.8	11729.2	351.2

ANID	MATERIAL	ISLAND	LOCATION	SC	SR	TA	TB	TH	ZN	ZR	AL	BA	CA	DY	K	MN	NA	TI	V
CHD247	POTTERY	YAP	C36-81-S	48.5948	0.00	0.2602	1.5710	0.4858	147.67	0.00	93199.2	0.0	14076.0	4.1671	3966.1	951.9	3446.0	12655.5	353.9
CHD248	POTTERY	YAP	C36-84-S	48.1738	0.00	0.4352	1.0370	0.5240	139.20	131.08	91172.3	0.0	13162.7	2.5407	5601.2	759.6	9283.7	13999.6	423.2
CHD249	POTTERY	YAP	C36-84-S	43.2585	0.00	2.1726	1.1238	0.5179	137.13	92.60	98587.8	0.0	36526.7	1.8136	4809.4	2370.1	4758.4	55821.1	501.5
CHD250	POTTERY	YAP	C36-72-S	38.3950	293.53	0.8356	1.3063	0.6001	128.03	0.00	80777.8	0.0	33858.4	2.7027	3842.3	1753.7	8142.5	18205.9	434.6
CHD251	POTTERY	YAP	C36-72-S	53.8467	0.00	0.4224	0.8990	0.3339	132.84	0.00	103935.5	47.7	4988.0	2.1827	0.0	838.9	2556.9	16388.7	569.7
CHD252	POTTERY	YAP	C36-71-II/9	46.9858	0.00	0.4841	1.3711	0.5597	130.47	165.23	84039.4	0.0	18322.3	3.3551	0.0	1757.6	2703.5	12861.8	373.3
CHD253	POTTERY	YAP	C36-71-II/8	33.4903	0.00	0.2135	1.5107	0.5413	129.32	0.00	90019.9	566.9	10256.0	2.2319	0.0	7838.2	4145.8	5805.0	194.6
CHD254	POTTERY	YAP	C36-71-II/5	36.2026	0.00	0.2172	1.2663	0.6978	130.07	0.00	101096.2	0.0	7170.9	3.1675	0.0	1384.8	4989.9	7227.6	272.4
CHD255	POTTERY	YAP	C36-83.1-I/12	34.4733	0.00	0.2201	1.1893	0.4589	131.37	0.00	93644.2	65.5	2849.3	3.8332	0.0	1232.0	4870.1	6099.0	214.8
CHD256	POTTERY	YAP	C36-22.1-II/2	43.6558	0.00	0.5775	1.1925	0.4961	168.79	138.21	82780.0	0.0	16931.3	3.5972	0.0	1234.6	3430.1	15918.6	531.5
CHD257	POTTERY	YAP	C36-22.1-I/6	50.2917	0.00	0.7864	0.9513	0.5991	128.84	147.30	99568.9	0.0	14816.1	1.1382	0.0	1080.8	5991.3	18638.1	510.1
CHD258	POTTERY	YAP	C36-22.1-I/6	54.9064	0.00	0.5031	0.5214	0.4520	182.24	0.00	96933.7	90.7	9520.5	2.7702	0.0	928.8	2077.5	14800.3	375.8
CHD259	POTTERY	YAP	C36-33-I/2	40.9949	0.00	0.4119	1.2654	0.4355	116.16	124.60	77555.4	0.0	30347.8	3.9647	4628.4	1112.7	4229.7	13657.0	346.4
CHD260	POTTERY	YAP	C36-27-I/2	54.0731	0.00	1.1097	0.0000	1.1105	147.92	0.00	115645.0	0.0	9812.1	1.0792	0.0	620.9	7535.8	11184.8	334.7
CHD261	POTTERY	YAP	C36-27-I/2	58.7144	0.00	0.7928	1.4851	0.6186	180.33	0.00	115521.9	0.0	10043.0	2.7999	1822.0	1130.1	5577.3	17549.3	549.8
CHD262	POTTERY	YAP	C36-06-I/3	37.4342	0.00	0.3674	1.2586	0.4372	119.51	84.00	72738.3	58.8	35389.1	3.4535	3915.8	1387.7	6644.1	11054.9	297.1
CHD263	POTTERY	MOGMOG	MOG-54-III/2	59.5407	0.00	0.5351	0.0000	0.6957	178.50	0.00	117099.2	0.0	10867.6	1.0632	0.0	399.8	1522.2	14870.4	446.4
CHD264	POTTERY	YAP	C36-76-I/3	52.2897	409.20	0.9886	2.1027	0.8034	159.26	166.88	104362.5	0.0	31527.9	5.6596	0.0	6166.3	7722.9	22447.5	506.4
CHD265	POTTERY	YAP	C36-76-I/9	37.4290	450.70	0.5417	0.7510	0.4355	102.60	87.15	78923.8	0.0	28346.4	1.6945	0.0	1246.7	7689.5	12885.5	368.1
CHD266	POTTERY	MOGMOG	MOG-22-III/1	39.8090	446.22	0.5822	1.6124	0.3828	110.56	0.00	75240.8	43.4	27169.5	3.7814	0.0	1944.0	10492.5	12433.8	417.7
CHD267	POTTERY	MOGMOG	MOG-22-V/2	37.6788	569.64	0.1683	1.6172	0.7012	162.97	71.27	111331.7	73.4	17396.0	3.7279	4303.9	849.6	4269.7	6994.6	167.7
CHD268	POTTERY	MOGMOG	MOG-22-III/1	42.2698	277.15	0.9256	1.5928	0.6003	132.83	0.00	81157.9	94.0	26480.4	3.8971	0.0	2084.9	4267.0	15078.2	424.3
CHD269	POTTERY	MOGMOG	MOG-25-V/1	37.3148	508.16	0.5443	2.2677	0.5901	118.14	92.03	72212.0	0.0	30712.7	2.9151	35081.2	878.8	18054.0	13905.7	716.9
CHD270	POTTERY	MOGMOG	MOG-25-II/1	58.6355	0.00	0.7559	0.7720	0.9415	229.08	149.70	109291.3	0.0	13923.6	2.3100	2738.7	334.2	11216.7	17164.5	358.6
CHD271	POTTERY	MOGMOG	MOG-53-IV/2	46.2597	580.99	0.6469	1.8077	0.4925	134.26	97.05	83368.8	0.0	26693.5	5.0247	5503.5	939.1	9787.4	13648.7	408.4
CHD272	POTTERY	YAP	C36-78-I/7	38.0151	0.00	0.3838	1.1942	0.3451	99.57	201.82	69675.2	94.2	29322.0	2.2281	1487.1	1326.9	4488.4	10720.2	370.5
CHD273	POTTERY	YAP	C36-77-I/3	54.1757	0.00	0.6169	0.0000	0.8648	145.44	112.26	103625.1	0.0	10049.4	1.1786	0.0	633.5	9957.4	18282.6	437.9
CHD274	POTTERY	YAP	C36-77-I/3	40.2180	0.00	0.2911	1.2114	0.5932	157.44	0.00	101312.1	50.3	4492.8	3.6691	3357.7	1202.9	5419.8	7647.0	213.6
CHD275	POTTERY	MOGMOG	MOG-43-III/4	36.7492	297.73	0.5545	1.2760	0.3704	143.18	0.00	68363.4	0.0	25773.7	2.5232	21110.7	1485.6	10977.0	15796.3	375.7
CHD276	POTTERY	MOGMOG	MOG-43-III/2	52.8832	781.82	0.6095	1.4551	0.4398	153.61	122.19	100322.6	59.7	25472.3	3.7567	2750.2	308.9	15999.5	19275.7	598.6
CHD277	POTTERY	MOGMOG	MOG-27-II/3	40.6935	0.00	0.4162	1.7381	0.5088	111.66	0.00	76819.6	0.0	30297.0	5.4594	1044.9	1872.1	4499.7	13104.6	369.8
CHD278	POTTERY	YAP	C36-16-I/5	33.1697	0.00	0.1973	1.2640	1.0975	157.65	119.83	135102.8	91.8	4335.0	3.4694	7344.6	188.1	8146.5	5607.0	169.9
CHD279	POTTERY	YAP	C36-16-I/5	33.5094	0.00	0.6923	1.9374	0.6033	108.49	103.11	66853.9	0.0	29694.6	2.9518	0.0	1541.2	5400.5	11093.6	345.5
CHD280	CLAY	YAP	C36-27-I/3	64.8201	0.00	0.6065	0.0000	2.6262	188.11	121.47	97329.4	0.0	3974.0	0.8370	0.0	3980.4	685.1	12941.5	341.0
CHD281	CLAY	YAP	C36-22.1-PROBE	10.9521	0.00	0.0000	0.1010	0.0000	69.65	0.00	10299.2	0.0	0.0	0.3380	0.0	804.6	200.5	0.0	41.8
CHD282	CLAY	YAP	C28-2-I/1	54.4346	0.00	0.0000	0.0000	0.3398	59.97	0.00	163250.4	0.0	4917.0	0.0000	0.0	637.0	372.1	6122.9	552.7
CHD283	CLAY	YAP	C36-16-II/3	81.5341	0.00	0.0000	0.0000	0.0000	221.75	0.00	39970.1	0.0	0.0	0.0000	0.0	5705.7	185.0	746.9	376.4
CHD284	POTTERY	MOGMOG	MOG-2.A6-I/1	35.6632	362.94	0.0000	0.3968	0.4315	158.94	0.00	91478.8	0.0	15081.7	3.2270	3969.1	202.3	10870.0	4409.7	233.9
CHD285	POTTERY	YAP	C36-77-I/2	49.7238	0.00	0.8312	0.5862	0.7241	71.36	119.00	96625.7	0.0	12593.0	4.3057	0.0	1273.0	4486.8	17432.4	477.0
CHD286	POTTERY	MOGMOG	MOG-27-III/1	63.7031	658.15	0.6082	0.6536	0.9304	93.46	0.00	104602.5	124.2	31145.6	4.4499	0.0	746.3	23508.8	12328.1	343.6
CHD287	POTTERY	YAP	C36-22.2-II/3	71.5764	0.00	0.8054	0.7732	1.0649	69.94	0.00	101262.0	58.1	9702.0	4.3999	0.0	1105.2	21337.9	16801.6	533.9
CHD288	POTTERY	YAP	C36-83.1-I/4	41.6748	116.62	0.5248	0.6588	0.3968	85.64	0.00	82317.1	0.0	32053.9	4.6923	0.0	1154.4	10510.4	14061.3	448.7
CHD289	POTTERY	YAP	C36-27-III/12	31.8748	0.00	0.4685	0.5270	0.5453	36.63	0.00	70194.3	0.0	26880.4	3.1796	0.0	4277.7	4433.3	14479.9	327.4
CHD290	130 IO	YAP	C36-27-III/12	40.4291	0.00	0.0000	0.6673	0.4924	115.52	0.00	102478.9	0.0	6755.0	4.3039	0.0	2802.3	4831.4	5143.4	305.4
CHD291	130 PASTE	YAP	C36-27-III/12	38.5896	0.00	0.0000	0.5931	0.4609	105.67	62.99	99705.9	0.0	5514.0	3.0692	0.0	2782.8	5174.7	4120.9	260.3
CHD292	130 GROG	YAP	C36-27-III/12	41.5022	106.66	0.0000	0.7891	0.3326	114.91	0.00	110542.7	0.0	5091.0	3.2426	0.0	1767.9	4827.2	5256.5	233.1
CHD293	254 IO	YAP	C36-71-II/5	38.9816	0.00	0.0000	0.6626	0.5197	124.11	103.67	90705.3	0.0	7064.3	5.3059	0.0	1257.9	4221.4	5653.1	385.6
CHD294	254 PASTE	YAP	C36-71-II/5	34.4721	182.95	0.2533	0.5328	0.6022	112.14	0.00	100810.1	109.5	7546.0	3.1487	2839.1	764.5	5168.7	7381.1	236.3
CHD295	254 GROG	YAP	C36-71-II/5	35.5344	80.07	0.1736	0.5330	0.6678	118.08	79.78	99817.6	112.3	8781.0	3.4931	0.0	988.8	5606.6	7098.2	229.1
CHD296	184 IO	MOGMOG	MOG-27-II/3	41.1619	503.68	0.0000	0.8834	0.6005	169.78	133.97	97119.8	0.0	14368.9	5.6049	0.0	1139.8	3689.4	5789.6	455.1
CHD297	184 PASTE	MOGMOG	MOG-27-II/3	38.0266	432.45	0.1584	0.6217	0.7163	107.74	91.67	118049.3	0.0	18621.0	3.8827	2382.7	323.7	5287.9	7707.2	174.4
CHD298	184 GROG	MOGMOG	MOG-27-II/3	39.0948	471.15	0.1918	0.6583	0.7857	246.27	141.36	113383.2	77.3	16247.0	4.2653	2214.1	328.8	5458.7	6780.1	183.3
CHD299	CLAY	YAP	WENTARA	55.6884	0.00	0.6938	0.0000	0.5983	67.11	0.00	125529.9	0.0	5440.0	0.7781	0.0	1109.1	5718.1	23487.1	659.3
CHD300	CLAY	YAP	NLUL	45.6216	0.00	0.1467	0.4297	0.1478	127.96	0.00	101909.0	152.8	7608.0	3.2295	13739.4	1004.3	2191.0	4916.4	338.3
CHD301	CLAY	YAP	NLUL	40.9271	0.00	0.0000	0.2173	0.2122	92.57	0.00	89155.8	623.8	2731.0	1.5704	14286.2	322.5	1440.1	3285.3	359.0
CHD302	CLAY	YAP	GOOCHOL	62.8490	0.00	1.0779	0.0000	1.3830	81.29	0.00	111033.0	0.0	4581.0	0.9891	0.0	665.7	1410.0	13461.1	413.2
CHD303	CLAY	YAP	MUYUB	48.2551	0.00	0.4980	0.2998	0.4782	84.71	0.00	91027.4	0.0	6480.0	2.3042	0.0	766.4	1043.8	14332.8	372.6
CHD304	CLAY	YAP	MAKI	54.7763	0.00	0.7898	1.2291	0.5662	137.18	178.79	97113.6	0.0	19815.0	5.0710	0.0	779.9	4622.1	17658.3	601.9
CHD305	CLAY	YAP	AYRECH	37.3455	0.00	0.9765	0.7903	0.5887	103.45	102.78	79983.6	0.0	22719.8	4.4886	0.0	1220.3	5641.2	21553.1	595.3
CHD306	CLAY	YAP	TABELANG	32.8256	0.00	0.5370	0.8750	0.4635	114.74	88.72	63906.7	0.0	37924.0	4.2766	3441.2	1353.9	7716.3	12484.0	352.1
CHD307	CLAY	YAP	KADAY	43.8849	0.00	0.4071	0.9619	0.3966	116.51	113.74	79510.4	0.0	18148.0	3.5333	0.0	2548.0	5096.4	13795.8	433.1
CHD308	CLAY	YAP	KADAY	62.2570	0.00	0.9643	0.6574	0.6436	153.91	152.27	106558.8	0.0	7212.0	1.8276	0.0	403.8	3012.8	19832.6	626.7
CHD309	CLAY	YAP	ARINGEL	46.8257	0.00	0.5638	1.0052	0.3467	132.09	123.08	82343.1	0.0	10994.0	5.3174	0.0	521.2	6428.1	15825.8	510.2
CHD310	CLAY	YAP	DACHANGER	43.4721	0.00	0.9792	1.7242	0.6410	145.96	100.91	83661.9	0.0	19464.0	6.1009	0.0	2065.7	6184.4	23971.4	448.6
CHD311	CLAY	YAP	GITAM	53.4570	0.00	1.0958	0.7441	0.9241	142.48	89.94	105446.0	0.0	6511.0	1.7790	0.0	686.8	2432.6	19537.7	495.4
CHD312	CLAY	YAP	BAANIMAUT	40.8204	0.00	0.9138	1.5682	0.5542	125.42	109.72	81506.3	0.0	24802.0	5.9872	0.0	1206.0	5126.3	18290.4	429.7
CHD313	CLAY	YAP	NEL	57.5588	0.00	0.0000	0.0000	0.3945	211.10	0.00	159851.7	0.0	4073.0	0.0000	0.0	1130.8	443.7	6119.3	421.9
CHD314	CLAY	YAP	FUNECHU	55.8899	0.00	0.0000	1.0930	0.3033	145.37	0.00	123749.3	0.0	4575.0	5.2306	0.0	1842.2	461.0	6383.4	539.3
CHD315	CLAY	YAP	BURUDEMIC	26.1404	0.00	0.1759	0.0000	0.4133	0.00	0.00	132244.5	0.0	2864.0	0.4424	0.0	455.5	334.7	8935.8	475.1
CHD316	CLAY	YAP	ARIMOW	29.2116	0.00	0.1419	4.3132	0.5322	217.58	96.46	98969.6	0.0	34511.0	19.0361	7567.0	1886.5	307.3	5613.6	216.1
CHD317	POTTERY	CHUUK	TKFE-1-TP4	28.2296	833.14	2.4344	0.6141	2.4541	81.91	344.53	91170.0	0.0	67928.0	3.3634	0.0	565.8	1362.6	25704.5	454.0
CHD318	POTTERY	CHUUK	TKFE-4-4	31.9624	264.64	5.7298	0.7659	3.4545	93.30	639.86	130932.9	0.0	10419.0	5.4806	0.0	760.8	6393.3	59549.8	491.3
CHD319	POTTERY	KOSRAE	LELU	40.4677	3193.06	5.3051	1.9584	6.5020	168.86	350.78	93557.1	211.2	22861.6	8.4515	3642.4	635.2	5991.5	35679.8	585.3
CHD320	POTTERY	KOSRAE	LELU	38.0002	2230.73	5.3652	1.0147	6.5948	148.15	402.07	87824.7	244.3	22401.0	8.0393	4947.8	547.1	9644.8	34006.7	512.2
CHD321	POTTERY	KOSRAE	LELU 210-230	39.3568	2429.07	5.4836	2.0092	6.9129	140.77	384.60	100416.2	243.6	22712.0	9.4853	4722.4	562.2	9184.2	34508.3	514.6
CHD322	POTTERY	KOSRAE	LELU 210-230	44.0083	2420.91	6.3577	2.4470	7.5843	168.14	367.31	113683.3	282.3	26501.2	9.9965	3593.7	676.8	10117.1	44219.0	663.1

Bibliography

Alkire, W. H.
1960 Cultural adaptation in the Caroline Islands. *Journal of the Polynesian Society* 69:123-150.

1977 *An Introduction to the Peoples and Cultures of Micronesia.* Second edition. Cummings Publishing Company, Meno Park, California.

1978 *Coral Islanders.* AHM Publishing Corporation, Arlington Heights, Illinois.

1980 Technical Knowledge and the Evolution of Political Systems in the Central and Western Islands of Micronesia. *Canadian Journal of Anthropology* 1(2):229-237.

1981 Traditional Exchange Systems and Modern Political Developments in the Yap District of Micronesia. In *Persistence and Exchange: Papers from a symposium on Ecological Problems of the Traditional Societies of the Pacific Region*, edited by R. W. Force and B. Bishop, pp. 15-24. Pacific Science Association, Honolulu.

1989 [1965] *Lamotrek Atoll: Inter-island socioeconomic ties.* Second edition. Waveland Press Inc., Prospect Heights, Illinois.

Allen, J.
1985 Comments on complexity and trade: a view from Melanesia. *Archaeology in Oceania* 20:49-57.

Ambrose, W. R.
1978 The Loneliness of the Long Distance Trader in Melanesia. *Mankind* 11(3):326-333.

Arnold, D., H. Neff, and R. L. Bishop
1991 Compositional Analysis and "Sources" of Pottery: An Ethnoarchaeological Approach. *American Anthropologist* 93(1):70-90.

Athens, J. S.
1995 Landscape Archaeology: Prehistoric Settlement, Subsistence, and Environment of Kosrae, Eastern Caroline Islands, Micronesia. Archaeological Data Recovery Investigations for the Kosrae Wastewater Project. International Archaeological Research Institute Inc., Honolulu.

Athens, J. S. and J. V. Ward
2002 Paleoenvironmental Evidence for Early Human Settlement in Palau: The Ngerchau Core. In *Pacific 2000: Proceedings of the Fifth International Congress on Easter Island and the Pacific*, edited by C. M. Stevenson, G. Lee, and F. J. Morin, pp. 165-177. Easter Island Foundation, Los Osos, California.

Ayres, W. S.
1990 Pohnpei's position in eastern Micronesian prehistory. *Micronesica Supplement* 2:187-212.

Ayres, W. S., A. E. Haun, and C. Severance
1981 *Ponape Archaeological Survey: 1978 Research.* Micronesian Archaeological Survey Report No. 4. Historic Preservation Office, Trust Territory of the Pacific Islands, Saipan.

Ayres, W. S., G. G. Goles, and F. Beardsley
1997 Provenance study of lithic materials in Micronesia. In *Prehistoric Long-Distance Interaction in Oceania: An Interdisciplinary Approach*, edited by M. I. Weisler, pp. 53-67. New Zealand Archaeological Association Monograph 21. New Zealand Archaeological Association, Auckland.

Barratt, G.
1988 *Carolinean Contacts with the Islands of the Marianas: The European Record.* Micronesian Archaeological Survey, Report Number 25. Division of Historic Preservation, Saipan.

Barrau, J.
1961 *Subsistence agriculture in Polynesia and Micronesia.* Bernice P. Bishop Museum Bulletin 223, Honolulu.

Bashkow, I.
1991 The Dynamics of Rapport in a Colonial Situation: David Schneider's Fieldwork on the Islands of Yap. In *Colonial Situations: Essays on the Contextualization of Ethnographic Knowledge*, edited by G. W. Stocking, Jr., pp. 170-242. The University of Wisconsin Press, Madison.

Baugh, T. G. and J. E. Ericson
1992 Trade and Exchange in a Historical Perspective. In *The American Southwest and Mesoamerica: Systems of Prehistoric Exchange*, edited by J. E. Ericson and T. G. Baugh, pp. 1-20. Plenum Press, New York.

Beardsley, F., W. S. Ayres, and G. G. Goles
1992 Characterization of Easter Island Obsidian. *Bulletin of the Indo-Pacific Prehistory Association* 2(11):179-187.

de Beauclair, I.
1963 The Stone Money of Yap Island. *Bulletin of the Institute of Ethnology, Academia Sinica* 16:147-160.

1967 Infant Burial in Earthenware pots and the Pyramidal Grave on Yap. *Bulletin of the Institute of Ethnology, Academia Sinica* 24:35-39.

1974 Studies on Botel Tabago and Yap. *Asian Folklore and Social Life* Monographs 19, Taipei.

Bellwood, P.
1978 *Man's Conquest of the Pacific*. Collins, Auckland.

1985 *Prehistory of the Indo-Malaysian Archipelago*. Academic Press, Sydney.

Berg, M. L.
1988 The Wandering Life Among Unreliable Islanders. *Journal of Pacific History* 23(1):95-101).

1991 Jürgen Habermas in the Western Caroline Islands. *Anthropos* 86(4-6):397-411.

1992 Yapese Politics, Yapese Money and the Sawei Tribute Network before World War I. *The Journal of Pacific History* 27(2):150-164.

Biersack, A.
1991 Introduction: History and Theory in Anthropology. In *Clio in Oceania: Toward a Historical Anthropology*, edited by Aletta Biersack, pp. 1-36. Smithsonian Institution Press, Washington and London.

Bintliff, J.
1991 The Contribution of an *Annaliste*/structural history approach to archaeology. In *The Annales School and Archaeology*, edited by J. Bintliff, pp. 1-33. New York University Press, Washington Square.

Bishop, R. L., R. L. Rands, and G. R. Holley
1982 Ceramic Compositional Analysis in Archaeological Perspective. *Advances in Archaeological Method and Theory* 5:275-330.

Blinman, E. and C. D. Wilson
1992 Ceramic Perspecitives on Northern Anasazi Exchange. In *The American Southwest and Mesoamerica: Systems of Prehistoric Exchange*, edited by J. E. Ericson and T. G. Baugh, pp. 65-94. Plenum Press, New York.

Bloom, A. L.
1970 Paludal Stratigraphy of Truk, Ponape, and Kusaie, Eastern Caroline Islands. *Geological Society of America Bulletin* 81(7):1895-1904.

Bourdieu, P.
1977 [1972] *Outline of a Theory of Practice*. Translated by Richard Nice. Cambridge University Press, Cambridge.

Braudel, F.
1972 *The Mediterranean and the Mediterranean World in the Age of Philip II*. Translated by Sian Reynolds. 2 vols. Harper and Row, New York.

1980 *On History*. Translated by Sarah Matthews. University of Chicago Press, Chicago.

Bryson, R.
1989 *Ceramics and Spatial Archaeology at Nan Madol, Pohnpei*. Unpublished Ph.D. dissertation, Department of Anthropology, University of Oregon.

Buck, P. H.
1938 *Vikings of the sunrise*. J. B. Lippincot, New York.

Butler, B. M.
1990 Pots as Tools: The Marianas Case. *Micronesica Supplement* 3:33-46.

1995 *Archaeological investigation in the Achugao and Matansa areas of Saipan, Mariana Islands*. Micronesian Archaeology Survey Report 30. Division of Historic Preservation, Department of Community and Cultural Affairs, Commonwealth of the Northern Mariana Islands, Saipan.

Cantova, J. A.
1728 Lettre du P. Jean Cantova, Missionaire de la Compagnie de Jésus au R. P. Guillaume Daubenton, March 20, 1722. In *Lettres édifiantes et curieuses, écrites des missions étrangères par quelques missionaires de la Compagnie de Jésus* 18:188-247.

Carrasco, F.
1881 Carolinas: Descubbrimiento y descripcion de las islas Garbanzos. *Boletin de la Sociedad geografica de Madrid* X(1):263-279.

Carucci, L. M.
1988 Small fish in a big sea: Geographical dispersion and sociopolitical centralization in the Marshall Islands. In *State and Society: The Emergence and Development of Social Hierarchy and Political Centralization*, edited by J. Gledhill, B. Bender, and M. T. Larsen, pp. 33-42. Unwin Hyman, London.

Childe, V. G.
1934 *New Light on the Most Ancient East: The Oriental Prelude to European Prehistory*. Kegan Paul, London.

Christian, F. W.
1899 *The Caroline Islands: Travel in the Sea of the Little Lands*. Methuen & Co., London.

Christmann, H., P. H. and D. A. Ballendorf
1991 *Die Karolinen-Inseln in deutscher Zeit: Eine kolonialgeschichtliche Fallstudie*. Bremer Asien-Pazifik Studien, Bd. 1. Münster, Hamburg.

Claridge, G. C.
1985 The Mineralogy of Clay Samples from Yap. In *Archaeological Investigations in the Yap Islands, Micronesia: First Millennium B.C. to the Present Day*, edited by M. Intoh and F. Leach, pp. 194-198. BAR International Series 277. British Archaeological Reports, Oxford.

Clifford, J. and G. E. Marcus (editors)
1986 *Writing Culture: The Poetics and Politics of Ethnography*. A School of American Research Advanced Seminar. University of California Press, Berkeley.

Cogswell, J., H. Neff, and M. D. Glascock
1996 The Effect of Firing Temperature on the Elemental Characterization of Pottery. *Journal of Archaeological Science* 23:283-287.

1998 Analysis of Shell-Tempered Pottery Replicates: Implications for Provenance Studies. *American Antiquity* 63(1):63-72.

Cordy, R.
1986 *Archaeological Settlement Pattern Studies on Yap*. Micronesian Archaeological Survey Report Series, Number 16. Office of Historic Preservation, Commonwealth of the Northern Marianas, Saipan.

Cowgill, G. L.
1975 On Causes and Consequences of Ancient and Modern Population Changes. *American Antiquity* 77(3):505-525.

Craib, J.
1980 *Archaeological Survey of Ulithi Atoll, Western Caroline Islands*. Pacific Islands Institute, Agana, Guam.

1981 Settlement on Ulithi Atoll, Western Caroline Islands. *Asian Perspectives* 24(1):47-55.

1983 Micronesian Prehistory: An Archaeological Overview. *Science* 219(4587):922-927.

Craib, J. and S. Price
1978 *Archaeological Survey of the Map Powerline*. MS Report to Historic Preservation Office, Trust Territory of the Pacific Islands, Saipan.

Dalton, G.
1977 Aboriginal Economies in Stateless Societies. In *Exchange Systems in Prehistory*, edited by T. K. Earle and J. E. Ericson, pp. 191-212. Academic Press, New York and London.

Damm, H.
1938 *Zentralkarolinen: Ifaluk - Aurepik - Faraulip - Sorol - Mogemog*. Halbband II. In *Ergebnisse der Südsee Expedition 1908-1910*, edited by Georg Thilenius. Friederichsen, De Gruyter, & Co., Hamburg. Human Relations Area Files unedited translated manuscript.

Davidson, J.
1967 Archaeology on Coral Atolls. In *Polynesian Culture History: Essays in Honor of Kenneth P. Emory*, edited by G. A. Highland, R. W. Force, A. Howard, M. Kelly, and Y. H. Sinoto, pp. 363-376. Bernice P. Bishop Museum Special Publication 56, Honolulu.

1968 Nukuoro: Archaeology on a Polynesian Outlier in Micronesia. In *Prehistoric Culture in Oceania: A Symposium*, edited by I. Yawata and Y. H. Sinoto, pp. 51-66. Eleventh Pacific Science Congress, Tokyo, Japan, 1966. Bishop Museum Press, Honolulu.

1971 *Archaeology on Nukuoro Atoll: A Polynesian Outlier in the Eastern Caroline Islands*. No 9. Bulletin of the Auckland Institute and Museum city, Auckland.

1988 Archaeology in Micronesia Since 1965: Past Achievements and Future Prospects. *New Zealand Journal of Archaeology* 10:83-100.

DeMarrais, E., L. J. Castillo, and T. Earle
1996 Ideology, materialization, and power strategies. *Current Anthropology* 37(1):15-31.

Descantes, C.
2001 Contained Identities: The Demise of Yapese Clay Pots. *Asian Perspectives* 40(2): 227-243.

2004 The Martyrdom of Father Juan Cantova on Ulithi Atoll: the Hegemonic Struggle between Spanish Colonialism and a Micronesian Island Polity. *Missionalia* 32(3).

Descantes, C., H. Neff, and M. D. Glascock
2002 Yapese Prestige Good: The INAA Evidence for an Asian 'Dragon Jar'. In *Geochemical Evidence for Long-Distance Exchange*, edited by M. D. Glascock pp. 229-256. Volume 3. Scientific Archaeology for the Third Millennium Series. Bergin & Garvey Inc., Westport, Connecticut.

Descantes, C., M. Intoh, H. Neff, and M. D. Glascock
2004 Chemical Characterization of Yapese Clays and Ceramics by Instrumental Neutron Activation Analysis. *Journal of Radioanalytical and Nuclear Chemistry* 262(1):83-91.

Descantes, C., H. Neff, M. D. Glascock, and W. R. Dickinson
2001 Chemical Characterization of Micronesian Ceramics Through Instrumental Neutron Activation Analysis: A Preliminary Provenance Study. *Journal of Archaeological Science* 28(11):1185-1190.

Dickinson, W. R.
1982 Temper sands from prehistoric sherds excavated at Pemrang site on Yap and from nearby Ngulu Atoll. *Bulletin of the Indo-Pacific Prehistory Association* 3:115-117.

1984 Indigenous and Exotic Sand Tempers in Prehistoric Potsherds From the Central Caroline Islands. In Caroline Islands Archaeology, edited by Y. H. Sinoto, pp. 131-135. *Pacific Anthropological Records*, No. 35,. Department of Anthropology, Bishop Museum, Honolulu.

1994 Origins of temper sands in prehistoric potsherds from Fais and other locales in the Caroline Islands. *William R. Dickinson Petrographic Report* 106:1-2. June 12, 1993. Final revision January 12, 1994.

1997a Petrography of sherds from Ulithi. *William R. Dickinson Petrographic Report* 134:1-2. May 10, 1997.

1997b Appraisal of Micronesian Sherds Selected for NAA Analysis. *William R. Dickinson Petrographic Report* 156:1-7. July 13, 1997.

1999 Holocene Sea-Level Record on Funafuti and Potential Impact of Global Warming on Central Pacific Atolls. *Quaternary Research* 51:124-132.

2001 Paleoshoreline record of relative Holocene sea levels on Pacific islands. *Earth-Science Reviews* 55:191-234.

Dickinson, W. R. and R. Shutler Jr.
1971 Temper Sands in Prehistoric Pottery of the Pacific Islands. *Archaeology and Physical Anthropology in Oceania* 6(3):191-203.

1979 Petrography of Sand Tempers in Pacific Islands Potsherds. *Geological Society of America Bulletin* 90(2):1644-1701.

Dodson, J. and M. Intoh
1999 Prehistory and Palaeoecology of Yap, Federated States of Micronesia. *Quaternary International* 59:17-26.

Dumond, D.
1965 Population growth and cultural changes. *Southwestern Journal of Anthropology* 21:302-324.

Dye, T. (editor)
1987 *Marshall Islands Archaeology*. Pacific Anthropological Records, No. 38. Department of Anthropology, Bernice P. Bishop Museum, Honolulu.

Dye, T.
1994 Apparent ages of marine shells: Implications for archaeological dating in Hawai'i. *Radiocarbon* 36(1):51-57.

Earle, T. K.
1977 A Reappraisal of Redistribution: Complex Hawaiian Chiefdoms. In *Exchange systems in prehistory*, edited by T. K. Earle and J. E. Ericson, pp. 213-232. Academic Press, New York.

1982 Prehistoric Economics and the Archaeology of Exchange. In *Contexts for Prehistoric Exchange*, edited by J. E. Ericson and T. K. Earle, pp. 1-15. Cambridge University Press, Cambridge.

1991 The evolution of chiefdoms. In *Chiefdoms: Power, Economy, and Ideology*, edited by T. K. Earle, pp. 1-12. Academic Press, New York.

Edwards, A. J.
1995 Impact of Climatic Change on Coral Reefs, Mangroves, and Tropical Seagrass Ecosystems. In *Climate Change: Impact on Coastal Habitation*, edited by D. Eisma, pp. 209-234. Lewis Publishers, Boca Raton.

Egloff, B. J.
1978 The Kula Before Malinowski: A Changing Configuration. *Mankind* 11(3):429-435.

Fajans, J.
1993 Introduction. In *Exchanging Products: Producing Exchange*, edited by J. Fajans, pp. 1-13. Oceania Monographs, No. 43. University of Sydney Press, Sydney.

Falanruw, M. V. C
1990 Traditional adaptation to natural processes of erosion and sedimentation on Yap Island. In *Research Needs and Applications to Reduce Erosion and Sedimentation in Tropical Steeplands*, edited by R. R. Ziemer, C. L. O'Loughlin, L. S. Hamilton, pp. 231-237. IAHS Publication No. 192. IAHS Press, Washington, D.C.

Falanruw, M. C., J. E. Maka, T. G. Cole, and C. D. Whitesell
1990 *Common and Scientific Names of Trees and Shrubs of Mariana, Caroline, and Marshall Islands*. Forest Service, U.S. Department of Agriculture Resource Bulletin PSW-26. U.S. Department of Agriculture and the Pacific Southwest Forest and Range Experiment Station.

Falanruw, M. C., C. D. Whitesell, T. G. Cole, C. D. MacLean, and A. H. Ambacher
1987 *Vegetation Survey of Yap, Federated States of Micronesia*. Forest Service, U.S. Department of Agriculture and the Pacific Southwest Forest and Range Experiment Station in cooperation with the Pacific Northwest Forest and Range Experiment Station.

Feinman G.
1997 Thoughts on New Approaches to Combining the Archaeological and Historical Records. *Journal of Archaeological Method and Theory* 4(3/4):367-377.

Figirliyong, J.
1976 *The Contemporary Political System of Ulithi Atoll*. Unpublished Masters thesis, California State University, Fullerton.

Firth, R.
1959 *Economics of the New Zealand Maori*. Second Edition. Government Printer, Wellington.

Fitzpatrick, S. M.
2001 Archaeological investigation of Omis Cave: a Yapese stone money quarry in Palau. *Archaeology in Oceania* 36:153-162.

2002 AMS Dating of Human Bone from Palau: New Evidence for a Pre-2000 BP settlement. *Radiocarbon* 44 (Nr1):217-221.

Frankenstein, S. and M. J. Rowlands
1978 The Internal Structure and Regional Context of Early Iron Age Society in South-western Germany. *London University Institute of Archaeology Bulletin* 15:73-112.

Fried, M.
1967 The Evolution of Political Society: An Essay in Political Anthropology. Random House, New York.

Friedman, J.
1981 Notes on Structure and History in Oceania. *Folk* 23:275-295.

1982 Catastrophe and Continuity in Social Evolution. In *Theory and Explanation in Archaeology: The Southhampton Conference*, edited by C. Renfrew, M. J. Rowlands, and B. Abbott Segraves, pp. 175-96. Academic Press, New York.

Fujimura, K. and W. Alkire
1977 Recent Excavations on three atolls in the Caroline Islands: A note. *Journal of the Polynesian Society* 86(3):413-414.

1984 Archaeological Test Excavations on Faraulep, Woleai, and Lamotrek in the Caroline Islands of Micronesia. In *Caroline Islands Archaeology*, edited by Y. Sinoto, pp. 65-129. Pacific Anthropological Records, No. 35, Department of Anthropology, Bishop Museum, Honolulu.

Gewertz, D.
1983 *Sepik River Societies: A Historical Ethnography of the Chambri and Their Neighbors*. Yale University Press, New Haven.

Giddens, A.
1979 *Central Problems in Social Theory: Action, Structure, and Contradiction in Social Analysis*. University of California Press, Berkeley.

1995 *A Contemporary Critique of Historical Materialism*. Second Edition. Stanford University Press, Stanford.

Gifford, E. W. and D. S. Gifford
1959 *Archaeological Excavations in Yap*. Anthropological Records 18(2):149-224. University of California Press, Berkeley and Los Angeles.

Gillilland, C. L.
1975 *The Stone Money of Yap: A Numismatic Survey*. Smithsonian Studies in History and Technology No. 23. Smithsonian Institution Press, Washington, D.C.

Gladwin, T.
1958 Canoe Travel in the Truk Area: Technology and its psychological correlates. *American Anthropologist* 60:893-899.

Glascock, M. D.
1992 Characterization of Archaeological Ceramics at MURR by Neutron Activation Analysis and Multivariate Statistics. In *Chemical Characterization of Ceramic Pastes in Archaeology*, edited by H. Neff, pp. 11-26. Monographs in World Archaeology, No. 7. Prehistory Press, Madison.

Glascock, M. D., H. Neff, J. W. Cogswell, and R. S. Herrera
1996 *Neutron Activation Analysis for Archaeological Applications*. Ms. on file, Missouri University Research Reactor Archaeometry Laboratory. Columbia, Missouri.

Godelier, M.
1988 *The Mental and the Material: Thought Economy and Society*. Translated by M. Thom. Verso, London.

Goles, G. G.
1978 Instrumental methods of neutron activation analysis. In *Physical Methods of Determinative Mineralogy*, edited by J. Zussman, pp. 343-369. Academic Press, London.

Gosden, C.
1989 Prehistoric social landscapes of the Arawe Islands, West New Britain Province, Papua New Guinea. *Archaeology in Oceania* 24(2):45-58.

1996 Transformations: history and prehistory in Hawaii. *Archaeology in Oceania* 31(3):165-172.

Graves, M. W., T. L. Hunt and D. Moore
1990 Ceramic production in the Mariana Islands: Explaining Change and Diversity in Prehistoric Interaction and Exchange. *Asian Perspectives* 29(2):211-233.

Great Britain Hydrographic Department
1987 Ocean passages for the world. 4th ed. Hydrographer of the Navy, Taunton, Somerset, England.

Gregory, C. A.
1982 *Gifts and Commodities*. Academic Press, London.

1992 Review of *Exchange in Oceania: A Graph Theoretic Analysis*, by P. Hage and F. Harary. *Man* 27(2):425-426.

Green, R. C.
1991 Near and remote Oceania – Disestablishing "Melanesia" in culture history. In *Man and a Half: Essays in Pacific anthropology and ethnobiology in honour of Ralph Bulmer*, edited by A. Pawley, pp. 491-502. Memoirs of the Polynesian Society 48. The Polynesian Society, Auckland.

1996 Prehistoric Transfers of Portable Items During the Lapita Horizon in Remote Oceania: A Review. *Bulletin of the Indo-Pacific Prehistory Association* 15:119-130.

Green, R. C. and P. V. Kirch
1997 Lapita exchange systems and their Polynesian transformations: seeking explanatory models. In *Prehistoric Long-Distance Interaction in Oceania: An Interdisciplinary Approach*, edited by M. I. Weisler, pp. 19-37. New Zealand Archaeological Association Monograph 21. New Zealand Archaeological Association, Auckland.

Gumerman, G. J.
1986 The role of competition and cooperation in the evolution of island societies. In *Island societies: Archaeological approaches to evolution and transformation*, edited by P. V. Kirch, pp. 42-49. Cambridge University Press, Cambridge.

Hage, P. and F. Harary
1991 Exchange in Oceania: A graph theoretic analysis. Clarendon Press, Oxford.

1996 Island networks: Communication, kinship, and classification structures in Oceania. Cambridge University Press, Cambridge.

Hambruch, P.
1912 *Die Schiffahrt Auf Den Karolinen- Und Marshallinseln*. Meereskunde, Sammlung Volkstumlicher Vortrage, Zum Verstandnis Der Nationalen Bedeutung Von Meer Und Seewesen Heft 66. Königliche Hofbuchhandlung, Kochstrasse, pp. 68-71. Ernst Siegfried Mittler Und Sohn, Berlin.

Harding, T. G.
1967 *Voyagers of the Vitiaz Strait: A Study of a New Guinea Trade System*. University of Washington Press, Seattle.

Hatcher, L.
1994 *A Step-by-Step Approach to Using the SAS® System for Factor Analysis and Structural Equation Modeling*. SAS Institute Inc., Cary, NC.

Hawkins, J. and R. Batiza
1977 Metamorphic rocks from the Yap arc-trench system. *Earth Planetary Science Letters* 37(2):216-229.

Helms, M.
1993 Craft and the Kingly Ideal: Art, Trade, and Power. University of Texas Press, Austin.

Hess, H. H.
1948 Major structural features of the Western North Pacific, an interpretation of H.O. chart 5485 (Bathymetric Chart Korea to New Guinea): *Geological Society of America Bulletin* 59(5):417-445.

Hezel, F. X.
1983 *The First Taint of Civilization: A History of the Caroline and Marshall Islands in Pre-Colonial Days, 1521-1885*. Pacific Islands Monograph Series, No. 1. University of Hawaii Press, Honolulu.

Hezel, F. X. and M. T. del Valle
1972 Early European Contact with the Western Carolines: 1525-1750. *Journal of Pacific History* 7:26-44.

Howells, W. W.
1973 *The Pacific Islanders*. Weidenfeld & Nicolson, London.

Hunt, T. L.
1989 *Lapita Ceramic Exchange in the Mussau Islands, Papua New Guinea*. Unpublished Ph.D. dissertation, University of Washington, Seattle.

Hunt, T. L. and M. W. Graves
1990 Some Methodological Issues of Exchange in Oceanic Prehistory. *Asian Perspectives* 29(2):107-115.

Hunter-Anderson, R. L.
1983 *Yapese Settlement Patterns: An Ethnoarchaeological Approach*. Pacific Studies Institute, Agana, Guam.

1986 Indigenous Fresh Water Management Technology of the Yap Islands, Micronesia. *Water & Energy Research Institute Technical Report* 63, University of Guam, Mangilao.

Hunter-Anderson, R. L. and Y. Zan
1996 Demystifying the *Sawei*, A traditional Interisland Exchange System. *ISLA: A Journal of Micronesian Studies* 4(1):1-45.

de Ibáñez y Garcia, L.
1992 [1887] *History of the Marianas, Caroline, and Palau Islands: From the Time of their Discovery by Magellan in 1521 to the Present*. Translated and annotated by M. G. Driver. MARC Educational Series No. 12. Micronesian Area Research Center, University of Guam, Mangilao.

Intoh, M.
1981 Reconnaissance archaeological research on Ngulu atoll in the Western Caroline Islands. *Asian Perspectives* 24(1):69-80.

1988 *Changing Prehistoric Yapese Pottery Technology: A Case Study of Adaptive Transformation*. Unpublished Ph.D. dissertation, University of Otago, Dunedin.

1990 Ceramic Environment and Technology: A Case Study in the Yap Islands in Micronesia. *Man and Culture in Oceania* 6:35-52.

1992 Why were pots imported to Ngulu Atoll? A consideration of subsistence strategy. *Journal of the Polynesian Society* 101(2):159-168.

1996 Multi-Regional Contacts of Prehistoric Fais Islanders in Micronesia. *Bulletin of the Indo-Pacific Prehistory Association* 15:111-117.

1997 Human Dispersals into Micronesia. *Anthropological Science* 105(1):15-28.

Intoh M. and W. R. Dickinson
1994 A petrological study of prehistoric pottery from Fais Island in Micronesia. *Anthropological Science* 102(2):167.

2002 Prehistoric Pottery Movements in Western Micronesia: Technological and Petrological Study of Potsherds from Fais Island. In *Fifty years in the Field. Essays in Honour and Celebration of Richard Shutler Jr's Archaeological Career*, edited by S. Bedford, C. Sand, and D. Burley, pp. 123-134. New Zealand Archaeological Association Monograph 25. New Zealand Archaeological Association, Auckland.

Intoh, M. and F. Leach
1984 *The Pottery Traditions of the Yap Islands*. Preliminary report of the survey work conducted in the Yap Islands. Historic Preservation Office, Saipan. Unpublished manuscript. Department of Anthropology, University of Otago, Dunedin.

1985 *Archaeological Investigations in the Yap Islands, Micronesia: First Millennium B.C. to the Present Day*. BAR International Series 277. British Archaeological Reports, Oxford.

Irwin, G.
1978 Pots and entrepôts: a study of settlement, trade and the development of economic specialization in Papuan prehistory. *World Archaeology* 9(3):299-319.

1985 *The Emergence of Mailu: as a central place in coastal Papuan prehistory*. Terra Australis 10. Department of Prehistory, Research School of Pacific Studies, The Australian National University, Canberra.

1992 The Prehistoric Exploration and Colonisation of the Pacific. Cambridge University Press, Cambridge.

Jensen, J. T.
1977 *Yapese-English Dictionary*. University Press of Hawaii, Honolulu.

Johnson, C., R. Alvis, and R. Hetzler
1960 *Military geology of Yap Islands*. U.S. Geological Survey under the direction of the Chief of Engineers, U.S. Army.

Jones, R. E.
1986 *Greek and Cypriot pottery: a review of scientific studies*. Fitch Laboratory Occasional Paper 1. British School at Athens, Athens.

Kawachi, Y
1985 Mineralogical examination of fired clay samples from Yap. In *Archaeological Investigations in the Yap Islands, Micronesia: First Millennium B.C. to the Present Day*, edited by M. Intoh, and F. Leach, pp. 199-200. BAR International Series 277. British Archaeological Reports, Oxford.

Kirch, P. V.
1984 *The Evolution of the Polynesian Chiefdoms*. Cambridge University Press, Cambridge.

1986 Exchange systems and inter-island contact in the transformation of an island society: the Tikopia case. In *Island societies: Archaeological approaches to evolution and transformation*, edited by P. V. Kirch, pp. 33-41. Cambridge University Press, Cambridge.

1987 Lapita and Oceanic Cultural Origins: Excavations in the Mussau Islands, Bismarck Archipelago, 1985. *Journal of Field Archaeology* 14:163-180.

1988 Long-distance Exchange and Island Colonization: The Lapita Case. *Norwegian Archaeological Review* 21(2):103-117.

1991 Prehistoric Exchange in Western Melanesia. *Annual Review of Anthropology* 20:141-165.

1992 *The Archaeology of History*. In *Anahulu: The Anthropology of a History in the Kingdom of Hawaii. The Archaeology of History*, edited by P. V. Kirch and M. Sahlins. Volume 2. Chicago University Press, Chicago.

Kirch, P. V. and R. C. Green
1987 History, Phylogeny, and Evolution in Polynesia. *Current Anthropology* 28(4):431-456.

Klein, P.
1707 Lettre écrite de Manille le 10. de Juin 1697. Par le Père Paul Clain de la Compagnie de Jésus, au Révérend Père Thyrse Gonzalez, Général de la même Compagnie, sur la nouvelle découverte qu'on a faite de trende-deux Îles au Sud des Îles Marianes. In *Lettres édifiantes et curieuses, écrites des missions étrangères par quelques missionaires de la Compagnie de Jésus* 1:112-136.

Knapp, A. B.
1992a Preface. In *Archaeology, Annales, and Ethnohistory*, edited by A. B. Knapp, pp. xv-xvi. Cambridge University Press, Cambridge.

1992b Archaeology and *Annales*: time, space, and change. In *Archaeology, Annales, and Ethnohistory*, edited by A. B. Knapp, pp. 1-21. Cambridge University Press, Cambridge.

1992c Independence and imperialism: politico-economic structures in the Bronze Age Levant. In *Archaeology, Annales, and Ethnohistory*, edited by A. B. Knapp, pp. 83-98. Cambridge University Press, Cambridge.

Krämer, A.
1937 *Zentralkarolinen*. In *Ergebnisse der Südsee Expedition 1908-1910*, edited by G. Thilenius, 1917-1918. II, B; Bd. 10/1. L. Friederichsen & Co., Hamburg.

Kubary, J. S.
1889 Ueber das einheimische Geld auf der Insel Yap und auf den Pelau-Inseln. *Ethnographische Beiträge zur Kenntnis des Karolinen Archipels*, edited by J. D. E. Schmeltz, I:1-28, heft. Verlag Von P. W. M. Trap, Leiden.

1895 *Ethnographische Beiträge zur Kenntnis des Karolinen Archipels*, edited by J. D. E. Schmeltz. Verlag Von P. W. M. Trap, Leiden.

Labby, D.
1976 *The Demystification of Yap: Dialectics of Culture on a Micronesian Island*. University of Chicago Press, Chicago.

La Lone, D. E.
1982 The Inca as a Nonmarket Economy: Supply on Command versus Supply and Demand. In *Contexts for Prehistoric Exchange*, edited by J. E. Ericson and T. K. Earle, pp. 291-316. Academic Press, New York.

Lauer, P.
1971 Changing Patterns of Pottery Trade in the Trobriand Islands. *World Archaeology* 3:197-209.

Leonard, R. D.
1993 The Persistence of an Explanatory Dilemma in Contact Period Studies. In *Ethnohistory and Archaeology: Approaches to Postcontact Change in the Americas*, edited by J. D. Rogers and S M. Wilson, pp. 31-43. Plenum Press, New York.

Le Roy Ladurie, E.
1979 *The Territory of the Historian*. University of Chicago Press, Chicago.

Lessa, W. A.
1950a *The Ethnography of Ulithi Atoll*. Coordinated Investigation of Micronesian Anthropology (CIMA) Report no.28. Pacific Science Board, Washington, D.C.

1950b The Place of Ulithi in the Yap Empire. *Human Organization* 9(1):16-18.

1950c Ulithi and the Outer Native World. *American Anthropologist* 52(1):27-52.

1956 Myth and Blackmail in the Western Carolines. *Journal of the Polynesian Society* 65(1):66-74.

1961 *Tales from Ulithi Atoll: A Comparative Study in Oceanic Folklore*. Folklore Studies: 13. University of California Press, Los Angeles.

1962a The Decreasing Power of Myth on Ulithi. *Journal of American Folklore* 75(296):153-159.

1962b An Evaluation of Early Descriptions of Carolinian Culture. *Ethnohistory* 9(4):313-403.

1968 The Social Effects of Typhoon Ophelia (1960) on Ulithi. In *Peoples and Cultures of the Pacific*, edited by A. P. Vayda, pp. 330-379. The Natural History Press, Garden City, New York.

1977 Traditional Uses of the Vascular Plants of Ulithi Atoll, with Comparative Notes. *Micronesica* 13(2):129-190.

1980 *More Tales from Ulithi Atoll: A Content Analysis*. Folklore and Mythology Studies: 32. University of California Press, Los Angeles.

1986 [1966] *Ulithi: A Micronesian Design for Living*. Waveland Press, Inc. Prospect Heights, Illinois.

1987 Comments on Settlement on Ulithi Atoll. *Asian Perspectives* 25(2):127-132.

Lévesque, R. (editor)
1992 *History of Micronesia: A Collection of Source Documents*, vol. I. Lévesque Publications, Gatineau, Québec.

1995 *History of Micronesia: A Collection of Source Documents*, vol. IV. Lévesque Publications, Gatineau, Québec.

Lilley, I
1988 Prehistoric Exchange across the Vitiaz Strait, Papua New Guinea. *Current Anthropology* 29(3):513-516.

Lingenfelter, S. G.
1975 *Yap, Political Leadership and Culture Change in an Island Society*. University Press of Hawaii, Honolulu.

Malinowski, B.
1922 *Argonauts of the Western Pacific: An Account of Native Enterprise and Adventure in the Archipelagoes of Melanesian New Guinea*. George Routledge and Sons, Ltd., London.

Mason L.
1968 Suprafamilial Authority and Economic Process in Micronesian Atolls. In *Peoples and Cultures of the Pacific*, edited by A. P. Vayda, pp. 299-329. The Natural History Press, Garden City, New York.

Marx, K.
1973 *Grundrisse*. Penguin, Harmondsworth.

Mauss, M.
1967 [1925] *The Gift: Forms and Functions of Exchange in Archaic Societies*. Translated by Ian Cunnison. W W Norton & Company Inc., Glencoe, New York.

Moreland, J. F.
1992 Restoring the dialectic: settlement patterns and documents in medieval central Italy. In *Archaeology, Annales, and Ethnohistory*, edited by A. B. Knapp, pp. 112-129. Cambridge University Press, Cambridge.

Müller (Wismar), W.
1917 *Yap*. In *Ergebnisse der Südsee Expedition 1908-1910*, edited by G. Thilenius, 1917-1918. II: Ethnographie, B: Mikronesien; Bd. 2/1. L. Friederichsen & Co., Hamburg. Translated for Yale Cross Cultural File, 1942; Human Relations Area Files, 1962.

1918 *Yap*. In *Ergebnisse der Südsee Expedition 1908-1910*, edited by G. Thilenius, 1917-1918. Bd. 2/2. L. Friederichsen & Co., Hamburg.

Munn, N.
1986 *The Fame of Gawa: A Symbolic Study of Value Transformation in a Massim (Papua New Guinea) Society*. Cambridge University Press, Cambridge.

Narotzky, S.
1997 *New Directions in Economic Anthropology*. Pluto Press, London.

Neff, H.
1992 Introduction. In *Chemical Characterization of Ceramic Pastes in Archaeology*, edited by H. Neff, pp. 1-10. Monographs in World Archaeology, No. 7. Prehistory Press, Madison, Wisconsin.

Neff, H., R. L. Bishop, and E. V. Sayre
1988 A Simulation Approach to the Problem of Tempering in Compositional Studies of Archaeological Ceramics. *Journal of Archaeological Science* 15:159-172.

1989 More Observations on the Problem of Tempering in Compositional Studies of Archaeological Ceramics. *Journal of Archaeological Science* 16:57-69.

Neff, H., D. O. Larson, and M. D. Glascock
1997 The Evolution of Anasazi Ceramic Production and Distribution: Compositional Evidence from a Pueblo III Site in South-Central Utah. *Journal of Field Archaeology* 24(4):473-492.

Pavlish, L. A., R. G. V. Hancock, D. Snyder, and L. Lucking
1986 INAA Study of Pottery from Palau, Micronesia. In *Proceedings of the 24th International Archaeometry Symposium*, edited by J. Olin and M. J. Blackman, pp. 381-387. Smithsonian Institution Press, Washington, D.C.

Peabody Museum of Archaeology and Ethnology
1949 *The Micronesians of Yap and Their Depopulation. Report of the Peabody Museum Expedition to Yap Island, Micronesia, 1947 - 1948*. Peabody Museum, Harvard University, Cambridge.

Peattie, M. R.
1988 *Nanyo: The Rise and Fall of the Japanese in Micronesia, 1885-1945*. Pacific Monograph Series, No. 4. University of Hawaii Press, Honolulu.

Petersen, G.
1982 *One man cannot rule a thousand: Fission in a Ponapean chiefdom*. University of Michigan Press, Ann Arbor.

Pirazzoli, P. A.
1991 *World Atlas of Holocene Sea-Level Changes*. Elsevier Oceanography Series, 58. Elsevier Science Publishers B. V., Amsterdam.

Plog, F. T.
1977 Modeling economic exchange. In *Exchange systems in prehistory*, edited by T. K. Earle and J. E. Ericson, pp. 127-140. Academic Press, New York.

Plog, S.
1986 Change in Regional Trade Networks. In *Spatial Organization and Exchange: Archaeological Survey on Northern Black Mesa*, edited by S. Plog, pp. 282-309. Southern Illinois University Press, Carbondale and Edwardsville.

Polanyi, K.
1965 *Trade and Market in the Early Empires: Economies in History and Theory*. Second Edition. The Free Press, New York.

Pollock, N. J.
1992 *These Roots Remain: Food Habits in Islands of the Central and Eastern Pacific since Western Contact*. The Institute for Polynesian Studies, Laie, Hawaii.

Poyer, L.
1995 Yapese Experiences of the Pacific War. *ISLA: A Journal of Micronesian Studies* 3(2):223-255.

Price, S. T.
1975 *The Transformation of Yap: Causes and Consequences of Socio-Economic Change in Micronesia*. Unpublished Ph.D. dissertation, Washington State University, Pullman.

Rainbird, P.
1994 Prehistory in the Northwest Tropical Pacific: The Caroline, Mariana, and Marshall Islands. *Journal of World Prehistory* 8(3):293-349.

Renfrew, C.
1975 Trade as Action at a Distance: Questions of Integration and Communication. In *Ancient Civilization and Trade*, edited by J. A. Sabloff and C. C. Lamberg-Karlovsky, pp. 3-59. University of New Mexico Press, Albuquerque.

Renfrew, C. and J. F. Cherry
1986 Introduction: Peer Polity Interaction and Socio-political Change. In *Peer Polity Interaction and Socio-Political Change*, edited by C. Renfrew and J. F. Cherry, pp. 1-18. Cambridge University Press, Cambridge.

Rice, P. M.
1987 *Pottery Analysis: A Sourcebook*. The University of Chicago Press, Chicago.

Ross, M.
1996 Is Yapese Oceanic? In *Reconstruction, Classification, Description. Festschrift in Honor of Isidore Dyen*, edited by Bernd Nothofer Volume III, pp. 121-166. Abera Verlag, Hamburg.

Russell, S.
1983 The Sea People: In Search of Iron and Land. *Glimpses of Micronesia* 23(4):22-23.

Rytuba, J. J. and W. R. Miller
1990 Geology and geochemistry of epithermal precious metal vein systems in the intra-oceanic arcs of Palau and Yap, Western Pacific. *Journal of Geochemical Exploration* 35:413-447.

Sahlins, M.
1965 On the Sociology of Primitive Exchange. In *The Relevance of Models for Social Anthropology*, edited by M. Banton, pp. 139-236. Tavistock, London.

1972 *Stone Age Economics*. Aldine Atherton, Inc., Chicago and New York.

1981 *Historical Metaphors and Mythical Realities: Structure in the Early History of the Sandwich Islands Kingdom*. A. S. A. O. Special Publication No. 1. University of Michigan Press, Ann Arbor.

1985 *Islands of History*. University of Chicago Press, Chicago.

1988 Cosmologies of Capitalism: The Trans-Pacific Sector of 'The World System'. *Proceedings of the British Academy* 74:1-51.

1992 *Historical Ethnography*. In *Anahulu: The Anthropology of a History in the Kingdom of Hawaii. The Archaeology of History*, edited by P. V. Kirch and M. Sahlins. Volume 1. Chicago University Press, Chicago.

Salesius, P. [F. S. Haas]
1907 *Die Karolinen-Insel Jap: Ein Beitrag zur Kenntnis von Land und Leuten in Unseren Deutschen Südsee-Kolonien*. William Süsserott, Berlin. Translated for Yale Cross Cultural File, 1942. Human Relations Area Files, 1963.

Schneider, D. M.
1949 *The Kinship System and Village Organization of Yap*. Unpublished doctoral dissertation, Harvard University, Cambridge.

1957 Typhoons on Yap. *Human Organization* 16(2):10-15.

1968 Abortion and Depopulation on a Pacific Island. In *Peoples and Cultures of the Pacific*, edited by A. P. Vayda, pp. 383-406. The Natural History Press, Garden City, New York.

1974 Depopulation and the Tap *Tabinau*. In *Social Organization and the Applications of Anthropology: Essays in Honor of Lauriston Sharp*, edited by R. J. Smith, pp. 94-113. Cornell University Press, Ithaca.

Schortman, E. M.
1989 Interregional Interaction in Prehistory: The Need for a New Perspective. *American Antiquity* 54(1): 52-65.

Senfft, A.
1903 Ethnographische Beiträge über die Karolineninsel Yap. *Petermanns Geographische Mitteilungen* 49:49-60, 83-87. Translated for Yale Cross Cultural File, 1942, Human Relations Area Files, 1962.

Seymour-Smith, C. (editor)
1986 *Dictionary of Anthropology*. G. K. Hall, Boston.

Shennan, S.
1997 *Quantifying Archaeology*. Second Edition. University of Iowa Press, Iowa City.

Sheppard, P. J.
1997 Characterisation of cherts from sites in southwest Tasmania. *Archaeology in Oceania*. 32(1):47-53.

Shineberg, D. (editor)
1971 *The Trading Voyages of Andrew Cheyne 1841-1844*. Australia National University Press, Canberra.

Shun, K. and Athens, J. S.
1990 Archaeological investigations on Kwajalein Atoll, Marshall Islands, Micronesia. *Micronesica Supplement* 2:231-240.

Silva, A. P. Duarte and A. Stam
1995 Discriminant Analysis. In *Reading and Understanding Multivariate Statistics*, edited by L. G. Grimm and P. R. Yarnold, pp. 277-318. American Psychological Association, Washington, D.C.

Small, D. B.
1995 Heterarchical Paths to Evolution: The Role of External Economies. In *Heterarchy and the Analysis of Complex Societies*, edited by R. M. Ehrenreich, C. L. Crumley, J. E. Levy, pp. 71-85. Archeological Papers of the American Anthropological Association No. 6. American Anthropological Association, Washington, D.C.

Smith, C. W.
1983 *Soil Survey of Islands of Yap, Federated States of Micronesia*. Soil Conservation Service, U.S. Department of Agriculture, Washington, D.C.

Smith, D. R.
1983 *Palauan Social Structure*. Rutgers University Press, New Brunswick.

Snyder, D.
1989 *Towards Chronometric Models for Palauan Prehistory: Ceramic Attributes*. Unpublished doctoral dissertation, Southern Illinois University, Carbondale.

Spoehr, A.
1957 *Marianas prehistory: archaeological survey and excavation on Saipan, Tinian, and Rota*. Fieldiana: Anthropology Vol. 48. Field Museum of Natural History, Chicago.

Stafford, T.W. Jr., A.J. Jull, K. Brendel, R.C. Duhamel, and D. Donahue
1987 Study of bone radiocarbon dating accuracy at the University of Arizona NSF accelerator facility for radioisotope analysis. *Radiocarbon* 29(1):24-44.

Stein, A., M. L. Van Der Plas, P. W. Van Den Broeke, and L. Van Der Plas
1991 Chemical Homogeneity and Representativeness of Prehistoric Pottery Sherds Relative to their Assemblage. *Journal of Quantitative Anthropology* 3:261-277.

Stuiver, M. and T. F. Brazuinas
1993 Modeling atmospheric ^{14}C influences and ^{14}C ages of marine samples to 10,000 B.C. *Radiocarbon* 35(1):137-189.

Strathern, A. J.
1971 *The Rope of Moka*. Cambridge University Press, Cambridge.

1991 Struggles for Meaning. In *Clio in Oceania: Toward a Historical Anthropology*, edited by Aletta Biersack, pp. 205-230. Smithsonian Institution Press, Washington and London.

Streck, C. F. Jr.
1990 Prehistoric settlement in eastern Micronesia: archaeology in Bikini Atoll, Republic of the Marshall Islands. *Micronesica Supplement* 2:247-260.

Summerhayes, G. R.
1997 Losing your temper. *Archaeology in Oceania* 32(1):108-117.

Takayama, J.
1982a A Brief Report on Archaeological Investigations of the Southern Part of Yap Island and Nearby Ngulu Atoll. In *Islanders and their Outside World: A Report of the Cultural Anthropological Research in the Caroline Islands of Micronesia in 1980-1981*, edited by M. Aoyagi, pp. 77-104. Committee for Micronesian Research, St. Paul's (Rikkyo) University, Tokyo.

1982b Archaeological Research in Micronesia During the Past Decade. *Bulletin of the Indo-Pacific Prehistory Association* 3:95-114.

Terrell, J. E., T. L. Hunt, and C. Gosden
1997 The Dimensions of Social Life in the Pacific: Human Diversity and the Myth of the Primitive Isolate. *Current Anthropology* 38(2):155-195.

Tetens, A.
1958 [1888] *Among the Savages of the South Seas: Memoirs of Micronesia, 1862-1868*. Translated by F. Spoehr, Stanford University Press, Stanford.

Tetens, A. and J. Kubary
1873 Die Carolineninsel Yap Oder Guap nach den Mittheilungen von Alfred Tetens und Johann Kubary. Prepared by Dr. E. Gräffe. *Journal des Museum Godeffroy* I:84-130. Translated for Yale Cross Cultural File, 1942, Human Relations Area Files, 1962.

Thilenius, G.
1927 *Allgemeines: Der Plan Der Expedition*. In the *Ergebnisse der Südsee-Expedition 1908-1910*, Vol. I, edited by G. Thilenius. L. Friederichsen & Co., Hamburg.

Thomas, N.
1991 *Entangled Objects: Exchange, Material Culture, and Colonialism in the Pacific*. Harvard University Press, Cambridge.

1992 Politicised values: the cultural dynamics of peripheral exchange. In *Barter, exchange and value: An Anthropological Approach*, edited by C. Humphrey and S. Hugh-Jones, pp. 21-41. Cambridge University Press, Cambridge.

1995 Exchange Systems, Political Dynamics, and Colonial Transformations. In *The Austronesians: Historical and Comparative Perspectives*, edited by P. Bellwood, J. J. Fox, and D. Tryon, pp. 269-290. Department of Anthropology, Research School of Pacific and Asian Studies, Australian National University, Canberra.

1996 *Out of Time: History and Evolution in Anthropological Discourse*. Second Edition. University of Michigan Press, Ann Arbor.

Thomas, W. L. Jr.
1967 The Pacific Basin: An Introduction. In *The Pacific Basin: A History of Its Geographical Exploration*, edited by H. R. Friis, pp. 3-26. Special Publication No. 38. American Geographical Society, New York.

Torrence, R.
1986 *Production and Exchange of Stone Tools: Prehistoric Obsidian in the Aegean*. New Studies in Archaeology. Cambridge University Press, Cambridge.

Torrence, R. and G. R. Summerhayes
1997 Sociality and the short distance trader: intra-regional obsidian exchange in the Willaumez region, Papua New Guinea. *Archaeology in Oceania* 32(1):74-84.

Trigger, B. G.
1984 Archaeology at the Crossroads: What's New? *Annual Review of Anthropology* 13:275-300.

Ueki, T.
1990 Formation of a Complex Society in an Island Situation. *Micronesica Supplement* 2:303-316.

Upham, S.
1982 *Polities and Power: An Economic and Political History of the Western Pueblo*. Academic Press, New York.

1987 The Tyranny of Ethnographic Analogy in Southwestern Archaeology. In *Coasts, Plains and Deserts: Essays in Honor of Reynold J. Ruppé*, edited by S. W. Gaines, pp. 265-279. Anthropological Research Papers No. 38. Arizona State University, Tempe.

1990 Analog or digital?: Toward a generic framework for explaining the development of emergent political systems. In *The Evolution of Political Systems: Sociopolitics in Small-Scale Sedentary Societies*, edited by S. Upham, pp. 87-115. Cambridge University Press, Cambridge.

Upham, S., G. M. Feinman, and L. M. Nichols
1992 New Perspectives on the Southwest and Highland Mesoamerica: A Macroregional Approach. *Review* 15(3):427-451.

Ushijima, I.
1982 The Control of Reef and Lagoons; Some Aspects of the Political Structure of Ulithi Atoll. In *Islanders and their Outside World. A report of the cultural anthropological research in the Caroline Islands of Micronesia in 1980-1981*, edited by M. Aoyagi, pp. 33-79. St. Paul's (Rikkyo) University, Tokyo.

1987a Political Structure and Formation of Communication Channels on Yap Island: A Case Study of the Fanif District. In *Cultural Uniformity and Diversity in Micronesia*, edited by I. Ushijima and K. Sudo. Senri Ethnological Studies 21:177-203.

1987b A Reinterpretation of the Sawai Overseas Exchange System of the Caroline Islands. In *Cultural Adaptation to Atolls in Micronesia & West Polynesia*. A report of the cultural anthropological research in Caroline, Marshall, and Ellice Islands, 1985, edited by E. Ishikawa, pp. 55-79. Tokyo Metropolitan University, Tokyo.

Van der Plicht, J.
1993 The Gröningen radiocarbon calibration program. *Radiocarbon* 35(1) 231-237.

Von Chamisso, A.
1986 [1835] *A Voyage Around the World with the Romanzov Exploring Expedition in the Years 1815-1818 in the Brig Rurik, Captain Otto von Kotzebue*, edited and translated by Henry Kratz. University of Hawaii Press, Honolulu.

Von Kotzebue, O.
1821 *A Voyage of Discovery into the South Sea and Beering's Straits, for the Purpose of Exploring a North-East Passage, Undertaken in the Years 1815-1818, at the Expense of his Highness the Chancellor of the Empire, Count Romanzoff, in the Ship Rurick, Under the Command of the Lieutenant in the Russian Imperial Navy, Otto von Kotzebue*. Volume 3. Longman, Hurst, Rees, Orme, and Brown, London.

Wallerstein, I.
1974 *The Modern World-System: Capitalist Agriculture and the Origins of the European Wold-Economy in the Sixteenth Century*. Academic Press, New York.

Walleser, P. S.
1913 Religiöse Anschauungen und Gebräuche der Bewohner von Jap (Deutsche Südsee). *Anthropos* 8:607-629, 1044-1068. Religious Beliefs and Practices of the Inhabitants of Yap (German South Seas). Translated from the German by the Jesuit Bureau in 1967, Buffalo, NY.

Weigand, G. Harbottle, and E. V. Sayre
1977 Turquoise Sources and Source Analysis: Mesoamerica and The Southwestern U.S.A. In *Exchange Systems in Prehistory*, edited by T. K. Earle and J. E. Ericson, pp. 15-34. Academic Press, New York and London.

Weiner, A. B.
1988 *The Trobrianders of Papua New Guinea*. Holt, Rinehart and Winston, New York.

Weisler, M. I.
1997 Prehistoric Long-Distance Interaction at the Margins of Oceania. In *Prehistoric Long-Distance Interaction in Oceania: An Interdisciplinary Approach*, edited by M. I. Weisler, pp. 149-172. New Zealand Archaeological Association Monograph 21. New Zealand Archaeological Association, Auckland.

Weisler, M. I. and P. V. Kirch
1996 Interisland and interarchipelago transfer of stone tools in prehistoric Polynesia. *Proceedings of the National Academy of Science* 93:1381-1385.

Wheeler, K.
1979 *The Road to Tokyo*. World War II. Volume 19. Time-Life Books, Alexandria, Virginia.

White, J. P. and M.-N. Harris
1997 Changing sources: early Lapita period obsidian in the Bismarck Archipelago. *Archaeology in Oceania* 32(1):97-107.

Wickler, S.
2002 The Colonization of Western Micronesia and Early Settlement in Palau. In *Pacific 2000: Proceedings of the Fifth International Congress on Easter Island and the Pacific*, edited by C. M. Stevenson, G. Lee, and F. J. Morin, pp. 185-196. Easter Island Foundation, Los Osos, California.

Wiens, H. J.
1962 *Atoll Environment and Ecology*. Yale University Press, New Haven.

Wilson, S. M.
1993 Structure and History: Combining Archaeology and Ethnohistory in the Contact Period Caribbean. In *Ethnohistory and Archaeology: Approaches to Postcontact Change in the Americas*, edited by J. D. Rogers and S M. Wilson, pp. 19-30. Plenum Press, New York.

Wylie, A.
1985 The Reaction against Analogy. *Advances in Archaeological Method and Theory*, vol. 8, edited by M. B. Schiffer, pp. 63-111. Academic Press, New York.

Yanaihara, T.
1934 Nanyo-gunto-min no kyoiku ni tsuite. (The educational system in South Sea Islands.) *Rin-re Koen-shu*, (May):67-85. Human Relations Areas Files archives, translated. Ms. No. 1576. New Haven.

www.ingramcontent.com/pod-product-compliance
Lightning Source LLC
Chambersburg PA
CBHW041704290426
44108CB00027B/2849
* 9 7 8 1 8 4 1 7 1 6 9 0 9 *